Human Rights and Civil Liberties
in the 21st Century

IUS GENTIUM

COMPARATIVE PERSPECTIVES ON LAW AND JUSTICE

VOLUME 30

For further volumes:
http://www.springer.com/series/7888

Yves Haeck • Eva Brems
Editors

Human Rights and Civil Liberties in the 21st Century

Springer

Editors
Yves Haeck
Human Rights Centre
Ghent University
Ghent, Belgium

Eva Brems
Human Rights Centre
Ghent University
Ghent, Belgium

ISBN 978-94-007-7598-5 ISBN 978-94-007-7599-2 (eBook)
DOI 10.1007/978-94-007-7599-2
Springer Dordrecht Heidelberg New York London

Library of Congress Control Number: 2013954376

Printed on acid-free paper

Springer is part of Springer Science+Business Media (www.springer.com)

Contents

Contributors

Adam Bodnar is an Associate Professor, holding the Chair of Human Rights at Warsaw University, Faculty of Law and Administration, and the Vice-President of the Board and the Head of Legal Division of the Helsinki Foundation for Human Rights, Warsaw, Poland. E-mail: a.bodnar@wpia.uw.edu.pl

Eva Brems is a Professor of International Human Rights Law at the Human Rights Centre of Ghent University, Ghent, Belgium. E-mail: Eva.Brems@UGent.be

Clara Burbano-Herrera is a Co-Lecturer of Human Rights in Developing Countries at the Human Rights Centre of Ghent University, Ghent, Belgium, and a Postdoctoral Research Fellow at the Research Foundation Flanders, Brussels, Belgium. E-mail: Clara.BurbanoHerrera@UGent.be

Katherine Cleary is the Assistant Director of the War Crimes Research Office at American University Washington College of Law, Washington DC, United States of America. E-mail: kcleary@wcl.american.edu

Jasmine Coppens is an Assistant at the Department of Public International Law of Ghent University, Ghent, Belgium. E-mail: Jasmine.Coppens@UGent.be

Helena de Vylder is a Lawyer at the Law Office of Simont Braun, Brussels, Belgium, and a Voluntary Research Fellow at the Human Rights Centre of Ghent University, Ghent, Belgium. E-mail: Helena.DeVylder@UGent.be

Marlies Eggermont is a Lecturer at the Artevelde University College of Ghent, Ghent, and a Practice Assistant at the Department of Social Law of Ghent University, Ghent, Belgium. E-mail: Marlies.Eggermont@UGent.be

Eric M. Freedman is a Maurice A. Deane Distinguished Professor of Constitutional Law, Maurice A. Deane School of Law of Hofstra University, United States of America. E-mail: Eric.M.Freedman@Hofstra.edu

Yves Haeck is a Professor of International Human Rights Law at the Human Rights Centre of Ghent University, Ghent, Belgium. E-mail: Yves.Haeck@UGent.be

Laurens Lavrysen is a Research Fellow at the Human Rights Centre of Ghent University, Ghent, Belgium. E-mail: Laurens.Lavrysen@UGent.be

Cesare Pitea is an Assistant Professor of International Law and a Senior Research Fellow at the Department of Law of the University of Parma, Parma, Italy. E-mail: cesare.pitea@unipr.it

Susana SáCouto is the Director of the War Crimes Research Office of American University Washington College of Law, Washington DC, United States of America. E-mail: ssacouto@wcl.american.edu

Mortimer N. S. Sellers is Regents Professor at the University System of Maryland, Baltimore, and Visiting Professor at the Georgetown University Law Center, Washington DC, United States of America. E-mail: mortimer.sellers@gmail.com

Frans Viljoen is the Director of the Centre for Human Rights and a Professor of International Human Rights Law at the University of Pretoria, Pretoria, Republic of South Africa. E-mail: frans.viljoen@up.ac.za

Introduction

Worldwide, civil rights and human rights are and will remain a very hot and interesting topic well within the twenty-first century. Contemporary discussions center both around historical and philosophical as well as procedural and substantial legal issues on different continents. This edited collection, which arose from a conference held at the Faculty of Law of Ghent University on 23 May 2012 under the aegis of the European and American Consortium for Legal Education (EACLE), an intercontinental network of law schools in the Americas and Europe, deals with a number of these hot items, which have only partially been dealt with in existing literature and around which legal scholars and academics from the Americas, Africa, and Europe have gathered their views and thoughts.

Cesare Pitea talks about the flawed relationship between European human rights law and international law, by taking a look at the interpretation and application of the European Convention on Human Rights in the broader context of international law. The intimate connection between universal human rights and the American legal tradition, in which federal courts are viewed as the most legitimate and accurate authorities on rights due to their well-developed case-law and perceived impartiality, but where foreign and international tribunals, which are developing deeper and more sophisticated rights traditions, are gathering ground and are thus being taken more into account by American law and courts, is dealt with by Mortimer Sellers. As to Europe, Helena De Vylder and Yves Haeck are analyzing the alarming unwillingness of certain member states to the European Convention on Human Rights to faithfully collaborate with the European Court of Human Rights during the proceedings in Strasbourg, by highlighting the situations where the duty to cooperate is violated as well as how the European Court reacts or should react when such incompliance is established. Laurens Lavrysen critically looks at the ever-evolving role of positive obligations in the case-law of the European Court to develop a legal framework to adequately protect the rights guaranteed by the European Convention on Human Rights, by examining both the substantive and the procedural guarantees that are encompassed by this legal framework and by comparing the European Court's approach with the one taken by the US Supreme Court.

Subsequently, Susana SáCouto and Katherine Cleary take a critical look at the approach of the International Criminal Court's Trial Chamber I in the Lubanga Case, by examining the time factor, the lack of clarity as to certain aspects of the crimes with which Lubanga was charged, and the relationship among factors relevant to the sentence and the means by which the majority of the Chamber reached its conclusion that 14 years was the appropriate length of the sentence, and finally, the purpose and timing of the Chamber's decision relating to reparations. Afterward, Clara Burbano-Herrera and Frans Viljoen provide some critical insights on the underdeveloped use of the legal instrument of interim measures before the African Commission on Human and Peoples' Rights, by comparing it to the use of the same instrument by its inter-American counterpart, i.e. the Inter-American Commission on Human Rights. Jasmine Coppens sheds light on push-back policies in Europe toward people trying to cross the Mediterranean in small boats, through the lens of the European Convention on Human Rights, but also through the lens of the Law of the Sea. In turn, Eric Freedman explores the possible new frontiers of capital punishment litigation in the United States, while Marlies Eggermont tackles the impact of the European Convention on Human Rights in the area of childbirth. Lastly, in view of the growing importance of the European Court of Human Rights' judgments, Adam Bodnar deals with the legal effect of such judgments beyond the parties to the proceedings before the European Court of Human Rights.

The editors would like to express their sincere gratitude to all the people involved in this conference, and especially to Prof. Dr. Hans De Wulf (Director of International Relations, Faculty of Law, Ghent University) and Veronique Christophe (International Relations Office, Faculty of Law, Ghent University), for making this conference possible. Finally, we would also like to thank Mrs. Kristien Van Ingelgem for the language review and Mrs. Martine Dewulf for ensuring that all the footnotes throughout the volume were in style and consistent with the guidelines.

Ghent, 1 June 2013

Yves Haeck
Eva Brems

Chapter 1
Interpretation and Application of the European Convention on Human Right in the Broader Context of International Law: Myth or Reality?

Cesare Pitea

Abstract The European Court of Human Rights (the Court) has progressively developed a method of interpretation of the European Convention of Human Rights which takes into account the evolving normative environment of international law. This methodology has been summarized by the Grand Chamber of the Court in the *Demir and Baykara* judgment. This chapter identifies two rationales for the Court's approach: "systemic integration", as it may be considered a tool to ensure coherence in a fragmented system of international law, and "evolutive interpretation", as far as it underpins with objective standards the adaptation of its interpretation to the evolving social and legal context. It then analyses two critical aspects of the Court's approach. On the one hand, it underlines the unnecessary use by the Court of expressions denoting its willingness to deviate from generally accepted rules on treaty interpretation, as codified by the Vienna Convention on the Law of Treaties. On the other hand, it brings a few examples of the inconsistent application of this interpretative approach. It concludes by observing that, if the practice of relying on "other" international law to interpret the Convention is a "reality", its contribution to the unity of international law and to the enhancement in consistency and predictability of the Court's jurisprudence remains, to a large extent, a "myth".

1.1 Introductory Remarks

The dramatic development of international human rights law since 1948 has been driven by two normative forces. On the one hand, State practice, at different levels, continuously contributes to expanding and deepening the normative environment through the adoption of new legal instruments, whether binding or not. On the other

C. Pitea (✉)
Department of Law, University of Parma, Parma, Italy
e-mail: cesare.pitea@unipr.it

Y. Haeck and E. Brems (eds.), *Human Rights and Civil Liberties in the 21st Century*, Ius Gentium: Comparative Perspectives on Law and Justice 30,
DOI 10.1007/978-94-007-7599-2_1, © Springer Science+Business Media Dordrecht 2014

hand, international judicial and quasi-judicial practice adapts the interpretation and application of State-created standards to the evolving social and legal background.

The European Court of Human Rights (the Court) has been a pioneering international tribunal in underlying – as early as 1975 in the *Golder* judgment[1] – the importance of placing an international human rights treaty, the European Convention on Human Rights,[2] in the broader context of international law. Ever since, in interpreting and applying the Convention, it has constantly referred to a great variety of sources of international law. In the *Demir and Baykara* judgment, a Grand Chamber of the Court has made an attempt at systematizing this scattered practice, through the elaboration of a general methodology of interpretation of the Convention in the light of other international instruments.

1.2 *Demir and Baykara v. Turkey*: Towards a Theory of Interpretation of the ECHR in the Light of Other International Instruments

In the judgment, the Grand Chamber, summarizing well-established principles of its own case law, recalled that, in interpreting the Convention, the Court "is guided *mainly* by the rules of interpretation provided for in Articles 31–33 of the Vienna Convention on the Law of Treaties".[3] The Convention has to be interpreted "in a manner which renders its rights practical and effective, not theoretical and illusory" and must be read "as a whole (…) in such a way as to promote internal consistency and harmony between its various provisions".[4] Furthermore, by direct reference to Article 31.3.c VCLT,[5] the Court added that it "has never considered the provisions of the Convention as the sole framework of reference for the interpretation of the rights and freedoms enshrined therein. On the contrary, it must also take into account any relevant rules and principles of international law applicable in relations between the Contracting Parties."[6] Referring to the "living" nature of the Convention and to the need to interpret it in the light of present-day conditions, the Court underlined

---

[1] ECtHR 21 February 1975, No. 4451/70, *Golder* v. *the United Kingdom*, para. 35.

[2] European Convention on Human Rights and Fundamental Freedoms (Rome, 4 November 1950, entered into force on 3 September 1953, amended by Protocols No. 11 and 14; hereinafter ECHR or "the Convention").

[3] ECtHR [GC] 12 November 2008, No. 34503/97, *Demir and Baykara v. Turkey*, para. 65, emphasis by the author. Vienna Convention on the Law of Treaties (Vienna, 22 May 1969, entered into force on 27 January 1980; hereinafter VCLT).

[4] Ibid., para. 66.

[5] Art. 31.3.c VCLT reads as follows: "There shall be taken into account, together with the context: (…) (c) any relevant rules of international law applicable in the relations between the parties". For an early analysis of the relevance of this provision, see P. Sands, "Treaty, Custom and the Cross-fertilization of International Law", 86 *Yale Human Rights & Development Law Journal* (1998) 85–105.

[6] ECtHR *Demir and Baykara v. Turkey*, supra, note 3, para. 67.

that, in past decisions, "it has taken account of evolving norms of national and international law in its interpretation of Convention provisions."[7]

In subsequent paragraphs of the judgment, the Court thoroughly reviewed the precedents in which it has used international external sources[8] as interpretative tools, pointing at their differences in scope and in nature,[9] and without establishing any order or hierarchy among them.[10]

The Court then observed that "when it considers the object and purpose of the Convention provisions, it also takes into account the international law background to the legal question before it. Being made up of a set of rules and principles that are accepted by the vast majority of States, the *common international* [...] *law standards of European States* reflect a reality that the Court cannot disregard when it is called upon to clarify the scope of a Convention provision that *more conventional means of interpretation* have not enabled it to establish with a sufficient degree of certainty."[11]

The reasoning concludes as follows:

> 85. The Court, in defining the meaning of terms and notions in the text of the Convention, can and must take into account elements of international law other than the Convention, the interpretation of such elements by competent organs, and the practice of European States reflecting their common values. The consensus emerging from specialized international instruments and from the practice of contracting States may constitute a relevant consideration for the Court when it interprets the provisions of the Convention in specific cases.
>
> 86. In this context, it is not necessary for the respondent State to have ratified the entire collection of instruments that are applicable in respect of the precise subject matter of the case concerned. It will be sufficient for the Court that the relevant international instruments denote a continuous evolution in the norms and principles applied in international law (...) and show, in a precise area, that there is common ground in modern societies.

1.3 A Two-Fold Rationale for the Court's Methodology

From the foregoing, one may infer that reliance on "external" sources to interpret and apply the ECHR has a two-fold rationale.

---

[7] Ibid., para. 68.

[8] In some cases, the judgment also contains references to domestic practices and decisions. The present contribution does not aim to discuss either the appropriateness of such references in this context or their implications.

[9] In particular, the Court divides its analysis between general international law – a heading under which multilateral human rights treaties are included! – and Council of Europe instruments. Practice covers customary norms, general principles of law, treaties, soft-law instruments, the jurisprudence of international courts and tribunals and the interpretative practice of supervisory bodies. See ECtHR *Demir and Baykara v. Turkey*, supra, note 3, paras. 69–75.

[10] G. Cohen-Jonathan and J.F. Flauss, "La Cour européenne des droits de l'homme et le droit international", 55 *Annuaire français de droit international*(2009) 765–780 at 767.

[11] ECtHR *Demir and Baykara v. Turkey*, supra, note 3, para. 76, emphasis by the author.

1.3.1 Systemic Integration

The first theoretical framework within which one may analyze the Court's methodology is the debate on the "proliferation" of international courts and tribunals and the ensuing risks of "fragmentation" of international law. Launched by the then president of the International Court of Justice (ICJ),[12] the theme has attracted a wealth of attention by scholars[13] over the last decades and, in its substantive aspects, has been on the agenda of the International Law Commission (ILC) since 2000, leading to the well-known report drafted by Martti Koskenniemi in 2009.

The Court, sometimes singled out as a judicial body whose jurisprudence threatens the unity of international law, may fairly be considered as a precursor of the ILC in resorting to Article 31.3.c VCLT as a means to incorporate "other international law" into a given treaty through interpretation: indeed the above-mentioned provision, allegedly expressing an interpretative principle of "systemic integration", is singled out by the ILC's anti-fragmentation "toolkit" as the "master-key" to international law building.[14]

According to the ILC, "systemic integration" is based upon the premise that "whatever their subject matter, treaties are a creation of the international legal system and their operation is predicated upon that fact".[15] Therefore, "international obligations are interpreted by reference to their normative environment ("system")".[16] The principle requires "the integration into the process of legal reasoning – including reasoning by international courts and tribunals – of a sense of coherence and meaningfulness".[17] In other words, it aims at ensuring that international law achieves the minimum degree of material coherence required to be characterized as a legal system and not, as H.L.A. Hart's well known definition suggests, a mere "set of rules".[18]

---

[12] See, in particular, *The Proliferation of International Judicial Bodies: The Outlook for the International Legal Order*, Speech by H.E. Judge Gilbert Guillaume, President of the International Court of Justice, to the Sixth Committee of the General Assembly of the United Nations (27 October 2000), available at: www.icj-cij.org/court/index.php?p1=1&p2=3&p3=1. (Accessed 29 April 2012). Judge Guillaume referred explicitly to the ECtHR jurisprudence on the validity of territorial reservations to unilateral declarations of acceptance of the Court's jurisdiction as a prominent example of such risks, ECtHR 23 March 1995, No. 15318/89, *Loizidou v. Turkey*.

[13] Among the numerous writings dealing with the issues of proliferation of international courts and tribunals and fragmentation of international law, see T. Treves, "Fragmentation of International Law: the Judicial Perspective", 23 *Comunicazioni e studi* (2007) 821–876.

[14] *Fragmentation of International Law: Difficulties Arising from the Diversification and Expansion of International Law*, Report of the Study Group of the International Law Commission finalized by Martti Koskenniemi, UN doc. A/CN.4/L.682 (13 April 2006); hereinafter "Koskenniemi Report".

[15] *Fragmentation of International Law: Difficulties Arising from the Diversification and Expansion of International Law*, Report of the Study Group of the International Law Commission, UN doc. A/CN.4/L.702 (18 July 2006); hereinafter "ILC Fragmentation Report" at 14.

[16] Koskenniemi Report, supra, note 14, para. 413.

[17] Ibid., para. 419.

[18] H.L.A. Hart, *The Concept of Law* (Cambridge University Press: Cambridge, 1961), p. 229.

Thus, by promoting cross-fertilization with general international law and other international human rights regimes, the Court's methodology may be analyzed as an attempt at preventing the fragmentation of the international legal system, especially in the field of human rights protection.

1.3.2 Evolutive Interpretation

The second conceptual issue intimately connected with the Court's methodology is that of dynamic or evolutive interpretation. As it is well-known, the Court since the *Tyrer* case, has adopted an interpretative principle, which is commonly found in national constitutional jurisprudence, according to which the Convention, a law-making or normative treaty[19] creating objective and non-reciprocal obligations[20] and "a constitutional instrument of European public order (*ordre public*)",[21] is a "living instrument which (…) must be interpreted in the light of present-day conditions".[22] This is an aspect of the principle of effective interpretation, based on the assumption that the Convention "is intended to guarantee not rights that are theoretical or illusory but rights that are practical and effective".[23]

This interpretative technique has attracted some criticism insofar as it would amount to a conceptual device used by the Court to trespass the boundaries of treaty interpretation, as defined in Arts 31–33 VCLT, thus engaging in "judicial legislation"[24] against the "sacred" principle of States' consent to be bound.[25] Moreover, it is allegedly used inconsistently in order to reach judicial policy objectives unattainable through a straightforward application of the VCLT rules on treaty interpretation,[26] at the expenses of legal certainty and predictability.

These arguments may be countered by observing that the development of the law is part of the judicial mandate of any international tribunal,[27] and the progressive reinforcement of human rights protection is a fundamental aspect of the object and purpose

[19] ECtHR 27 June 1968,No. 2122/64, *Wemhoff v. Germany*, para. 8.

[20] ECtHR 18 September 1978, No. 5310/61, *Ireland v. United Kingdom*, para. 42.

[21] ECtHR, *Loizidou v. Turkey*, supra, note 12, para. 25.

[22] ECtHR 25 April 1978, No. 5856/72, *Tyrer v. United Kingdom*, para. 31.

[23] ECtHR 9 October 1979, No. 6289/73, *Airey v. Ireland*, para. 24.

[24] L. Hoffman, "The Universality of Human Rights", 125 *Law Quarterly Review* (2009), 416–432 at 428 (arguing that the "living instrument" doctrine "is the banner under which the Strasbourg court has assumed power to legislate what they consider to be required by "European public order").

[25] See, generally, M. Fitzmaurice, "Dynamic (Evolutive) Interpretation of Treaties, Part I", 21 *Hague Yearbook of International Law* (2008) 101–153 at 131–153.

[26] G. Gaja, "Does the European Court of Human Rights Use Its Stated Methods of Interpretation?", in *Divenire sociale e adeguamento del diritto*: *Studi in onore di Francesco Capotorti*, vol. 1, (Giuffré: Milan, 1999) 213–227 at 225–227.

[27] See T. Treves, "Judicial Lawmaking in an Era of "Proliferation" of International Courts and Tribunals: Development or Fragmentation of International Law?", in R. Wolfrum and V. Röben (eds), *Developments of International Law in Treaty Making*, (Springer: Berlin, 2005) 587–620.

of a human rights treaty.[28] Furthermore, one may also argue that, by conferring and progressively deepening and enlarging the competence of a judicial body as the "guardian of a common plan",[29] States Parties to the ECHR have implicitly accepted that they must face the effects of such developments beyond their initial expectations.[30]

Finally, it should be recalled that the power of the ECtHR to interpret the ECHR dynamically is constrained by several factors. In a large sense, it is limited by the Court's need to maintain legitimacy *vis-à-vis* its constituency, primarily the community of States parties. The Court is aware of this need, for example when it resorts to the so-called "consensual interpretation" in examining whether States have overstepped the margin of appreciation they enjoy in applying the Convention. From the narrower perspective of interpretation techniques, the flexibility conferred by the teleological approach is not unlimited. However, far from being limited by the original intention of the Parties, it is defined by the actual text of the Convention: the Court does not read into conventional provision meanings that textual and contextual elements plainly exclude.[31]

As much as the so-called "comparative" interpretation, the Court's reliance on external sources of international law by linking the inherently dynamic interpretation of the Convention to objective elements of State practice, may be considered an additional factor protecting the authority of the Court against allegations of "judicial law-making".

1.4 Two Critical Aspects of the Court's Methodology and of Its Application

The systematization of a generally applicable methodology on the use of "other" international law in interpreting the Convention and its application in judicial practice and reasoning, could help streamlining judicial reasoning and foster the external and internal coherence of the Court's jurisprudence.

---

[28] In this respect, the reference in the Preamble to the Convention to the objective of the "further realization of human rights" ("développement des droits de l'homme" in the French text) is often recalled, see F. Tulkens, "Commentaire sur Touzé, Les techniques interprétatives des organes de protection des droit de l'homme", 115 *Revue générale de droit international public* (2011) 533–540 at 534 and P.M. Dupuy, "Evolutionary Interpretation of Treaties: Between Memory and Prophecy", in E. Cannizzaro (ed.), *The Law of Treaties Beyond the Vienna Convention*, (Oxford: Oxford University Press, 2011) 123–137 at 133.

[29] Dupuy 2011, supra, note 28, at 125 (arguing that in such cases, i.e. when the international judge "does not simply act as an arbitrator", "the institutional mandate conferred upon the judge will provide him with the necessary authority and legitimacy" to further such a collective plan through interpretation).

[30] R. Bernhardt, "Evolutive Treaty Interpretation, Especially of the European Convention of Human Rights", 42 *German Yearbook of International Law*(1999) 11–25 at 24 (arguing that States have generally accepted evolutive interpretation by the Court "either by acting in conformity with the pronouncement of the Court or by ratifying additional protocols like Protocol No. 1").

[31] See, for example, ECtHR, *Wemhoff v. Germany*, supra, note 19; ECtHR 7 July 1989, No. 14038/88, *Soering v. United Kingdom*; ECtHR 29 April 2002, No. 2346/02, *Pretty v. United Kingdom*.

However, the potential for "external coherence", i.e. the development of the Court's case law in harmony with other international law and jurisprudence, is curtailed by the growingly isolationist stance of the Court in developing "special" hermeneutic canons, allegedly not grounded in the customary rules on treaty interpretation, codified in the VCLT. Moreover, the technique appears to be selectively and inconsistently used by the Court, thus undermining "internal coherence", i.e. harmony in the reasoning and predictability in the actual outcome of the Court's decisions in similar cases.

1.4.1 Systemic Integration Through the Disintegration of Customary Rules on Treaty Interpretation?

At first sight, the Court's theory determines a paradox, at least if one assumes that harmony in material international (human rights) law is one of the objectives it pursues.[32]

The Court seemingly admits going beyond the VCLT in treaty interpretation: the very wording of the *Demir and Baykara* judgment suggests that the Court resorts "mainly", therefore not exclusively, to the VCLT, feeling free to use "less conventional" means of interpretation when the result of the ordinary interpretative process is unsatisfactory. In other words, the Court seems to be ready to bend generally accepted rules of interpretation to a breaking point and beyond, in order to achieve the coherence of substantive human rights law and an appropriate degree of human rights protection: it thus purports to create a "special rule of interpretative connection" between the ECHR and the surrounding normative environment.[33]

In doing so, it seems to contradict the "systemic integration" paradigm. Rules on treaty interpretation are (or should be) among the most resilient fabric ensuring the unity of international law: as long as the methods according to which a conventional text is interpreted are generally shared by the epistemic community of international lawyers, actual divergences as to the results of the interpretative process may be considered inherent in the nature of this legal system. This is especially true if one keeps in mind that within customary rules on treaty interpretation, different and sometimes contradictory principles coexist,[34] and that international law is characterized

---

[32] R.C. Nordeide, "Demir & Baykara v. Turkey: app. no. 34503/97", 103 *American Journal of International Law* (2009) 567–574 at 573 ("the Court supports the idea of a structural relationship between the Convention and other international law").

[33] This expression is used by L. Gradoni, "Regole di interpretazione difficili da interpretare e frammentazione del principio di integrazione sistemica", 93 *Rivista di diritto internazionale* (2010) 809–817 at 813–814, commenting on the use of art. 31.3.c VCLT by the WTO Panel in the Biotech case (WTO (Panel Report) 29 September 2006, No. WT/DS291-293/R, *EC – Measures Affecting the Approval and Marketing of Biotech Products*, para. 7.70).

[34] J.M. Sorel, "Article 31 – Convention de 1969", in O. Corten and P. Klein(eds), *Les Conventions de Vienne sur le droit des traités. Commentaire article par article*, (Brussels: Bruylant, 2006) 1289–1334 at 1332 ("la Convention [de Vienne] juxtapose des principes parfois contradictoires qui peuvent aboutir – avec les mêmes instruments – à des conclusions fort éloignées").

by institutional and normative pluralism, and a reasonable degree of disagreement has to be accepted.

Therefore, the coherence of rules on interpretation is a precondition for attaining the objective of systemic integration, and the conclusion that the ECtHR is willfully creating special rules on interpretation is not one that should be reached easily. An attempt at conceptualizing the process followed by the Court against the background and within the boundaries of Articles 31–33 VCLT, should first be made.

If the analysis moves exclusively from the narrow perspective of Article 31.3.c VCLT, which is often assumed to be the normative reference for the principle of systemic integration, the Court's theory appears to be in sharp contrast to the requirements and conditions set forth therein: at least some of the international materials referred to for interpretative purposes hardly fall within the notion of "rules of international law applicable in the relations between the parties". This consideration applies especially to soft-law instruments – radically excluded from the scope of Article 31.3.c. VCLT, which refers to binding norms deriving from formal sources of international law[35] – and to treaties which are not binding (at least) on the respondent State in the relevant case.

As far as "external" agreements are concerned, the central and most debated[36] issue to be settled in the perspective of Article 31.3.c VCLT is whether the rule to be used for interpretation is "applicable in the relations between the parties". In the narrowest view, the term "parties" must be interpreted "as requiring consideration of those rules of international law which are applicable in the relations

[35] H. Waldock, "Sixth Report on the Law of Treaties", in *Yearbook of the International Law Commission*, vol. II, UN doc. A/CN.4/SER.A/1966/add. 1 (1967) at 97, para. 10. See also J. Cazala,"Le rôle de l'interprétation des traités à la lumière de toute autre 'règle pertinente de droit international applicable entre les parties' en tant que 'passerelle' jetée entre systèmes juridiques différents", in H. Ruiz Fabri H and L. Gradoni L (eds), *La circulation des concepts juridiques. Le droit international de l'environnement entre mondialisation et fragmentation*, (Paris: Société de législation comparée, 2009) 95–136 at 11 ff.; R. Gardiner, *Treaty Interpretation*, (Oxford: Oxford University Press, 2008) 260–263. In this context, it should be noted that when the Court cites art. 31.3.c VCLT, it reformulates its wording as including, besides "rules", also "principles" of international law. However, this semantic divergence does not seem to be decisive, as confirmed by the widespread reliance on "general principles of law" or "principles of customary international law" as permitted interpretative tools, see WTO (Appellate Body Report) 12 October 1998, No. WT/DS58/AB/R, *United States – Import Prohibition of Certain Shrimp and Shrimp Products*, para. 158 and footnote 157 (the principle of good faith as a general principle of law and a general principle of international law); PCA Arbitral Tribunal 12 March 2004,*Apurement des comptes entre le Royaume des Pays-Bas et la République Française en application du Protocole du 25 septembre 1991 additionnel à la Convention relative à la protection du Rhin contre la pollution par les chlorures du 3 décembre 1976* (Netherlands/France), para. 103 (rejecting the interpretative relevance of the polluter pays principle on the basis of its status under customary international law and the treaty to be interpreted, rather than because of its nature as a principle). See also Koskenniemi Report, supra, note 14, paras. 463–469 at 233–237.

[36] See C. McLachlan, "The Principle of Systemic Integration and Article 31(3)(c) of the Vienna Convention", 54 *International and Comparative Law Quarterly* (2005) 279–320 at 313–315.

between all parties to the treaty which is being interpreted."[37] In the broadest interpretation, the treaty used for interpretative purposes should at least be binding on the parties to the actual dispute in which the interpretative issue arises.[38] However, this approach is only suitable for application to synallagmatic treaties not establishing obligations *erga omnes partes*, and thus not to human rights treaties,[39] since otherwise the applicable standard of protection would vary from one party to another, depending on their respective commitment to other treaties.

Soft-law instruments and agreements not "applicable in the relations between the parties" can be relied upon under Article 31.3.c VCLT insofar as they are singled out as evidence of an established customary rule or principle. In this respect, the notion of "common international [...] law standards of European States" used by the Court is to a certain extent akin to that of a regional custom.[40] However, it is doubtful whether the kind and generality of practice and *opinio iuris* normally referred to by the Court is sufficient to conclude that a custom has emerged in every instance in which this concept is used. In most cases, the expression points at an emerging custom[41] or an evolving standard which is not per se sufficient to be taken into account as an established rule.[42]

The exclusion of certain "international materials" from the scope of Article 31.3.c VCLT does not deny altogether their relevance in the interpretative process. In some instances, such materials may qualify as "practice in the application of the treaty which establishes the agreement of the parties regarding its interpretation"

---

[37] WTO: *EC – Biotech Products*, supra, note 33, para. 7.70. See also U. Linderfalk, "Who Are 'the Parties'? Article 31 § 3(c) of the 1969 Vienna Convention, and the 'Principle of Systemic Integration' Revisited", 55 *Netherlands International Law Review* (2008) 343–364, E. Cannizzaro "Il rilievo di accordi esterni nell'interpretazione degli accordi OMC", in A. Ligustro and G. Sacerdoti (eds), *Problemi e tendenze del diritto internazionale dell'economia. Liber amicorum in onore di Paolo Picone*, (Napels: Editoriale Scientifica, 2011) 513–524 at 521 and, with some qualifications, C. McLachlan 2005, supra, note 36, at 315.

[38] The ILC has criticized the restrictive approach, since it would nullify the effect of the provision in the relations between multilateral regimes, where a perfect coincidence of parties is very unlikely, if not impossible, see Koskenniemi Report, supra, note 14, paras. 450 and 470–471, at 227–228 and 237–238. L. Gradoni 2010, supra, note 33, at 812 speaks of "neutralizzazione funzionale" of the principle of systemic integration.

[39] Koskenniemi Report, supra, note 14, para. 472, at 238–239.

[40] D. Rietiker, "The Principle of Effectiveness in the Jurisprudence of the European Court of Human Rights: Its Different Dimensions and Its Consistency with Public International Law – No Need for the Concept of Treaty Sui Generis", 79 *Nordic Journal of International Law* (2010) 245–277 at 275.

[41] V.P. Tzevelekos, "The Use of Article 31(3)(C) of the VCLT in the Case Law of the ECtHR: An Effective Anti-Fragmentation Tool or a Selective Loophole for the Reinforcement of Human Rights Teleology? Between Evolution and Systemic Integration", 31 *Michigan Journal of International Law* (2010) 621–690 at 654.

[42] PCA Arbitral Tribunal 2 July 2003, *Access to Information under Article 9 of the OSPAR Convention* (Ireland v. United Kingdom), paras. 93–105 (hereinafter: *Mox OSPAR Arbitration*), paras. 93–105.

(Art. 31.3.b VCLT), as it might be the case of soft-law instruments elaborated in the context of the Council of Europe, including resolutions adopted without opposition by the Committee of Ministers, conventions not yet in force and the practice of treaty and expert bodies.[43]

More generally, it is submitted that the specific function of Article 31.3.c VCLT is to *mandate* the interpretative reference to a broadened context, since the rules of international law referred to therein "*shall* be taken into account, together with the context".[44] Accordingly, the provision should not be read as merely allowing such a reference, thus limiting the list of potentially relevant sources. Therefore, the narrow scope of Article 31.3.c VCLT does not prevent the use, for interpretative purposes, of a wider normative environment,[45] including emerging trends in international law. In this context, in determining the ordinary meaning of an expression, apart from relying on customary law,[46] the interpreter of a conventional text may find guidance in the sense it assumes in other international instruments.[47] According to the ILC, this approach[48] "gives effect to the sense in which certain multilateral treaty notions or concepts, though perhaps not found in treaties with identical membership, are adopted nevertheless widely enough so as to give a good sense of a "common

[43] On which, see J. Polakiewicz, "Alternatives to Treaty-Making and Law-Making by Treaty and Expert Bodies in the Council of Europe", in R. Wolfrum and V. Röben (eds), supra, note 27, 245–290.

[44] D. French, "Treaty Interpretation and the Incorporation of Extraneous Legal Rules", 55 *International and Comparative Law Quarterly* (2006) 281–314 at 301 ("article 31(2) and (3) are not discretionary add-ons, but prescriptive and mandatory aspects of the 'general rule'").

[45] Cannizzaro 2011, supra, note 37, argues that art. 31.3.c VCLT is only one of the interpretative tools for coordinating legal regimes and describes as "global interpretation" the technique allowing the use of "external sources" beyond the narrowly construed boundaries of this provision (ibid., at 522). He underlines that this technique, as much as the "evolutive interpretation", can hardly be characterized as the expression of a single method of interpretation among those explicitly incorporated by art. 31 VCLT (objective, subjective, functional). It is rather a combination of, and a supplement to, each and all of them (*ibid.*, at 518).

[46] Koskenniemi Report, supra, note 14, paras. 467–468 at 235–236 (underlying that "[h]ere it is really immaterial whether a tribunal chooses to invoke article 31 (3) (c) [VCLT]").

[47] Cazala 2009, supra, note 35, at 102–103 (evoking analogical interpretation techniques).

[48] Adopted in particular in the context of the WTO, see WTO: *United States – Shrimp*, supra, note 35, para. 130 at 48–49 (referring to the United Nations Convention on the Law of the Sea (Montego Bay, 10 December 1982, entered into force on 16 November 1994, hereinafter UNCLOS), and to the Convention on Biological Diversity (Rio de Janeiro, 5 June 1992, entered into force on 29 December 1993) to include living resources within the meaning of the expression "exhaustible natural resources" under art. XX GATT 1947); WTO (Appellate Body Report) 14 January 2002, *United States – Tax Treatment for "Foreign Sales Corporations"* (Article 21.5), WT/DS108/AB/RW, paras. 141–145 (especially footnote 123) (referring to several bilateral and regional trade agreements to define the meaning of the expression "foreign-source income" in footnote 59 of the Agreement on Subsidies and Countervailing Measures). See also ICJ 25 September 1997, *Gabčíkovo-Nagymaros Project* (Hungary/Slovakia), para. 140; PCA: *Mox OSPAR Arbitration*, supra, note 42, dissenting opinion Gavan Griffith QC, paras. 9–19 (an unratified treaty may be of "normative and evidentiary value to the extent that regard may be had to it to inform and confirm the content" of the provision to be interpreted).

understanding" or a "state of the art" in a particular technical field without necessarily reflecting formal customary law."[49]

The resemblance with the Court's approach and terminology is evident.

The third and final limb of the argument relates to another debated aspect of the principle of systemic interpretation, namely the critical date at which the normative environment has to be considered when interpreting a conventional provision. As we have already noted in the Court's interpretative theory and practice, this question is easily resolved by reference to the notion of the ECHR as a "living instrument" and therefore to the issue of dynamic (evolutive) interpretation.[50] For our purposes, it is sufficient to recall that human rights treaties possess *prima facie* those features characterizing an instrument calling for evolutive interpretation in general international law.[51]

From the foregoing, one may observe that although the Court, in pursuance of its own "interpretive ethic",[52] undoubtedly bends customary rules on treaty

---

[49] Koskenniemi Report, supra, note 14, para. 472, p. 239. Similarly, McLachlan 2005, supra, note 36, at 315 (other treaties are not used as sources of binding international law, but "as a rather elaborate law dictionary"). In both cases, the approach is seen as a qualification or particular application of art. 31.3.c VCLT. However, the present author considers that this approach may be better justified under art. 31.1 VCLT.

[50] The link between systemic integration and evolutive interpretation is often underlined; see in particular, G. Distefano, "L'interprétation évolutive de la norme internationale", in 115 *Revue générale de droit international public* (2011) 373–396.

[51] R. Higgins, "A Babel of Judicial Voices? Ruminations from the Bench", 55 *International and Comparative Law Quarterly* (2006) 791–804 at 797–798. The Koskenniemi Report concluded that "the treaty language itself […] provide[s] for the taking into account of future developments" (para. 478, p. 242) when: the terms used are inherently "not static, but evolutionary" (referring to ICJ 21 June 1971, *Legal Consequences for States of the Continued Presence of South Africa in Namibia (South West Africa) notwithstanding Security Council Resolution 276 (1970)*, para. 53) or simply generic (*Koskenniemi Report*, supra, note 14, para. 478 at 242, referring to ICJ 19 December 1978, *Aegean Sea Continental Shelf* (Greece v. Turkey), para. 78 (a generic term is "intended to follow the evolution of the law and to correspond with the meaning attached to the expression by the law in force at any given time") when the object and purpose of the treaty suggests that "the parties have committed themselves to a project of progressive development" (ICJ *Gabčíkovo-Nagymaros Project* (Hungary/Slovakia), supra, note 48, paras. 132–147 and Separate Opinion of Judge Weeramantry at 113–115. See also Bernhardt 1999, supra, note 30, at 16. In other cases the ICJ has rather referred to the presumed intention of the parties to give an evolutive meaning to a treaty or certain of its terms (ICJ 13 July 2009, *Navigational and Related Rights* (Costa Rica v. Nicaragua), para. 64 and 20 April 2010, *Pulp Mills on the River Uruguay* (Argentina v. Uruguay), para. 204). However, it has been observed that such an intention should be primarily inferred from the object and purpose of the treaty (Distefano 2011, supra, note 50 at 394). See also PCA Arbitral Tribunal 24 May 2005, *Iron Rhine ("IJzeren Rijn") Railway* (Belgium/Netherlands), para. 80 ("an evolutive interpretation, which would ensure an application of the treaty that would be effective in terms of its object and purpose, will be preferred to a strict application of the intertemporal rule") and when the obligation concerned is couched in very general terms WTO (Appellate Body Report) 12 October 1998, WT/DS58/AB/R, *United States – Import Prohibition of Certain Shrimp and Shrimp Products*, para. 130 (with reference to the expression "necessary to protect human, animal and plant life or health" used in art. XX GATT).

[52] G. Letsas, "Strasbourg's Interpretive Ethic: Lessons for the International Lawyer", 21 *European Journal of International Law* (2010) 503–541(arguing that the Court dismisses both intentionalism and textualism to favour a "moral reading" of the Convention's rights).

interpretation, these seem to be flexible enough to sustain the stress without breaking.[53] In particular, the specific interpretative needs deriving from special features of human rights treaties are accommodated through the emphasis placed on the teleological approach, one of the fundamental elements of the general rule of interpretation.[54] The ensuing conclusion is that, by taking unnecessary isolationist stances in developing "special" hermeneutic canons, allegedly not grounded in the customary rules on treaty interpretation, in order to take into account the wide international normative environment, the Court curtails the potential for "external coherence" of its own methodology.

1.4.2 Does the Court Apply Consistently its Own Methodology?

The second critical aspect of the Court's methodology is that, insofar as it aims at enhancing coherence and predictability of its evolving jurisprudence, it should be applied consistently. A glance at some recent cases cast serious doubt on the possibility of answering positively to this question.

In one of the most controversial cases considered by the "new" Court, the *Banković* case, the decisive issue was whether the Convention was applicable to allegations of violations of human rights as a consequence of the NATO air strikes over Belgrade during the NATO Kosovo campaign in 1999. The Court had to determine whether the applicants fell within a contracting Party's "jurisdiction" under Article 1 of the Convention. In finding that the notion of jurisdiction was "primarily territorial", the Court was satisfied that this was the ordinary meaning of the notion of State jurisdiction "from the standpoint of public international law".[55] No relevance was given to the comparative analysis with other international human rights instruments, such as the UN covenants on Civil and Political Rights and on Economic, Social and Cultural Rights.[56] In practical terms, reliance on general international law to interpret the Convention was the basis for a restrictive, and

[53] M. Villiger, (2011) "The Rules on Interpretation: Misgivings, Misunderstandings, Miscarriage? The 'Crucible' Intended by the International Law Commission", in E. Cannizzaro (ed.), supra, note 28 at 122.

[54] Letsas 2010, supra, note 52, at 514 ("[the general rule of treaty interpretation] is abstract enough to allow for different interpretive 'techniques' or 'methods' depending on the object and purpose of each treaty").

[55] ECtHR [GC] 12 December 2011, No. 52207/99, *Banković and others v. Belgium and 16 other Contracting States*, para. 59.

[56] On this issue, see ICJ 9 July 2004, *Legal Consequences of the Construction of a Wall in the Occupied Palestinian Territory*, paras. 107–113, HRC 29 July 1981,No. 52/1979,*López Burgos v. Uruguay*), UN doc. Supp. No. 40 (A/36/40), 1981 at 176 ss, para. 12). See also HRC: General Comment No. 31, Nature of the General Legal Obligation Imposed on States Parties to the Covenant, UN doc. CCPR/C/21/Rev.1/Add.13 (26 May 2004) ("a State party must respect and ensure the rights laid down in the Covenant to anyone within the power or effective control of that State Party, even if not situated within the territory of the State Party").

lately criticized, understanding of the territorial applicability of the Convention, in a politically controversial case.[57]

In the *Demir and Baykara* case, the Court had to answer the question whether municipal civil servants, whose right to organize and to collective bargaining was at stake, qualified as "members (...) of the administration of the State". In fact, Article 11(2) of the last sentence of the Convention states that the freedom of association protected therein "(...) shall not prevent the imposition of lawful restrictions on the exercise of these rights by members of the armed forces, of the police or of the administration of the State". On the basis of the very same "methodology" that the Court had explained few paragraphs earlier in the same judgment, and having in mind the *Banković* precedent, one would have expected the Court to take, as a starting point, the notion of "State" under public international law, that would clearly cover central as well as local authorities. Quite surprisingly, no mention of a similar reasoning can be found in the judgment. Quite to the opposite, the Court, as a supplementary argument, simply considers that municipal civil servants who are not engaged in the administration of the State as such, cannot in principle be treated as "members of the administration of the State".[58]

The "methodology" is then resumed to engage in a comparative review of international treaties dealing with the matter, and to come to the more radical conclusion that "members of the administration of the State" cannot be excluded from the scope of Article 11. At most, the national authorities are entitled to impose "lawful restrictions" on those members in accordance with Article 11 § 2", namely when the restriction has a legitimate aim, and is necessary in a democratic society to reach such a legitimate objective.

In two recent cases dealing with the issue of attribution to the State of conducts, allegedly violating the Convention by persons not qualifying as State agents, the Court has shown a cautious approach to the relevance of general international law. In the recent Grand Chamber judgment in the case of *Kotov v. Russia*, the Court had to decide whether the acts of the liquidator in a winding-up procedure (or trustee in bankruptcy, as in certain legal systems it would be called) was to be attributed to Russia in order to establish the latter's direct responsibility for violations committed by the former. In the factual part of the judgment, the Court recalled the applicable customary international law on State responsibility as codified by the ILC,[59] but refrained to make any reference to general international law when dealing with the issue in its reasoning. This, in turn, led the Court to conclude that "the liquidator did not act as a State agent" in the case before it.

[57] The Court has nuanced its jurisprudence in following cases, see ECtHR [GC] 7 July 2011, No. 55721/07, *Al-Skeini and others v. the United Kingdom* e No. 27021/08, *Al-Jedda and others v. the United Kingdom*.

[58] ECtHR, *Demir and Baykara v. Turkey*, supra, note 3, para. 97.

[59] ECtHR [GC] 3 April 2012, No. 54522/00, *Kotov v. Russia*, paras. 30–32, quoting the ILC Draft Articles on Responsibility of States for Internationally Wrongful Acts (2001), *Yearbook of the International Law Commission*, vol. II, Part Two) and the commentary thereof.

Few months before, the Court had dealt with a similar issue, the case of *Kuzmin v. Russia*. A well-known Russian politician, a retired general of the army, and formerly the holder of posts of responsibility in the Russian administration while running for the post of governor of a Russian region, made statements during a TV broadcast describing the applicant, a civil servant indicted for rape, as a "criminal" deserving to be put to the "cage" and promising to put him into jail if elected. Russia argued that these statements, which were arguably prejudicial to the presumption of innocence, were made by a person not holding, at the material time, any public office. Therefore, responsibility for them could not be attributed to the State. The Court, without any reference to the international law on attribution of international wrongful acts to the State, concluded that "in the very specific circumstances of the case (…) the statements were to be considered as made by a public official".[60]

The case law reviewed is too limited to be conclusive and further and in-depth research is needed. Nevertheless, some signals should be considered. Generally speaking, the Court is often criticized for applying some of its own interpretative doctrines *à la carte*. This is the case, for instance, of the margin of appreciation and the connected comparative method to determine the existence of a common normative ground in Europe regarding the solution of a given controversial issue. The above-mentioned case law seems to suggest that the same attitude may prevail in the actual resorting to other rules of international law in the process of interpretation and application of the Convention: indeed, international law seems to be occasionally used to enhance legitimacy of a given decision, rather than its very rationale, while its relevance is downplayed if not neglected in other cases. The perils of inconsistency undermine from its very foundation the potential of the methodology elaborated by the Court in promoting internal coherence of the Court's jurisprudence.

1.5 Concluding Remarks

The aforementioned considerations suggest a provisional answer to the question posed in the title of this chapter. The growing use of international law to interpret the Convention has long become a reality. However, the contribution given by the systematization of this practice into a "methodology" to the unity of international law and to the enhancement of consistency and predictability of the Court's jurisprudence remains, to a large extent, a myth.

---

[60] ECtHR 18 March 2010, No. 58939/00, *Kuzmin v. Russia*, paras. 60–63. The judgment is available only in French. The English translation was made by the author of the present chapter.

Chapter 2
Universal Human Rights Law in the United States

Mortimer N.S. Sellers

Abstract Universal human rights provided the primary legal justification for the American Revolution and have therefore been at the heart of the American law from the earliest years of the Republic. The inherent and inalienable rights of all human beings were cited in the Declaration of Independence of the United States, protected in the federal Bill of Rights and independently guaranteed by the separate constitutions of every state in the Union. American law and American lawyers consider support for universal rights to be the ultimate basis of all legitimate government, everywhere. So intimate is the connection between universal rights and the American legal tradition that in the eyes of the American government and courts most international declarations and covenants recognizing universal rights are simply restatements of existing United States law and established constitutional guarantees. This leads to a persistent and lingering suspicion of international authorities and tribunals that presume to revise or improve upon settled American understandings of human rights law. For the most part Americans view their federal courts as the most legitimate and accurate authorities on rights, because of their well-developed jurisprudence and perceived impartiality. As foreign and international tribunals develop deeper and more sophisticated rights traditions, American law and courts will take these more into account, as has already occurred in several recent Supreme Court decisions. Authority will flow to whichever officials and courts prove the most accurate in identifying and protecting universal human rights.

This chapter is adapted from an essay on the same subject first published in a supplement to the American Journal of Comparative Law in 2010.

M.N.S. Sellers (✉)
Regents Professor at the University System of Maryland, Baltimore, MD, USA

Visiting Professor at the Georgetown University Law Center, Washington, DC, USA
e-mail: mortimer.sellers@gmail.com

Y. Haeck and E. Brems (eds.), *Human Rights and Civil Liberties in the 21st Century*, Ius Gentium: Comparative Perspectives on Law and Justice 30,
DOI 10.1007/978-94-007-7599-2_2, © Springer Science+Business Media Dordrecht 2014

2.1 Introduction: Universal Human Rights in the Law of the United States

The founding legal principles and separate political existence of the United States of America began with the claim that "all men" are born with certain "unalienable rights," including rights to "life, liberty, and the pursuit of happiness."[1] The United States' Declaration of Independence from Great Britain rested on this assertion that human rights are universal and binding on all human beings, nations, and states and that it is only to secure these rights that governments legitimately exist, so "that whenever any form of government becomes destructive of these ends, it is the right of the people to alter or to abolish it."[2] The political architects of the United States believed that by violating fundamental human rights, the British king had made himself a "tyrant…unfit to be the ruler of a free people," and therefore subject to replacement by a "new government" more suited to the "safety and happiness" of its citizens.[3] Universal human rights are, will be, and always have been deeply embedded in the law of the United States, and binding in all American tribunals of justice.

There was not at the beginning, is not now, and never can be for Americans any question whether human rights are universal and binding, because universal human rights supply the theoretical foundations that support the United States Federal and separate State governments and necessarily provide, in the American view, the ultimate basis of all legitimate government anywhere.[4] John Adams, the leading constitutional lawyer of the American Revolution, took it for granted as early as 1765 that "many of our rights are inherent and essential, agreed on as maxims, and established as preliminaries, even before a parliament existed."[5] When the North American States established their own independent governments, most followed Adams' advice by supporting their new written constitutions with detailed declarations of rights, listing some of the "inherent rights," of which no government or state can presume to "deprive" or "divest" its subjects.[6]

---

[1] The Unanimous Declaration of the thirteen United States of America (4 July 1776).

[2] Ibid.

[3] Ibid.

[4] On American conceptions of rights in the era of independence, see B.A. Shain (ed.), *The Nature of Rights at the American Founding and Beyond* (Charlottesville, University of Virginia Press, 2007); T.H. Breen, *The Lockean Moment: the Language of Rights on the Eve of the American Revolution* (Oxford, Oxford University Press, 2001); J.P. Reid, *Constitutional History of the American Revolution: The Authority of Rights* (Madison, University of Wisconsin Press, 1986); W.P. Adams, *The First American Constitutions: Republican Ideology and the Making of the State Constitutions in the Revolutionary Era*, trans. R. Kimber and R. Kimber (Chapel Hill, University of North Carolina Press, 1980); M.G. White, *The Philosophy of the American Revolution* (New York, Oxford University Press, 1978); P.A. Hamburger, "Natural Rights, Natural Law, and American Constitutions", 102 *Yale Law Journal* (1993) 907–960; W.F. Dana, "The Declaration of Independence as Justification for Revolution", 13 *Harvard Law Review* (1900) 319–343.

[5] J. Adams, *A Dissertation on the Canon and Feudal Law* (1765) in C. F. Adams, (ed.) *The Works of John Adams, Second President of the United States: with a Life of the Author, Notes and Illustrations,* volume III (Boston: Little & Brown,1865) at 463.

[6] These quotations are from the *Virginia Declaration of Rights* (12 June 1776).

These declarations of the newly independent American States were no innovation. They followed the example of such famous documents as the Pennsylvania Charter of Privileges of 1701 or the Massachusetts Body of Liberties of 1641,[7] and would be replicated on a larger scale by the French *Déclaration des droits de l'Homme et du citoyen* of 1789, the United States Bill of Rights of 1791, and finally the Universal Declaration of Human Rights of 10 December 1948.[8] The Universal Declaration, like the American declarations, threatened "rebellion against tyranny and oppression" unless human rights were "protected by the rule of law"[9] and insisted that "all human beings are born free and equal in dignity and rights."[10] So intimate is the relationship between universal human rights and the rights protected by the United States Constitution, that in the eyes of the United States government and courts most international covenants and treaties recognizing universal human rights are simply restatements of existing United States law and established constitutional guarantees.[11] To the extent that international documents and scholarly or other interpretations of universal human rights depart from traditional American understandings of these ancient guarantees, American officials have usually preferred their own longstanding precedents to more recent (and less well-established) interpretations of human rights law.[12]

This last point is particularly important in understanding the role that universal human rights play in the legal systems of the United States of America. While there is no question that human rights are universal and binding throughout the United States, there have been strong and persistent disagreements about who has the authority to prescribe or to identify these rights in detail, to enforce their requirements against violations in practice, and to adjudicate legal disputes that arise from their enforcement. There are international, Federal (United States), and State constitutions and declarations purporting to identify and to protect universal human rights, and international, Federal (United States) and State authorities with simultaneous and often overlapping responsibility to implement and protect the fundamental

---

[7] On these and other antecedents of the American declarations of rights, see B. Schwartz, *The Great Rights of Mankind: A History of the American Bill of Rights* (expanded ed. Madison: Madison House, 1992).

[8] For a collection of such texts, *see* F. Mari (ed.), *The Universal Declaration of Human Rights and its Predecessors (1679–1948)*, (Leiden: ej Brill, 1949). Cf. J. Morsink, *The Universal Declaration of Human Rights: Origins, Drafting, and Intent* (Philadelphia: University of Pennsylvania Press, 1999).

[9] *The Universal Declaration of Human Rights* (10 December, 1948), Preamble.

[10] Ibid. Article 1.

[11] See e.g., Message of President Jimmy Carter to the United States Senate, 23 February 1978 (concerning the International Convention on the Elimination of All Forms of Racial Discrimination, signed on behalf of the United States on 28 September 1966; *The International Covenant on Economic, Social and Cultural Rights*, signed on behalf of the United States on 5 October 1977; *The International Covenant on Civil and Political Rights*, signed on behalf of the United States on 5 October 1977; and the *American Convention on Human Rights*, signed on behalf of the United States on 1 June 1977).

[12] See e.g., ibid. and *U.S. reservations, declarations, and understandings, International Covenant on Civil and Political Rights*, 138 *Congressional Record* S4781-01 (daily ed. 2 April 1992).

rights of the people. This discussion will consider State, Federal, and international documents and authorities in the order in which they first asserted their jurisdiction through courts, beginning with the separate State institutions.

2.2 Human Rights in the States

The United States of America forms a Union of otherwise independent States, which have delegated certain powers to a Federal government, but reserve the rest.[13] Each of the United States has its own constitution, and each of the State constitutions has its own bill or declaration of rights.[14] The constitutions of five of the most influential States can be taken here as useful and typical examples of these various State provisions. Thus, the Massachusetts,[15] Pennsylvania,[16] Virginia,[17] Texas,[18] and California[19] constitutions all contain their own lists of fundamental rights, which are to be protected by courts and public officials (who must take an oath to do so).[20] The State constitutions describe these rights as "natural, essential, and unalienable" (Massachusetts),[21] the "inherent rights of mankind" (Pennsylvania),[22] "inherent rights, of which… they cannot, by any compact, deprive or divest their posterity" (Virginia),[23] because "All people are by nature free and independent and have inalienable rights" (California),[24] which must be maintained by their "free and

[13] This point is clarified in the United States Constitution by Amendment X, ratified on 15 December 1791.

[14] These may be found easily on-line through the various State websites.

[15] *Constitution of the Commonwealth of Massachusetts, A Declaration of the Rights of the Inhabitants of Massachusetts.*

[16] *Constitution of the Commonwealth of Pennsylvania*, Article 1, *Declaration of Rights.*

[17] *Constitution of Virginia*, Article 1, *Bill of Rights.*

[18] *The Texas Constitution*, Article 1, *Bill of Rights.*

[19] *Constitution of California*, Article 1, *Declaration of Rights.*

[20] For example, in California all members of the legislature, and all public officials and employees, executive, legislative, and judicial, except such inferior officers and employees as may be by law exempted, must "before they enter upon the duties of their respective offices, take and subscribe the following oath or affirmation." The oath reads: "I, …, do solemnly swear (or affirm) that I will support and defend the Constitution of the United States and the Constitution of the State of California against all enemies, foreign and domestic; that I will bear true faith and allegiance to the Constitution of the United States and the Constitution of the State of California; that I take this obligation freely, without any mental reservation or purpose of evasion; and that I will well and faithfully discharge the duties upon which I am about to enter." *Constitution of the State of California*, Article 20. California public officials must further swear or affirm that they belong to no party or organization that advocates the overthrow of the government by force or violence.

[21] *Constitution of the Commonwealth of Massachusetts*, Article CVI.

[22] *Constitution of the Commonwealth of Pennsylvania*, Article 1, Sect. 1.

[23] *Constitution of Virginia*, Article I, Sect. 1.

[24] *California Constitution*, Article 1, Sect. 1.

independent State[s], subject only to the Constitution of the United States, and the maintenance of our free institutions" (Texas).[25]

The bills and declarations of rights of the existing American States served as the model for the United States Bill of Rights, which was added to the Constitution by amendment, as a condition of that document's ratification.[26] Many feared that the United States government under the new constitution might "deprive them of the liberty for which they valiantly fought and honorably bled"[27] and wanted the same protections at the federal level of "those safeguards which they have long been accustomed to have interposed between them and the magistrate who exercises the sovereign power."[28] James Madison, who proposed the United States Bill of Rights to Congress, cited possible threats to liberty not only from the federal executive and legislature, but also from the people of the United States themselves, "operating by the majority against the minority."[29]

The hope expressed for the Federal, as for the State bills of rights, was that the "independent tribunals of justice" would consider themselves to be "the guardians of those rights"[30] and an "impenetrable bulwark" against every improper "encroachment upon rights"[31] enumerated in the "declaration of the rights" of the people.[32] The most persuasive argument offered against the Federal Bill of Rights was that such lists of rights, however carefully drafted, might seem to "disparage" those rights not explicitly set down.[33] James Madison averted this danger by proposing what became the Ninth Amendment to the United States Constitution, which provides that "The enumeration in the Constitution, of certain rights, shall not be construed to deny or disparage others retained by the people."[34] The citizens of the United States were united from the beginning in seeking to "fortify the rights of the people against the encroachments of the Government."[35]

The relationship between the duty of the separate State governments to protect the natural and inherent rights of the people, and the duty of the Federal government

---

[25] *The Texas Constitution*, Article 1, Sect. 1.

[26] Preamble of the "Bill of Rights," as proposed by the United States Congress to the States (4 March 1789).

[27] James Madison discussed this viewpoint in his speech to the Congress proposing a Bill of Rights. *The Annals of Congress, House of Representatives, First Congress, 1st Session* (8 June 1789) at 449.

[28] Ibid. at 450.

[29] Ibid. at 455.

[30] Ibid. at 457.

[31] Ibid.

[32] Ibid.

[33] Ibid. at 456.

[34] On the Ninth Amendment see D.A. Farber, *Retained by the People* (New York: Basic Books, 2007); C.O. Prince, *The Purpose of the Ninth Amendment to the Constitution of the United States* (Lewiston, N.Y.: Edwin Mellen Press, 2005); R. Barnett, *Rights Retained by the People: The History and Meaning of the Ninth Amendment* (Fairfax: George Mason University Press, 1991).

[35] J. Madison in *The Annals of Congress, House of Representatives, First Congress, 1st Session* (8 June 1789) at 459.

to do the same was highly contested at first. The famous Kentucky[36] and Virginia Resolutions of 1798[37] denied both that the protection of fundamental rights in the States was the province of the Federal government[38] and that the United States government should be the final arbiter of its own jurisdiction in these or any other circumstances.[39] Kentucky claimed the right to "nullify" any Federal Acts that overstepped the proper limits of Federal control,[40] insisting that "it is jealousy, and not confidence which prescribes limited constitutions."[41] Both State and the Federal authorities claimed to protect fundamental rights and justice, without being certain at first which jurisdiction had ultimate control.

Chief Justice John Marshall concluded in the famous case of *Barron v. City of Baltimore* (1833) that the "liberty of the citizen" was a subject on which the States remained the judges "exclusively"[42] under the United States Constitution. Marshall suggested that the purpose of listing fundamental rights in the Federal Constitution was solely to constrain the United States government, while the State courts, constitutions and legislature had primary responsibility for keeping their own governments in check.[43] This did not mean that the fundamental and inherent rights of all persons did not apply against the State governments, but rather that the United States courts were not responsible for their enforcement against the States' own public officials.[44] The "fundamental" guarantees, "which belong, of right, to the citizens of all free governments," have been enjoyed by the citizens of the American States "from the time of their becoming free, independent, and sovereign,"[45] and generally protected by the State courts.[46] The famous Federal cases of *Calder v. Bull* (1788) and *Corfield v. Coryell* (1823) confirmed that State governments have a duty to respect "that security for personal liberty, or private property, for the protection whereof government was established" *(Calder)*[47] and to uphold those rights which are "in their nature, fundamental" (*Corfield*).[48]

The United States discovered in the eighteenth and nineteenth centuries what has become apparent to the world since the Second World War, which is that local ("national" or "sovereign") enforcement of the "great rights of mankind" fails in the

---

[36] *Resolutions of the Kentucky Legislature* (10 November 1798).

[37] *Resolution of the Virginia Senate* (24 December 1798).

[38] *Resolutions of the Kentucky Legislature* (10 November 1798) No.3.

[39] Ibid., Resolution no. 1.

[40] Ibid., Resolution no. 8.

[41] Ibid.

[42] *Barron v. City of Baltimore*, 32 U.S. 243, 248 (1833).

[43] Ibid. at 250-1.

[44] The Constitution itself referred to the "privileges and immunities of citizens in the several states", *Constitution of the United States* (1787), Article IV, Sect. 2.

[45] *Corfield v. Coryell,* 6 Fed. Cas. 546, no. 3230 C.C.E.D. Pa. (1823).

[46] See *Calder v. Bull*, 3. U.S. 386, 388 (1798) for those acts "which the Federal, or State, Legislature cannot do, without exceeding their authority."

[47] *Calder v. Bull*, 3 U.S. 386, 388 (1798).

[48] *Corfield v. Coryell*, 6 Fed. Cas. 546, no. 3230 C.C.E.D. Pa. (1823).

face of petty prejudice and the parochial self-interest of local ethnic, religious and political factions.[49] For example, the Court of Appeals of Kentucky held in the case of *Amy, a woman of color, v. Smith* (1822) that "free negroes and mulattoes" are a "degraded race of people"[50] and therefore not entitled to any of those "ordinary rights of personal security and property" enjoyed by others in the Commonwealth.[51] The same was true in Tennessee, which considered any "man of color" to belong to an "inferior caste in society" and "scarcely" worthy of enjoying "a single right in common with the mass of citizens of the State."[52] All this in spite of constitutional clauses in their State bills or declarations of rights, which guaranteed that "no free man shall be… deprived of his life, liberty of property, but by … the law of the land."[53]

The disregard by the southern States in the American Union of the universal or "inherent" rights of humanity, as applied not only to their slaves, but also to free African Americans, led to increasingly sharp conflicts with other States and their representatives in the United States legislature and in the courts.[54] United States Chief Justice Roger B. Taney tried to settle the question, and to strengthen the slaveholders' position, by extending the reasoning of the *Amy* and *Claiborne* cases to the United States as a whole in the infamous decision of *Dred Scott v. Sandford* (1857),[55] in which Taney argued that the "self-evident" truths of the Declaration of Independence, although they "would seem to embrace the whole human family," were never intended to extend to the "African Race."[56]

The promotion of such reasoning, and principled resistance against it, let in time to a great Civil War (1861–1865), and ultimately to the passage of three new amendments to the United States Constitution, prohibiting slavery (Amendment XIII),[57] extending the vote to African Americans (Amendment XV),[58] and prohibiting the States from depriving "any person of life, liberty, or property, without due process of law" or denying "any person within its jurisdiction the equal protection of the laws"

---

[49] James Madison saw this already when he proposed the Bill of Rights to the First Congress and observed that he thought "there is more danger of those powers being abused by the State Governments than by the Government of the United States." James Madison, in *The Annals of Congress, House of Representatives, First Congress, First Session* (8 June 1789) at 458. For "the great rights of mankind," see p. 449.

[50] *Amy, a woman of color, v. Smith*, 11 Ky. 326; 1 Litt. 326, 334.

[51] Ibid. at 333.

[52] *The State v. Claiborne*, 19 *Tenn*. 331, 1 Meigs 331, 340. "An emancipated slave is called a freeman in common parlance … but in reference to the conditions of a white citizen, his condition is still that of degraded man, aspiring to no equality of rights with white men, and possessing a very few only of the privileges pertaining to a 'freeman'." Ibid. at 341.

[53] State of Tennessee, *Constitution of 1835*, Article I, *Declaration of Rights*, Sect. VIII. Cf. Magna Carta, Chap. 39.

[54] For the vast literature on the antebellum conflict over fundamental human rights, *see* R. Barnett, *Restoring the Lost Constitution* (Princeton: Princeton University Press, 2004).

[55] *Dred Scott v. Sandford*, 60 U.S. (19 How.) 393 (1857).

[56] Ibid. at 410.

[57] The Thirteenth Amendment was ratified on 6 December 1865.

[58] The Fifteenth Amendment was ratified on 3 February 1870.

(Amendment XIV).[59] These provisions had the effect of overturning *Dred Scott v. Sandford*, which had protected legal discrimination against African Americans, but also reversed *Barron v. Baltimore*, because the Fourteenth Amendment gave the United States Congress the power to enforce the provisions of the amendment "by appropriate legislation."[60]

The Fourteenth Amendment to the United States Constitution did not limit or in any way compromise the separate duty of the governments and courts in each of the United States to protect and respect the universal, inherent and inalienable rights of humanity, as recognized by the Declaration of Independence and in the various State constitutions and bills of rights.[61] States continue to apply their own bills and declarations of rights directly, through their own courts.[62] But the imposition of the Fourteenth Amendment gave the Federal government and courts full power to intervene when states invade or fail to protect the "life, liberty, or property" of any person subject to their jurisdiction. State governments and courts can and often do protect rights (including universal rights) more broadly and generously than has yet been required by United States courts, but they cannot now diminish the rights of their citizens by narrow or parochial constructions of universal human rights.[63]

2.3 Federal Protections of Human Rights

The United States government did not at first fully exercise the powers conferred by the Fourteenth Amendment,[64] and even when the United States did act, such action was not at first supported by the courts, which were slow to accept the vastly expanded jurisdiction of the Federal authorities.[65] United States courts recognized that some "additional guarantees of human rights" were provided by the Fourteenth Amendment, along with "additional powers" for the Federal government, and the "additional restraints" upon the States[66] concerning "fundamental rights" as

---

[59] The Fourteenth Amendment was ratified on 9 July 1868.

[60] United States Constitution, Amendment XIV, Sect. 5.

[61] See W.J. Jr. Brennan, "The Bill of Rights and the States, The Revival of State Constitutions as Guardians of Individual Rights" in 61 *New York University Law Review* (1986) 535; Ibid., "State Constitutions and the Revival of Individual Rights" in 90 *Harvard Law Review*(1977) 489.

[62] See, e.g., M.H. Marshall, "Wise Parents Do Not Hesitate to Learn from their Children: Interpreting State Constitutions in an Age of Global Jurisprudence" in 79 *New York Law Review* (2004) 1633.

[63] H.A. Linde, "E Pluribus – Constitutional Theory and State Courts" in 18 *Georgia Law Review*(1984) 165, H.A. Linde, "First things First – Rediscovering the States' Bills of Rights" 9 *University of Baltimore Law Review*(1980) 379.

[64] The first major attempt to enforce the Fourteenth Amendment to protect Civil Rights in the States was the Civil Rights Act of 1871 (also known as the "Enforcement Act" or the "Ku Klux Klan Act") (17 *Stat*. 13).

[65] For example, the Civil Rights Act of 1875 (18 *Stat*. 335) was struck down as unconstitutional by the United States Supreme Court in *The Civil Rights Cases,* 109 U.S. 3 (1883).

[66] *Slaughter-House Cases*, 83 U.S. 36, 67–68 (1873).

described in the old case of *Corfield v. Coryell.*[67] But the Supreme Court could not at first accept that the Federal government should really have the power to enforce "the entire domain of civil rights heretofore belonging exclusively to the States."[68] The whole history of United States human rights law since the Supreme Court first interpreted the Fourteenth Amendment in the *Slaughter-House Cases* in 1873 has been the story of gradual progress towards broader acceptance by the Federal Courts and Congress that the Fourteenth Amendment did indeed "radically change[] the whole theory of the relations of the State and Federal governments to each other,"[69] by protecting "the rights of person and property" against the arbitrary power of the States.[70]

American judges disagreed initially, not about the existence of "natural and inalienable" rights,[71] "which of right belong to the citizens of all free governments,"[72] but about whether the Federal Constitution protected these "common rights" against State action.[73] Gradually over decades Federal judges and other American public officials came to accept that the Fourteenth Amendment "was intended to give practical effect to the declaration of 1776 of inalienable rights, rights which are the gift of the Creator, which the law does not confer, but only recognizes."[74] Put more prosaically, more than a century after the ratification of the Fourteenth Amendment to the United States Constitution, the Federal and other United States courts now fully accept that "all fundamental rights comprised within the term liberty are protected by the Federal Constitution from invasion by the States"[75] through the section of the Fourteenth Amendment which declares that no State shall "deprive any person of life, liberty or property without due process of law." The controlling word in most such cases is "liberty."[76]

The protection of liberty "against executive usurpation," "tyranny," and "arbitrary legislation,"[77] has been the business of American courts from the beginning, often resting on the ancient promise of the English Magna Carta that "No freeman shall

---

[67] "Rights which belong of right to the citizens of all free governments" and "embrace nearly every civil right for the protection of which civil government is instituted." Ibid. at 75–76. Cf. above on *Corfield v. Coryell.*

[68] *Slaughter-House Cases,* supra, note 67 at 77.

[69] Ibid. at 78.

[70] Ibid. at 82.

[71] Ibid. (Field dissent) at 96.

[72] Ibid. (Field dissent) at 97.

[73] Ibid. (Field dissent) at 89.

[74] Ibid. (Field dissent) at 105.

[75] Justice O'Connor, Justice Kennedy, and Justice Souter, writing for the majority in *Planned Parenthood of Southeastern Pennsylvania v. Casey*, 505 U.S. 833, 847 (1992) quoting Justice Brandeis' concurring opinion in *Whitney v. California*, 274 U.S. 357, 373 (1927).

[76] *Planned Parenthood v. Casey*, supra, note 76 at 846.

[77] Ibid. at 847 quoting Justice Harlan, dissenting on jurisdictional grounds in *Poe v. Ullman* 367 U.S. 497, 541 (1961), in which Justice Harlan quoted the case of *Hurtado v. California,* 110 U.S. 516, 537 (1884).

be taken or imprisoned, or be disseized of his freehold or liberties or free customs, or be outlawed or exiled, or any otherwise destroyed… but by the law of the land."[78] This final phrase, "*per legem terrae,*" was understood by English whigs and by the American constitutional writers who followed them, to protect life, liberty and property from deprivation except through the "due process of law."[79] Some such protection and guarantee appears in most American State bills of rights, in the United States Bill of Rights (Amendment V), and in the Fourteenth Amendment to the United States Constitution, which requires that no State shall "deprive any person of life, liberty, or property, without due process of law."

The historical antecedents of the phrases "liberty" and "due process" in the Fourteenth Amendment have colored their interpretation from the beginning. The Supreme Court of the United States, in its most detailed recent discussion of the meaning of the word "liberty" in the Due Process clause of the Fourteenth Amendment, cited Magna Carta and quoted the phrase "*per legem terrae*" as interpreted by Supreme Court jurisprudence going back to the nineteenth century.[80] The Supreme Court has construed this fundamental "liberty" to encompass most of the rights enumerated in the United States Bill of Rights,[81] but also other fundamental human rights, such as the rights to marry,[82] to procreate,[83] to pursue an education,[84] or to enjoy "privacy" as privacy relates to abortion[85] and to homosexuality.[86] To determine the scope of such rights, United States courts have looked to the concepts of "personal dignity" and "autonomy" that are "central to the liberty protected by the Fourteenth Amendment."[87]

The United States executive, congress and the courts feel a responsibility to strengthen and to advance the American legal tradition of "liberty,"[88] "having regard to what history teaches are the traditions from which it developed as well as the traditions from which it broke."[89] This includes concern for judicial precedents in United States courts protecting "personal autonomy,"[90] but also the protection of

---

[78] *Magna Carta*, 39 (1215).

[79] See e.g., Justice Bradley's dissent in the *Slaughter-House Cases* supra, note 67 at, 50. Cf. *Planned Parenthood v. Casey*, supra, note 75 at 847.

[80] *Planned Parenthood v. Casey*, supra, note 76, quoting Justice Harlan's dissent in *Poe v. Ullman*, supra, note 78, which itself quoted *Hurtado v. California,* supra, note 78.

[81] See e.g., *Planned Parenthood v. Casey*, supra, note 76; *Duncan v. Louisiana*, 391 U.S. 145, 147–148 (1968).

[82] *Loving v. Virginia*, 388 U.S. 1, 12 (1967).

[83] *Skinner v. Oklahoma*, 316 U.S. 535, 541–542 (1942).

[84] *Pierce v. Society of Sisters*, 268 U.S. 510, 535 (1925); *Meyer v. Nebraska*, 262 U.S. 390 (1923).

[85] *Roe v. Wade*, 410 U.S. 113, 153 (1973); *Planned Parenthood v. Casey,* supra, note 76.

[86] *Lawrence v. Texas*, 539 U.S. 558, 564 (2003).

[87] *Planned Parenthood v. Casey*, supra, note 76.

[88] See e.g., *Planned Parenthood v. Casey,*850, supra, note 76, quoting Justice Harlan dissenting in *Poe v. Ullman*, supra, note 78 at 542.

[89] Ibid.

[90] *Planned Parenthood v. Casey,* supra, note 76 at 857, 860.

other rights implicit in the concept of ordered "liberty."[91] A persistent but isolated minority of judges on United States courts has sometimes seen the concept of "tradition" as a limitation on "liberty" and fundamental rights.[92] Such attitudes misunderstand the role of liberty in the American legal tradition, which protects fundamental human rights, not because they are "traditional," but because they are just – and "unalienable" by any person or government official.[93] Tradition, precedent and American legal history play a central role in clarifying the meaning of liberty and universal human rights in United States courts, not because American legal precedents *create* rights, but because the American legal system and judges seeking to understand its promise of liberty have studied individual human rights for so long, so carefully, and so well.[94]

The role of American tradition in understanding the meaning of "liberty" becomes particularly important when the Supreme Court of the United States must overturn its own mistaken precedents concerning fundamental rights, as it did recently in the cases of *Lawrence v. Texas* (2003) regarding homosexuality[95] and *Roper v. Simmons* (2005) regulating the death penalty for juvenile offenders.[96] In both cases the Court looked for support to decisions made by State courts interpreting their own bills or declarations of rights,[97] but also to the practices of foreign and international tribunals interpreting universal rights as applied to their own jurisdictions.[98] When the Supreme Court overturned its own recent precedents[99] to hold in *Lawrence v. Texas* that homosexual adults must be left free to engage in "private conduct in the exercise of their liberty under the Due Process clause of the Fourteenth Amendment to the Constitution,"[100] the rationale for this holding depended on the Court's own evolving jurisprudence,[101] but also on the jurisprudence of the European Court of Human Rights, which had recognized similar protection of consensual homosexual conduct under the European Convention on Human Rights.[102] The *Roper v. Simmons* case invalidating the juvenile death penalty in the United States cited the United Nations Convention on the Rights of the Child (to

[91] Ibid. at 869.

[92] See e.g., Chief Justice Rehnquist, dissenting in *Planned Parenthood v. Casey*, supra, note 76, 951–952, 981.

[93] See e.g., the United States Declaration of Independence (1776) on "unalienable rights" and the *Constitution of the United States* (1787) Preamble on "Justice" and "the Blessings of Liberty."

[94] See *Planned Parenthood v. Casey,* supra, note 76 at 848.

[95] *Lawrence v. Texas*, supra, note 87.

[96] *Roper v. Simmons*, 543 U.S. 551 (2005).

[97] *Lawrence v. Texas,* supra, note 87.

[98] Ibid.

[99] *Bowers v. Hardwick,* 478 U.S. 186 (1986).

[100] *Lawrence v. Texas*, supra, note 87 at 564.

[101] Ibid. at 564–566.

[102] Ibid. at 573, citing ECtHR 22 October 1981, No. 7525/76, *Dudgeon v. United Kingdom*, para 52.

which the United States is not a party)[103] and the views of "leading members of the Western European community."[104]

Cases such as these, interpreting the fundamental requirements of "liberty" under the Due Process clause of the Fourteenth Amendment to the United States Constitution, cite foreign opinions to establish "civilized standards,"[105] not because the opinion of the world community "controls" the outcome of American cases,[106] but because "the express affirmation of certain fundamental rights by other nations and peoples … underscores the centrality of those same rights within our own heritage of freedom."[107] American judges interpreting "values we share with a wider civilization"[108] have been guided in some cases by foreign jurisdictions towards better understanding which rights (or which applications of known rights) should be protected "as an integral part of human freedom."[109] This direct reference by American courts to the fundamental and inalienable requirements of human liberty is often described (and sometimes criticized) as establishing the "substantive" due process of law.[110]

The Constitution of the United States was intended by its drafters to constitute, and accepted by the States that ratified it as having constituted, the "supreme Law of the Land," not only in itself, but also through all laws or treaties made under its provisions.[111] With the ratification of the Fourteenth Amendment in 1868, the Supreme Court of the United States became the final arbiter of all "fundamental rights" requiring judicial protection under the concept of "liberty" confirmed by the due process clause of the United States Constitution.[112] To understand which rights liberty requires, judges and other officers of the State have looked to the United States Bill of Rights,[113] to the practices of the American State governments and courts,[114] to the opinions of the broader world community,[115] and directly to the "purpose and function" of liberty and rights in

---

[103] *Roper v. Simmons*, supra, note 97 at 576.

[104] Ibid. at 561.

[105] Ibid.

[106] Ibid. at 578.

[107] Ibid.

[108] *Lawrence v. Texas*, supra, note 87 at 576.

[109] Ibid.

[110] Justice Scalia dissenting in *Lawrence v. Texas*, supra, note 87 at 593.

[111] *Constitution of the United States*, (1787) Article VI.

[112] On the Fourteenth Amendment, see G. Epps, *Democracy Reborn: The Fourteenth Amendment and the Fight for Equal Rights in Post-Civil War America* (New York: Henry Holt, 2006); W.E. Nelson, *The Fourteenth Amendment: From Political Principle to Judicial Doctrine* (Cambridge, Mass.: Harvard Univ. Press, 1988); M.K. Curtis, *No State Shall Abridge: The Fourteenth Amendment and the Bill of Rights* (Durham, N.C.: Duke Univ. Press, 1986).

[113] *Roper v. Simmons*, supra, note 97 at 555.

[114] Ibid. at 568.

[115] Ibid. at 576, 578.

the "constitutional design."[116] This allows judicial and other public understandings of the rights protected by constitutional liberty to "evolve" as society "progresses" and "matures."[117]

2.4 International Human Rights Standards

The Supreme Court of the United States puzzled some observers when it cited the United Nations Convention on the Rights of the Child (a treaty the United States never ratified)[118] and the International Covenant on Civil and Political Rights (to which the United States had made a specific reservation on this precise issue)[119] in concluding that the imposition of the death penalty on juveniles under State law would violate "liberty" rights protected by the Fourteenth Amendment.[120] Such references by American courts to treaty provisions that are not in themselves directly binding on the United States, raises the broader question how American courts, legislators and government officials apply generally accepted international human rights standards to American circumstances.[121] American courts and American public officials have usually weighed foreign evidence of the requirements of universal human rights according to the legitimacy, importance and probative value of the treaty, judicial decision, custom, or academic opinion advanced to substantiate the suggested universal standard.[122]

The use by American courts (and other public officials) of non-American authorities to better understand fundamental rights protected by the United States Constitution, reflects a broader American tradition of looking beyond purely American precedents to clarify the requirements of international law.[123] The most detailed exposition of this American attitude was set out by the Supreme Court of the United States in the case of *The Paquete Habana* in 1900, which negated the seizure of two Cuban fishing boats as contrary to the law of nations.[124] To substantiate this "rule of international law" against the seizure of coastal fishing vessels, even in time of war, the Supreme Court referred (*inter alia*) to the practices of

[116] Ibid. at 560.

[117] Ibid. at 561.

[118] Ibid. at 576.

[119] Ibid.

[120] See the florid dissent of Justice Scalia in *Roper v. Simmons*, supra, note 97 at 622 for his strongly worded objections to considering the views of such "like-minded foreigners." Ibid. at 608.

[121] Ibid.

[122] *Roper v. Simmons*, supra, note 97 at 578, the most prominent recent case to make such a judgment, looks to the "express affirmation of certain fundamental rights by other nations and peoples" to underscore "the centrality of those same rights within our own heritage of freedom."

[123] For the early history, see M.W. Janis, *The American Tradition of International Law: Great Expectations, 1789–1914* (Oxford: Clarendon Press, 2004).

[124] *The Paquete Habana*, 175 U.S. 677 (1900).

English and French kings,[125] to treaties among various European nations,[126] to French declarations,[127] to a United States treaty with Prussia[128] and to Richard H. Dana's edition of Henry Wheaton's treatise on the *Elements of International Law*.[129] The Court suggested that, taken together, such authorities tend to indicate a consensus among "civilized nations" concerning the requirements of international law.[130] The concept of what constitutes a "civilized nation" is to a large extent circular, but still plays a significant role in Supreme Court jurisprudence concerning fundamental human rights.[131] Foreign States that generally respect universal human rights and the requirements of international law thereby show themselves to be "civilized," and their views and practices are taken as good evidence of what fundamental human rights and international law require of them and others.[132]

The United States have long recognized that "International law is part of our law" and "must be ascertained and administered by the courts of justice of appropriate jurisdiction as often as questions of right depending upon it are duly presented" for determination.[133] But United States courts will generally look to controlling acts of the United States' own executive or legislative powers to determine the requirements of international law in practice.[134] This reflects in part the natural deference of the judiciary to legislative and executive authority, but also the positive grant to Congress by the United States Constitution of the power "to define and punish… offenses against the law of nations."[135] This can lead to serious tension, where congressional or executive conceptions of the requirements of international law are at variance with the more widely held views or practices of other nations. But even in such cases, when they concern universal human rights, the positive requirements of existing United States laws and the Constitution have usually been sufficient to maintain general compliance with widely accepted international standards.[136]

The most difficult question facing Americans and United States Courts in seeking to implement universal human rights in practice, has been to determine which international institutions or foreign (or American) authorities deserve deference

---

[125] Ibid. at 687.

[126] Ibid. at 687–688.

[127] Ibid. at 688–689.

[128] Ibid. at 690–691.

[129] Ibid. at 691.

[130] Ibid. at 686.

[131] See *Roper v. Simmons*, supra, note 97 at 561, citing *Thompson v. Oklahoma* 487 U.S. 815, 826 (1988).

[132] The Supreme Court usually looks to "the Western European community" and to "other nations that share our Anglo-American heritage." Ibid.

[133] *The Paquete Habana*, supra, note 125 at 700.

[134] Ibid.

[135] *United States Constitution*, Article I, Sect. 8.

[136] See e.g., *Hamdan v. Rumsfeld* 548 U.S. 557 (2006), which relied on Federal law and the Uniform Code of Military Justice to require the United States government to respect the humanitarian requirements of the Geneva Conventions.

(or at least consideration) in specific cases.[137] For example, in the recent case of *Medellin v. Texas*, the Supreme Court of the United States concluded not only that the International Court of Justice had no binding authority to order the review and reconsideration of Texas State court convictions and (ensuing death-penalty sentences) as violations of the Vienna Convention on the Law of Treaties, but also that the President of the United States had no authority to require Texan compliance with what he judged to be the nation's binding obligations under international law.[138] The underlying conflict arose from a difference of opinion between American and Mexican public officials about the right to life as applied to the death penalty, but this difference expressed itself in jurisdictional claims relating to the proper domain and democratic legitimacy of the International Court of Justice.[139] In the *Medellin* case, the Supreme Court held both that the judgments of the International Court of Justice are *not* directly enforceable as domestic law in the United States[140] *and* that the President of the United States cannot order the States to treat them as such[141] without first securing Federal implementing legislation to give separate domestic effect to international obligations already created by the treaty itself.[142]

The *Medellin* case is particularly revealing, because the Supreme Court stressed the significance of the United States' Security Council veto in limiting the authority of the International Court of Justice.[143] The United States has not – and according to this rationale *should not* – cede the same authority to the United Nations or to its organs that the States ceded to the Federal government with the ratification of the Fourteenth Amendment to the United States Constitution.[144] Certain international tribunals may enjoy a special status because of implementing legislation enacted by Congress, but otherwise their power is (and should be) limited.[145] Even the President of the United States may not act in such cases, without prior Congressional legislation that would empower him to do so.[146] The pronounced aversion of United States courts and public officials to ceding final control over the meaning or interpretation of international law or human rights guarantees to foreign authorities or

---

[137] See e.g., "The Use of Foreign Law in American Constitutional Adjudication: A Revealing Colloquy between Justices Scalia and Breyer" on the American University website and discussed in M.G. Dorf, *No Litmus Test: Law versus Politics in the Twenty First Century* (Lanham, Maryland: Rowland 1 Littlefield, 2006), 213–219.

[138] *Medellin v. Texas*, 128 S. Ct. 1346 (2008).

[139] On American worries concerning the democratic legitimacy and general reliability of international courts, see D.M. Amann and M.N.S. Sellers, "The United States of America and the International Criminal Court" in 50 *American Journal of Comparative Law* (Supplement) 381 (2002).

[140] *Medellin v. Texas,* supra, note 139 at 1353.

[141] Ibid.

[142] Ibid. at 1357.

[143] Ibid. at 1359.

[144] Ibid. at 1360.

[145] Ibid. at 1365–1366.

[146] Ibid. at 1367–1368.

to international tribunals, might seem at first to contradict the insight of the Fourteenth Amendment that local perceptions of universal human rights are necessarily incomplete.[147] What makes the circumstance different (from the American perspective) is that international tribunals have not yet secured the judicial autonomy or democratic legitimacy of the United States Supreme Court or other institutions of the United States Federal government.[148]

United States attitudes towards the International Criminal Court provide a striking recent example of American distrust of what some perceive as the insufficiently liberal and democratic foundations of many international institutions.[149] The United States government refused to ratify the Rome Statute establishing the International Criminal Court (ICC) on the theory (as it was expressed in the United States Senate) that ICC decision-making "will not be confined to those from democratic countries with the rule of law."[150] The fear was that since each state party to the ICC has one vote in the Assembly of States Parties,[151] this will make the selection and removal of the prosecutor and judges,[152] the development of the rules of procedure and evidence,[153] and the alteration of the treaty through amendment,[154] all ultimately subject to the influence of undemocratic and illiberal regimes.[155] As a general rule, the United States has been hesitant to cede judicial, legislative or enforcement authority to any international institution or tribunal that is not subject (as in the United Nations) to the veto power of the United States.[156]

The confidence of Americans in their own constitutional protections of universal human rights has been so great that the United States has joined in proposed international articulations or clarifications of universal human rights only with the greatest reluctance, always taking care to maintain its own existing Federal

---

[147] Ibid. at 1367. "Nothing in the text, background, negotiating and drafting history, or practice among signatory nations suggests that the President or Senate intended the improbable result of giving the judgments of an international tribunal a higher status than that enjoyed by 'many of our most fundamental constitutional protections'."

[148] European Courts have showed a similar hesitancy to defer to less-than-democratic international institutions in cases affecting fundamental human rights, see the joined cases of *Yassin Abdullah Kadi and Al Barakaat International Foundation v. Council of the European Union and Commission of the European Communities* in the Court of Justice of the European Communities (C-402/05 P and C-415/05 P) (2008).

[149] On American attitudes towards the International Criminal Court, see D.M. Amann and M.N.S. Sellers, "The United States of America and the International Criminal Court," in 50 *American Journal of Comparative Law* (Supplement) (2002) 381.

[150] "Is a U.N. International Criminal Court in the National Interest?", Hearing on the International Criminal Court before the International Operations Subcommittee of the U.S. Senate Foreign Relations Committee (July 23, 1998) (statement of Senator Rod Grams).

[151] Rome Statute of the International Criminal Court, U.N. Doc. A/CONF. 183/9 (1998), art 112.

[152] Ibid., Arts. 36(6)(a); 46(2)(a); 42(4); and 46(2)(b).

[153] Ibid., Arts. 9(1) and 51(1).

[154] Ibid., Arts. 121; 122.

[155] See Amann and Sellers, "International Criminal Court" supra, note 150 at 389.

[156] See *Medellin v. Texas*, supra, note 139 and particularly the remarks by Chief Justice Roberts.

constitutional understandings intact.[157] Whenever the United States has taken the unusual step of ratifying an international treaty governing or defining universal human rights, the motive has been to encourage greater respect for fundamental rights in other nations, rather than to change existing American constitutional guarantees.[158] For example, when the United States ratified the International Covenant on Civil and Political Rights, it was with express reservations preserving existing American conceptions of the right of free speech,[159] the right to life,[160] the prohibition of cruel or degrading treatment or punishment,[161] the punishment of juvenile offenders,[162] and racial and other discrimination,[163] as well as a general statement that "Nothing in this covenant requires or authorizes legislation, or other action, by the United States of America prohibited by the Constitution of the United States as interpreted by the United States."[164]

The United States ratified the United Nations conventions against Torture,[165] against the Crime of Genocide,[166] and against All Forms of Racial Discrimination,[167] but all with restrictive reservations, declarations and understandings similar to those that applied in the case of the Covenant on Civil and Political Rights, protecting existing understandings of the United States Bill of Rights and providing that the treaties would in any case be "non-self-executing," requiring that implementing legislation pass through the United States Congress before United States courts would apply the human rights conventions directly to United States cases and controversies.[168] The general policy of the United States with respect to all new multilateral human rights treaties has been to view the great majority of their substantive provisions as consistent with the existing United States Constitution and

---

[157] See e.g., Message of the President of the United States, Transmitting Four Treaties Pertaining to Human Rights, S. EXEC. Docs. C, D, E and F, 95th Congress 2d. Session at III (23 February 1978).

[158] See e.g., the statement of the American delegate Eleanor Roosevelt, *On the Adoption of the Universal Declaration of Human Rights*, United Nations General Assembly (December 9, 1948).

[159] U.S. Reservations, Declarations, and Understandings, International Covenant on Civil and Political Rights, 138 *Congressional Record* S4781-01 (daily ed., 2 April 1992) at I(1).

[160] Ibid. at I (2).

[161] Ibid. at I (3).

[162] Ibid. at I (5).

[163] Ibid. at II (1).

[164] Ibid. at IV.

[165] U.S. Reservations, Declarations, and Understandings, Convention Against Torture and Other Cruel, Inhuman or Degrading Treatment or Punishment, 101st Congress, 2d session in 136 *Congressional Record* S17486 (27 October 1990).

[166] U.S. Reservations, Declarations, and Understandings, Convention on the Prevention and Punishment of the Crime of Genocide, *Congressional Record* S1355-01 (19 February 1986).

[167] U.S. Reservations, Declarations, and Understandings, International Convention on the Prevention of All Forms of Racial Discrimination, *Congressional Record* S14326 (24 June 1994).

[168] See also Message from the President of the United States, Transmitting Four Treaties Pertaining to Human Rights, S. EXEC. Docs. C, D, E and F, 95th Congress 2d. Session at III (23 February 1978).

laws, but to the extent that the treaties are not consistent with existing practice, to require a modifying reservation, understanding or declaration before giving the treaty legal effect in the courts of the United States.[169]

2.5 Conclusion and Prospects for the Future

The courts and people of the United States have been committed throughout their history to the proposition that human rights are universal, binding and enforceable by law – or even by extra-legal action and revolution when rights are not protected fully by the State. Americans and American judges have also become accustomed through their own history and in light of the American experience of oppression, revolution and civil war, to cede jurisdiction over the protection of fundamental rights to inter-State institutions, such as the United States Congress and the Federal judiciary. Americans demanded, when they created their Federal Union, that the United States Constitution should guarantee the same protection of inalienable human rights already present in their own State constitutions, and they required in due course that the United Nations Organization must also declare its commitment to fundamental human rights[170] and to protect "universal respect for, and observance of, human rights and fundamental freedoms for all without distinction as to race, sex, language, or religion."[171]

The first United States delegate to the United Nations General Assembly, Eleanor Roosevelt, played a leading role in securing the creation and unanimous approval of the Universal Declaration of Human Rights in 1948.[172] Speaking on behalf of the United States to the General Assembly of the United Nations, Roosevelt embraced the Universal Declaration as a "great event ... in the life of mankind"[173] and expressed her nation's hope that "this Universal Declaration of Human Rights may ... become the International Magna Carta of all men everywhere," a document as significant for all humanity as the Bill of Rights had been for the people of the United States.[174] Then, as now, the government of the United States embraced "basic principles of human rights and freedoms," applicable to "all peoples of all nations," without wishing thereby to alter in any way American law or the existing "legal obligation" of the United States.[175]

---

[169] Ibid.

[170] *Charter of the United Nations* (1945), Preamble.

[171] Ibid., Art. 55.

[172] M.A. Glendon, *A World Made New: Eleanor Roosevelt and the Universal Declaration of Human Rights* (New York: Random House, 2001).

[173] E. Roosevelt, *On the Adoption of the Universal Declaration of Human Rights*, United Nations General Assembly (9 December 1948).

[174] Ibid.

[175] Ibid.

The American commitment to liberty and inalienable human rights that animated the Revolution, the constitutions (State and Federal) and the legal system of the United States, has two primary components: substantive and procedural. The substantive rights of humanity are enumerated (to the extent that this is possible) in the State declarations of rights, the United States Bill of Rights, the international covenants and Universal Declaration of Human Rights. The procedural commitments to democratic deliberation, to the separation of powers, to legislative and executive checks and balances, and to an independent judiciary have been much more important in securing the rights and liberty of American citizens. As James Madison well expressed it in the *Federalist*, explaining the Constitution of the United States to the People of New York, "parchment barriers" against despotism will not be effective without "divided and balanced" institutions, so that each part of government can effectively "check" and "restrain" the excesses of the others.[176]

The independence of the judiciary has played a particularly important role in the procedural protection of universal human rights in the United States, since judges have always had the last word in interpreting the Constitution of the United States, including the Fourteenth Amendment guarantees of "liberty" and the "due process of law."[177] The drafters of the United States Constitution made sure that judges would serve "during good behavior,"[178] which is to say for life, and that their salaries "shall not be diminished" during their continuance in office.[179] Americans knew (and know) this to be "the best expedient which can be devised in any government, to secure a steady, upright, and impartial administration of the laws."[180]

Alexander Hamilton, in his essays in favor of the United States Constitution, praised judicial independence and long judicial terms in office as an "excellent barrier" against despotism[181] and insisted (quoting Montesquieu) that "there is no liberty if the power of judging be not separated from the legislative and executive powers."[182] Then, as now, judges in the United States needed "complete independence" to exercise properly their power "to declare all acts contrary to the manifest tenor of the Constitution void."[183] The framers of the United States Constitution knew that "without this, all reservations of particular rights or privileges would amount to nothing."[184] Alexander Hamilton and other architects of the United States

---

[176] "Publius" [James Madison], *The Federalist* No. 48 in the *New York Packet* (1 February 1788).

[177] This judicial authority was famously confirmed by the United States Supreme Court in the case of *Marbury v. Madison*, 5 U.S. (1 Cranch) 137 (1803), when Chief Justice John Marshall declared for the Court that "It is emphatically the province and duty of the judicial department to say what the law is" and reiterated that "the Constitution is superior to any ordinary act of the legislature."

[178] *Constitution of the United States*, Article III, Sect. I.

[179] Ibid.

[180] "Publius" [Alexander Hamilton], *Federalist* 78 in the *Independent Journal* (14 June 1788).

[181] Ibid.

[182] Ibid., citing Charles de Secondat, Baron de la Brède et de Montesquieu, *The Spirit of the Laws*, volume I, p. 181.

[183] "Publius" [Alexander Hamilton], *Federalist* 78 in the *Independent Journal* (14 June 1788).

[184] Ibid.

legal system saw the independence of judges as absolutely necessary to protect the "rights of individuals" against "serious oppressions of the minor party in the community."[185] None of this could be expected "from judges who hold their offices by a temporary commission."[186]

United States judges interpreting the United States Constitution in United States Courts have been the greatest guardians of fundamental human rights throughout the history of the United States of America, and they are unlikely to cede their jurisdiction to international institutions until the procedural safeguards of liberty in international organizations, courts and tribunals have reached a considerably higher stage of development.[187] American States have ceded ultimate authority over the universal and inalienable rights of their people to the Federal government, which establishes a precedent for similar deference to international courts, but the limited terms in office of judges on most international tribunals,[188] and the participation of illiberal and undemocratic regimes in the selection of judges,[189] makes it unlikely that any such American move towards global federation will take place at any time in the near future.

The United States Supreme Court is the final arbiter of the fundamental rights required by liberty and the due process of law under the Fourteenth Amendment to the United States Constitution, and the highest State courts have similar authority over their own bills and declarations of rights. But these documents, in both instances, depend ultimately upon universal and inalienable liberties, which apply to all peoples, everywhere. American judges and United States public officials are far more likely to *refer* to the *substantive* views of foreign and international authorities on the requirements of universal human rights than they are to *defer* to their *procedural* authority. Because "liberty" is an absolute and universal value guaranteed by the Constitution of the United States, American judges properly can and often do consider international and foreign perceptions of liberty and fundamental human rights, including views expressed in documents and tribunals to which the United States has never been a party.

Human rights are universal and binding in United States law and United States courts. They are protected by each of the States in their separate bills and declarations of rights, by the Federal government in the United States Bill of Rights and Fourteenth Amendment, and by the law of nations, which is part of the law of the United States and of the law of each of the States in the Union. To understand the requirements of liberty and the fundamental and inalienable rights of humanity, United States Courts and public officials consider all sources that illuminate the

---

[185] Ibid.

[186] Ibid.

[187] See the remarks of Chief Justice Roberts in *Medellin v. Texas*, supra, note 139 at 1367.

[188] Judges on the International Court of Justice serve for renewable 9-year terms. *Statute of the International Court of Justice*, Article 13(1).

[189] Judges on the International Court of Justice are elected by the General Assembly and Security Council of the United Nations, Ibid., Article 4(1).

requirements of "life, liberty, and the pursuit of happiness," including international conventions and foreign judicial opinions. International courts and international organizations cannot, as yet, exercise effective jurisdiction, judicial or otherwise, over United States law, even as it applies to fundamental human rights, but United States law itself incorporates the requirements of universal human rights. "A decent respect to the opinions of mankind" has always illuminated American understandings of the rights of Americans.[190] The law of the United States seeks to secure the "Blessings of Liberty" for all its subjects.[191]

[190] *Declaration of Independence of the United States of America* (4 July 1776).

[191] *Constitution of the United States* (1787), Preamble.

Chapter 3
The Duty of Cooperation of the Respondent State During the Proceedings Before the European Court of Human Rights

Helena De Vylder and Yves Haeck

Abstract The right of individual petition under Article 34 ECHR is the cornerstone of the European Convention on Human Rights, but it is rather odd that its efficiency can be so easily undermined by member states. Indeed, without the states' cooperation in clarifying the facts, it is impossible for the European Court of Human Rights to adjudicate the case. Therefore, Article 38 ECHR obliges respondent states to furnish all necessary facilities to the European Court. Eventually, the ultimate goal in this provision is thus to conserve the effective character of the substantive rights in the ECHR. Statistical data reveal a growing unwillingness of certain member states to faithfully collaborate with Court in relation to certain fundamental rights, which is an alarming trend. A comprehensive case law analysis on the one hand reveals the exact situations where member states are failing in their duty to cooperate and their reasons for acting in that way, but it also shows the ingenuity with which the Court is expanding the scope of the protection under Article 38, and the legal consequences which it attaches to the establishment of a violation of the provision, and is thereby for the first time 'giving teeth' to this under-explored provision. While the Court's interpretation of Article 38 aims to counter the erosion of the right of individual petition and thus renders the substantive rights in the Convention efficient, this contribution offers some suggestions to improve the current system.

H. De Vylder (✉)
Lawyer at the Law Office, Simont Braun, Brussels, Belgium

Voluntary Research Fellow at the Human Rights Centre, Ghent University, Ghent, Belgium
e-mail: Helena.DeVylder@UGent.be

Y. Haeck
Professor of International Human Rights Law at the Human Rights Centre, Ghent University, Ghent, Belgium
e-mail: Yves.Haeck@UGent.be

Y. Haeck and E. Brems (eds.), *Human Rights and Civil Liberties in the 21st Century*, Ius Gentium: Comparative Perspectives on Law and Justice 30,
DOI 10.1007/978-94-007-7599-2_3, © Springer Science+Business Media Dordrecht 2014

3.1 Introduction

The coming into being of the European Convention of Human Rights (hereinafter ECHR) in 1950 and its entry into force in 1953 – followed by the acceptance by a number of member states of the right to application before the former European Commission of Human Rights (hereinafter European Commission or Commission) and the competence of the European Court of Human Rights (hereinafter European Court or Court) – created the possibility for individuals to question a violation of their rights guaranteed under the ECHR and its Protocols before an international (quasi-)judicial mechanism. Although redress is theoretically secured, the efficiency of this mechanism is open to question. That the execution of judgments is problematic, is widely recognised and discussed,[1] but the often less than optimal cooperation during the proceedings before the European Court has, in contrast, been virtually ignored in legal literature so far.[2] This is exactly the topic we are focusing on.

Article 34 ECHR and Article 38 ECHR serve as a starting point. Where the final phrase of Article 34 prohibits the member states to "hinder in any way the effective exercise of the right of individual application", Article 38 ECHR emphasizes their duty to cooperate, in that:

> [t]he Court shall examine the case together with the representatives of the parties and, if need be, undertake an investigation, for the effective conduct of which the High Contracting Parties concerned shall furnish all necessary facilities.

While Article 38 ECHR lays down a positive obligation on the member states to furnish the necessary facilities to the European Court, Article 34 ECHR originally only contained a negative duty to refrain from interference. Without losing sight of

[1] See e.g. D. Baluarte and C.M. Vos, *From Judgment to Justice. Implementing International and Regional Human Rights Decisions* (New York: Open Society Foundations, 2010) 198; E. Bates, "Supervising the Execution of Judgments Delivered by the European Court of Human Rights: The Challenges Facing the Committee of Ministers", in T.A. Christou and J.P. Raymond (eds.) *European Court of Human Rights. Remedies and Execution of Judgments*, (London: British Institute of International and Comparative Law, 2005) 49–106; E. Lambert Abdelgawad, "L'execution des arrets de la Cour européenne des droits de l'homme", *Revue trimestrielle des droits de l'Homme,*77 (2007), 669–705, 78 (2008), 647–686, 79 (2009), 651–682, 2010, 793–814, 81 (2011), 939–958; M. Marmo, "The execution of judgments of the European Court of Human Rights – a politicalbattle", 15 *Maastricht Journal of European and Comparative Law* 2008, 235–276; X. Ruedin, *Exécution des arrêts de la Cour européenne des droits de l'homme. Procédure, obligations des Etats, pratique et réforme* (Brussels: Bruylant, 2009) 244.

[2] For the odd (partial) exception, see O. Chernishova and N. Vajic, "The Court's evolving response to the states' failure to cooperate", in D. Spielmann (ed.), *The European Convention on Human Rights: a living and dynamic instrument – liber amicorum in honour of judge Rozakis*, (Brussels: Bruylant 2011) 47–79, 58–79; J. Măckić, "Artikel 38 EVRM [Article 38 ECHR]", in J. Gerards, Y. Haeck, de Hert, A. Woltjer, M. Tjepkema and J. van der Velde (eds.), *EVRM Rechtspraak & Commentaar [ECHR Case Law & Commentary]* (The Hague: Sdu Publishers, loose-leaf) 1–18, 11–17; J. Vande Lanotte and Y. Haeck, *Handboek EVRM Deel 1. Algemene Beginselen [Handbook ECHR. Part 1. General Principles]*, (Antwerp: Intersentia, 2005) 361–369.

Article 34 ECHR (*lex generalis*), which lays the foundation for the duty of the government to cooperate under Article 38 ECHR (*lex specialis*), but which does not include the right to obtain the cooperation of governments in proceedings before the European Court, the major point of analysis will be the aforementioned positive obligation encapsulated in Article 38 ECHR. Where a state action makes it more difficult for the applicant to exercise his or her right of application resulting for example from instances of intimidation, or restrictions on communication through mail or on the lawyer-client contact, this will be seen by the Court as an obstacle to the applicant's right of application and be dealt with under Article 34 ECHR,[3] and therefore not be considered as a failure to cooperate with the Court under Article 38 ECHR.[4] In contrast, a failure of the State, for example, to submit information and witnesses considered to be necessary by the Court for the proceedings, will be essentially dealt with under Article 38 ECHR and not under Article 34 ECHR.[5]

In this contribution, firstly the origin and the evolution of the positive duty to cooperate with the Court will be analysed, and the evolvement of the application of Article 38 ECHR in the Court's case law over time will be illustrated with statistics. Secondly, the context(s) within which violations of the duty to cooperate under Article 38 ECHR take place, will be clarified. In this part, both the division of the cases over the different member states where Article 38 ECHR has been deemed violated, and the connection to the substantive ECHR rights at stake in these cases, will be examined, and numerical data will be provided. Thirdly, in view of the intimate relation between the actual proceedings before the European Court and Article 38 ECHR, two issues during the admissibility stage are discussed, i.e. is the 6-month time limit valid when complaining about a breach of Article 38, and is Article 38 applicable in the stage before the admissibility decision? Fourthly, during the merits stage before the European Court, the exact scope of the application of Article 38 ECHR is defined, as are the means of defense used and usable by member states wishing to deny their alleged uncooperative behaviour. Lastly but very interestingly, the legal consequences of the establishment of a violation of Article 38 ECHR for the aggrieved party and the member state are scrutinised. We will illustrate that the potential influence of a violation of Article 38 ECHR on the burden of proof can be as far-reaching as a (near) reversal of the burden. Moreover, one may logically claim that the establishment of a violation of Article 38 should impact upon the amount of just satisfaction awarded to the victim, and at least one case proofs that it is possible for the European Court to oblige a member state to compensate useless costs made by the Court. Eventually, the current system will be evaluated in the light of the efficiency and capacity to remedy violations of the ECHR, and some suggestions to improve the system will be made.

---

[3] ECtHR 28 October 1998, No. 24760/94, *Assenov v. Bulgaria*, para. 170 (discouraging to submit an application).

[4] ECtHR 25 September 1997, No. 23178/94, *Aydin v. Turkey*, para. 120 (intimidation).

[5] ECtHR 18 June 2002, No. 25656/94, *Orhan v. Turkey*, para. 402.

3.2 Origin and Evolution of Article 38 ECHR

3.2.1 The Creation and the Evolution of the 'Duty to Cooperate'

During the 1948 Congress of Europe in the Hague the idea to establish a European Court of Human Rights linked to the adoption of a European Convention on Human Rights, was launched. The discussions leading to the eventual adoption of the ECHR in 1950 were dominated by the contrasting visions of the so-called maximalists and minimalists. The former, led by France, were pleading for an in-depth cooperation, while the latter, led by the United Kingdom and fearing for a loss of sovereignty on behalf of the member states, stood up for a lesser cooperation as to protection of human rights. The question whether or not to create an individual right of application was one of the core issues of the discussion. Eventually, and while originally four different draft conventions had been submitted to the Committee of Ministers of the Council of Europe created in 1949,[6] the negotiating governments were able to agree on the acceptance of an individual and facultative right of application, as well as the creation of an European Commission of Human Rights, as well as an European Court of Human Rights, the access to which would also be optional.[7]

The origin of the obligation to cooperate may only be vaguely traced and uncovered through the *Travaux Préparatoires* to the European Convention. To draw the evolution over time, the Explanatory Reports to the respective Amending Protocols to the European Convention are helpful. The very first Draft Convention, prepared by the European Movement – a consortium of pro-European NGOs – and presented to the Committee of Ministers on 12 July 1949,[8] contains an Article 10(c) that forms the basis of the current Article 38 ECHR, which reads:

> The Commission may on a decision taken by a majority of two-thirds of its members conduct an enquiry within the territory of any state a party to this Convention for the purpose of investigating a petition. *Such State shall afford full facilities necessary for the efficient conduct of such an enquiry.* [emphasis added]

It is a pity that the *Travaux Préparatoires* do not shed any specific light on the origin of this provision in general, or on the last sentence in particular, as they remain silent on the concrete motives of the parties to include such a provision.

---

[6] Collected edition of the "Travaux préparatoires" of the European Convention on Human Rights/Council of Europe (henceforth: Travaux Préparatoires) Vol. 4. Committee of Experts (30 March–17 June 1950) (The Hague: Martinus Nijhoff, 1977) 18–19.

[7] Art. 19 ECHR. The Commission was elected on 18 May 1954 and met for the first time on 12 July 1954, while the Court was set up on 21 January 1959.

[8] Travaux Préparatoires Vol. 1, Appendix.

The same observation applies to the so-called '*Teitgen* Report', elaborated by the Parliamentary Assembly's Committee on Legal and Administrative Questions.[9] Article 13 of the Report reproduces the obligation for the parties to lend their assistance when the Commission undertakes an investigation of a petition, be it in different and less compelling wording:

> The Commission shall then undertake:
>
> 1. An investigation of the application *with the assistance of the representatives of either party*;
> 2. If necessary, an enquiry. [emphasis added]

Although the question on whether or not to create a right of individual petition was debated extensively in the aforementioned Report, when deciding on the actual establishment, it is quite remarkable that no one questioned or at least shed any doubts as to the willingness of states to fully cooperate with the (former) Commission.

A quote of the then Secretary-General of the Council of Europe on another issue (i.e. once a violation would be established, a state would immediately provide restitution) seems to indicate that the drafters of the European Convention took it for granted that all the member states would be queuing to lend their good services to the Commission to establish the facts in pending cases before the Commission.[10]

The lack of any (procedural) tools for the (former) Commission to act in case of unwillingness by states to cooperate, may be deemed a huge shortcoming. It is after all self-evident that opponents or moderate lovers of a right of individual petition are, or may be, rather uncooperative as to the establishment of the facts, when that same right is exercised against them.

Finally, the negotiations led to the adoption of the European Convention without further discussion on the topic.

Article 28 para.1 (a) ECHR includes both parts of the above-mentioned drafts and states:

> In the event of the Commission accepting a petition referred to it:
>
> (a) It shall, with a view to ascertaining the facts, undertake together with the representatives of the parties an examination of the petition and, if need be, an investigation, for the effective conduct of which the States concerned shall furnish all necessary facilities, after an exchange of views with the Commission.[11]

[9] Travaux Préparatoires Vol. 1 Sitting of the Committee of Legal and Administrative Questions (22 August–5 September 1949) 154.

[10] "Furthermore, the European States were governed by the rule of law: the rare cases of violation, once established by the Commission, would give rise to immediate restitution by the Member States, who were all anxious that human rights should be respected."Travaux Préparatoires Vol. 3 Committee of Experts (2 February–10 March 1950) 18.

[11] Travaux Préparatoires Vol. 6 Consultative Assembly 64.

It is remarkable that, except for two minor changes, no real substantive amendments have since been made to the original provision. The two small changes are the modification of the article numbers[12] and the addition by the Committee of Experts (after having taken into account Articles 26 and 27 of the 1949 draft UN Covenant on Civil and Political Rights) of the final part of the last sentence, providing for the fact that States should cooperate in an investigation 'after an exchange of views with the Commission'(as opposed to the UN Covenant provision requiring member states' prior consent);in fact, this last minor change may even be considered as a concession of the maximalists in favour of the national sovereignty championed by the minimalists.

During the 1990s, Protocol No. 8[13] and Protocol No. 11,[14] which entered into force in 1990 and 1998 respectively, amended Article 28 ECHR, however, without making any amendments to the 'obligation to cooperate', besides the fact that Article 28 was renamed Article 38 (by the latter Protocol).

More recently, Protocol No. 14,[15] which entered into force in 2010, did make a slight amendment to Article 38, to the effect that the wording 'if the Court declares the application inadmissible' was deleted. Therefore, since 1 June 2010, the member states are formally obliged to lend the necessary facilities from the start of the proceedings before the Court.

Unfortunately, the drafters of Protocol No. 14 did not consider it necessary to amend and further strengthen Article 38 ECHR, in order to better prevent any unwillingness by states to comply with Article 38 ECHR. The Explanatory Report to Protocol No. 14 states that Article 38 already contains strong legal obligations for the member states, and that additionally, if states would still not comply, the case could be brought before the Committee of Ministers, which could take every step it deems necessary.[16]

[12] Article 13 became Article 14: Travaux Préparatoires Vol. 3 Committee of Experts (2 February–10 March 1950) 196; Article 14 became Article 18: Travaux Préparatoires Vol. 3 Committee of Experts (2 February – 10 March 1950) 236; Article 18 became Article 24: Travaux Préparatoires Vol. 3 Committee of Experts (2 February–10 March 1950) 328. In the four alternative draft conventions drawn up by the Committee of Experts: Article 24 or 26; Travaux Préparatoires Vol. 4 Committee of Experts. Eventually this becomes Article 28: Travaux Préparatoires Legal Committee, Ad Hoc Joint Committee, Committee of Ministers, Consultative Assembly (23 June–28 August 1950) 88.

[13] Protocol No. 8 to the Convention for the Protection of Human Rights and Fundamental Freedoms, 19 March 1985, ETS No. 118.

[14] Protocol No. 11 to the Convention for the Protection of Human Rights and Fundamental Freedoms, restructuring the control machinery established thereby, 11 May 1994, ETS No. 155.

[15] Protocol No. 14 to the Convention for the Protection of Human Rights and Fundamental Freedoms, amending the control system of the Convention, Strasbourg, 13 May 2004, ETS No. 194.

[16] Explanatory Report to the Protocol No. 14 to the ECHR, para. 90.

3.2.2 *The Evolution of the Number of (Allegations of) Violations of the Duty to Cooperate*

Until 31 January 2012, Article 38 ECHR (the duty to cooperate)[17] has appeared in 63 judgments and seven decisions of the European Court. These are not only the result of formal allegations of violations of Article 38 ECHR made by individuals, since the Court sometimes applies Article 38 on its own initiative.

In 42 of the aforementioned cases, the Court established a violation of the said provision, in 15 cases no violation was found, and seven other cases were declared inadmissible. The residual category mostly contains cases in which the Court only mentions Article 38 without further using the provision for legal purposes, or where the Court deemed it unnecessary to explore the compliance with Article 38, given that the same shortcoming(s) was/were already established under another Article.[18]

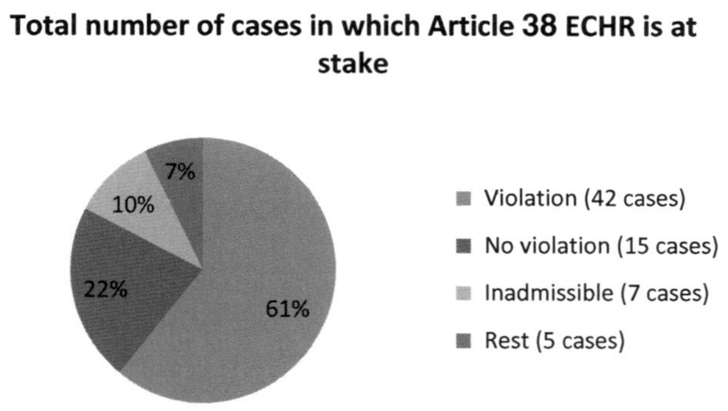

The first time an applicant alleged a violation of Article 38 ECHR and the Court agreed with the applicant, dates back from 1999, i.e. the case of *Tanrikulu v. Turkey.*[19] In this landmark case, the Court draws once and for all the attention to the major importance of Article 38 ECHR.

Since the beginning of the twenty-first century, the total number of cases in which a violation of Article 38 has been alleged, as well as the number of established violations of Article 38, are continually on the rise.

When one takes into account these facts, there seems to be indeed an increasing problem as to incompliance by states with their duty to cooperate with the Court, and not just a rise of allegations of incompliance. While the number of violations seems to have gone down since 2008, which would be an indication of an improved willingness of states to collaborate with the Court, it is clearly too early to speak of a permanent drop in violations.

---

[17] Including the former Articles 28 ECHR and 38(1)(a) ECHR.

[18] It often concerns the procedural limb under Article 2 and 3 ECHR, next to Article 34 ECHR.

[19] ECtHR 8 July 1999, No. 23763/94, *Tanrikulu v. Turkey.*

Chronological Evolution of Article 38 ECHR cases

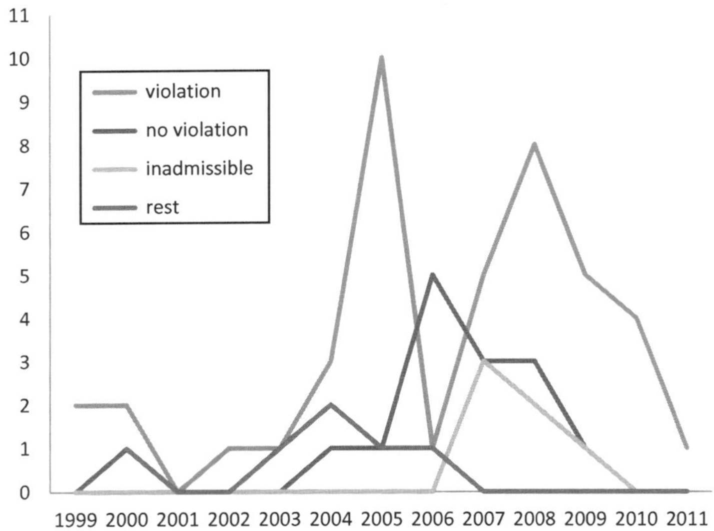

3.3 Context of Violations

3.3.1 Division of Violations of the Duty to Cooperate Under Article 38 ECHR by Member State

The number of cases in which a violation of Article 38 ECHR has been established is not proportionally spread over all the ECHR member states. Russia and Turkey clearly take the lead with a total of 39 and 24 cases respectively. The other cases in which violations have been found are mostly held against Eastern European and Caucasian states, though none of them has been condemned more than twice.

Number of violations by member state

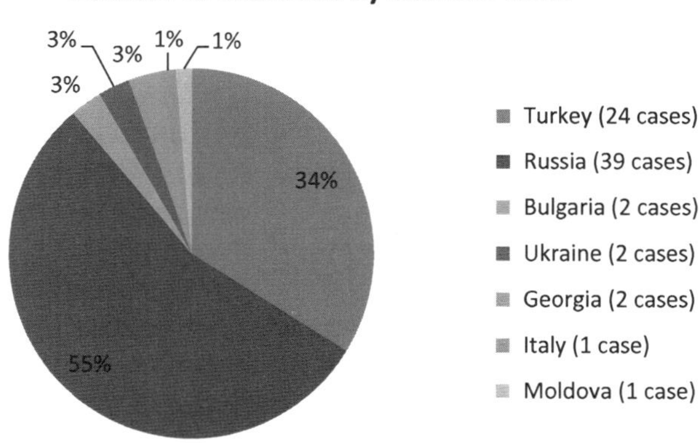

In order to be able to conclude that the unwillingness of cooperation of Turkey and Russia with the European Court is worse than in other states, it is necessary to take a look at the proportion of violations in the total number of applications. It appears that Russia is responsible for 55 % and Turkey for 34 % of the total number of violations. The problem is thus evident.

However, all cases relating to Turkey and Russia in which Article 38 has been held to be violated are context-related. The Turkish cases have occurred in a context of government state violence against the Kurdish minority in East- and Southeast-Turkey. In each of these cases the Turkish government claimed to behave legitimately in order to protect the population from PKK-members.[20] In the Russian cases, the security forces were fighting against alleged Chechen rebels.[21]

3.3.2 *Division of Violations of the Duty to Cooperate Under Article 38 ECHR by Substantive Convention Article*

A few substantive ECHR rights appear in large numbers in the same cases as Article 38 ECHR. It is mainly Article 2 (right to life), Article 3 (prohibition of torture), Article 13 (right to an effective remedy) and Article 5 (right to liberty) ECHR which are being invoked next to allegations of a violation of Article 38. Not only are they often invoked together, but the division of cases in the chart below also proves that the above-mentioned material rights, i.e. first generation civil rights which are constructive to democracy and rule of law, are also the most often violated. That every detriment to those basic rights should be prevented or remedied, is obvious.

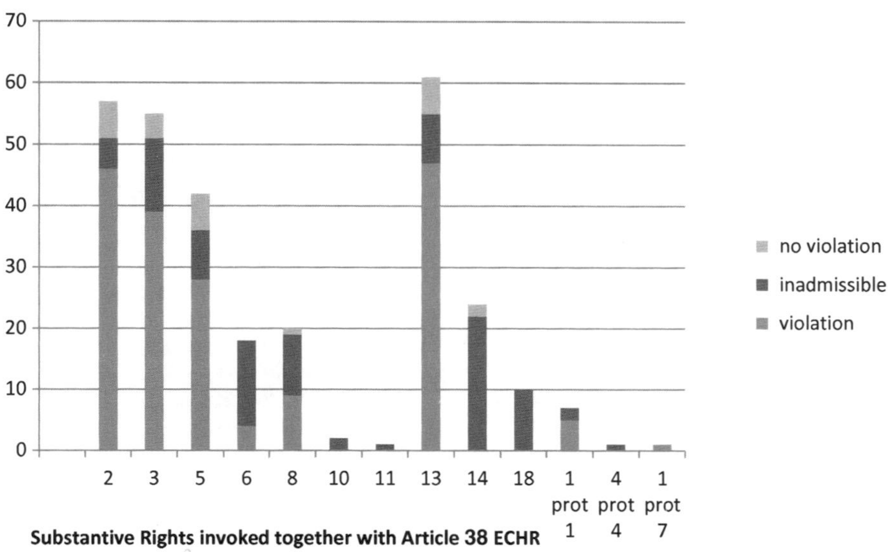

[20] In 96 % of cases.

[21] In 85 % of cases.

3.4 Admissibility

Since Article 38 ECHR is a procedural right, the admissibility conditions are not simply applicable. Two questions arise: (a) Is it required to fulfill the admissibility conditions – in particular the 6-month time limit – in order to allege a violation of Article 38?; (b) Is the admissibility of a case a condition to apply Article 38, meaning is Article 38 applicable in the *stage before the admissibility decision?*

3.4.1 Is It Required to Fulfill the Admissibility Conditions in Order to Allege a Violation of Article 38 ECHR

The question arises whether, supposing that the applicant submits a violation of Article 38 ECHR after the expiration of the 6 month time limit while the complaint of substantive rights is submitted within the time limit, the alleged violation of Article 38 can still be established?

The Court has confirmed that a violation of Article 34 ECHR is possible outside the 6-month time limit, since Article 34 is a right of a procedural nature.[22] Although there is no explicit statement yet by the Court with regard to Article 38, since Article 38 is a procedural right as well, one may conclude by analogy that the 6-month time limit is not applicable. Moreover, in the case of *Tahsin Acar v. Turkey,*[23] the Court implicitly holds that there is an analogy between both provisions, by stating that "[t]he Court has jurisdiction to examine the applicant's complaints under articles 34 and 38 of the Convention in respect of events that took place both before and after the Commission's decision on admissibility of 30 June 1997." To this, one may add the fact that the time limit is incompatible with the Court's practice[24] to apply Article 38 without formal complaint of the applicant. But above all, applying the 6-month time limit would be in contradiction with the *ratio legis* of the time limit, i.e. to

[22] ECtHR 20 February 2007, No. 35865/03, *Al-Moayad v. Germany*, para. 107; ECtHR 12 April 2005, No. 36378/02, *Shamayev and others v. Georgia and Russia*, para. 407; ECtHR 20 July 1998, No. 23818/94, *Ergi v. Turkey*, para. 105; R. Toma, "The Sanctioning of Hindrances to the Exercise of the Right of Individual Petition before the European Court of Human Rights: Is it Effective?", in E. Lambert Abdelgawad (ed.), *Preventing and sanctioning hindrances to the right of individual petition before the European Court of Human Rights* (Antwerp: Intersentia, 2011)34. But see ECtHR 23 November 2003, Nos. 23145/93 and 25091/94, *Elci and others v. Turkey*, para. 716, where the 6-month limit was applied. See also ECtHR 28 October 2010, No. 23284/04, *Boris Popov v. Russia*, para. 117, where an Article 34 case was declared inadmissible as being manifestly ill-founded.

[23] ECtHR 8 April 2004, No. 26307/95, *Tahsin Acar v. Turkey*, para. 252.

[24] E.g. ECtHR 28 March 2000, No. 22492/93, *Kilic v. Turkey*; ECtHR 4 July 1999, No. 23657/94, *Cakici v. Turkey*; ECtHR 14 November 2000, No. 24396/94, *Tas v.* Turkey; ECtHR 9 March 2004, No. 22494/93, *Hasan Ilhan v. Turkey.*

avoid that facts that have happened a long time ago would be discussed in the light of the objective to ensure legal security.[25]

3.4.2 Is Article 38 Applicable in the Pre-admissibility Stage?

In order to answer the question whether Article 38 ECHR is applicable in the pre-admissibility stage, it is necessary to distinguish between the period before and the period after Protocol No. 14 came into force. Before the entry into force of Protocol No. 14, the former Article 38 ECHR limited the duty to cooperate with the Court under Article 38 to cases already declared admissible. In most cases, the Court held on to this requirement, either explicitly[26] or implicitly.[27] The Court, for example, often noticed the shortcomings in cooperation before the admissibility decision, but did not establish a violation if those shortcomings were remedied during the merits stage.

In other cases, though, the Court seemed to keep Article 38 ECHR in mind during both stages, to conclude that there was a violation. In *Tanrikulu v. Turkey,* the Court pointed out that"[w]here the applicants raise the issue of the effectiveness of the investigation, the documents of the criminal investigation are fundamental to the establishment of the facts, and their absence may prejudice the Court's proper examination of the complaint both at the admissibility and at the merits stage."[28] The Court thus acknowledged a lacuna in the Convention: the absence of cooperation during the admissibility stage may have consequences, though there was formally no obligation to cooperate. Moreover, In *Khadisov and Tsechoyev v. Russia,*[29] the Court seems to oblige the parties to furnish all facilities independent of the phase of the investigations, when it stated that "[t]his obligation requires the Contracting States to furnish all necessary facilities to the Court, whether it is conducting a fact-finding investigation or performing its general duties as regards the examination of applications."

Though in other cases the Court stated that the obligation was only valid after the admissibility decision, the Court often added that *in casu* the shortcomings prior to the decision on admissibility did not prejudice the establishment of the facts or otherwise prevented the proper examination of the case.[30] The Court seemed to

---

[25] E.g. ECtHR 1 November 2000, No. 25760/94, *Ipek v. Turkey*; J. Vande Lanotte and Y. Haeck, *Handboek EVRM Deel 1. Algemene Beginselen [Handbook ECHR. Part 1. General Principles]*, (Antwerp: Intersentia, 2005) 606.

[26] E.g. ECtHR 24 January 2008, No. 48804/99, *Osmanoglu v. Turkey*, para. 44; ECtHR 5 April 2007, No. 74237/01, *Baysayeva v. Russia*, para. 167; ECtHR 5 Juli 2007, No. 68007/01, *Alikhadzhiyeva v. Russia*, para. 104.

[27] E.g. ECtHR 26 January 2006, No. 77617/01, *Mikheyev v. Russia*, para. 144.

[28] ECtHR 8 July 1999, No. 23763/94, *Tanrikulu v. Turkey*, para. 70.

[29] ECtHR 5 February 2009, No. 21519/02, *Khadisov and Tsechoyev v. Russia*, para. 177.

[30] E.g. ECtHR 26 July 2007, Nos. 57941/00 58699/00 60403/00, *Musayev and others v. Russia*, para. 183. ECtHR 27 July 2006, No. 69481/01, *Bazorkina v. Russia*, paras. 172–174.

suggest that in case of a lack of cooperation that causes damage, even before the admissibility decision, Article 38 may have effects.

Protocol No. 14 changed this situation fundamentally. Even before this change, it was common practice to take decisions on admissibility and merits jointly, though Article 29(3) ECHR reserved this for exceptional cases. Protocol No. 14 formalizes this legal practice[31] and omits the admissibility requirement in Article 38. The cases[32] submitted after the entry into force of Protocol No. 14 reflect and incorporate this novelty, and do not make a difference between the different phases as to the applicability of Article 38. Therefore, a violation of Article 38 ECHR can be established related to the pre-admissibility stage. Only the Georgian judge Adeishvili criticizes this change in a partly dissenting opinion under the *Enukidze and Girgvliani v. Georgia* case.[33] He mistakenly denies the Court the possibility to find a violation of Article 38 ECHR before the admissibility decision is taken, because to do so would clearly contradict the wording of Protocol No. 14. To underscore his view, the Georgian judge points to the imaginable danger that states will not remedy any shortcomings in a later phase (the merits stage) anymore, since the establishment of a violation of a Convention article, i.e. Article 38, would already be inevitable.

3.5 Scope of Article 38 ECHR

3.5.1 What Are Investigative Measures?

For a long time it remained rather unclear what the Convention meant by 'the necessary facilities'. A starting point to determine these are the investigative measures found in the Annex to the Rules of Court. The Annex not only concretizes the measures in the Court's power, but it clarifies the obligation of the parties to assist the Court as well. This minimum has to be respected by the state, otherwise its abidance by Article 38 ECHR may be in jeopardy.

Rule A1(1) Annex to the Rules of Court (hereinafter Annex) holds:

> The Chamber leading the investigation can adopt any investigation measure which it considers capable of clarifying the facts of the case. The Chamber may, inter alia, invite the parties to produce documentary evidence and decide to hear as a witness or expert in any other capacity any person whose evidence or statement seems likely to assist it in carrying out its tasks.

Moreover, the Chamber can organize a fact-finding mission in the state concerned (Rule A1(3) Annex). The Annex guarantees the Court and the delegation it has sent

[31] Explanatory Report to the 14th Protocol to the ECHR, para. 73.

[32] ECtHR 28 October 2010, No. 35079/04,*Sasito Israilova and others v. Russia*; ECtHR 7 October 2010, No. 41840/02, *Sadykov v. Russia*; ECtHR 26 April 2011, No. 25091/07, *Enukidze and Girgvliani v. Georgia.*

[33] Partly dissenting opinion of judge Adeishvili under ECtHR 26 April 2011, No. 25091/07, *Enukidze and Girgvliani v. Georgia.*

out a wide discretionary power to take investigative measures and to ensure the state's cooperation. Rule A2 Annex further clarifies the parties obligations:

> The applicant and any Contracting Party concerned shall assist the Court as necessary in implementing any investigative measures. The Contracting Party on whose territory on-site proceedings before a delegation take place shall extend to the delegation the facilities and co-operation necessary for the proper conduct of the proceedings. These shall include, to the full extent necessary, freedom of movement within the territory and all adequate security arrangements for the delegation, for the applicant and for all witnesses, experts and others who may be heard by the delegation. It shall be the responsibility of the Contracting Party concerned to take steps to ensure that no adverse consequences are suffered by any person or organisation on account of any evidence given, or of any assistance provided, to the delegation.

In short, this rule specifies the state's and the applicant's obligations under Article 38 ECHR, while the concrete interpretation is for the Court to decide.

As a conclusion, the term 'investigation' includes an entire set of measures, ranging from the examination of documentary evidence to securing the attendance of witnesses in proceedings before the Court, possibly during fact-finding missions.

3.5.2 *Quantitative Overview of Types of Violations Under Article 38 ECHR*

The bulk of violations of Article 38 ECHR relate to a refusal to submit documents, as those documents most often are part of a criminal investigation file against the applicant, and concern e.g. detention and custody records, expulsion orders,[34] medical files of detainees,[35] and reports considering military operations.[36] Next to pure refusals, delays in submitting documents form a major part of violations as well. Those two often go hand in hand, as in 47 % of the cases, the respondent member state submits a part of the requested file late, but refuses to submit another part.

In almost one out of ten cases, the member state refuses to submit information, e.g. information considering names and phone numbers,[37] the course of the facts[38] or procedures,[39] etc.

Another common practice is impeding witnesses' appearances before the Court.[40] There is a difference as to whether witnesses are connected to or appointed by the state, or not. Police officers, military personnel and (investigating) judges, for

[34] ECtHR 12 February 2009, No. 2512/04, *Nolan and K v. Russia.*

[35] ECtHR 5 April 2005, No. 54825/00, *Nevmerzhitsky v. Ukraine*, paras. 76–77; ECtHR 5 July 2005, No. 49790/99, *Trubnikov v. Russia*, para. 52.

[36] ECtHR 18 June 2002, No. 25656/94, *Orhan v. Turkey.*

[37] Ibid, para. 270.

[38] ECtHR 6 April 2004, No. 21689/93, *Ahmet Ozkan and others v. Turkey*, paras. 481–482.

[39] ECtHR 20 September 2005, No. 27309/95, *Dizman v. Turkey*, paras. 57–66.

[40] ECtHR 13 June 2000, No. 23531/94, *Timurtas v. Turkey*, para. 70.

example, are state officials, while the victim's family members, locals and prisoners are not state-connected.

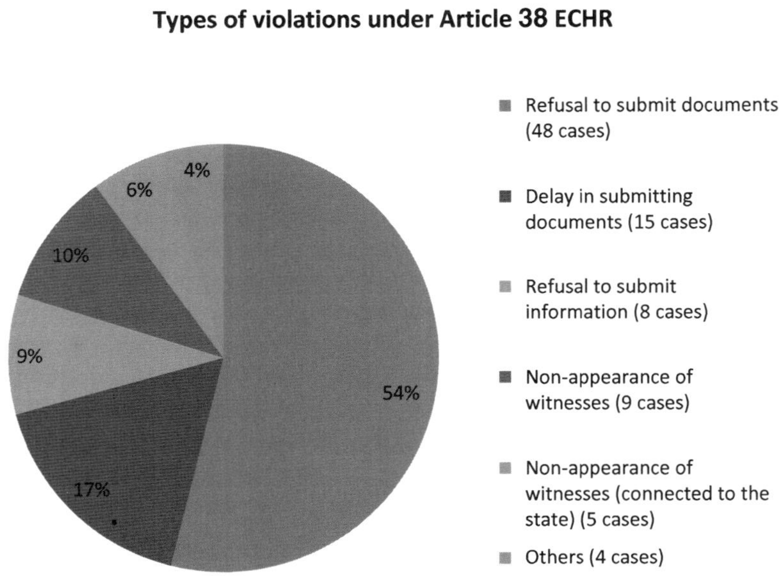

3.5.3 Qualitative Overview of Types of Violations Under Article 38 ECHR

3.5.3.1 Failure to Submit Documents and Information

When the European Court's request for documents is followed by a refusal by the respondent member state, the Court is in the possibility to convict this state for a violation of Article 38.

In the first ever case before the Court where Article 38 ECHR (former Article 28(1)(a)) was considered, i.e. *Tanrikulu v. Turkey,*[41] the Court's expectations are clearly high: all documents have to be submitted to avoid a breach of Article 38 (former Article 28(1)(a)) ECHR. Later case law, however, shows that the Court does not stay this rigorous, as in some cases providing certain documents is deemed sufficient. However, in *Tanrikulu* the Court states in its deliberations that Turkey fell short of its obligations under Article 28 (current Article 38) ECHR, but it does not consider it relevant to repeat this statement in its final conclusions ('For this reasons…') of the case. This common practice did not change until 2003.

[41] ECtHR 8 July 1999, No. 23763/94, *Tanrikulu v.* Turkey, para. 71.

In *Timurtas v. Turkey*,[42] the government failed to submit the original version of an operation report to the Court, which the applicant had submitted. Moreover, the government claimed that the document had disappeared or had not even existed. This ambiguous attitude contributed to the establishment of a violation of Article 38 ECHR, since only Turkey had access to the information capable of corroborating or refuting these allegations, and no satisfactory explanation was given.

The Court sharpened the duty upon governments to submit documents in *Ahmet Ozkan and others v. Turkey*,[43] where it criticizes the government's unhelpful and passive attitude in submitting documents which it did not explicitly ask for, but which the government should have known were unquestionably of fundamental importance for elucidating disputed facts. The Court thus suggests that not just 'explicitly' requested documents should be submitted to it for states to fulfill their duty to cooperate with the Court under Article 38 ECHR. However, Turkey was finally not convicted since the government submitted the documents once explicitly asked for by the Court, and above all, the applicant's lack of cooperation caused a delay as well.

Moreover, in *Khashiyev and Akayeva v. Russia*,[44] the Court stated for the first time that a member state cannot refuse to submit documents on the pretext of some documents allegedly not being relevant to the cases. The question of whether certain documents are relevant or not, cannot be unilaterally decided by the respondent government. And the same applies to the appearance of witnesses.[45]

In various cases the respondent government only submits part of the requested documents. In these circumstances the Court does not per se conclude that there is a violation of Article 38 ECHR, but has developed certain criteria in its case law to evaluate the situation:

Firstly, the Court concluded that if the documents lacking do not preclude the establishment of the facts, Article 38 ECHR is not breached. In *Karov v. Bulgary*,[46] the government did not contest the applicant's statements as to violations of substantive provisions, thus the confidential documents not submitted did not amount to a breach of Article 38 ECHR.

Secondly, the Court lowered its standards in *Giuliani and Gaggio v. Italy*.[47] Even though the Italian government had given false and incomplete answers and omitted details of essential circumstances, since the incomplete nature of the requested information did not prevent the examination of the case, Italy did not fail to fulfill its obligations under Article 38 ECHR.

---

[42] ECtHR 13 June 2000, No. 23531/94, *Timurtas v. Turkey*, paras. 66 and 70.

[43] ECtHR 6 April 2004, No. 21689/93, *Ahmet Ozkan and others v. Turkey*, paras. 479–482.

[44] ECtHR 24 February 2005, No. 57942/00 57945/00, *Khasashiyev and Akayeva v. Russia*, para. 138. Repeated in ECtHR 26 July 2007, No. 57941/00 58699/00 60403/00, *Musayev and others v. Russia*, para. 146.

[45] ECtHR 24 May 2005, No. 25660/94, *Suheyla Aydin v. Turkey*.

[46] ECtHR 16 November 2006, No. 45964/99, *Karov v. Bulgary*, paras. 97–98.

[47] ECtHR 25 August 2009, No. 23458/02, *Giuliani and Gaggio v. Italy*, paras. 269–271; ECtHR 24 March 2011, No. 23458/02, *Gialiani and Gaggio v. Italy*, para. 344.

Thirdly, the Court further decreased the standard to fulfill Article 38 in *Chitayev and Chitayev v. Russia* and *Khatsiyeva and others v. Russia.*[48] In these cases the Court concluded that although not all relevant documents had been submitted, the documents that were submitted considerably facilitated the examination of the case and therefore, Article 38 was not breached.

What is sure, however, is that the submittal of only procedural documents, i.e. documents instituting, suspending and reopening criminal proceedings, letters informing the applicant thereof …, will never fulfill the requirement of Article 38, following *Kukayev v. Russia* and four other cases.[49] In this series of cases the Court did not explore whether the submitted documents facilitated the examination of the case or not, as procedural documents never suffice.

Following the Court in *Lyanova and Aliyeva v. Russia*, the possibility provided by the respondent state to consult documents in the place where the preliminary investigation is conducted instead of submitting the documents concerned to the Court, does not meet the requirements of Article 38 ECHR either.[50]

3.5.3.2 Delay in Submitting Documents and Information

In many cases the Court has to repeatedly request documents to respondent states. The question arises in how far the Court accepts delays in the submission of documents, before Article 38 ECHR is deemed violated?

Since the changes under Protocol No. 14,[51] Article 38 is applicable both before and after the declaration of admissibility. A delay before the admissibility decision can thus not be justified anymore.

It is often difficult to discover which delays are accepted by the Court, since in many cases delays go hand-in-hand with refusals, and the Court does not usually indicate what exact document contributes to the establishment of a violation.

Other cases teach us that a delay only causes a violation of Article 38 if it causes significant consequences for the investigation. For example, in *Tas v. Turkey,*[52] the delay in submitting information on special officers involved in the disappearance of the victim, created an impossibility to summon important witnesses.

---

[48] ECtHR 18 January 2007, No. 59334/00, *Chitayev and Chitayev v. Russia*, para. 207; ECtHR 17 January 2008, No. 5108/02, *Khatsiyeva and others v. Russia*, para. 207.

[49] ECtHR 15 November 2007, No. 29361/02, *Kukayev v. Russia*, para. 121; ECtHR 29 November 2007, No. 57935/00, *Tangiyeva v. Russia*, paras. 73–78; ECtHR 24 January 2008, No. 839/02, *Maslova and Nalbandov v. Turkey*, paras. 127–128; ECtHR 10 January 2008, No. 67797/01, *Zubayrayev v. Russia*, paras. 74–77; ECtHR 29 May 2008, No. 29133/03, *Utsayeva and others v. Russia*, paras. 149–153.

[50] ECtHR 2 October 2008, No. 12713/02 28440/03, *Lyanova and Aliyeva v. Russia*, paras. 143–147.

[51] See supra, note 10 and 4. Admissibility, sub 4.2. Is Article 38 applicable in the pre-admissibility stage?

[52] ECtHR 14 November 2000, No. 24396/94, *Tas v. Turkey*, para. 54.

The same happened in *Suheyla Aydin v. Turkey,*[53] where some documents were only submitted after the end of the fact-finding mission, which made it impossible for the former European Commission to identify and question certain potentially important witnesses.

In most cases, the Court has not gone so far as to find a violation of the State's obligations under Article 38 ECHR whenever the documents were provided by the State to the Court in the end.[54]

3.5.3.3 Absence of Witnesses

During a fact-finding mission, the delegation may decide to hear witnesses (Rule A7(1) Annex). The member state on whose territory such proceedings are held shall, if so requested, take all reasonable steps to facilitate the witnesses' attendance (Rule A5(5) Annex). Moreover, if persons are summoned who are under the member states' authority or control, this state shall further take all reasonable steps to ensure their attendance (Rule A5(4) Annex).

It does not come as a surprise that some member states are not very cooperative in the summoning of witnesses. Except in *Hasan Ilhan v. Turkey,*[55] the Court always considered Article 38 ECHR violated when one or more of the summoned witnesses did not appear. Furthermore, the Court states repeatedly that it is its sole responsibility to decide whether witnesses are relevant or not.[56]

As the Annex to the Rules of Court suggests, the member state has a stronger responsibility if witnesses are under the states' authority or control. This is certainly true when it concerns public servants. That explains why Turkey got convicted for the failure to make a colonel and public prosecutor appear in *Cakici v. Turkey,*[57] although the Turkish government agent declared that he was not in the possibility to oblige the unwilling witnesses. In another case,[58] neither a cancelled plane, nor an annual holiday could serve for the Turkish government as an excuse for its failure to ensure the appearance of a governor and public prosecutor.

---

[53] ECtHR 24 May 2005, No. 25660/94, *Suheyla Aydin v. Turkey*, paras. 138–142.

[54] ECtHR 27 July 2006, No. 69481/01, *Bazorkina v. Russia*, para. 171; O. Chernishova and N. Vajic, "The Court's evolving response to the states' failure to cooperate", in D.Spielmann (ed.), *The European Convention on Human Rights: a living and dynamic instrument – liber amicorum in honour of judge Rozakis*, (Brussels: Bruylant, 2011) 67.

[55] ECtHR 9 March 2004, No. 22494/93, *Hasan Ilhan v. Turkey*: in this case 1 out of 11 summoned witnesses did not appear, but the witness sent a letter stating that he only played a limited role.

[56] ECtHR 18 June 2002, No. 25656/94, *Orhan v. Turkey,* para. 271; ECtHR 1 November 2000, No. 25760/94, *Ipek v. Turkey*, para. 124; ECtHR 24 May 2005, No. 25660/94, *Suheyla Aydin v. Turkey,* para. 142; ECtHR 1 July 2010, No. 17674/02 39081/02, *Davydov and others v. Ukraine*, para. 174.

[57] ECtHR 8 July 1999, No. 23657/94, *Cakici v. Turkey*, para. 43.

[58] ECtHR 28 March 2000, No. 22492/93, *Kilic v. Turkey,* para. 35.

Thus, on the one hand, when a witness connected to the state refuses to testify, the state will be held to have breached Article 38. On the other hand, when a witness unrelated to a state institution does not testify, and the member state took all reasonable steps to facilitate his attendance, the state is absolved. But in *Ipek v. Turkey,*[59] the Court opens Pandora's box by deciding that Article 38 is not violated, because the former mayor who did not appear before the Court is no longer an agent of the state at the time of the hearing. This dangerous reasoning creates a loophole for respondent states by providing the possibility to dismiss state agents from appearing and for the states to avoid being found in breach of Article 38 ECHR.

3.5.3.4 Diverse

Considering the investigative measures in the Court's potential, it is obvious that most Article 38 ECHR violations relate the non-submission or late submission of documents or the non-appearance of witnesses. But the scope of Article 38 is not limited to these kinds of shortcomings.

The *Shamayev and others v. Georgia and Russia* case[60] deserves special mention for its impact on the consequences of the finding of a breach of Article 38 (see infra), but next to this, it widens the scope of Article 38 cases as well. In this case, the delegation members of the Court were refused access to the detained applicants, and Russia consequently obstructed the fact-finding mission, causing the establishment of a violation of Article 38. The particular issue here is that Russia was convicted to compensate the costs for the fact-finding mission as a consequence (see infra).

3.5.4 Means of Defense by Respondent States Not to Cooperate Under Article 38 ECHR

3.5.4.1 Means of Defense to Refuse the Submitting of Documents

Article 161 Russian Code of Criminal Proceedings Prevent Submission of Information

On a regular basis, the Russian government refers to Article 161 of its Code of Criminal Procedure (hereinafter CCP) to justify its unwillingness to submit certain documents. This provision states:

> Article 161. Inadmissibility of Divulging the Data of the Preliminary Inquisition
>
> (…)

---

[59] ECtHR 1 November 2000, No. 25760/94, *Ipek v. Turkey,* paras. 119–121.

[60] ECtHR 12 April 2005, No. 36378/02, *Shamayev and others v. Georgia and Russia*, paras. 492–504.

> 3. The data of the preliminary inquisition may be revealed only with the permission of the public prosecutor, the investigator and the inquirer, and only in that volume, in which they recognize this as admissible, if such divulgence does not contradict the interests of the preliminary inquisition and is not connected with a violation of the rights and lawful interests of the participants in the criminal court proceedings. The divulgence of the data on the private life of the participants in the criminal court proceedings without their consent shall be inadmissible.

Contrary to what the Russian government asserts, the Court is convinced that this Article does not include an absolute prohibition to disclose documents from a pending investigation file, but rather sets out a procedure and limits.[61] A literal reading of the article in question would lead to the same result.

Following settled Strasbourg case law since *Mikheyev v. Russia,*[62] Russia needs to state *in concreto* why Article 161 is applicable, hence the reason why the revelation of documents is contradictory to the interests of the preliminary inquiry, or violates the rights and lawful interests of the participants in criminal court proceedings. Furthermore, *Baysayeva v. Russia*[63] adds that it is necessary to specify the nature of the documents to explain the use of Article 161.

In not even one case, the Court has been convinced by the Russian government's appeal to Article 161, even though Russia states that the criminal investigation file contains sensitive information about the location and actions of military personal, or that it concludes personal information about the parties.[64] Thus, even though a legitimate appeal to Article 161 is not excluded *de jure*, *de facto* it is. As an alternative, the Court refers to the fact that Rule 33(2) of its Rules of Court provide for the possibility to restrict public access to (parts of) documents in the interests of morals, public order or national security, the interests of juveniles or the protection of the private life of the parties or of any person concerned, or where publicity would prejudice the interests of justice (see also infra Lack of Confidentiality in Rules of Court Prevent Submission of Information). However, Russia makes such high demands as to confidentiality, meaning that Rule 33(2) does not suffice in the eyes of the Russian government, since there are no guarantees in the form of sanctions to preclude the disclosure of the confidential documents by the applicant.[65]

---

[61] E.g. ECtHR 12 October 2006, No. 60272/00, *Estamirov and others v. Russia*, para. 104; ECtHR 9 November 2006, No. 7615/02, *Imakayeva v. Russia*, para. 123; ECtHR 26 January 2006, No. 77617/01, *Mikheyev v. Russia*, para. 104; ECtHR 21 June 2007, No. 57953/00 37392/03, *Bitiyeva and X v. Russia*, para. 125.

[62] ECtHR 26 January 2006, No. 77617/01, *Mikheyev v. Russia*, para. 104.

[63] ECtHR 5 April 2007, No. 74237/01, *Baysayeva v. Russia*, para. 166. And *inter alia* ECtHR 15 November 2007, No. 29361/02, *Kukayev v. Russia*, para. 121; ECtHR 29 November 2007, No. 57935/00, *Tangiyeva v. Russia*, para. 76.

[64] ECtHR 23 April 2009, No. 57953/00 37392/03, *Bitiyeva and X v. Russia*, paras. 124–125.

[65] ECtHR 4 December 2008, No. 27243/03, *Musikhanova and others v. Russia*, para. 104; ECtHR 12 February 2009, No. 7654/02, *Ayubov v. Russia*, para. 108; ECtHR 7 October 2010, No. 41840/02, *Sadykov v. Russia*, para. 280; ECtHR 28 October 2010, No. 35079/04, *Sasita Israilova and others v. Russia*, para. 142.

Clerical Errors and Communication Problems Within Respondent State Prevent Submission of Information

The Turkish government defends itself regularly by referring to clerical errors and communication problems, meaning that the national authorities cooperate badly and subordinate officers make mistakes, leading to significant delays in submitting information.

In not even one case does the Court accept this defense, which seems logical because state liability is interpreted wide in the Court's case law. A member state is responsible for events occurring anywhere on its national territory. Moreover, the higher authorities of a state are under a duty to require their subordinates to comply with the Convention, and cannot shelter behind their inability to ensure that it is respected.[66]

State Secrets Prevent Submission of Information

Turkey,[67] as well as Russia[68] and Bulgaria[69] often refuse to submit documents in the name of state secrecy. This has only been accepted in the *Karov v. Bulgaria* case, in view of the fact that *in casu* the lack of documents did not hinder the establishment of the facts. The case of *Noland and K v. Russia* on the other hand illustrates that the character of state secrets cannot usually be accepted, since Article 38 implies putting in place any procedures as a necessity for unhindered communication and exchange of documents with the Court. In these circumstances, a mere reference to the structural deficiency of domestic law which renders impossible the communication of sensitive documents to international bodies, is an insufficient explanation to justify the withholding of key information requested by the Court.

Lack of Confidentiality in Rules of Court Prevent Submission of Information

Likewise, under Article 161 Russian CCP, the Court does not accept a perceived lack of confidentiality in its proceedings as a reason for not having to submit documents. The Court also refers to the possibility to invoke Rule 33(2) of its Rules of Court to request confidentiality (see also supra Article 161 Russian Code of Criminal Proceedings Prevent Submission of Information). Although Russia complains that the confidentiality in the Court's proceedings is not sufficiently guaranteed by a lack

[66] ECtHR 8 April 2004, No. 71503/01, *Assanidze v. Georgia*, para. 146.

[67] E.g. ECtHR 13 June 2000, No. 23531/94, *Timurtas v. Turkey*, para. 28.

[68] E.g. ECtHR 12 February 2009, No. 2512/04, *Nolan and K v. Russia*, para. 56; ECtHR 9 November 2006, No. 7615/02, *Imakayeva v. Russia*, para. 92.

[69] ECtHR 16 November 2006, No. 45964/99, *Karov v. Bulgaria*, para. 97.

of sanctions or liability for international lawyers, the Court is convinced that the confidentiality requirement is sufficiently far-reaching.[70]

Information Is Unnecessary or Irrelevant

The question of whether certain documents are relevant or not, cannot be unilaterally decided by the respondent government[71] (see supra Article 161 Russian Code of Criminal Proceedings Prevent Submission of Information).

3.5.4.2 Means of Defense Against the Absence of Witnesses

Impossible to Locate Witnesses

The respondent member state has an obligation to ensure the attendance of state agents, and will thus violate Article 38 ECHR if they do not appear.[72] If other witnesses do not appear, the Court examines whether the state did facilitate the attendance of these non-state agents. In all cases in which the state did not fulfill this requirement, the Court always found other means for the state to locate the witness. For example, in *Cakici v. Turkey*[73] and *Tepe v. Turkey,*[74] the Court held that ex-prisoners should have been possible to pinpoint through the registers of local courts. According to the Court, it should be possible to locate former prison guards as well, since they enjoy a state pension.[75]

Impossible to Identify Witnesses

In three different cases, the Turkish government refused to identify certain relevant witnesses: police agents that took the victim to the local court,[76] someone who heard the victim via telephone,[77] and the head of a boarding school where a detention had taken place.[78] The Court does not accept this refusal in any case, but it is striking,

---

[70] ECtHR 8 January 2009, No. 27251/03, *Shakhgiriyeva and others v. Russia*, para. 136.

[71] ECtHR 19 December 2002, No. 57942/00 57945/00, *Khashiyev and Akayeva v. Russia*, para. 138.

[72] E.g. ECtHR 8 July 1999, No. 23763/94, *Tanrikulu v. Turkey;* ECtHR 24 May 2005, No. 25660/94, *Suheyla Aydin v. Turkey*.

[73] ECtHR 4 July 1999, No. 23657/94, *Cakici v. Turkey,* para. 43.

[74] ECtHR 9 May 2003, No. 27244/95, *Tepe v. Turkey*, para. 133.

[75] ECtHR 1 July 2010, No. 17674/02 39081/02, *Davydov and others v. Ukraine*, paras. 33 and 162.

[76] ECtHR 24 May 2005, No. 25660/94, *Suheyla Aydin v. Turkey*, para. 13.

[77] ECtHR 2 August 2005, No. 65899/01, *Tanis and others v. Turkey*, paras. 8–9 and 160.

[78] ECtHR 18 July 2002, No. 25656/94, *Orhan v. Turkey*, para. 272.

though, that in every case there is a clear unwillingness and no real impossibility on behalf of the state to identify a person. It is thus not sure if the Court would make a distinction between both factual situations, if there is a real impossibility for the state to identify a witness.

Government Cannot Compel Witnesses to Attend

The Turkish government claims not to be in the possibility to compel witnesses to attend a hearing organised by a (former Commission) delegation. The Court, though, does not accept such reasoning.[79]

Unnecessary or Irrelevant Witnesses

See supra Information Is Unnecessary or Irrelevant.

Diverse

A few other means of defense were used by the respondent states. Though none of those were ever accepted as legitimate by the Court, they are mentioned for their value as a precedent.

Mandatory exercises in the context of a military service,[80] nor annual holidays[81] were ever accepted to justify the absence of a person. Even absence due to a sudden heavy snowfall – force majeure – did not convince the Court.[82]

3.6 Legal Consequences of Violations of Article 38 ECHR

Article 38 ECHR is a procedural right. In contrast to the substantive rights, in case of the finding of a violation, the legal consequences are not described in the Convention or an adjacent document. It is thus unclear if the triple obligation contained in the duty to execute or implement final judgments (Article 46 ECHR) and the just satisfaction provision (Article 41 ECHR) are applicable. On the other hand, it is sure that the overall impact of state compliance with Article 38 on the establishment of breaches of a material right is massive: with sufficient proof – a

[79] ECtHR 4 July 1999, No. 23657/94, *Cakici v. Turkey*, para. 43.

[80] ECtHR 8 July 1999, No. 23763/94, *Tanrikulu v. Turkey* para. 39.

[81] ECtHR 28 March 2000, No. 22492/93, *Kilic v. Turkey*, para. 35.

[82] ECtHR 28 March 2000, No. 22492/93, *Kilic v. Turkey*.

result of the cooperation of the parties with the Court – material violations can be found, but without proof – a result of the lack of cooperation of the parties with the Court – no violations can be found. Logically this reasoning means that violations of Article 38 ECHR will have consequences for the burden of proof.

3.6.1 Burden of Proof

In the cases referred to it, the European Court examines all the material before it, whether originating at the time from the former European Commission, the parties or other sources, and, if necessary, obtains material *proprio motu*.[83] *De jure* the parties do not have a burden of proof, but in fact a heavy duty rests on the applicant, since the Court's role is usually limited to requesting additional documents. Therefore, the applicant has to bear the burden of proof (*affirmanti incumbit probation*), and in order for something to be proven there may be no reasonable doubt.[84] Proof beyond reasonable doubt can result from the coexistence of sufficiently strong, clear and concordant inferences or of similar unrebutted presumptions of fact. In this context, the conduct of the Parties when evidence is being obtained has to be taken into account.[85] In the case of *Timurtas v. Turkey*, the Court takes the conduct of the parties into account:

> The Court emphasises that Convention proceedings do not in all cases lend themselves to rigorous application of the principle of *affirmanti incumbit probatio*. The Court has previously held that it is of the utmost importance for the effective operation of the system of individual petition instituted under former Article 25 of the Convention (now replaced by Article 34) that States should furnish all necessary facilities to make possible a proper and effective examination of applications. It is inherent in proceedings relating to cases of this nature, where an individual applicant accuses State agents of violating his rights under the Convention, that in certain instances solely the respondent State has access to information capable of corroborating or refuting these allegations. A failure on a Government's part to submit such information as is in their hands without a satisfactory explanation may not only reflect negatively on the level of compliance by a respondent State with its obligations under Article 38 § 1 (a) of the Convention, but may also give rise to the drawing of inferences as to the well-foundedness of the allegations.[86]

A failure from the state to provide information in its exclusive realm may give rise to the drawing of inferences. Moreover, a delay in submitting information may give rise to the drawing of inferences as well.[87]

---

[83] ECtHR 18 January 1978, No. 5310/71, *Ireland v. UK*, para. 160.

[84] E.g. ECtHR 28 June 1998, No. 23818/94, *Ergi v. Turkey*, paras. 77–78; ECommHR, 5 November 1969, *Denmark, Norway, Sweden and the Netherlands v. Greece*, Yearbook, Vol. XII bis, 196.

[85] ECtHR 18 January 1978, No. 5310/71, *Ireland v. UK*, para. 161.

[86] ECtHR 13 June 2000, No. 23531/94, *Timurtas v. Turkey*, para. 66.

[87] ECtHR 18 June 2002, No. 25656/94, *Orhan v. Turkey.*

These consequences considering the burden of proof may appear independent from the conclusion considering a violation. In certain cases, no violation is established, although it is possible to draw inferences[88] or vice versa.[89]

In certain cases the burden of proof is shifting from the applicant to the respondent state:

> [W]here the events in issue lie wholly, or in large part, within the exclusive knowledge of the authorities, as in the case of persons under their control in custody, strong presumptions of fact will arise in respect of injuries and death occurring during that detention. Indeed, the burden of proof may be regarded as resting on the authorities to provide a satisfactory and convincing explanation.[90]

The Court later draws a parallel between the situation of detainees and persons found injured or dead in an area within the exclusive control of the authorities of the state.[91] In all those cases, the respondent state will be held responsible for a violation of Article 2 or Article 3 ECHR when the non-disclosure of documents in the exclusive possession of the government prevents the Court from establishing the facts.[92]

Thus, the Court states that strong presumptions of fact may arise, and the burden of proof may shift to the respondent state in limited cases. The question rises under which circumstances this may be the case?

In *Estamirov v. Russia* the Court states:

> Where the applicant makes out a *prima facie* case and the Court is prevented from reaching factual conclusions for lack of such documents, it is for the Government to argue conclusively why the documents in question cannot serve to corroborate the allegations made by the applicants, or to provide a satisfactory and convincing explanation of how the events in question occurred.[93]

But which standards have to be met in order to classify as a *prima facie* case? In the Court's opinion, "the distribution of the burden of proof is intrinsically linked to the specific of the facts, the nature of the allegation made and the Convention right at stake."[94]

The Court's first case law requires sufficiently strong, clear and concordant inferences or of similar unrebutted presumptions of facts, based on concrete elements[95] to make out a *prima facie* case and to shift the burden of proof. Following this theory, the Russian government was held responsible for the detention of a Chechen

[88] E.g. ECtHR 19 December 2002, No. 57942/00 57945/00, *Khashiyev and Akayeva v. Russia*, para. 139.

[89] E.g. ECtHR 8 July 1999, No. 23763/94, *Tanrikulu v. Turkey*.

[90] ECtHR 2 August 2005, No. 65899/01, *Tanis and others v. Turkey*, para. 160.

[91] ECtHR 24 March 2005, No. 21894/93, *Akkum and others v. Turkey*, para. 211.

[92] Ibid.

[93] ECtHR 12 October 2006, No. 60272/00, *Estamirov and others v. Russia*, para. 122.

[94] ECtHR 24 January 2008, No. 48804/99, *Osmanoglu v. Turkey*, para. 45.

[95] ECtHR 27 July 2006, No. 69481/01, *Bazorkina v. Russia*, para. 106.

citizen, based on a CNN film showing a general ordering the victim's execution, without any further proof, while Russia refused to submit any documents.

In contrast, in *Togcu v. Turkey,*[96] the Court found a violation of Article 38, but could not draw any consequences considering the burden of proof. The applicant and his family members presented contradictory versions of the events. In concordance with the refusal to submit documents, this made it impossible for the Court to establish who was responsible and thus to make out a *prima facie* case. In another forced disappearance case, on the other hand, the Court states that not all contradictions exclude a *prima facie* case. The contradictions in the applicant's submissions and the other testimonies considering the chronology of the events had no influence on the credibility of their testimonies, given that their cultural background makes it inevitable that dates and other details (in particular numerical details) lack precision.[97]

In *Tangiyeva v. Russia,*[98] the Court abandons the need for concrete elements to establish a *prima facie* case. The applicant argued that the murder of her relatives was linked to other murders which had occurred in the same district in January 2000 and proved this on the basis of other cases. Without the need of any further eyewitnesses or concrete elements, the Court adopts the applicant's version of the facts, since the government refuses to submit any documents and this shifts the burden of proof. It is not surprising that judges Kovler and Hajiyev are not convinced that the burden of proof beyond reasonable doubt is met, but presume that the applicant does not establish a *prima facie* case.

Not even 2 months after its judgment in *Tangiyeva*, the Court strengthens or sharpens its criteria to make out a *prima facie* case. In *Zubayrayev v. Russia,*[99] the applicant could not establish a *prima facie* case simply based on indirect proof and the government's refusal to disclose evidence. In this case it was discussed whether the assassins were Russian special forces or fundamentalist wahabites. Based on the statement that the killers were armed, spoke Russian and wore camouflage uniforms, the Court could not shift the burden of proof.

In contrast, in *Ayubov v. Russia,*[100] the Court accepts the facts presented by the applicant on the basis of the same evidence as in *Zubayrayev*. Based on the existence of mere indirect evidence, Russia is convicted for the detention and disappearance of the applicant's son. Thus, the Court opens the way for the need of less proof, but the future will show us how the case law will evolve.

Cherchishova and Vajic conclude that"[w]ithout drawing generalisations that are too broad, [...] in cases where facts are in dispute and the domestic proceedings have been ineffective, the applicant's own submissions to the Court, witness testimonies collected by them and copies of their submissions to the domestic authorities in the aftermath of the event become primary sources of evidence. Besides that, depending

[96] ECtHR 31 May 2005, No. 27601/95, *Togcu v. Turkey*, para. 96.

[97] ECtHR 9 March 2004, No. 22494/93, *Hasan Ilhan v. Turkey* paras. 82, 87.

[98] ECtHR 29 November 2007, No. 57935/00, *Tangiyeva v. Russia*, para. 80.

[99] ECtHR 10 January 2008, No. 67797/01, *Zubayrayev v. Russia*, paras. 82–83.

[100] ECtHR 12 February 2009, No. 7654/02, *Ayubov v. Russia*, paras. 65 and 67.

on the circumstances of the case, the Court can examine medical documents and other expert reports produced within the national investigation, contemporary reports by the media and other public sources, such as NGO reports and other documents."[101]

3.6.2 Just Satisfaction

Article 41 ECHR allows the Court to award just satisfaction if (a) it finds a violation of the Convention or the additional protocols and (b) national law affords no reparation or only partial reparation to be made. This provision covers both pecuniary damages, non-pecuniary (moral) damages and costs and expenses. But the causal link between the loss and the wrongdoing has to be demonstrated, and only exceptionally has the Court accepted this link in cases considering procedural rights.[102]

On the one hand, the Court grants compensation for material damage. This depends on the factual background, and is not influenced by the member state's level of cooperation. It is obvious and logical that the decision to award compensation for pecuniary damage does not take a possible negative attitude of a member state into account. Moreover, the Court has stated that taking Article 34 ECHR into account when granting just satisfaction would be contrary to its rejection to award exemplary and punitive damages.[103] By analogy, one can assume that the Court would conclude the same in a case considering Article 38, since Article 34 relates to Article 38 as a *lex generalis* relating to a *lex specialis*.

On the other hand, the faulty cooperation may have an influence on the non-pecuniary damage. In a few forced disappearance cases, victims' relatives were awarded moral compensation because the state refused to cooperate sufficiently, and they were found to be a victim of Article 3 ECHR for the emotional distress and anguish they endured. In the Court's opinion, the finding of violations in themselves could not compensate for the loss.[104] But other cases prove that even without finding a violation of Article 3, Article 38 may be taken into account for awarding moral compensation.[105]

---

[101] O. Chernishova and N. Vajic, "The Court's evolving response to the states' failure to cooperate", in D.Spielmann (ed.), *The European Convention on Human Rights: a living and dynamic instrument – liber amicorum in honour of judge Rozakis*, (Brussels: Bruylant, 2011) 76.

[102] ECtHR 16 December 1997, No. 25528/94, *Canea Catholic Church v. Greece*, paras. 42 and 55.

[103] ECtHR 9 May 2003, No. 27244/95, *Tepe v. Turkey*, paras. 214–218.

[104] ECtHR 15 November 2007, No. 6846/02, *Khamila Isayeva v. Russia*, paras. 181–183; ECtHR 4 December 2008, No. 27243/03, *Musikhanova and others v. Russia*, para. 116; ECtHR 15 November 2007, No. 29361/02, *Kukayev v. Russia*, paras. 128–130.

[105] ECtHR 12 February 2009, No. 7654/02, *Ayubov v. Russia*; para. 122; ECtHR 7 October 2010, No. 41840/02,*Sadykov v. Russia*, para. 291. Compare: ECtHR 4 February 2005, Nos. 46827/99 46951/99, *Mamatkulov and Askarov v. Turkey*, para. 134, where non-pecuniary damage was awarded following the establishment of a violation of Article 34 ECHR, in order to remedy the harm caused by the incompliance with the aforementioned provision.

The question arises as to what the concrete influence of Article 38 is on the non-pecuniary compensation? To grant a moral compensation, the Court needs to find a violation which has a causal link to feelings of anxiety, confusion, frustration, fear, insecurity, loss of reputation and the lack of access to justice. Since poor cooperation contributes to those negative emotions, the Court takes it into account. The violation of Article 38 is thus not decisive, though of interest, possible as an aggravating factor, since it aggravates the negative emotions. The influence in terms of money is impossible to establish since it is especially hard to determine the exact damage, and therefore the Court usually awards just and fair satisfaction.

3.6.3 Compensation of Useless Costs

In *Shamayev and others v. Georgia and Russia,*[106] the Court condemns a non-cooperative member state – where a fact-finding mission was to take place[107] – to restitute the non-satisfactory costs that result from the refusal to cooperate. In this case, the Court delegation had to annul a planned fact-finding mission, since the Russian authorities refused the Court delegation access to the detained applicants. The Russian government had to restitute the incurred costs, but these amounted only to 1,600€ since the annulled plane tickets were insured.

This case is a pure application of the liability doctrine: there is a refusal to cooperate, the incurred costs constitute a(n) fault/error and harm/damage, and there is a causal link between both. It should be noted that the Court has not compensated ineffective costs in other cases; a wider use would be possible, however the profit is questionable, taking into account the low sum.

3.6.4 Duty to Execute

In none of the cases where Article 38 ECHR was deemed violated, reference is made to the duty to execute a judgment under Article 46 ECHR. The threefold obligation, i.e. (a) to end the violation, (b) to remedy the victim and (c) to take measures to ensure that in the future no similar violations occur, and especially the third aspect would, however, necessarily imply that a condemned state has to prevent similar violations of Article 38 from occurring in the future by taking structural measures, such as the removal of legislation contravening the Convention

[106] ECtHR 12 April 2005, No. 36378/02, *Shamayev and others v. Georgia and Russia*, paras. 492–504.

[107] In fact, it is the only fact-finding mission which was ever planned in the Northern Caucasus regions (i.e. the Chechen region).

or embarking in law-making. In that regard, the controversial Article 161 of the Russian CCP, would in our opinion arguably not survive the third obligation under Article 46 ECHR.

3.7 Conclusions

The right of individual application forms the cornerstone of the European Convention on Human Rights. It enables private individuals to bring their case before an international Court in order to remediate the human rights violations they suffered. While the exercise of the right of petition is an important source of protection, its functioning demands the goodwill of the member states. In order for the Court to adjudicate a case, it is necessary for the facts to be clarified, for which the member state's cooperation is fundamental. For this reason, Article 38 ECHR obliges the respondent member state to lend the necessary facilities to the Court. This contribution's final goal is thus the conservation of the effective character of the substantive rights in the Convention.

This provision did not involve any concrete obligations at the time the Convention entered into force, as the drafters presumed a good cooperation of the states with the supervisory bodies. Nor did the amending protocols or the explanatory reports thereby provide a lot of clarification or specification to the duty to cooperate. The duty has been entirely constructed through the case law before Rules 44A until C were introduced into the Rules of Court in 2004 as a concretization of the duty under Article 38 ECHR. These rules allow, among a confirmation of the duty to cooperate (Rule 44A[108]), for the President of the Chamber to take any steps he considers appropriate (Rule 44B[109]) and for the Court to draw inferences from an ineffective participation (Rule 44C[110]). But these Rules barely explain what member states may expect in case of faulty cooperation. They do not state which inferences may follow, nor which concrete steps can be taken. The Explanatory Report to Protocol No. 14 states that the Committee of Ministers can take necessary steps,[111]

[108] Rule 44A (Duty to cooperate with the Court) states: "The parties have a duty to cooperate fully in the conduct of the proceedings and, in particular, to take such action within their power as the Court considers necessary for the proper administration of justice. This duty shall also apply to a Contracting Party not party to the proceedings where such cooperation is necessary."

[109] Rule 44B (Failure to comply with an order of the Court) states: "Where a party fails to comply with an order of the Court concerning the conduct of the proceedings, the President of the Chamber may take any steps which he or she considers appropriate."

[110] Rule 44C (Failure to participate effectively) states: "1. Where a party fails to adduce evidence or provide information requested by the Court or to divulge relevant information of its own motion or otherwise fails to participate effectively in the proceedings, the Court may draw such inferences as it deems appropriate. 2. Failure or refusal by a respondent Contracting Party to participate effectively in the proceedings shall not, in itself, be a reason for the Chamber to discontinue the examination of the application."

[111] Explanatory Report to Protocol No. 14 to the ECHR, para. 90.

but it does not elucidate which steps can be taken. A non-limitative enumeration may in our opinion be desirable, for the sake of legal certainty, without touching upon the possibility of further jurisprudential clarification or addition.

Quantitative research proves the need for a better cooperation, though. Not only has the number of violations of Article 38 ECHR increased since 1999, the context in which violations are happening is 'grave'. Turkey and Russia are responsible for the major part of Article 38 violations; these occur in the context of state-driven force against the Kurdish and Chechen part of their population respectively. Moreover, the violations go hand-in-hand with violations of essential first generation civil rights, such as the right to life and the prohibition of torture, which are all absolutely fundamental for the maintenance of democracy and rule of law.

Since Article 38 ECHR is not a substantive but a procedural right, the admissibility conditions are not *an sich* applicable, since likewise, with regard to Article 34, the 6-month time limit is not applicable. Protocol No. 14 eliminated the need to wait for the admissibility decision to be taken in order to invoke Article 38. This responded to the Court's practice to take the decision on the merits and admissibility together. Moreover, the case law eased this strict requirement even before the entry into force of Protocol No. 14. So, for the sake of procedural efficiency, Article 38 indeed has to be met even before the decision on admissibility.

Considering the general character of Article 38, the Court has determined the scope of provision through its case law, only aided by the text on investigative measures in the Annex to its Rules of Court. When a member state refuses to submit documents, Article 38 will be deemed violated, even though the respondent member state considers these documents as irrelevant to the case. Only when the establishment of the facts is not obstructed, or the submitted documents already considerably facilitate the case, will Article 38 not be deemed to have been breached. Furthermore, procedural documents by themselves will never be sufficient to fulfill the requirement, just as documents which are only submitted after the fact-finding mission. Also, in most cases where the respondent state fails to make a material witness appear at a hearing, he will probably violate Article 38. If the absent witness is linked to the state, the duty upon the state to ensure the attendance of the witness is even more strict. Only when a witness has no bonds with the state's authority and the state took all reasonable steps to ensure his attendance, will the state be released from its responsibility under Article 38.

All means of defense which have until now been invoked by respondent states to escape their responsibility under Article 38 have been considered very poor by the Court. Russia cannot base a defense on Article 161 of the Russian CCP: firstly, the Court doubts that this prohibits the submitting of documents of pending cases; and secondly, the Court points to the possibility of Rule 33(2) Rules of Court to provide confidentiality. It is clear that respondent states cannot base a defense on a perceived lack of confidentiality either, since they could have invoked Rule 33(2) Rules of Court. Since the member state is responsible as one entity, internal communication problems and miscommunication cannot justify any shortcoming as to the duty under Article 38. Finally, the absence of witnesses at a Court hearing cannot be justified because it would be impossible to identify or locate them.

It is obvious that faulty cooperation could preclude the establishment of facts, and thus the finding of violations of substantive rights. Therefore, another very important evolution is the drawing of consequences by the Court in case of a non-cooperative attitude on the part of the state. The Court shifts the burden of proof to the respondent member state if the applicant makes out a *prima facie* case. In its most liberal case law, the Court shifts the burden of proof to the state, although the applicant only submitted indirect evidence to make out a *prima facie* case, but later on the Court seemed to return to its former case law.

On the one hand, the bad cooperation from the state with the Court resulting in the establishment of a violation of Article 38 ECHR can influence the level of just satisfaction awarded for moral damages, due to the increasing negative emotions that the applicant experiences. On the other hand, the pecuniary just satisfaction will not and cannot be influenced since this would contradict the prohibition on punitive and exemplary damages.

The violation of Article 38 does – in contrast to the violation of substantive rights – not provoke a duty to execute the judgment under Article 46 ECHR. The obligation to take individual or structural measures to ensure that in the future no similar violations occur, could serve the Court well, though. This would obligate the member state(s) concerned to modify or withdraw objectionable laws or practices, such as Article 161 Russian CCP. Applying the duty to execute on the violation of procedural rights would mean an improvement, though it is sure that it would be hard or even impossible to ensure the enforceability.

The creation of strict obligations under Article 38 ECHR and a stricter case law can only be welcomed, as the Court is under increasing pressure due to the high number of applications and its backlog. The Council of Europe's Parliamentary Assembly emphasized the failing cooperation by (certain) member states in its Resolution 1571,[112] Resolution DH (2006)45[113] and Recommendation 1809.[114] Though the Assembly complimented the Court with its more assertive case law, it stated that attention should be drawn to the unwilling member states. It encourages the member states to cooperate on the Court's request, and take positive measures on their own initiative to protect applicants and make internal procedures just and efficient. Furthermore, the 'High Level Conferences on the future of the European Court of Human Rights' resulting in the 'Interlaken Declaration',[115] the 'Izmir Declaration'[116] and the 'Brighton Declaration'[117] state that the right of individual

[112] Resolution 1571 (2007) Council of Europe member states' duty to co-operate with the European Court of Human Rights.

[113] Resolution Res DH (2006) 45 States' obligation to co-operate with the European Court of Human Rights.

[114] Recommendation 1809 (2007) Council of Europe member states' duty to co-operate with the European Court of Human Rights.

[115] Interlaken Declaration (2010), High Level Conference on the future of the European Court of Human Rights.

[116] Izmir Declaration (2011) on the future of the European Court of Human Rights.

[117] Brighton Declaration (2012), High Level Conference on the future of the European Court of Human Rights.

application is a shared responsibility. Moreover, the securing of human rights is the primary responsibility of the member states. The latter have to meet the standards in the Convention and the Court's interpretation. In case of the establishment of a violation by the Court, it is the member state's responsibility to remedy the violation, to keep the Court vital. It is impossible not to forget this is *sensu stricto* only a reactive system. The member state's initiative is especially important, both proactive – to preclude violations – and reactive – to restore violations at the national level.

Chapter 4
Protection by the Law: The Positive Obligation to Develop a Legal Framework to Adequately Protect ECHR Rights

Laurens Lavrysen

Abstract The European Court of Human Rights has recognized positive obligations to develop a legal framework to adequately protect the rights guaranteed by the European Convention on Human Rights ('protection by the law'). This article examines both the substantive and the procedural guarantees that are encompassed by this legal framework. The article examines the rationale behind, as well as the extent of substantive and procedural 'protection by the law', thereby identifying the general principles that can be induced from the European Court's jurisprudence. Where possible, the article compares the European Court's approach with the one taken by the United States Supreme Court, and with the theoretical account of 'protection by the law' as provided by the German Constitutional law theorist Robert Alexy. The article further argues that 'protection by the law' could be the key to the proper application of the European Court's margin of appreciation doctrine. Moreover, 'protection by the law' could be seen as a step in the direction of a more 'constitutionalized' positive obligations jurisprudence.

4.1 Introduction

The aim of this article is to examine the case law of the European Court of Human Rights (hereinafter the European Court) regarding the so-called positive obligation to develop a legal framework to adequately protect the rights provided for in the European Convention of Human Rights (hereinafter ECHR or the Convention).

This contribution has been funded by the Research Foundation Flanders (FWO) and has been written within the framework of the European Research Council funded project 'Strengthening the European Court of Human Rights: More Accountability through Better Legal Reasoning'.

L. Lavrysen (✉)
Human Rights Centre, Ghent University, Ghent, Belgium
e-mail: Laurens.Lavrysen@UGent.be

Y. Haeck and E. Brems (eds.), *Human Rights and Civil Liberties in the 21st Century*, Ius Gentium: Comparative Perspectives on Law and Justice 30,
DOI 10.1007/978-94-007-7599-2_4, © Springer Science+Business Media Dordrecht 2014

'Protection by the law', as one could paraphrase this positive obligation, arguably is the domain in which the Convention requirements restrict the freedom to act of national legislatures in the most far-reaching way, as it prescribes states to develop both substantive and procedural guarantees to pro-actively protect Convention rights. This paper examines the theoretical foundations and application of 'protection by the law'. As the edited volume of which this contribution forms part stems from a transatlantic encounter of American and European scholars, the paper will compare, where possible, the European Court's approach with the one taken by the U.S. Supreme Court. While there certainly are notable differences between both Courts – not in the least the fact that the European Court is a supranational court, whereas the Supreme Court is a traditional constitutional court[1] – there is sufficient common ground to allow for a meaningful comparison: both Courts' established fundamental rights jurisprudence.

This paper first briefly discusses the conceptual relationship between rights and duties/obligations (Sect. 4.2). Thereafter, Sect. 4.3 examines the different categories of obligations generated by (human) rights, with a particular focus on the obligation to protect, because of the major differences between the case law of the European Court and the U.S. Supreme Court. Section 4.4 gives a general introduction to the topic of 'protection by the law', while the subsequent parts deal with substantive 'protection by the law' (Sect. 4.5) and procedural 'protection by the law' (Sect. 4.6). Finally, in Sect. 4.7, some remarks are given on the relationship between 'protection by the law' and the European Court's doctrine of the margin of appreciation.

4.2 Rights and Duties

According to Joseph Raz, a proponent of the so-called 'interest model' of rights, "'x has a right' means that, other things being equal, an aspect of x's well-being (his interest) is a sufficient reason for holding some other person(s) to be under a duty."[2] There is no need to settle the fierce debate between legal theorists here and now, on whether rights are best seen as being interest-based or not. For the sake of this discussion, it is clear that the interest model best explains rights as they have been set out in the European Convention of Human Rights,[3] while this is not necessarily the case with respect to the U.S. Bill of Rights, which arguably is more

[1] This is, for example, relevant with respect to the margin of appreciation doctrine as developed by the European Court (see Sect. 4.7), which is an instrument of deference based on the Court's position as a supranational court.

[2] J. Raz, "Right-Based Moralities" in J. Waldron, *Theories of Rights* (Oxford Readings in Philosophy) (New York: Oxford University Press, 1984), 183.

[3] Similarly G. Letsas, *A Theory of Interpretation of the European Convention on Human Rights* (Oxford: Oxford University Press, 2007), 104.

abuse-of-power-oriented, rather than simply focusing on the protection of interests.[4] What, however, is of importance for this discussion, is that Raz's conception perfectly grasps our common sense feeling that if one labels something a right, then the right-holder must be able to claim this right vis-à-vis a corresponding duty-bearer. Under a rights-based theory, which a theory of human rights must necessarily be, rights generate derivative duties.[5] Rights and duties, however, do not stand on a simple one-to-one correlation, and it may be difficult to specify exactly on whom the duty to respect/protect/fulfill[6] a given rights rests,[7] as well as the extent of this duty to protect this right. The latter holds particularly true under the interest model, where, in George Letsas' words, "[s]omeone's interest or well-being may be served to a lesser or greater extent."[8] Furthermore, both under the ECHR and the United States Constitution (hereinafter the Constitution), rights are conceived as claims of individuals vis-à-vis the state, and therefore these documents – although they may generate strong moral duties for third parties – strictly speaking only generate legal duties on the state.[9]

These duties may be positive (a duty of the state to do something) or negative (a duty of the state to refrain from doing something). The existence of negative duties is not very controversial, and these duties are conceptually relatively easy to define, as the relationship between the right and the corresponding duty is arguably quite easy to establish. Take the example of the right to privacy, as protected by Art. 8 ECHR: the individual has a right that protects his or her interest in privacy and therefore the state has the corresponding negative duty not to 'interfere' with any

[4] E.g. S. Bandes, "The Negative Constitution: A Critique", 88 *Michigan Law Review* (1989–90), 2285. The rejection of the interest model is reflected in Ronald Dworkin's metaphor of 'rights as trumps' that block reasons that are based on corrupted utilitarian calculations (R. Dworkin, "Rights as Trumps" in J. Waldron, *Theories of Rights* (New York: Oxford University Press, 1984), 153–167) and in a stronger focus on exclusionary reasons (see, for example, R. Pildes, "Avoiding Balancing: The Role of Exclusionary Reasons in Constitutional Law", 45 *Hastings Law Journal* (1993–94), 711–751, in which Richard H. Pildes considers rights to be "means of defining the reasons for state action that are appropriate in a particular sphere" (724)). However, there are American scholars such as Richard H. Fallon who do consider constitutional rights to be interest-based, see R. Fallon, "Individual Rights and the Powers of Government", 27 *Georgia Law Review* (1992–93), 352–360. The interest model is also not incompatible with Frederick Schauer's metaphor of 'rights as shields' that require the state to provide a higher burden of justification, see F. Schauer, "A Comment on the Structure of Rights", 27 *Georgia Law Review* (1992–93), 428–431.

[5] Dworkin, supra, note 5, 171. Dworkin distinguishes between right-based, duty-based and goal-based political theories.

[6] For the distinction, see Sect. 4.3.

[7] H. Shue, *Basic Rights – Subsistence, Affluence and U.S. Foreign Policy (second edition)* (Princeton: Princeton University Press, 1996), 16.

[8] G. Letsas, "The Concepts of the Margin of Appreciation", 26 *Oxford Journal of Legal Studies* (2006), 718.

[9] The ECHR does not recognize the concept of *horizontal or third-party applicability (drittwirkung)*, i.e. the possibility of an individual to bring a claim against another individual directly based on the Convention. The ECHR, however, does require states to protect individuals against other individuals. See D. Harris, M. O'Boyle, E. Bates and C. Buckley, *Law of the European Convention on Human* Rights (Oxford: OUP, 2009), 20.

issue that falls within the protected 'sphere' of privacy (e.g. by searching an individual's house or tapping his or her telephone), unless and insofar the exceptions under paragraph 2 allow lawful state 'interference'.[10] There is a 'conceptual proximity' between right and duty, and the right/duty relationship approximates the simplified account of rights and duties as being on a simple one-to-one correlation.

The theoretical difficulties in dealing with positive duties stem exactly from the lack of such a 'conceptual proximity'.[11] In some cases, this lack of 'conceptual proximity' stems from the fact that state responsibility may only be engaged indirectly (in the case of obligations to protect, see Sect. 4.3) – unlike negative duties, where direct state responsibility is at stake. More generally, even when state responsibility can be engaged directly (in the case of obligations to fulfill, see Sect. 4.3), it may still be hard to establish the necessity and the required scope of state action[12] – unlike what is the case for negative duties, where non-interference is the rule and interference an exception requiring justification. Establishing the responsibility of the state as duty-bearer and the extent to which these duties arise, may thus prove to be particularly difficult, especially when there is a lack of knowledge on the part of the state regarding (the extent of) the threat to the individual's right, or when recognizing a positive duty would severely restrict the state's possibilities in pursuing other acceptable policy goals.

4.3 Respect, Protect, Fulfill

Before discussing the obligation to provide 'protection by the law', it is necessary to give a more general account of the kind of duties rights generate. Human rights law traditionally distinguishes between the negative obligation to respect on the one hand, and the positive obligations to protect and fulfill on the other.[13] The obligation

---

[10] Art. 8 ECHR: 1. Everyone has the right to respect for his private and family life, his home and his correspondence. 2. There shall be no interference by a public authority with the exercise of this right, except such as is in accordance with the law and is necessary in a democratic society in the interests of national security, public safety or the economic well-being of the country, for the prevention of disorder or crime, for the protection of health or morals, or for the protection of the rights and freedoms of others.

[11] Dimitris Xenos applies a similar concept of 'proximity' in relation with the element of knowledge (see below): "In general terms, the element of knowledge is evaluated in relation to two separate identity types that reflect two corresponding conditions of proximity which are critical in the determination of the state's obligations. (1) The identity of the individual(s) in need of human rights protection (the first condition of proximity); and/or (2) The source of the threat to human rights (the second condition of proximity)" (D. Xenos, *The Positive Obligations of the State under the European Convention of Human Rights* (Abingdon: Routledge, 2012), 75–76).

[12] The same applies to obligations to protect.

[13] The distinction between obligations to respect, to protect and to fulfill stems from the work of Asbjørn Eide; *The Right to Adequate Food as a Human Right*, Report prepared by A. Eide, UN Doc E/CN.4/Sub.2/1987/23. In the context of positive obligations under the European Convention on Human Rights, Dröge distinguishes between positive obligations of a horizontal dimension and positive obligations of a social dimension (C. Dröge, *Positive Verpflichtungen der Staaten in der Europäischen Menschenrechtskonvention* (Berlin: Springer, 2003), 381–382). This distinction generally coincides with the obligation to protect/fulfill distinction.

to protect requires that states protect the enjoyment of a human right against violations emanating from private perpetrators. The obligation to fulfill requires states to facilitate the individual's enjoyment of a human right by, for example, participation in the decision-making process and the provision of legal remedies, as well as to provide a certain good when this is necessary for the enjoyment of a human right.

Admittedly, the distinction between the obligations to respect, protect and fulfill is not always clear, and there may be overlaps. There may be cases in which the violation is partially caused by the state and partially by a private actor, thereby engaging both obligations to respect and obligations to protect. If a state, for example, gives a permit to a highly pollutive factory, it fails in its obligation to protect against private violations of the right to a healthy environment,[14] but it equally fails in its obligation to respect this right, as it is exactly the act of issuing a permit which enables the environmental nuisance. Or similarly, when a state authority has sanctioned a situation in which an individual's rights are violated by other individuals: while this is certainly a failure of an obligation to protect that individual, by sanctioning this situation the state becomes complicit in the human rights violation, which relates to an obligation to respect.[15] Or take cases concerning the lack of access to state-held information[16]: is this a question of an obligation to fulfill (i.e. to provide and facilitate access),[17] or is this a question of an obligation to respect (i.e. not to

[14] To a certain extent, such a right has been recognized under Art. 8 ECHR, the right to privacy, e.g. ECtHR (GC) 8 July 2003, No. 36022/97, *Hatton and Others v. the United Kingdom*. The ECtHR generally examines environmental cases under the obligation to protect.

[15] While some environmental cases illustrate the contrary, the European Court sometimes examines such cases as involving obligations to respect. For example, the case of ECtHR (GC) 13 August 1981, Nos. 7601/76; 7806/77, *Young, James and Webster v. the United Kingdom*, para. 49, in which the Court decided to examine a closed shop agreement as a matter of obligations to respect, because "it was the domestic law in force at the relevant time that made lawful the treatment of which the applicants complained." The same applied in a case in which a private television company refused to broadcast a commercial directed against industrial animal production because it was too political, in application of domestic law (ECtHR 28 June 2001, No. 24699/94, *VgT Verein Gegen Tierfabrieken v. Switzerland*, para. 47). See also ECtHR 16 December 2008, No. 23883/06, *Khursid Mustafa and Tarzibachi v. Sweden*, para. 34. The U.S. Supreme Court made a similar finding in the context of the 'negative' Due Process Clause in the case of U.S. Supreme Court 19 December 1921, *Truax v. Corrigan*, 257 U.S. 312: "The legislative power of a state can only be exerted in subordination to the fundamental principles of right and justice which the guaranty of due process in the Fourteenth Amendment is intended to preserve, and a purely arbitrary or capricious exercise of that power, whereby a wrongful and highly injurious invasion of property rights is practically sanctioned and the owner stripped of all real remedy, is wholly at variance with those principles."

[16] Or similarly, on access to abortion, see A. Timmer, "R.R. v. Poland: of reproductive health, abortion and degrading treatment", 31 May 2011, strasbourgobservers.com.

[17] The ECtHR examines such cases as involving positive obligations, e.g. ECtHR (GC) 7 July 1989, No. 10454/83, *Gaskin v. the United Kingdom*. With respect to access to information in the context of a trial, the Supreme Court on the other hand has held that "[i]t is not crucial whether we describe this right to attend criminal trials to hear, see, and communicate observations concerning them as a 'right of access' (...) or a 'right to gather information', for we have recognized that 'without some protection for seeking out the news, freedom of the press could be eviscerated.' The explicit, guaranteed rights to speak and to publish concerning what takes place at a trial would lose much meaning if access to observe the trial could, as it was here, be foreclosed arbitrarily" (U.S. Supreme Court 2 July 1980, *Richmond Newspapers, Inc. v. Virginia*, 448 U.S. 555).

hinder an individual in gaining access)?[18] What if a state not only fails to protect or fulfill a right, but also makes matters worse (i.e. a failure of an obligation to respect).[19] Can you examine both obligations separately or do they form an inseparable whole? And similarly, what if a state fails to take positive steps to mitigate the consequences of a state interference (i.e. a negative obligation)?[20] And what if – in a situation of 'privatization'[21] of public tasks – a private actor violates a human right while exercising powers that have been delegated by the state: does the state violate an obligation to respect by delegating those powers or is it rather a violation of an obligation to protect against that private actor?[22]

The problems in distinguishing between the negative obligation to respect on the one hand and the positive obligations to protect and fulfill on the other, is that they are based on the equally difficult action/inaction distinction. In a dissenting opinion

[18] The UN Committee on Economic, Social and Cultural Rights (CESCR), for example, considers the hindering of access to be a question of the obligation to respect. See, for example, CESCR 12 May 1999, General Comment No. 12 on the right to adequate food, para. 15, in which it held that "[t]he obligation to respect existing access to adequate food requires States parties not to take any measures that result in preventing such access." Similarly, in the context of the right to respect for family life (Art. 8 ECHR), the European Court held that "domestic measures hindering [the mutual enjoyment by parent and child of each other's company] amount to an interference with the right protected by Article 8" (ECtHR 5 February 2004, No. 60457/00, *Kosmopoulou v. Greece*, para. 47).

[19] For example, the case of ECtHR 31 May 2007, No. 7510/04, *Kontrová v. Slovakia*, concerning domestic violence. Not only was there a failure of the obligation to protect, but the state had also made matters worse, as a police officer had pressurized the victim to drop charges against her husband. One month later the husband killed both of their children.

[20] E.g. ECtHR 12 February 2009, No. 2512/04, *Noland and K. v. Russia*, concerning the separation of a father and son as a result of the refusal by the Russian authorities to allow the father to re-enter the territory after a short trip abroad. According to the Court, "[t]he period of separation was the direct consequence of a combination of the Russian authorities' actions (the decision to exclude the applicant from Russia) and omissions (failure to notify the applicant of that decision and to take measures that would enable his son to leave Russia)." The Court avoided the characterization problem, by stating that it was not necessary "to decide (…) whether it would be more appropriate to analyse the case as one concerning a positive or a negative obligation since it is of the view that the core issue is whether a fair balance was struck between the competing public and private interests involved." Other examples under Art. 8 ECHR, the right to respect for family life, are cases in which the state has placed children into public care (which raises an issue under an obligation to respect), but then fails to take positive steps to reunite the family as soon as possible, e.g. ECtHR 23 September 1994, No. 19823/92, *Hokkanen v. Finland*.

[21] Harris et al., supra, note 9, 20–21. Harris et al. argue that a state may be held directly responsible under the Convention "for the acts of private companies and other persons to whom powers that are traditionally state powers have been transferred by privatization, as in the case of private prisons."

[22] In the case of ECtHR 25 March 1993, No. 13134/87, *Costello-Roberts v. the United Kingdom*, the Court examined a case of corporal punishment of the applicant by the headmaster of an independent school as involving negative obligations. The Court held that "(…) the State cannot absolve itself from responsibility by delegating its obligations to private bodies or individuals" (para. 27). See similarly ECtHR 16 June 2005, No. 61603/00, *Storck v. Germany*, para. 103. In the case of Storck, the Court, however, did examine the case as one involving the obligation to protect.

in the ECtHR case of *Mouvement Raëlien Suisse v. Switzerland*,[23] judge Pinto de Albuquerque held that "the Court should ask itself if the absence of any action by the national authorities would have resulted in a violation of the Convention": if so, the case concerns positive obligations.[24] Similarly, Frank B. Cross proposed "(…) the following simple test for distinguishing between positive and negative rights – if there was no government in existence, would the right be automatically fulfilled?"[25] In line with Susan Bandes, I submit that such proposals are problematic for pragmatic reasons, as they assume "that the baseline should be complete lack of government involvement", which "is sharply at odds with the reality of government as pervasive regulator and architect of a vast web of social, economic, and political strategies and choices."[26] According to Bandes, "the distinction between action and inaction fails to reflect the distribution of power and the ways in which government can cause harm in the modern welfare state."[27] As illustrated by the access to information example, a fundamental problem of the action/inaction distinction, in the words of an American court, is that "(…) it is possible to restate most actions as corresponding inactions with the same effect, and to show that inaction may have the same effects as a forbidden action."[28] Furthermore, the obligation to fulfill includes the obligation to provide remedies to challenge a human rights violation – whether it stems from state or private action – and thus overlaps with the obligations to respect and protect. In this sense, Stephen Holmes and Cass Sunstein have argued that the negative/positive obligations distinction is inadequate, because all rights are meaningless without the provision of remedies, and therefore all obligations necessarily are positive.[29] More generally, Henry Shue has held that "[i]t is impossible (…) meaningfully and exhaustively to split all rights into two kinds based upon the nature of their implementing duties, because the duties are always a mixture of positive and negative ones."[30]

I have argued elsewhere that the European Court should apply a similar approach to negative and positive obligations, exactly because in practice it may prove to be

---

[23] ECtHR (GC) 13 July 2012, No. 16354/06, *Mouvement Raëlien Suisse v. Switzerland.*

[24] Judge Pinto de Albuquerque also recognizes "complementary action by the government (…) required to restore the applicant to the situation in which he found himself prior to that violation" as a positive obligation. "If a finding of a violation does not imply the need for any restorative action by the government, that indicates a negative obligation."

[25] F. Cross, "The Error of Positive Rights", 48 *UCLA Law Review* (2001), 866.

[26] Bandes, supra, note 4, 2284–2285.

[27] Bandes, supra, note 4, 2283. According to Bandes, "[t]he assumption that government can deprive individuals of protected rights only by its actions does not take into account government's pervasive influence through regulatory action and inaction, its displacement of private remedies, and, indeed, its monopoly over some avenues of relief."

[28] Bandes, supra, note 4, 2281, with reference to United States Court of Appeals, Seventh Circuit 23 May 1988, *Archie v. City of Racine*, 847 F.2d 1211.

[29] S. Holmes and C. Sunstein, *The Cost of Rights. Why Liberty Depends on Taxes* (New York: W.W. Norton, 1999), 48.

[30] Shue, supra, note 7, 155.

particularly difficult to distinguish between both categories.[31] Nonetheless, the tripartite classification of obligations to respect, protect and fulfill is helpful as an analytical framework to examine the case law of both the European Court and the Supreme Court. Before proceeding to the issue of 'protection by the law', it is necessary to first give a short comparison between the practice of both Courts with respect to positive obligations. Firstly, the totally different approach with respect to the positive obligation to protect will be examined. Secondly, a discussion of what I will call 'conditional' positive obligations provides insights in both Court's practice.

4.3.1 Positive Rights: ECHR v. United States Constitution

The case law concerning child protection against abusive parents perfectly illustrates the difference of approach between the European Court and the Supreme Court concerning the obligation to protect.[32] The Supreme Court case of *DeShaney* concerned the beating of 4-year old Joshua DeShaney by his father in March 1984, which resulted in brain damage that was so severe that he had to be confined to an institution for the intellectually disabled for the rest of his life. Social services had been aware of the abuse since a police report of child abuse and a hospital visit in January 1983. In the course of 1983, suspicion of child abuse was recorded five times by a social worker, in November 1983, a hospital report again reported child abuse suspicions, and in January and March 1984, the father refused to allow social workers to see the boy. Despite all this, social services had not undertaken any action to remove the boy from the father's custody. Joshua's mother, acting on behalf of her son, argued that the Winnebago County social services had failed to intervene and protect Joshua against the violence of which they were aware or should have been aware, in violation of Joshua's right to liberty under the due process clause of the Fourteenth Amendment. The Supreme Court, in a

[31] L. Lavrysen, "The Scope of Rights and the Scope of Obligations: Positive Obligations" (to be published in E. Brems and J. Gerards, *Shaping Rights in the ECHR – The Role of the European Court of Human Rights in Determining the Scope of Human Rights*, Cambridge University Press). In order to tackle criticism that it provides less protection when it considers a borderline case to involve positive rather than negative obligations, the Court generally holds that "[t]he boundaries between the State's positive and negative obligations (…) do not lend themselves to precise definition. The applicable principles are nonetheless similar. In particular, in both instances regard must be had to the fair balance to be struck between the competing interests" (e.g. ECtHR (GC) 4 December 2007, No. 44362/04, *Dickson v. the United Kingdom*). Despite this rhetoric, however, in reality the Court does provide less protection in the case of positive obligations, by allowing a wider margin of appreciation (e.g. ECtHR 3 February 2009, No. 31276/05, *Women on Waves and Others v. Portugal*) and by applying a looser proportionality test (a mere fair balance test, instead of a more structured proportionality analysis, as well as a lack of examination of the legality and the legitimacy of the interference).

[32] For a similar discussion, see K. Starmer, "Positive obligations under the Convention" in J.L. Jowell and J. Cooper (eds.), *Understanding Human Rights Principles* (Portland: Hart Publishing, 2001), 140–144.

majority opinion written by Justice Rehnquist, however, dismissed this claim, particularly because:

> (...) nothing in the language of the Due Process Clause itself requires the State to protect the life, liberty, and property of its citizens against invasion by private actors. The Clause is phrased as a limitation on the State's power to act, not as a guarantee of certain minimal levels of safety and security. It forbids the State itself to deprive individuals of life, liberty, or property without 'due process of law,' but its language cannot fairly be extended to impose an affirmative obligation on the State to ensure that those interests do not come to harm through other means. Nor does history support such an expansive reading of the constitutional text. Like its counterpart in the Fifth Amendment, the Due Process Clause of the Fourteenth Amendment was intended to prevent government 'from abusing [its] power, or employing it as an instrument of oppression'(...) Its purpose was to protect the people from the State, not to ensure that the State protected them from each other. The Framers were content to leave the extent of governmental obligation in the latter area to the democratic political processes.
>
> Consistent with these principles, our cases have recognized that the Due Process Clauses generally confer no affirmative right to governmental aid, even where such aid may be necessary to secure life, liberty, or property interests of which the government itself may not deprive the individual. (...)[33]

In the similar case of *Z and Others v. the United Kingdom*, the European Court applied an entirely different approach. The case concerned the serious abuse and neglect of four siblings by their parents. The social services had been aware of these problems, which were confirmed by numerous later reports, since October 1987. The children were only placed in emergency foster care in June 1992, on demand of their mother, who said that she would batter them if they were not removed from her care. Psychiatric analysis in 1993 revealed that the children, then aged 10, 8, 6 and 4 years, had suffered severe psychological damage as a result of the abuse and neglect. They unsuccessfully claimed damages against the social services before the domestic courts. The European Court, however, held that the social services' negligence amounted to a violation of Art. 3 ECHR, the prohibition of torture and of inhuman treatment or punishment, holding in particular that:

> The Court reiterates that Article 3 enshrines one of the most fundamental values of democratic society. It prohibits in absolute terms torture or inhuman or degrading treatment or punishment. The obligation on High Contracting Parties under Article 1 of the Convention to secure to everyone within their jurisdiction the rights and freedoms defined in the Convention, taken in conjunction with Article 3, requires States to take measures designed to ensure that individuals within their jurisdiction are not subjected to torture or inhuman or degrading treatment, including such ill-treatment administered by private individuals (...). These measures should provide effective protection, in particular, of children and other vulnerable persons and include reasonable steps to prevent ill-treatment of which the authorities had or ought to have had knowledge (...).
>
> (...) The Court acknowledges the difficult and sensitive decisions facing social services and the important countervailing principle of respecting and preserving family life. The present case, however, leaves no doubt as to the failure of the system to protect these applicant children from serious, long-term neglect and abuse.[34]

---

[33] U.S. Supreme Court 22 February 1989, *DeShaney v. Winnebago County*, 489 U.S. 189.

[34] ECtHR (GC) 10 May 2001, No. 29392/95, *Z and Others v. the United Kingdom*, paras. 73–74.

Unlike the Supreme Court, which only allows for direct responsibility, the European Court thus acknowledges that the state may have an indirect responsibility to protect an individual's right against violations by private actors. The Court first developed its doctrine of positive obligations in the case of *Marckx v. Belgium*:

> (…) the object of [Article 8 ECHR] is 'essentially' that of protecting the individual against arbitrary interference by the public authorities […]. Nevertheless it does not merely compel the State to abstain from such interference: in addition to this primarily negative undertaking, there may be positive obligations inherent in an effective 'respect' for family life.[35]

This is the application of the principle of effectiveness, a general interpretative principle the European Court applies when determining the extent of protection under the ECHR.[36] In the Court's words, the principle of effectiveness implies that "[t]he Convention is intended to guarantee not rights that are theoretical or illusory but rights that are practical and effective."[37] The principle of effectiveness or the need to provide effective protection, has since the *Marckx* judgment been the primary rationale for the development of positive obligations under almost every Convention article,[38] both with respect to obligations to protect (e.g. *Z and Others v. the United Kingdom*) as with respect to obligations to fulfill (e.g. *Marckx v. Belgium*). In the European Court's case law, the focus is on harm to individual interests. From this perspective, it is not decisive who is directly responsible for this harm. Therefore, to prevent such harm and thus to 'effectively' protect the rights guaranteed in the European Convention, the existence of positive obligations is necessary. Below I will more extensively discuss the proper application of the principle of effectiveness to 'protection by the law'.

The focus of the U.S. Constitution, however, arguably lies on the status of the individual as a member of a democratic society, rather than on harm to individual interests.[39] This status largely depends on the way authorities deal with individuals, and therefore the Constitution is not concerned with relations between an individual and other private parties. But such a restriction is not entirely convincing, because the way authorities protect individuals against other private parties necessarily also provides information about the individual's status as a member of democratic society. Such a conception seems to be at the basis of Justice Brennan's strong dissent in *DeShaney*:

> My disagreement with the Court arises from its failure to see that inaction can be every bit as abusive of power as action, that oppression can result when a State undertakes a vital duty and then ignores it. Today's opinion construes the Due Process Clause to permit a State

---

[35] ECtHR (GC) 13 June 1979, No. 6833/74, *Marckx v. Belgium*, para. 31.

[36] Harris et al., supra, note 9, 15.

[37] E.g. ECtHR 9 October 1979, No. 6289/73, *Airey v. Ireland*, para. 24.

[38] See A. Mowbray, *The Development of Positive Obligations under the European Convention on Human Rights by the European Court of Human Rights* (Oxford: Hart Publishing, 2004).

[39] See J.H. Ely, *Democracy and Distrust, a theory of judicial review* (Cambridge (Mass): Harvard University Press, 1980), 87.

> to displace private sources of protection and then, at the critical moment, to shrug its shoulders and turn away from the harm that it has promised to try to prevent. Because I cannot agree that our Constitution is indifferent to such indifference, I respectfully dissent.[40]

For the remaining part of this paper, it is necessary to keep in mind that, until *DeShaney* is overruled,[41] the U.S. Constitution does not generate positive obligations to protect. This is relevant because it equally restricts the obligation to provide 'protection by the law'. 'Protection by the law' against violations by private actors, procedural as well as substantive, is therefore not required under the U.S. Constitution, while it may flow from the European Convention.

4.3.2 'Conditional' Positive Obligations

In the introduction of an influential article on the distinction between negative and positive rights and its relevance in U.S. constitutional law, Susan Bandes wrote:

> The conventional wisdom distinguishes between negative rights to be free from governmental interference and positive rights to have government do or provide various things. The conventional wisdom is that the Constitution recognizes only the former. Individuals have no right to have government do anything at all; it must only refrain from harming or coercing them.[42]

This is clearly in line with what one would expect from the discussion of *DeShaney* above. However, as the term 'conventional wisdom' suggests, considering the Constitution to be exclusively negative does little justice to the truth.

---

[40] See in a similar vein, Bandes, supra, note 4, 2285: "Consider the proposition that government inaction is not actionable because it is not an abuse of power. This conclusory proposition begs the question of why inaction is not an abuse of power."

[41] For an overview of arguments in favor of overruling *DeShaney*, see. J.R. Howard, "Rearguing DeShaney", 18 *Thomas M. Cooley Law Review* (2001), 381–408. The Supreme Court confirmed *DeShaney* in the case of U.S. Supreme Court 27 June 2005, *Castle Rock v. Gonzales*, 545 U.S. 748. The case concerned the murder of a woman's three children by her husband, against whom she had obtained a restraining order, which the police had failed to enforce. The Court's reasoning focused primarily on rejecting the argument that, for the purposes of the Due Process Clause, the woman had a property interest in police enforcement of the restraining order. Notably, in the same case, the Inter-American Commission on Human Rights did find violations of the American Declaration of the Rights and Duties of Man (Inter-American Commission on Human Rights 21 July 2011, *Jessica Lenahan (Gonzales)* et al. *v. The United States*). The Commission held "that the State failed to act with due diligence to protect Jessica Lenahan and Leslie, Katheryn and Rebecca Gonzales from domestic violence, which violated the State's obligation not to discriminate and to provide for equal protection before the law under Article II of the American Declaration. The State also failed to undertake reasonable measures to prevent the death of Leslie, Katheryn and Rebecca Gonzales in violation of their right to life under Article I of the American Declaration, in conjunction with their right to special protection as girl-children under Article VII of the American Declaration. Finally, the Commission concludes that the State violated the right to judicial protection of Jessica Lenahan and her next of kin, under Article XVIII of the American Declaration."

[42] Bandes, supra, note 4, 2274.

Without attempting to be exhaustive, I will indicate some areas of the U.S. Supreme Court's case law that clearly illustrate that Constitutional rights can have a limited positive dimension.

The most illustrative area concerns prisoners' rights. In the case of *Estelle v. Gamble*, the Supreme Court held that a failure to provide a prisoner with medical care – clearly a positive obligation – may constitute cruel and unusual punishment in the sense of the Eight Amendment. Because prisoners cannot, by reason of their deprivation of liberty care for themselves, Justice Marshall in his majority opinion found that:

> We therefore conclude that deliberate indifference to serious medical needs of prisoners constitutes the 'unnecessary and wanton infliction of pain,' (...) proscribed by the Eighth Amendment. This is true whether the indifference is manifested by prison doctors in their response to the prisoner's needs or by prison guards in intentionally denying or delaying access to medical care or intentionally interfering with the treatment once prescribed.[43]

While there certainly are differences with respect to standards applied, the Supreme Court's approach is not essentially different from the one taken by the European Court, which has in numerous cases found violations of Art. 3 ECHR (the prohibition of torture and of inhuman or degrading treatment or punishment) on account of a lack of adequate medical treatment for prisoners.[44] Both the Supreme Court and the European Court have found the following problems to raise issues under the Eight Amendment and Art. 3 ECHR respectively: failure to provide acceptable detention conditions, particularly due to overcrowding[45]; lack of protection against violence by other prisoners[46]; lack of protection against health hazards in prison, in particular against passive smoking.[47] The Supreme Court has even recognized positive obligations outside the Eight Amendment sphere, such as the obligation to provide prisoners with law books based on the fundamental constitutional right of access to the courts.[48]

The rationale behind these decisions is that by locking up an individual, the state deprives him or her from other sources of aid.[49] The positive obligation is not freestanding, but depends on an earlier act of the state, i.e. the deprivation of liberty of the individual. Therefore, as opposed to a freestanding 'regular positive

---

[43] U.S. Supreme Court 30 November 1976, *Estelle v. Gamble*, 429 U.S. 97.

[44] E.g. ECtHR (GC) 26 October 2000, No. 30210/96, *Kudła v. Poland*.

[45] U.S. Supreme Court 23 May 2011, *Brown v. Plata*, 563 U.S. ___, and amongst many others ECtHR 6 March 2001, No. 40907/98, *Dougoz v. Greece*.

[46] U.S. Supreme Court 6 June 1994, *Farmer v. Brennan*, 511 U.S. 825, and amongst many others ECtHR 27 May 2008, No. 22893/05, *Rodić and 3 Others v. Bosnia and Herzegovina*. Fatal incidents in prison are examined under Art. 2 ECHR, the right to life, e.g. ECtHR 14 March 2002, No. 46477/99, *Paul and Audrey Edwards v. the United Kingdom*.

[47] U.S. Supreme Court 18 June 1993, *Helling v. McKinney*, 509 U.S. 25; ECtHR 14 September 2010, No. 37186/03, *Florea v. Romania*.

[48] U.S. Supreme Court 27 April 1977, *Bounds v. Smith*, 430 U.S. 817.

[49] Bandes, supra, note 4, 2295.

obligation', I will label such obligations as 'conditional' positive obligations.[50] In theory, the state can always release itself from such a 'conditional' positive obligation by simply refraining to act in a certain way. It is easy to reformulate such 'conditional' positive obligations as negative obligations: the positive obligation to provide healthcare to prisoners becomes the negative obligation not to imprison a person if one does not provide for the prisoner's healthcare. One could therefore say that, in such cases, the positive obligation is 'parasitical' on a negative obligation.

This parasitical character explains why the Supreme Court does recognize 'conditional' positive obligations, without abandoning the 'essentially negative nature' of the Constitution and despite its rejection of regular positive obligations in *DeShaney*. A closer look at David Currie's overview of 'affirmative duties' in the case law of the Supreme Court reveals that all of them that can genuinely be considered as positive obligations are 'conditional' ones.[51] In the case of *Goldberg v. Kelly*,[52] the Supreme Court held that the Due Process Clause of the Fourteenth Amendment required a certain procedure before welfare benefits could be terminated. This procedural positive obligation is a 'conditional' one: it depends on the government's earlier decision to grant the individual concerned welfare benefits, a decision which the state was not constitutionally obliged to take. In a similar vein, the positive obligation on the government to provide judicial remedies for its own violations of the Constitution[53] is a 'conditional' one: government can always avoid it by simply refraining from violating the Constitution. The Sixth Amendment's positive obligation to provide legal assistance is also a 'conditional' one: it depends on the government's initial decision to prosecute the individual.[54] Finally, Currie also discusses some cases decided on the basis of the Fourteenth Amendment's equal protection clause. In *Shapiro v. Thompson*,[55] the Supreme Court decided that it was unconstitutional for a state to exclude individuals from welfare benefits on the basis that they had not yet lived in that state for a year. Currie himself considered this to be a 'conditional affirmative duty': "if government undertakes to help A, it may have to help B as well."[56] While it may be better to consider such a case as involving a negative obligation not to discriminate, the finding of such discrimination indeed gives rise to what one could call a 'corrective' positive obligation to provide the

[50] While discussing the case of U.S. Supreme Court 22 November 1939, *Schneider v. State of New Jersey*, 308 U.S. 147, David Currie also labeled the alleged 'affirmative duty' concerned as a 'conditional' one, in the sense that it only arises after an initial decision by the state (i.e. to designate an area as public forum), see. D. Currie, "Positive and Negative Constitutional Rights", 53 *University of Chicago Law Review* (1986), 879.

[51] Currie, supra, note 50, 872–886. For a more recent discussion, see Cross, supra, note 26, 868–874.

[52] U.S. Supreme Court 23 March 1970, *Goldberg v. Kelly*, 397 U.S. 254.

[53] Currie refers to the case of U.S. Supreme Court 13 March 1908, Ex parte Young, 209 U.S. 123.

[54] Bandes, supra, note 4, 2277.

[55] U.S. Supreme Court 21 April 1969, *Shapiro v. Thompson*, 394 U.S. 618.

[56] Currie, supra, note 50, 881.

discriminated with the good concerned.[57] Insofar as one considers this to be a positive obligation, it can indeed only be a 'conditional' one: its existence depends solely on the government acting in such a way as to discriminatorily favoring another group.

The concept of 'conditional' positive obligations is thus crucial to understand certain lines of case law of the Supreme Court. It is equally helpful to better understand the European Court's positive obligation case law. All things being equal, 'conditional' positive obligations under the ECHR require enhanced protection compared with regular positive obligations. This explains the enhanced protection in the prisoner cases, for example, why the European Court requires high standards of healthcare with respect to prisoners, whereas it is very reluctant to require states to provide a certain level of healthcare to the population at large.[58] A reason for this may be that, all things being equal, there is more 'conceptual proximity' in cases of 'conditional' positive obligations: as the state is involved anyway, it is a smaller step to require it to remedy the complained of situation (in this example, the lack of appropriate healthcare).

4.4 'Protection by the Law'

So far, we have seen that, while the European Court has widely accepted the existence of positive obligations, the Supreme Court has been more reluctant to do so and has restricted itself to recognizing so-called 'conditional' positive obligations. Now we will turn to the issue of 'protection by the law'. In a broad sense, 'protection by the law' relates to the insight that certain guarantees contribute to the effective protection of rights against unjustified infringements – regardless of whether they are caused by actions or inactions. As we will see in the next parts, 'protection by the law', both in the case law of the European Court as in the case law of the U.S. Supreme Court, comprises substantive and procedural protection. This

---

[57] Also see O. Arnardóttir, "Discrimination as a Magnifying Lens: Scope and Ambit under Article 14 and Protocol 12" (to be published in E. Brems and J. Gerards, *Shaping Rights in the ECHR – The Role of the European Court of Human Rights in Determining the Scope of Human Rights*, Cambridge University Press).

[58] In the case of ECtHR (dec.) 21 March 2002, No. 65653/01, *Nitecki v. Poland*, the Court, for example, held that "(…) with respect to the scope of the State's positive obligations in the provision of health care, the Court has stated that an issue may arise under Article 2 where it is shown that the authorities of a Contracting State put an individual's life at risk through the denial of health care which they have undertaken to make available to the population generally (…)." In ECtHR (GC) 27 May 2008, No. 26565/05, *N. v. the United Kingdom*, para. 44, concerning the expulsion of a HIV-positive woman to Uganda, where her condition could rapidly deteriorate, the Court held that "(…) Article 3 does not place an obligation on the Contracting State to alleviate such disparities [between the level of treatment available in the Contracting State and the country of origin] through the provision of free and unlimited health care to all aliens without a right to stay within its jurisdiction. A finding to the contrary would place too great a burden on the Contracting States."

article will try to be faithful to the most simplified account of the distinction between substance and procedure: the former relates to the content of the decision and the latter to the steps taken in arriving at that decision.[59] Admittedly, the substance/procedure distinction is a crude one, as remedies (typically considered to be procedural) do not exist independent of substantive provisions and vice versa. Before turning to the content of 'protection by the law' in Sects. 4.4 and 4.5, the article will first give a brief theoretical account of 'protection by the law' (Sect. 4.4.1). The article will also give an introduction to 'protection by the law' under the ECHR, providing a short overview of legal literature on the subject, as well as a delimitation of the scope of this paper (Sect. 4.4.2).

4.4.1 A Theoretical Account of 'Protection by the Law'

One of the most influential theoretical accounts of how rights operate in an interest model, is Robert Alexy's theory of constitutional rights.[60] While his theory builds on the jurisprudence of the German Constitutional Court, it "has been widely recognised as a theory that helps to shed light on human and constitutional rights practice more generally"[61] and the rights entrenched in the ECHR more specifically.[62] As it is impossible to ignore Alexy's influential theory, this part will briefly discuss how Alexy conceptualizes rights in general and 'protection by the law' in particular.[63]

In Alexy's model, constitutional rights have both a rule-like and a principle-like character.[64] According to Alexy, principles are optimisation requirements: "they can be satisfied to varying degrees, and (...) the appropriate degree of satisfaction depends not only on what is factually possible but also on what is legally possible."[65] From this character as optimisation requirements, Alexy deduces the

[59] For a discussion, see L. May, *Global Justice and Due Process* (Cambridge: CUP, 2011), 47–52.

[60] R. Alexy, A Theory of Constitutional Rights (Oxford: OUP, 2002).

[61] M. Kumm, "Political Liberalism and the Structure of Rights: On the Place and Limits of the Proportionality Requirement" in G. Pavlakos (ed.), *Law, Rights and Discourse – The Legal Philosophy of Robert Alexy* (Oxford: Hart Publishing, 2007), 136.

[62] S. Greer, "'Balancing' and the European Court of Human Rights: A Contribution to the Habermas-Alexy Debate", 63 *Cambridge Law Journal* (2004), 433.

[63] See also Lavrysen, supra, note 31.

[64] Alexy, supra, note 60, 84–86. The rule-like element relates to the fact that the norm itself "is applicable without needing to be balanced by any other norm, and cases can be subsumed under it" (85). According to Alexy," rules are norms which are always either fulfilled or not": if a rule validly applies, one is required to do exactly what it says (48). When two rules conflict, either an exception is read into one of them or at least one of them is declared invalid (49). Conflicts between principles "are played out in the dimension of weight instead" (50): one principle outweighs the other principle based on the concrete facts of the case. The fact that a principle is outweighed does not imply that it is either invalid or that an exception must be read into it.

[65] Ibid., 47–48.

proportionality test, in which it is verified whether legal and factual considerations take precedence over the protected right or not.[66]

Alexy clusters procedural as well as some substantive aspects of 'protection by the law' in what he labels 'the right to organization and procedure'.[67] According to Alexy, "[n]orms of procedure and organization should be formulated in such a way that the outcome is with adequate probability and to an adequate extent constitutional."[68] With respect to procedural norms, but equally relevant with respect to substantive norms in general,[69] Alexy holds that "[w]herever procedural norms can raise the protection of constitutional rights they are prima facie required by constitutional principles. If no competing principles apply, then there is a definitive right to their application."[70] In Alexy's account, these principles can be substantive (e.g. competing rights) as well as formal (e.g. the sparing use of public resources or the competence of the democratically legitimated legislature).[71]

Transposed to the context of the ECHR, this would imply that 'protection by the law' of a certain Convention right is required – assuming that the procedural and substantive norms concerned effectively enhance the protection of that right[72] – unless it is outweighed by competing principles. This is essentially a question of proportionality.

The question whether 'protection by the law' in the jurisprudence of the European Court conforms to the optimisation conception as theorised by Alexy will be discussed later. At this point, however, it is important to note that the transposition of this optimisation conception to the ECHR is not without critics. Jonas Christoffersen,

---

[66] Ibid., 66–69. In the wide sense, the principle of proportionality consists of three sub-principles: suitability, necessity and proportionality in the narrow sense (balancing) (67).

[67] Ibid., 316. According to Alexy, 'the right to organization and procedure' "extends from rights to effective legal protection, which no one would refuse to call 'procedural rights', to 'organizational state measures' such as those relevant to the creation of academic committees in universities." A specific example of substantive protection is the requirement that certain private law norms have a certain content (324).

[68] Ibid.

[69] In Alexy's theory, not all substantive norms protecting rights fall under the 'right to organization and procedure'. Some substantive norms, for example, belong to the category of protective rights, which generally require "legal regulations to be structured in such a way as to limit the danger of constitutional rights infringements" (301), the most obvious example being the criminalisation of murder and manslaughter (302). This distinction, however, is of no interest here, as the mechanism that plays is the same: optimising rights as far as possible in the light of countervailing principles. Alexy's discussion of the mainly procedural 'right to organization and procedure' therefore is equally relevant for substantive protection.

[70] Ibid., 328. This is a specification of Alexy's general model of rights adjudication, in which he distinguishes between a first stage in which the question is addressed as to what is *prima facie* protected by the fundamental right, and a second stage which concerns the question of what is *definitively* protected after taking into account the possibility of limitations (196–200). According to Alexy, "constitutional protection always depends on a relationship between a reason for constitutional protection and some relevant contrary reason" (209).

[71] Ibid., 348 and 400.

[72] If not, these norms do not optimise the right concerned and therefore cannot be required by it.

for example, has rejected optimisation[73] because it is incompatible with the nature of the ECHR as a document providing a minimum level of protection, rather than imposing maximum limits on the state's implementation freedom.[74]

4.4.2 *'Protection by the Law' and the European Convention*

On the basis of his exhaustive examination of the European Court's positive obligations case law, Mowbray found with respect to the obligation to protect that "[a]t its most basic level this positive obligation may be satisfied by the respondent state having adequate domestic legal provisions criminalizing the conduct which threatens another's Convention rights."[75] More generally, Keir Starmer has held that"[t]he duty to put in place a legal framework which provides effective protection for Convention rights in many respects represents the minimum obligation of Contracting States under the Convention."[76] In Starmer's classification of positive obligations under the European Convention, 'protection by the law' is listed as the first and foremost positive obligation.[77] 'Protection by the law' requires that legislation is developed in such a way that violations of obligations to respect, protect and fulfill are prevented and remedied.

Dimitris Xenos similarly stresses the importance of 'protection by the law'. He holds that "[i]n most circumstances, a regulatory framework can be imposed as a core content of positive obligations under paragraph 1 of the Convention rights. Regulations of human rights standards to educate the behavior of private parties or to condition the operation of their activities are the first and most basic content of positive obligations."[78] Xenos identifies a second element of 'core content of positive obligations': "administrative structures to implement and enforce the human rights standards that have been regulated by the state in advance."[79] Both elements

[73] He specifically rejected the incorporation of a necessity or less restrictive means test – which in Alexy's model follows from the character of rights as optimisation requirements – as part of the proportionality test.

[74] J. Christoffersen, *Fair Balance: Proportionality, Subsidiarity and Primarity in the European Convention on Human Rights* (Leiden: Martinus Nijhoff Publishers, 2009), 132 and 135.

[75] Mowbray, supra, note 38, 225.

[76] Starmer, supra, note 32, 147. Starmer illustrated this obligation by the cases of ECtHR 26 March 1985, No. 8978/80, *X and Y v. the Netherlands*; ECtHR 22 October 1996, No. 22083/93, *Stubbings and Others v. the United Kingdom*; and *Young, James and Webster v. the United Kingdom*, supra, note 15.

[77] Starmer distinguishes between (1) a duty to put in place a legal framework which provides effective protection for Convention rights, (2) a duty to prevent breaches of Convention rights, (3) a duty to provide information and advice relevant to a breach of Convention rights, (4) a duty to respond to breaches of Convention rights, and (5) a duty to provide resources to individuals to prevent breaches of their Convention rights. The cases mentioned by Starmer under (4) and (5) are related to the broader conception of 'protection by the law' envisaged in this paper.

[78] Xenos, supra, note 11, 107.

[79] Xenos, supra, note 11, 110.

are explicitly reflected in the Court's case law with respect to the obligation to protect the right to life (Art. 2 ECHR). In the case of *Osman v. the United Kingdom,* for example, the Court stressed the state's "primary duty to secure the right to life by putting in place effective criminal-law provisions to deter the commission of offences against the person backed up by law-enforcement machinery for the prevention, suppression and sanctioning of breaches of such provisions."[80] For the sake of this article, I am primarily interested in Xenos' first element of 'core content': the way in which human rights oblige states to incorporate substantive as well as procedural guarantees in their domestic laws. The effective functioning of the administrative structures – the second element of 'core content' – is of course crucial for the implementation of the first element in practice.

As we will see in the discussion of the Court's case law, the need for substantive and procedural 'protection by the law' is very much related to the principle of effectiveness. The effective protection of human rights cannot solely depend on *ad hoc responses* to human rights claims, as human rights protection then risks to depend solely on wide discretionary powers of particular state authorities. Human rights do not depend on administrative goodwill, they are checks on what authorities are allowed *to do* or *not to do*. Therefore, individuals must be protected against arbitrary state actions or omissions infringing their human rights.

With regard to the obligation to protect, such a legal framework is moreover necessary to effectively prevent private actors from committing human rights violations. As explained, in the current state of the law, private actors are not under an international legal obligation to refrain from infringing human rights, and *ad hoc* responses to such violations might well run counter to the perpetrator's human rights. In a similar sense, Xenos has held that "[i]n the contexts of private interactions in which known issues of conflict of interests exist, the protection of human rights cannot solely be guaranteed by some positive reactive responses and *ad hoc* balances."[81] We will see that 'protection by the law' is particularly important in cases involving conflicting rights.

4.4.2.1 'Quality of the Law'

It should be noted at this point that the European Court generally does not analyze the 'conditional' obligation to provide 'protection by the law' against violations of obligations to respect as a positive obligation.[82] With a few exceptions, such as the

---

[80] ECtHR (GC) 28 October 1998, No. 23452/94, *Osman v. the United Kingdom*, para. 115.

[81] Xenos, supra, note 11, 137.

[82] Admittedly there are some exceptions. The Court has, for example, examined a case concerning shootings by the police (i.e. an obligation to respect) as raising questions as to the obligation to protect the right to life (Art. 2 ECHR) by law, by requiring regulations concerning the use of firearms by state agents, e.g. ECtHR (GC) 20 December 2004, No. 50385/99, *Makaratzis v. Greece*. An explanation may be that Art. 2 ECHR explicitly couples legality to a positive obligation in its first sentence: "Everyone's right to life shall be protected by law." According to Xenos, this sentence corresponds to the legality stage of other rights (Xenos, supra, note 11, 123).

prohibition of torture, the rights set out in the European Convention are not absolute. The Convention generally allows lawful state interference insofar as this interference satisfies the conditions of legality (does it have a legal basis?), legitimacy (does it serve a legitimate aim?) and proportionality (is there a relationship of proportionality between the interference and the legitimate aim?).[83] According to the European Court, the legality condition, however, does not only require a legal basis in the strict sense, but also requires that the law allowing for state interference with a Convention right is of sufficient 'quality'. The law must be 'accessible' and 'foreseeable', the law may not grant the executive 'unfettered power' to interfere with a Convention right and the interference must be subject to some form of adversarial proceedings before an independent body.[84] This 'quality of the law' condition thus requires both substantive and procedural safeguards, and is in essence not very different from the positive obligation to provide a legal framework that adequately protects Convention rights.[85]

Admittedly an important distinction between both situations is that the negative obligation involves an element of choice: the 'quality of the law' condition is relevant insofar as the state wishes to enable a certain state interference with a Convention right. In this sense, it can be considered as a 'conditional' positive obligation[86]: its existence is 'parasitical' on a negative obligation. If the state, for example, sees no need to allow deportation on national security grounds – an action that interferes with the individual's right to respect for family and/or private life (Art. 8 ECHR) – it, of course, does not have to develop substantive and procedural safeguards to ensure that such deportations do not violate human rights. Only if it does want to enable such deportations, the positive obligation is triggered.[87] Similarly, if a state wishes to enable secret surveillance techniques, it is under a positive obligation to provide protection against arbitrary interference.[88] The 'regular' positive obligation on the other hand is not 'optional'[89]: a threat to a human right arises or not, irrelevant

---

[83] These conditions are made explicit in the second paragraph (limitation clause) of Art. 8–11 ECHR, but is also implicit in most other Convention provisions.

[84] ECtHR 20 June 2002, No. 50963/99, *Al-Nashif v. Bulgaria*, paras. 119 and 123.

[85] See similarly Xenos, supra, note 11, 118–125. Xenos argues that "the protection of human rights cannot be organised through incidental questions of justifiability of acts of interference, without recognising that protection has already arisen as an obligation for the state much before the isolated interference" (119).

[86] See Sect. 4.3.2. As explained above: all things being equal, 'conditional' positive obligations under the ECHR require enhanced protection compared with regular positive obligations. This explains why the Court requires more 'protection by the law' under the 'quality of the law' condition than with respect to obligations to protect/fulfill.

[87] See *Al-Nashif v. Bulgaria*, supra, note 84, paras. 119–128.

[88] E.g. ECtHR (GC) 2 August 1984, No. 8691/79, *Malone v. the United Kingdom*.

[89] Similarly Xenos, supra, note 11: "Although in negative obligations cases the state always has a free choice of whether or not to pursue a legitimate aim of interference, the state's positive obligation to intervene in order to guarantee the protection of human rights is not optional" (139).

of whether or not the state chooses to enable such conduct.[90] Take the example of individuals invading the privacy of famous individuals: such a risk exists – regardless of the state's conduct – therefore protection of famous individuals' privacy is necessary.[91]

The importance of this distinction should, however, not be exaggerated. First of all, one should not overstate the 'optional' character of many state interferences: it is impossible to properly run a modern society without them. State interference may even be required in order to discharge a positive obligation: the obligation to protect under Art. 3 ECHR (the prohibition of torture and inhuman or degrading treatment or punishment) may require state authorities to take children into care in order to protect them against abusive or neglectful parents, even though this action interferes with Art. 8 ECHR (the right to respect for family life).[92] In many cases, the state thus has no genuine choice not to interfere. Secondly, as explained above, in many cases it may be difficult to distinguish between negative and positive obligations. Thirdly, the 'quality of the law' condition is primarily concerned with legal protection against arbitrary interference by state agents.[93] While the conduct of individual state agents is traditionally considered as *ipso facto* resulting in direct state responsibility – and thus as a question of negative obligations – it is possible to construct the 'quality of the law' condition as simply comprising a positive obligation to protect against lawful (in the formal sense) but arbitrary interferences by individual state agents. If one focuses on the individual conduct of state agents, there is, as such, not that much of a difference between this situation and situations in which individuals should be protected against the risk of abuse of power in interpersonal contexts, where the power comes from a different source than the participation to state authority.[94] Fourthly, in any event the mechanisms have essentially the same content and the same function: a minimum level of both substantive and procedural protection in order to protect against human rights violations, regardless of whether these are caused by violations of obligations to respect ('quality of the law') or of obligations to protect or fulfill ('general' positive obligations). The close resemblance between the positive obligation to protect on the one hand and the 'quality of the law' criterion on the other, has been acknowledged by the Court itself

[90] See, for example, the case of *Young, James and Webster v. United Kingdom*, supra, note 15, concerning closed-shop agreements that violated the applicant's freedom of association. The Court examined the case as one concerning negative obligations, exactly because it had enabled such conduct. According to the Court, "(…) it was the domestic law in force at the relevant time that made lawful the treatment of which the applicants complained. The responsibility of the respondent State for any resultant breach of the Convention is thus engaged on this basis" (para. 49).

[91] E.g. ECtHR 24 June 2004, No. 59320/00, *Von Hannover v. Germany*; ECtHR 9 October 2012, No. 42811/06, *Alkaya v. Turkey*.

[92] *Z and Others v. the United Kingdom*, supra, note 34, para. 74.

[93] E.g. *Malone v. the United Kingdom*, supra, note 88, para. 67.

[94] For example, the power imbalances that operate in cases of domestic violence (e.g. ECtHR 9 June 2009, No. 33401/02, *Opuz v. Turkey*) or domestic servitude (e.g. ECtHR 26 July 2005, No. 73316/01, *Siliadin v. France*).

in the context of Art. 5 ECHR, the right to liberty, in the case of *Cristian Teodoresco v. Romania*.[95]

As the European Court, however, does not consider 'protection by the law' against violations of obligations to respect (i.e. the 'quality of the law' condition) to be a positive obligation, this contribution will further focus on the legal framework required to comply with obligations to protect and obligations to fulfill under the European Convention. To be able to make a useful comparison, this paper will, however, discuss 'protection by the law' against violations of obligations to respect under the U.S. Constitution. Such a comparison is unproblematic, as 'protection by the law' is not in essence different depending on the type of obligation it must prevent.

4.5 Substantive 'Protection by the Law'

Substantive 'protection by the law' requires substantive safeguards to be in place to fulfill human rights and to prevent human rights violations. There are two rationales for the substantive 'protection by the law': effective prevention of human rights violations on the one hand and protection against arbitrariness in the protection of human rights on the other.

Firstly, the existence of such safeguards has an important preventive function and thus contributes to the effective protection of fundamental rights. This is in line with the principle of effectiveness, which is at the basis of the doctrine of positive obligations developed by the European Court. I will call this the instrumental function of substantive 'protection by the law'. This is particularly important with respect to obligations to protect: as human rights provided for in international legal documents do not bind private actors, human rights holders are in need of state assistance in order to be able to effectively claim respect for their rights in their relations with private actors. By developing substantive safeguards in domestic law, the state 'translates' the on private actors non-binding international legal obligation into binding domestic law. The most obvious example being that, while a murderer cannot be charged with a violation of Art. 2 ECHR (the right to life), he can be charged with the crime of murder under domestic law. The need to enable human rights holders to effectively claim their rights is equally relevant with respect to

[95] The Court held that "(…) la première phrase de l'article 5 § 1 doit être comprise comme imposant à l'Etat l'obligation positive de protéger la liberté des personnes relevant de sa juridiction et que les expressions «prévue par la loi» et «selon les voies légales» visent aussi la qualité de la loi qui constitue la base légale des mesures privatives de liberté qui peuvent les concerner (…)" (ECtHR 19 June 2012, No. 22883/05, *Cristian Teodorescu v. Romania*, para. 65). Also in other cases, the Court has applied clear protection-by-the-law-language in the context of the 'quality of the law' condition, for example in ECtHR 3 July 2012, No. 34806/04, *X v. Finland*, para. 221: "(…) the absence of sufficient safeguards against forced medication by the treating doctors deprived the applicant of the minimum degree of protection to which she was entitled under the rule of law in a democratic society (…)."

obligations to fulfill. The problem with these obligations is that they are seldom straightforward: while they do give the human rights holder an abstract claim to a certain good (e.g. the right to education, Art. 2 Protocol 1), providing him or her that good in practice often allows a wide range of possible implementation modalities (e.g. how to organize an educational system). The fulfillment of a right[96] thus equally requires 'translation' into domestic law.

Secondly, substantive guarantees protect against arbitrariness.[97] The protection of human rights cannot simply be made dependent of unfettered discretion of state authorities. Discretion and arbitrariness are two sides of the same coin: wide discretion in the protection of human rights encompasses the risk of arbitrary decision-making. Non-arbitrariness also has an instrumental function, in the sense that it contributes to a better protection of human rights. In the context of positive obligations, David Russell has clarified this instrumental function, by holding that "if the obligations imposed on duty-bearers are not explained clearly enough then there may be less diligence afforded to protecting human rights and so violations are ultimately more likely to occur."[98] More importantly, non-arbitrariness relates to what I call the intrinsic function of substantive 'protection by the law': regardless of its impact on the extent of human rights protection, we cherish non-arbitrariness primarily because it enhances our trust in the motives of decision-makers.[99] In this sense, non-arbitrariness is generally related to the rule of law[100]: we require from authorities that they make their decisions by applying known legal principles and not on the basis of questionable personal motives. The risk of arbitrariness is reduced when authorities have to discharge their obligations to protect and fulfill by applying a known legal framework to a particular case, rather than allowing them undue leeway in providing *ad hoc* responses to human rights violations. The European Court has also acknowledged the link between non-arbitrariness, as part of the principle of

[96] In other words, the 'prevention' of violations of obligations to fulfill.

[97] While arbitrariness is certainly an idea hard to define (see G. Wright, "Arbitrariness: Why the Most Important Idea in Administrative Law Can't Be Defined, and What This Means for the Law in General", 44 *University of Richmond Law Review* (2010), 839–865), it has undeniably penetrated the way we think about law in general and about rights in particular.

[98] D. Russell, "Supplementing the European Convention on Human Rights: Legislating for Positive Obligations", 61 *Northern Ireland Legal Quarterly* (2010), 281.

[99] On the importance of trustworthiness of decision-makers in human rights adjudication, see E. Brems and L. Lavrysen, "Procedural Justice in Human Rights Adjudication: the European Court of Human Rights", 35 *Human Rights Quarterly* (2013), 182.

[100] May, supra, note 59, 53. Joseph Raz acknowledges that the rule of law may contribute to the curbing of arbitrariness, but considers the problem of arbitrary power to be broader than the rule of law, as many forms of arbitrary rule are compatible with the rule of law, see J. Raz, *The Authority of Law* (Oxford: OUP, 1979), 219–220. Raz further holds that "[t]he rule of law is essentially a negative value. The law inevitably creates a great danger of arbitrary power – the rule of law is designed to minimize the danger created by the law itself" (224). It should be noted that, in Raz's conception, the rule of law is far from an absolute value: "Conformity to the rule of law is a matter of degree, and though, other things being equal, the greater the conformity the better – other things are rarely equal. A lesser degree is often to be preferred precisely because it helps realization of other goals" (228).

the rule of law, on the one hand, and the need to develop legal safeguards to protect against unfettered discretion on the other.[101]

Due to its concern with tackling questionable personal motives, non-arbitrariness can be considered to have a reason-blocking function, as in Ronald Dworkin's account of 'Rights as Trumps'.[102] In Dworkin's model, rights are not concerned with the protection of fundamental interests, they instead block reasons based on corrupted motives[103] (or external preferences[104]), which fail to protect the fundamental right of citizens to equal concern and respect, which lies at the basis of Dworkin's model.[105] While rights under the European Convention are primarily interest-based, this does not exclude that some of them may also, to a greater or lesser extent, have a reason-blocking function.[106] The reason-blocking function of the prohibition of arbitrariness under the European Convention is, however, broader than 'Rights as Trumps', as it is not only concerned with protection against the corruption of utilitarian considerations by the majority's external preferences, but more generally with protection against the risk that state authorities act on the basis of unacceptable motives.

4.5.1 General Principles from the European Court's Case Law

In general terms, substantive 'protection by the law' requires that states develop a legal framework that provides individuals with effective substantive protection that is in line with ECHR standards. This legal framework does not necessarily have to consist of law in the formal sense (i.e. norms that are passed by the legislature), 'protection by law' in the material sense (i.e. the entire body of law) is in principle sufficient,[107] unless 'effective protection' requires the latter.[108]

In the absence of effective 'protection by the law', the Court will generally find a violation of the Convention right concerned. For example, in *Von Hannover*

---

[101] E.g. ECtHR (GC) 14 September 2010, No. 38224/03, *Sanoma Uitgevers B.V. v. the Netherlands*, para. 82. More generally, non-arbitrariness can be considered as one of the foundational principles of human rights, e.g. E. Fox-Decent and E. Criddle, "The Fiduciary Constitution of Human Rights", 15 *Legal Theory* (2009), 301–336.

[102] Dworkin, supra, note 4, 153–167.

[103] Letsas, supra, note 3, 113 with reference to J. Waldron, "Pildes on Dworkin's Theory of Rights", 29 *Journal of Legal Studies* (2000).

[104] Dworkin, supra, note 4, 234–238.

[105] Ibid., 277.

[106] Letsas has, for example, identified Art. 14 ECHR, the prohibition of discrimination, as a reason-blocking mechanism, see Letsas, supra, note 3, 104.

[107] *Mutatis mutandis* the autonomous notion of 'law' applied under the legality test, e.g. ECtHR 25 March 1985, No. 8734/79, *Barthold v. Germany*. This is related to the fact that the choice of means to discharge a positive obligation in principle falls within the state's margin of appreciation, see below.

[108] For example, when protection by criminal law is required.

v. Germany, the Court found a violation of the right to privacy (Art. 8 ECHR), because the applicant, princess Caroline of Monaco, did not enjoy protection under German law against invasions of her privacy by German magazines – under German law, protection against the publication of images from the private sphere was excluded with respect to so-called figures of contemporary society 'par excellence'.[109] The Court requires that the domestic law contains 'appropriate safeguards' to prevent human rights violations, such as the disclosure of privacy intrusive information.[110] While the primary responsibility to provide substantive 'protection by the law' rests on the legislator, a more limited responsibility also extends to domestic courts: they "are obliged to apply the provisions of national law in the spirit of [the Convention] rights."[111]

Substantive 'protection by the law', however, is not limitless: not every substantive safeguard that enhances the protection of an individual's human rights will be required under the ECHR. Sometimes such protection will not be required due to a lack of 'conceptual proximity'. Matters may also get more complicated due to the presence of conflicting rights. On the other hand, when developing a legal framework to protect human rights, it is crucial to take certain elements into account: non-discrimination, proportionality as well as the need to provide protection of 'sufficient quality'. This part will further focus on some general principles that can be deduced from the Court's case law on how to deal with such issues.

4.5.1.1 Knowledge

A first important principle is the requirement of knowledge. Lack of knowledge of a human rights violation necessarily results in a lack of 'conceptual proximity' of the corresponding obligation to protect against that violation.[112] The required knowledge relates both to the source of threat to human rights, and to the identity of the individuals that need to be protected against that threat.[113] As I have argued elsewhere, positive obligations are essentially obligations of due diligence, and they can only arise insofar as the state is aware or ought to be aware of a (potential) human rights violation.[114] This necessarily also holds true for the positive obligation to develop a legal framework. This is perfectly illustrated by the case of *K.U. v. Finland*, which concerned the posting by an anonymous person of the picture and the contact details of a 12 year old boy on an internet dating site in 1999, which

---

[109] *Von Hannover v. Germany*, supra, note 91, paras. 72–75.

[110] ECtHR 17 July 2003, No. 25337/94, *Craxi (No.2) v. Italy*, 17 July 2003, para. 74.

[111] *Storck v. Germany*, supra, note 22, para. 93.

[112] Xenos also considers lack of knowledge to be a problem of proximity, see Xenos, supra, note 11, 76.

[113] Ibid.

[114] Lavrysen, supra, note 31.

exposed the boy to the interest of pedophiles. A police investigation was started, but it was unsuccessful as the service provider refused to divulge the necessary information because it considered itself legally bound by the principle of confidentiality of telecommunications, and Finish law did not require service providers to divulge such information. In Strasbourg, the boy claimed that thereby Finland had failed in its positive obligation to protect his right to respect for his private life (Art. 8 ECHR). On the issue of knowledge, the Court ruled that:

> The Court notes at the same time that the relevant incident took place in 1999, that is, at a time when it was well-known that the Internet, precisely because of its anonymous character, could be used for criminal purposes (...). Also the widespread problem of child sexual abuse had become well-known over the preceding decade. Therefore, it cannot be said that the respondent Government did not have the opportunity to put in place a system to protect child victims from being exposed as targets for paedophiliac approaches via the Internet.[115]

The judgment clearly illustrates the importance of knowledge. This knowledge is moreover not a static issue: it is the task of the state to adequately tackle new threats to human rights which may arise in a changing world, such as the human rights challenges posed by the emergence of the internet. The fact that the obligation to provide 'protection by the law' arises from the moment the state 'ought to be aware' of such threats, moreover implies that the state may not remain passive: it requires active anticipation. The knowledge spectrum from 'does not know and ought not to know' over 'does not know but ought to know' to 'does know', illustrates an increasing level of 'conceptual proximity'.

4.5.1.2 Conflicting Rights

A second principle that can be distilled from *K.U. v. Finland* is that the Court acknowledges that the need for 'protection by the law' is particularly necessary in cases of conflicting rights[116]:

> (...) it is (...) the task of the legislator to provide the framework for reconciling the various claims [i.e. protection of the right to respect for the private life of internet users, freedom of expression of internet users and confidentiality of telecommunications] which compete for protection in this context. Such framework was not however in place at the material time, with the result that Finland's positive obligation with respect to the applicant could not be discharged.[117]

The Court thus recognizes that legislators have a task to act as impartial arbitrators in reconciling conflicting rights. This is even more relevant because courts may not be the best *fora* to deal with such conflicts. Because of the problem of 'preferential

[115] ECtHR 2 December 2008, *K.U. v. Finland*, para. 48.

[116] See mutatis mutandis, with respect to procedural protection, Xenos, supra, note 11, 137 and.

[117] K.U., supra, note 115, para. 49.

framing' involved in the judicial adjudication of conflicts of rights,[118] Brems has argued that "legislators are in a better position than judges to deal with conflicting human rights. Legislators can treat both rights equally and are not hindered in the choice of criteria and arguments by a framework that focuses on one right only."[119]

In this respect, the Court's case law differs from Robert Alexy's theoretical model discussed above. According to Alexy, 'protection by the law' is *prima facie* required wherever it "(…) can raise the protection of constitutional rights (…). If no competing principles apply, then there is a definitive right to their application."[120] In Alexy's model, the freedom of expression of internet users and the confidentiality of telecommunications would count as competing principles that argue against 'protection by the law' of K.U.'s right to privacy. Conflicting rights thus result in less, rather than more need for 'protection by the law'. Thereby, Alexy's model fails to acknowledge the need for the legislator to act as an impartial arbitrator.

It should be noted that the Court acknowledges that it might be a very difficult task for the state to reconcile different competing rights, and that the state may be principally better placed to do so than a supranational court, due to its direct contact with societal values and needs. Therefore, as explicitly recognized in the case of *Chassagnou and Others v. France*, the Court generally only applies light scrutiny[121] with respect to the way the state balances these competing rights.[122] This, however, does not contradict with *K.U. v. Finland*. When rights conflict, it is more urgent for the state to establish a legal framework that balances these conflicting rights.[123] A lack of such a legal framework may lead to the finding of a violation of the Convention. If the state, however, does establish such a legal framework, then it will

[118] Stijn Smet considers 'preferential framing' to be the approach in which a court "addresses only the right invoked by the applicant and disregards to a lesser or greater extent the other right(s) involved", see S. Smet, "Freedom of Expression and the Right to Reputation: Human Rights in Conflict", 26 *American University International Law Review* (2011), 185.

[119] E. Brems, "Conflicting Human Rights: An Exploration in the Context of the Right to a Fair Trial in the European Convention for the Protection of Human Rights and Fundamental Freedoms", 27 *Human Rights Quarterly* (2005), 305.

[120] Alexy, supra, note 60, 328. This particular quote concerns procedural 'protection by the law', but arguably also reflects Alexy's view on substantive 'protection by the law'.

[121] By allowing the state a so-called 'wide margin of appreciation'. This concept will be addressed more elaborately in Sect. 4.7).

[122] ECtHR (GC) 29 April 1999, Nos. 25088/94, 28331/95 and 28443/95, *Chassagnou and Others v. France*, para. 113. In ECtHR (GC) 15 March 2012, Nos. 4149/04 and 41029/04, *Aksu v. Turkey*, para. 66, the Court acknowledged that in earlier cases in which it examined the width of the margin of appreciation, it "attached significant weight to the fact that the domestic authorities had identified the existence of conflicting rights and the need to ensure a fair balance between them." There are, however, exceptions in which the Court did develop detailed guidelines on how to solve a conflict of rights, such as in cases of anonymous witnesses involving a conflict between the right to examine witnesses (Art. 6(3)(d) ECHR) of the accused on the one hand, and the right not to incriminate oneself (implicit in Art. 6(1) ECHR) of the witness on the other, see Brems, supra, note 119, 309–311, with reference to ECtHR 27 February 2001, No. 33354/96, *Lucà v. Italy*.

[123] Similarly, see hereunder the discussed case of ECtHR (GC) 10 April 2007, No. 6339/05, *Evans v. the United Kingdom*, para. 84.

only violate the Convention in exceptional circumstances, when the importance of certain rights is manifestly disregarded.[124]

4.5.1.3 Non-discrimination

A third principle is that the legal framework must be developed in a non-discriminatory way. This relates to the discussion on non-arbitrariness above: the way in which a state chooses to provide substantive 'protection by the law' may not succumb to unacceptable motives.[125] The judgment of *Marckx v. Belgium* is an example in which the Court has tackled discriminatory 'protection by the law'. The case concerned the discrimination of 'illegitimate' children compared to 'legitimate' children in the field of affiliation and inheritance rights.[126] The case was examined both under Art. 8 ECHR (the right to respect for family life) separately and under Art. 8 in conjunction with Art. 14 ECHR (the prohibition of discrimination). According to the Court, "respect for family life implies in particular (...) the existence in domestic law of legal safeguards that render possible as from the moment of birth the child's integration in his family."[127] The Court thus considered the case to raise issues related to a lack of 'protection by the law'. Besides two violations of Art. 8 ECHR separately, the Court found three violations of Art. 8 ECHR in conjunction with Art. 14 ECHR.[128]

Another example is the case of *Christine Goodwin v. the United Kingdom*, which concerned the question whether the United Kingdom had "failed to comply with a positive obligation to ensure the right of the applicant, a post-operative male to female transsexual, to respect for her private life, in particular through the lack of legal recognition given to her gender re-assignment."[129] This case essentially concerned indirect discrimination: although the legal framework was apparently neutral, it had

---

[124] In ECtHR (GC) 7 February 2012, Nos. 40660/08 and 60641/08, *Von Hannover v. Germany (No.2)*, para. 107, the Court held: "Where the balancing exercise has been undertaken by the national authorities in conformity with the criteria laid down in the Court's case law, the Court would require strong reasons to substitute its view for that of the domestic courts."

[125] Letsas considers that Art. 14 ECHR has a reason-blocking function in the Dworkinian sense, Letsas, supra, note 3, 104.

[126] The discrimination was threefold: (1) maternal affiliation was only established by voluntary declaration by the mother or by a court declaration, instead of by application of the principle *mater semper certa est*; (2) no legal ties were established between such an 'illegitimate' child and the mother's family; (3) and there were restrictions on the child's capacity to receive property from the mother, as well as a total lack of inheritance rights on intestacy estates of the relatives on the side of the mother.

[127] Marckx, supra, note 35, para. 31.

[128] According to the Court, Art. 8 does not require that children are entitled to patrimonial rights in relation with their relatives and therefore dismissed this claim under Art. 8. The Court nonetheless found a violation of Art. 14 on the basis that the Belgian law discriminated between 'legitimate' and 'illegitimate' children.

[129] ECtHR (GC) 11 July 2002, No. 28957/95, *Christine Goodwin v. the United Kingdom*, para. 71.

an unjustified disproportionate impact on transsexuals.[130] The Court integrated an indirect discrimination analysis in finding a violation of Art. 8 ECHR[131] – therefore it did not find it necessary to make a separate analysis under Art. 14 ECHR.[132] The cases of *Marckx* and *Christine Goodwin* illustrate that substantive 'protection by the law' may not be provided in a discriminatory way – either directly or indirectly.

4.5.1.4 Seriousness

A fourth principle is that the required extent of 'protection by the law' depends on the seriousness of the human rights threat involved. This is clear from the case of *Uzun v. Germany,*[133] which concerned GPS surveillance of the car of a suspected terrorist.[134] While the Court generally requires rather strict standards in the context of surveillance of telecommunications, it did not find that normative framework applicable to GPS surveillance. The Court considered less protection compared with telecommunications surveillance acceptable in the light of the less intrusive nature of GPS surveillance.

The legal framework must thus be proportionate to the severity of the threat to human rights: more serious threats require more serious safeguards. If a threat to human rights is not considered to be serious enough, there may even be no need for 'protection by the law'. The latter is illustrated by the case of *Köpke v. Germany,*[135] which concerned the lack of a legal framework to protect the privacy of an employee at work. The applicant, who worked at a supermarket, was dismissed by her employer on suspicion of theft. She unsuccessfully challenged her dismissal before the Labor Court. The Labor Court allowed as evidence a covert video surveillance tape the employer had obtained with the help of a detective agency. According to the European Court, "a covert video surveillance at the workplace following substantiated suspicions of theft does not concern a person's private life to an extent which is comparable to the affection of essential aspects of private life by grave acts in respect of which the Court has considered protection by legislative provisions indispensable." According to the Court, it was sufficient that, in weighing the competing interests at

---

[130] The Court has accepted that indirect discrimination can violate Art. 14 ECHR in ECtHR (GC) 13 November 2007, No. 57325/00, *D.H. and Others v. the Czech Republic*.

[131] The Court held "that society may reasonably be expected to tolerate a certain inconvenience to enable individuals to live in dignity and worth in accordance with the sexual identity chosen by them at great personal cost" (*Christine Goodwin v. the United Kingdom*, supra, note 129, para. 91).

[132] *Christine Goodwin v. the United Kingdom*, supra, note 129, para. 108.

[133] ECtHR 2 September 2010, No. 35623/05, *Uzun v. Germany*, para. 66.

[134] Admittedly, this case concerns 'protection by the law' against violations of an obligation to respect, which the Court examined under the legality condition of Art. 8 ECHR (the right to privacy). As explained in Sect. 4.4.2, such an examination is, however, not essentially different from the one under the positive obligation to protect the law, and therefore it is relevant for this discussion.

[135] ECtHR (inadm.) 5 October 2010, No. 420/07, *Köpke v. Germany*.

stake, the domestic courts had considered the surveillance as a considerable intrusion into the employee's privacy.[136]

'Protection by the law' may require criminal law provisions to deter very serious infringements of human rights, particularly when physical integrity is at stake. In the case of *X and Y v. the Netherlands,*[137] concerning the sexual abuse of a mentally disabled girl by the son-in-law of the director of the home she stayed in, the Court held that:

> (...) the protection afforded by the civil law in the case of wrongdoing of the kind inflicted on Miss Y is insufficient. This is a case where fundamental values and essential aspects of private life are at stake. Effective deterrence is indispensable in this area and it can be achieved only by criminal-law provisions; indeed, it is by such provisions that the matter is normally regulated.[138]

The need for criminal law provisions does not, however, extend to every infringement of physical integrity, as is illustrated by the case of *Calvelli and Ciglio v. Italy*. The case concerned the death of a 2-day old baby because of complications at the delivery, which could have been prevented if the gynecologist had taken the necessary precautionary measures and if he had been present at the moment of delivery, while he was well aware of the risk of that particular delivery. The Court held that:

> (...) if the infringement of the right to life or to personal integrity is not caused intentionally, the positive obligation imposed by Article 2 to set up an effective judicial system does not necessarily require the provision of a criminal-law remedy in every case. In the specific sphere of medical negligence the obligation may for instance also be satisfied if the legal system affords victims a remedy in the civil courts, either alone or in conjunction with a remedy in the criminal courts, enabling any liability of the doctors concerned to be established and any appropriate civil redress, such as an order for damages and for the publication of the decision, to be obtained. Disciplinary measures may also be envisaged.[139]

The required strength of 'protection by the law' thus depends on the seriousness of the human rights violation. Very serious infringements of human rights require

---

[136] In my view, the Court has underestimated the seriousness of this intrusion, as well as ignored the need for the legislator to reconcile such conflicting interests.

[137] The applicant's case at the domestic level was actually dismissed for procedural rather than for substantive reasons. The victim's father had lodged a complaint against the son-in-law for abuse of dominant position to cause a minor to commit indecent acts with him. The complaint was dismissed because Dutch law required it to be lodged by the victim herself. This was, however, impossible because, being mentally handicapped, she was legally incapable of lodging such a complaint.

[138] *X and Y v. the Netherlands*, supra, note 76, para. 27. Compare with the case of Stubbings supra, note 76, concerning the dismissal of civil proceedings for being time-barred in a case concerning sexual abuse of minors, in which the Court held that *"(...)* Article 8 (art. 8) does not necessarily require that States fulfil their positive obligation to secure respect for private life by the provision of unlimited civil remedies in circumstances where criminal law sanctions are in operation" (para. 66).

[139] ECtHR (GC) 17 January 2002, No. 32967/96, *Calvelli and Ciglio v. Italy*, para. 51. This case illustrates that it may be difficult to distinguish between substantive and procedural protection. Access to a remedy is traditionally considered to be a procedural rather than a substantive issue. Protection by substantive legal provisions, however, will in most cases be a prerequisite for effective access to such remedy.

effective deterrence by criminal law provisions. With respect to infringement of physical integrity, intentional infringements are considered more serious than unintentional ones: the former require criminal law provisions, the latter not necessarily.[140] This is nothing more than the application of the principle of proportionality. The application of the principle of proportionality[141] to substantive 'protection by the law', is compatible with the optimisation conception of rights, as explained in the theoretical discussion above.

4.5.1.5 Level of Detail

It is established case law that "where the State is required to take positive measures, the choice of means is in principle a matter that falls within the Contracting State's margin of appreciation."[142] Consequently, if the Court establishes that there is a lack of substantive 'protection by the law', one would expect the Court to be fairly undetailed with respect to the content that should be given to the required legal provisions. In most cases, effective protection can be offered by a number of different legal provisions. Insofar as these different options all provide protection proportionate to the seriousness of the human rights violation, the Court generally does not oblige a state to choose a particular one.

This is perfectly illustrated by the just discussed case of *Calvelli and Ciglio*, in which the Court did not consider it appropriate to dictate Italy how it should provide legal protection: through civil or through criminal law.[143] Another example is the case of *Evans v. the United Kingdom.*[144] This case concerned a woman whose ovaries had to be removed because of a pre-cancerous condition. She and her partner

---

[140] With respect to more serious cases of death by negligence, effective protection may require criminal law provisions in order to satisfy the principle of proportionality. In the case of ECtHR (GC) 30 November 2004, No. 48939/99, *Öneryildiz v. Turkey* – concerning a methane explosion on a state-run dump which resulted in the flooding by waste of the slum dwellings situated below the dump and the death of 39 people – the Court found a violation of Art. 2 ECHR, the right to life, "on account of the lack, in connection with a fatal accident provoked by the operation of a dangerous activity, of adequate protection 'by law' safeguarding the right to life and deterring similar life-endangering conduct in future." This violation was procedural rather than substantive: there existed criminal law provisions that could potentially have provided sufficient deterrence; the problem was the lack of serious application of these provisions in practice, as those responsible for the management of the dump site were only convicted to small suspended criminal fines.

[141] This is not really surprising, as the proportionality principle in its broadest sense – i.e. the search for a fair balance between the demands of the general interest of the community and the requirement of the protection of the individual's fundamental rights – has been recognised as a general principle of Convention law (e.g. ECtHR (GC) 27 May 2008, No. 26565/05, *N. v. the United Kingdom*, para. 44).

[142] E.g. ECtHR 9 June 2005, No. 55723/00, *Fadeyeva v. Russia*, para. 96.

[143] Both options fall within a range of proportionate responses to death by medical negligence.

[144] *Evans v. the United Kingdom*, supra, note 123.

decided to have IVF-treatment. After the removal of her ovaries, she and her partner separated. Her partner withdrew his consent to the implantation of the created embryos and requested their destruction, which was his right under domestic law. Thereby, the applicant would have been prevented from ever becoming a genetically related parent. When examining the issue under Art. 8 ECHR, the right to privacy, the Court held that it is desirable that the state sets up a legal scheme which takes into account the possibility that there may be a substantial lapse of time between the creation of the embryo and its implantation. The Court, however, dismissed the applicant's complaint, because it did not consider it appropriate to decide on the content of this legal scheme. The Court acknowledged that it would have been possible to regulate the situation differently by, for example, providing exceptions for particular circumstances. This was, however, not required by virtue of Art. 8 ECHR.

There are, however, certain exceptional cases in which the Court did provide detailed guidance as to what 'protection by the law' requires. In the case of *M.C. v. Bulgaria*, the Court, for example, ruled that 'protection by the law' may require a particular definition of a criminal offence. The case concerned a 14-year old girl who was the victim of date rape by two men. The prosecutor decided not to start criminal proceedings, because there was insufficient evidence that M.C. had been compelled to have sex with the two men. According to the prosecutor, the use of force or threats had not been established beyond reasonable doubt and, in particular, no resistance by M.C. was established nor attempts to seek help from others. The European Court first considered that states "have a positive obligation inherent in Articles 3 [the prohibition of torture and of inhuman or degrading treatment or punishment] and 8 [the right to respect for private life] to enact criminal-law provisions effectively punishing rape and to apply them in practice through effective investigation and prosecution."[145] After an examination of a variety of comparative and international law standards, the Court specified what should be the focus of any member state's definition of the criminal offence of rape:

> (...) any rigid approach to the prosecution of sexual offences, such as requiring proof of physical resistance in all circumstances, risks leaving certain types of rape unpunished and thus jeopardising the effective protection of the individual's sexual autonomy. In accordance with contemporary standards and trends in that area, the member States' positive obligations under Articles 3 and 8 of the Convention must be seen as requiring the penalisation and effective prosecution of any non-consensual sexual act, including in the absence of physical resistance by the victim.[146]

In the case of *C.N. v. the United Kingdom*, the Court made a similar ruling with respect to domestic servitude. The applicant was a Nigerian woman who was kept in domestic servitude, in the sense of Art. 4 ECHR, by an elderly couple. The applicant's complaint was dismissed by the investigative authorities, because they held that the

---

[145] ECtHR 4 December 2003, No. 39272/98, *M.C. v. Bulgaria*, para. 153.

[146] Ibid., para. 166.

circumstances of her case did not appear to constitute the offence of trafficking people for the purposes of exploitation. The Court held that:

> (…) domestic servitude is a specific offence, distinct from trafficking and exploitation, which involves a complex set of dynamics, involving both overt and more subtle forms of coercion, to force compliance. A thorough investigation into complaints of such conduct therefore requires an understanding of the many subtle ways an individual can fall under the control of another. In the present case, the Court considers that due to the absence of a specific offence of domestic servitude, the domestic authorities were unable to give due weight to these factors.[147]

The Court found a violation of Art. 4 ECHR, because it found that "the investigation into the applicant's complaints of domestic servitude was ineffective due to the absence of specific legislation criminalising such treatment."[148] States thus have to incorporate a specific criminal offence of domestic servitude in their legislation.[149]

M.C. v. Bulgaria and *C.N. v. the United Kingdom* both illustrate why, despite its general policy of not entering into detail, the Court sometimes does give detailed directions with respect to the substantive content of 'protection by the law'. This will be the case with complex human rights violations, where the violations stem from a specific dimension of interpersonal conduct, in particular when they involve abuse of power relationships. In the case of rape, this specific dimension is the lack of consent. The specific dimension of servitude on the other hand is the presence of coercion, either overt or more subtle, in order to force compliance. If a human rights violation has such a specific dimension, legal protection necessarily has to tackle it. This may explain why the Court is more detailed with respect to required protection against such human rights violations, whereas it generally does not provide such detailed guidance.

The Court may also provide detailed guidance if effective protection requires not only a mere prohibition of a certain conduct – for example, through criminalization – but instead requires a holistic approach through various fields of the law. In the human trafficking case of *Rantsev v. Cyprus and Russia*, for example, the Court held that:

> (…) in addition to criminal law measures to punish traffickers, Article 4 requires member States to put in place adequate measures regulating businesses often used as a cover for human trafficking. Furthermore, a State's immigration rules must address relevant concerns relating to encouragement, facilitation or tolerance of trafficking.[150]

While Cyprus did have the required criminal law provisions, protection was ineffective because the 'cabaret artiste' visa regime was abused by traffickers to

---

[147] ECtHR 13 November 2012, No. 4239/08, *C.N. v. the United Kingdom*, para. 80.

[148] Ibid., para. 81.

[149] Similarly, in the earlier case of *Siliadin* v. France, supra, note 94, the Court found a violation of Art. 4 ECHR. The applicant was a Togolese girl who had been kept in servitude as a housemaid for a French family. Under French law there was no specific offence of servitude. The Court dismissed the French government's argument that the servitude was criminally punishable on other grounds, because "those provisions do not deal specifically with the rights guaranteed under Article 4 of the Convention, but concern, in a much more restrictive way, exploitation through labour and subjection to working and living conditions that are incompatible with human dignity."

[150] ECtHR 7 January 2010, No. 25965/04, *Rantsev v. Cyprus and Russia*, para. 284.

legally bring thousands of young foreign women to Cyprus, where they were exploited sexually and otherwise by their employers.

Another example of a case in which the Court provides detailed guidance is *Redfearn v. the United Kingdom.* The case concerned the dismissal of a bus driver for a private company, because he was elected as local councilor for the racist British Nationalist Party. The applicant could not complain about his dismissal, because he had no claim under the Employment Rights Act 1996, which is only applicable in case of continuous employment for a period of not less than 1 year before the effective date of termination. The Act contained some exemptions from the 1-year qualifying period, such as dismissal on account of race, sex or religion. Political opinion or affiliation were, however, not included in this list of exemptions. The Court found a violation of Art. 11 ECHR, the right to freedom of association, because it considered that "in the absence of judicial safeguards a legal system which allows dismissal from employment solely on account of the employee's membership of a political party carries with it the potential for abuse."[151] To redress this situation, the Court held that "it was incumbent on the respondent State to take reasonable and appropriate measures to protect employees, including those with less than 1 year's service, from dismissal on grounds of political opinion or affiliation, either through the creation of a further exception to the 1-year qualifying period or through a free-standing claim for unlawful discrimination on grounds of political opinion or affiliation."[152] The reason why the Court was so detailed was probably because the source of the violation was easy to identify: an existing means of protection was cut off by the 1-year qualifying period that did not allow for sufficient exemptions.

4.5.1.6 Position of the State

As with any positive obligation, the European Court also takes into account the position of the state as a duty-bearer. In this respect, when listing the factors that are relevant for the assessment of the content of positive obligations, in *A, B and C v. Ireland*, the Court held that:

> Some factors concern the position of the State: whether the alleged obligation is narrow and defined or broad and indeterminate (...); and the extent of any burden the obligation would impose on the State (...).[153]

The latter relates to the fact that the effective enforcement of any legal framework places a financial and organizational burden on the state, and thereby limits the state in pursuing other social goals. Due to the importance of what is at stake, effective

---

[151] ECtHR 6 November 2012, No. 47335/06, *Redfearn v. the United Kingdom*, para. 55.

[152] Ibid., para. 57. While the case was argued as one involving procedural protection, it is more appropriate to consider it as one involving substantive protection: the judgment requires the state to prohibit employers from dismissing their employees during the 1-year qualifying period on grounds of political opinion or affiliation.

[153] ECtHR (GC) 16 December 2010, No. 25579/05, *A, B and C v. Ireland*, para. 248.

protection of human rights must nonetheless be prioritized in policy making, unless and to the extent that necessary protective measures would entail social costs that cannot reasonably be required.[154]

The former aspect – whether the alleged obligation is narrow and defined or broad and indeterminate – is best illustrated by the case of *Botta v. Italy.*[155] This case concerned a physically disabled person who complained about the lack of access to private bathing establishments during his stay at a seaside resort at the Adriatic coast, which was caused by the absence of special access ramps for wheelchairs and specially equipped lavatories and washrooms. Although the complaint was not framed that way, it essentially concerned the question whether the Italian state should have developed a legal framework to protect disabled persons against denial of reasonable accommodation[156] by private actors. The European Court held that there must be "a direct and immediate link between the measures sought by an applicant and the latter's private and/or family life", before a positive obligation under Art. 8 ECHR (the right to respect for private life) would arise. The Court, however, dismissed the applicant's complaint, because it concerned "interpersonal relations of such broad and indeterminate scope that there can be no conceivable direct link between the measures the State was urged to take in order to make good the omissions of the private bathing establishments and the applicant's private life."

The *Botta* judgment reflects the problem of 'conceptual proximity' discussed above: if the obligation to protect a given right is broader and more indeterminate, then there is less 'conceptual proximity' between right and obligation. At a certain point, there is so little 'conceptual proximity' that it is unreasonable to hold the state to be under that particular obligation. The criterion of narrow and defined vs. broad and indeterminate is in any event more of a scale than of a black-and-white-distinction. It is also not a decisive criterion as such, but should be balanced against other criteria, such as the seriousness of the issue or the existence of competing rights. The Court should in any event be careful not to rely too heavily on this criterion, as it thereby risks to underestimate the seriousness of the issue at stake. This has led Xenos to reject the *Botta* test, on the grounds that elements of 'directness' and/or 'immediacy' will always be difficult to establish "when individuals claim assistance from the state due to their own personal vulnerability in order to be able to enjoy human rights."[157]

It would be better to accommodate the problem of the lack of 'conceptual proximity' in the proportionality test. The imposition of too 'broad and indeterminate' positive

[154] See, for example, *N. v. the United Kingdom*, supra, note 141, para. 44, in which the Court held that the provision of free and unlimited health care to all aliens without a right to stay "would place too great a burden on the Contracting states."

[155] ECtHR 24 February 1998, No. 153/1996/772/973, *Botta v. Italy*.

[156] In the Convention on the Rights of Persons with Disabilities (2006), reasonable accommodation is defined as "necessary and appropriate modification and adjustments not imposing a disproportionate or undue burden, where needed in a particular case, to ensure to persons with disabilities the enjoyment or exercise on an equal basis with others of all human rights and fundamental freedoms" (Art. 2).

[157] D. Xenos, "The human rights of the vulnerable", 13 *International Journal of Human Rights* (2009), 598.

obligations risks placing an excessive burden on the state and should – together with 'the extent of any burden the obligation would impose on the State' – as such be taken into account as an element in the proportionality analysis.[158] With respect to the extent of the burden, the Court has, for example, done so in the above discussed case of *K.U. v. Finland*, in which it held, in the context of the proportionality analysis, that "(...) a positive obligation must be interpreted in a way which does not impose an impossible or disproportionate burden on the authorities or, as in this case, the legislator."[159] The extent of such a burden will, however, depend on the nature of the particular positive obligation and it may be outweighed by the seriousness of the human rights issue at stake.

4.5.1.7 'No Significant Flaws' Versus Effective Protection

The recent case of *E.S. v. Sweden* may have introduced a new element in the Court's case law: the 'no significant flaws' test. At the age of 14 years old, the applicant discovered that her stepfather had hidden a video camera in the laundry basket in the bathroom, directed towards the spot where she normally undressed. The stepfather was prosecuted for sexual molestation, but was acquitted on appeal. The appeal court accepted that his motive had been to film his stepdaughter for a sexual purpose, but he could not be convicted because the offence of sexual molestation required intent, in particular the intent that the girl would find out about the filming. Besides, there was no general prohibition against filming an individual without his or her consent in Swedish law. A charge of attempted child pornography was apparently not possible in this case, because the video tape had been destroyed by the applicant's mother.

The applicant complained that the lack of protection by Swedish law amounted to a violation of Art. 8 ECHR, the right to privacy. When listing the general principles applicable to the case, the Court held that:

> It must also be kept in mind that only significant flaws in legislation and practice, and their application, would amount to a breach of the State's positive obligations under Article 8.[160]

---

[158] I have made a similar argument in Lavrysen, supra, note 31. As explained in that paper, this would be more in line with an Alexian conception of rights (see Sect. 4.4.1).

[159] *K.U. v. Finland*, supra, note 115, para. 48.

[160] ECtHR 21 June 2012, No. 5786/08, *E.S. v. Sweden*, para. 59. Bizarrely, while the Court lists this 'no significant flaws' test as a general principle, it provides no references to earlier case law to justify this. The Court did mention the notion of 'significant flaws' in the earlier cases of *M.C. v. Bulgaria*, supra, note 145, para. 167 (Art. 3 and 8 ECHR), *Siliadin v. France*, supra, note 94, para. 130 (Art. 4 ECHR) and ECtHR 27 September 2011, No. 29032/04, *M. and C. v. Romania*, para. 112 (Art. 3 and 8 ECHR). In these cases, this notion merely signified that domestic law and practice must provide effective protection, and, unlike in *E.S. v. Sweden*, it was not applied as a separate test. While not explicitly rejecting the 'no significant flaws' test, the dissenting judges Spielmann, Villiger and Power-Forde consider the appropriate question to be whether "there is a lacuna in the legislation which fails to protect these values."

According to the Court, the relevant question to determine whether there had been a 'significant flaw' was:

> (...) should the legislators have foreseen that in a case of attempted covert filming of a minor for a sexual purpose, where the film was subsequently destroyed without anyone having seen it, and where the person who filmed did not intend the minor to find out about the filming, the provision of sexual molestation could not cover the act, and a charge of attempted child pornography offence would not necessarily be brought.[161]

The Court did not find that the legislators should have foreseen this.[162] For the Court it was sufficient that the disputed act of the stepfather was 'in theory' covered by the offences of sexual molestation and attempted child pornography, to find that there had not been a violation of Art. 8 ECHR.

The judgment is problematic for a number of reasons. Firstly, the application of the 'no significant flaws' test is overly deferential. In its case law the Court has always stressed that "[t]he Convention is intended to guarantee not rights that are theoretical or illusory but rights that are practical and effective."[163] In this light, it is strange that the Court accepts the argument that Swedish criminal law 'in theory' – rather than in practice – provided sufficient protection. Secondly, by introducing the 'no significant flaws' test, the state's positive obligation is in a sense 'negativised': it becomes an obligation *not to do something* (i.e. allowing significant flaws in legislation), rather than an obligation *to do something* (i.e. providing effective protection). As such, this may not be so problematic, on condition that there is sufficient certainty with respect to the content of this 'negative' criterion. However, in the absence of any criteria as to what amounts to a 'significant flaw', the Court's judgment does not provide any guidance as to what does amount to sufficient 'protection by the law'.

Thirdly and most importantly, introducing the 'no significant flaws' test is difficult to reconcile with the principle of effectiveness. This principle has always been the rationale behind the Court's doctrine of positive obligations.[164] The same holds true with respect to the necessary legal framework: states are under a positive obligation to provide *effective* 'protection by the law'. Effective protection does not imply that the state must prevent every violation of a human right: positive obligations are generally considered to be obligations of means rather than obligations of result.[165] While total protection is not required, the principle of effectiveness, however, does

---

[161] Ibid., para. 68.

[162] This relates to the criterion of knowledge discussed above.

[163] *Airey v. Ireland*, supra, note 37, para. 24.

[164] See Sect. 4.3.1.

[165] E.g. Dröge, supra, note 13, 388. With respect to the positive obligation to investigate violations of Art. 2 ECHR, the right to life, the Court has explicitly acknowledged this: "[t]he investigation must also be effective in the sense that it is capable of leading to a determination of whether the force used was or was not justified in the circumstances (...) and to the identification and punishment of those responsible (...). This is not an obligation of result, but of means" (E.g. Paul and Audrey Edwards, supra, note 46, para. 71).

require that the state strives to provide as much protection as can reasonably be expected from them.[166] According to Xenos, "the choice of measures is reviewed against the standard of effectiveness, which aims, consciously or unconsciously, at an end/complete result (...)",[167] in particular the end result "not to suffer a violation of human rights by a given activity."[168] Turning back to the theoretical discussion above, the principle of effectiveness thus operates, to a certain extent, as an element of optimisation in the Alexian sense.

The ECHR rights, however, do not operate as full-fledged optimisation requirements. As minimum guarantees, the ECHR rights do not require a state to always adopt the most protective measure.[169] As explained above, the choice of means to protect a certain right generally falls within the state's margin of appreciation. The state is free to adopt the means it prefers, insofar as these means are proportionate to the (potential) human rights violation. Thereby, the Court avoids the pitfall inherent to Alexy's model that optimisation inevitably leads to imposing only one solution: the adoption of the most protective measure, taking into account the competing legal and factual elements. One could therefore say that the principle of effectiveness reconciles both Alexy's and Christoffersen's positions, as discussed above: the principle is at the middle ground between the 'maximum perspective' of optimisation on the one hand and the 'minimum perspective' of ECHR rights as minimum requirements on the other.[170]

Introducing a 'no significant flaws' test in the Court's positive obligation case law, however, disturbs that balance, as it denies the element of optimisation inherent in the principle of effectiveness. Effective protection in the Court's case law has never simply meant the absence of 'significant flaws'. In the above discussed case of *K.U. v. Finland*, which bears some resemblance to *E.S. v. Sweden*,[171] the Court has, for example, applied an 'impossible or disproportionate burden' test, which surely requires more than simply the absence of 'significant flaws' in legislation.[172] A standard

[166] In the context of the preventive positive obligation under Art. 2 ECHR, the Court has held that, in order to find a violation, "it is sufficient for an applicant to show that the authorities did not do all that could be reasonably expected of them to avoid a real and immediate risk to life of which they have or ought to have knowledge" (e.g. *Osman v. the United Kingdom*, supra, note 80, para. 116).

[167] Xenos, supra, note 11, 118.

[168] Ibid., 102.

[169] Presuming that one can determine what 'the most protective measure' is, as this inevitably involves some degree of speculation.

[170] On minimum and maximum perspectives, see E. Brems, "Human Rights: Minimum and Maximum Perspectives", 9 *Human Rights Law Review* (2009), 349–372.

[171] Both concern lack of protection of a minor against (potential) sexual abuse. In *K.U.*, the Court held "(...) that sexual abuse is unquestionably an abhorrent type of wrongdoing, with debilitating effects on its victims. Children and other vulnerable individuals are entitled to State protection, in the form of effective deterrence, from such grave types of interference with essential aspects of their private lives" (*K.U. v. Finland*, supra, note 115, para. 46).

[172] Ibid., para. 48. Also see above.

comparable with 'no significant flaws' has moreover been dismissed in the context of the preventive positive obligation under Art. 2 ECHR, where the government argued that the standard under Art. 2 ECHR was whether there had been 'gross negligence' or 'wilful disregard of the duty to protect life'. According to the Court, such standards were incompatible with the need to provide effective protection.[173] On a spectrum, protection is not either effective or 'significantly flawed': between both points on the spectrum, there are other positions in which unacceptably low protection is offered. As the 'no significant flaws' test would not find a violation with respect to these other positions, the test thus amounts to the lowering of standards in the Court's jurisprudence.

The case of *E.S. v. Sweden* potentially signifies a major step backwards in the Court's positive obligations case law. The Court, however, still has the opportunity to correct this mistake, as the case has been referred to the Grand Chamber.[174]

4.5.1.8 'Quality of the Law'

Related to the principle of effectiveness is the need to provide protection of 'sufficient quality'. In negative obligations cases, the 'quality of the law' is an element that is traditionally examined under the legality criterion. The 'quality of the law' condition requires that the law is 'accessible' and 'foreseeable', and that it does not grant an 'unfettered power' to the executive[175] – the latter relates to the principle of non-arbitrariness. In a dissenting opinion to the Chamber judgment of *Evans v. the United Kingdom*, judges Traja and Mijović held that:

> The fact that the case is analysed as one concerning positive obligations and not as one involving an interference by the State with the applicant's right, should make no difference as to the requirement for law of a certain quality. If the case had been decided as one involving the State's interference, as the domestic courts did, then the Court would feel the need to review the quality of the law. The same must apply when the case is seen from the angle of positive obligations.[176]

[173] *Osman v. the United Kingdom*, supra, note 80, para. 116: "[t]he Court does not accept the Government's view that the failure to perceive the risk to life in the circumstances known at the time or to take preventive measures to avoid that risk must be tantamount to gross negligence or willful disregard of the duty to protect life (…). Such a rigid standard must be considered to be incompatible with the requirements of Article 1 of the Convention and the obligations of Contracting States under that Article to secure the practical and effective protection of the rights and freedoms laid down therein, including Article 2."

[174] This was decided on 19 November 2012 by the Grand Chamber panel of five judges. Before the Grand Chamber, the name of the case was changed to *Söderman v. Sweden*.

[175] See Sect. 4.4.2.

[176] ECtHR 7 March 2006, No. 6339/05, *Evans v. the United Kingdom*.

In a similar sense, Xenos has argued that "core positive obligations (...) can be incorporated as legal safeguards that have to be 'prescribed by law'",[177] i.e. as an element in the application of the legality test to positive obligations. According to Xenos, those legal safeguards have to be prescribed by the law in a foreseeable and certain manner.[178] This reflects an important aspect of the required 'quality of the law' in negative obligations cases (see above): the foreseeability and certainty of the law. Similarly, 'protection by the law' arguably has to comply with the 'quality of the law' requirement of accessibility: it is hard to see how a law can provide effective protection if it is not accessible.[179]

While the cases in which the Court has examined whether 'protection by the law' was of sufficient quality are rare, some privacy cases are illustrative. In the above discussed case of *Von Hannover v. Germany*, the Court stressed the lack of foreseeability of protection – due to the distinction under German law in protection of privacy with respect to figures of contemporary society 'par excellence' and 'relatively' public figures. According to the Court, such distinctions have to be "clear and obvious so that, in a State governed by the rule of law, the individual has precise indications as to the behaviour he or she should adopt. Above all, they need to know exactly when and where they are in a protected sphere or, on the contrary, in a sphere in which they must expect interference from others, especially the tabloid press."[180] In the case of *Mosley v. the United Kingdom*, on the other hand, the Court did not find the requested measure – a pre-notification requirement for the

---

[177] Xenos, supra, note 11, 121. Xenos argues to also apply this as a separate test in positive obligation cases. This is in line with the symmetrical model I proposed in Lavrysen, supra, note 31. If a state fails to comply with or fails to enforce the laws it has enacted to fulfill its positive obligations, the Court should find a violation. The Court has done so in many environmental cases, e.g. ECtHR 9 December 1994, No. 16798/90, *López Ostra v. Spain*, paras. 54–58 (failure to shut down a waste-treatment plant operating without the legally required license); ECtHR 16 November 2004, No. 4143/02, *Moreno Gómez v. Spain*, paras. 59–63 (failure to enforce the designation of an area as an acoustically saturated zone); ECtHR 9 November 2010, No. 2345/06, *Deés v. Hungary*, paras. 22–24 (failure to enforce domestic standards concerning traffic noise pollution). As domestic authorities may still fulfill their positive obligation by other means than by applying a particular measure provided by domestic law, the Court has, however, stated that "domestic legality should be approached not as a separate and conclusive test, but rather as one of many aspects which should be taken into account in assessing whether the State had struck a fair balance." (*Fadeyeva v. Russia*, supra, note 142). I am convinced that the legality principle in positive obligations cases consists at least of an obligation of means that requires domestic authorities to take all the reasonable steps possible to enforce compliance with domestic law (*mutatis mutandis Osman v. the United Kingdom*, supra, note 80, para. 116). I am, however, not convinced that the 'quality of the law' in cases of positive obligations should be examined at the separate legality test, as it is impossible to distinguish the question of the requisite 'quality' from the principle of effectiveness and the context in which the human rights violation takes place – such a question is more appropriately addressed at the proportionality stage.

[178] Xenos, supra, note 11, 121.

[179] The 'quality of the law' also encompasses the requirement of an element of procedural protection against arbitrariness, this relates to Sect. 4.6 on procedural 'protection by the law'.

[180] *Von Hannover v. Germany*, supra, note 91, para. 73.

press – necessary in order to provide effective 'protection by the law' of the applicant's right to privacy (Art. 8 ECHR), because of the lack of certainty of the effectiveness of that measure.[181] As the case concerned a conflict of rights, the lack of certainty could have resulted in insufficient protection of the right to privacy on the one hand, but also in an excessive restriction of press freedom (Art. 10 ECHR) on the other. Both cases illustrate that substantive 'protection by the law' requires that law to have a certain 'quality'.

4.6 Procedural 'Protection by the Law'

A second aspect of 'protection by the law' is procedural protection. It should be noted at this point that it may not always be easy to distinguish between substantive and procedural protection: as held above, the substance/procedure distinction is a crude one. As with substantive protection, it is possible to distinguish between an instrumental and an intrinsic function of procedural protection.[182] The instrumental function is premised on the idea that fair procedures are more likely to lead to fairer results.[183] With respect to the European Convention, this is very much related to the principle of effectiveness: we need procedures because they contribute to the effective protection of substantive human rights.

However, the instrumental function is only part of the picture: we also value procedure because procedural fairness has an intrinsic value. This intrinsic function is explained by social psychological research: procedures define the internal features of a group and thereby give people information about their social connection to groups and to group authorities.[184] In that way, procedural fairness has an important impact on status recognition.[185] The research of Tom Tyler further illustrates that a perception of procedural fairness does not only contribute to feelings of self-worth of the individual concerned, but also has a crucial impact on strengthening the legitimacy of legal institutions and in gaining compliance with the law.[186] Tyler has

[181] ECtHR 10 May 2011, *Mosley v. the United Kingdom*, paras. 121 and 125–129.

[182] Similarly May, supra, note 59, 50.

[183] In the context of negative obligations, Başak Çali stressed this intrinsic function, by recognizing as one of the rationales underlying procedural fairness that "authorities are required to be more stringent with their own reasoning and empirical evidence to demonstrate the necessity and the degree of restriction" (B. Çali, "Balancing Human Rights? Methodological Problems with Weights, Scales and Proportions", 29 *Human Rights Quarterly* (2007), 267).

[184] E.A. Lind and T.R. Tyler, *The Social Psychology of Procedural Justice* (New York: Plenum, 1988), 231; T.R. Tyler, P. Degoey and H.J. Smith, "Understanding Why the Justice of Group Procedures Matters: A Test of the Psychological Dynamics of the Group-Value Model", 70 *Journal of Personality and Social Psychology* (1996), 914.

[185] T.R. Tyler and E.A. Lind, "A Relational Model of Authority in Groups", in M. Zanna (ed.) *Advances in Experimental Social Psychology* (Vol. 25) (New York: Academic Press, 1992), 141.

[186] T.R. Tyler, *Why People Obey the Law* (Princeton: Princeton University Press, 2006).

further demonstrated that this feeling of procedural fairness is influenced by four distinct procedural justice judgments: participation, neutrality, respect and trust.[187] Elsewhere, Brems and I have argued that human rights adjudication bodies, and the European Court in particular, should consistently take these principles into account.[188] The European Court must ensure that, when human rights are at stake, procedures are enacted and applied in such a way as to contribute to a sense of procedural justice.

4.6.1 European Court Versus Supreme Court: The Abortion Cases

Before examining the European Court's case law more into detail, it would be interesting to first discuss an area in which there have been remarkable differences between the European Court's approach and the one taken by the Supreme Court: the abortion cases. The ECtHR case of *A, B and C v. Ireland* concerned three women who were obliged to go to the United Kingdom to obtain an abortion. Two of them complained that the fact that Irish law did not allow abortion for health and/or well-being reasons violated Art. 8 ECHR (the right to privacy). The third woman was in remission of cancer and feared that there was a risk that her pregnancy would cause a relapse of cancer. She claimed a violation of Art. 8 ECHR on the grounds that, although the Irish Constitution allowed for abortion in order to protect the life of the mother, there was no procedure through which she could have had such a risk established and therefore she was denied access to a legal abortion.

The Court accepted first of all that, due to its impact on the private life of the woman, the regulation of abortion comes within the scope of Art. 8 ECHR. The Court, which generally exercises judicial constraint in cases where public morals are at stake, however, dismissed the first complaint that Art. 8 ECHR guarantees a right to abortion for health and/or well-being reasons:

> (...) having regard to the right to lawfully travel abroad for an abortion with access to appropriate information and medical care in Ireland, the Court does not consider that the prohibition in Ireland of abortion for health and well-being reasons, based as it is on the profound moral views of the Irish people as to the nature of life (...) and as to the consequent protection to be accorded to the right to life of the unborn, exceeds the margin of appreciation accorded in that respect to the Irish State. In such circumstances, the Court finds that the impugned prohibition in Ireland struck a fair balance between the right of the first and second applicants to respect for their private lives and the rights invoked on behalf of the unborn.[189]

---

[187] T.R. Tyler, "Procedural Justice and the Courts", 44 *Court Review* (2007–2008), 30–31.

[188] Brems and Lavrysen, supra, note 99, 182–185.

[189] *A, B and C v. Ireland*, supra, note 153, para. 241.

The second complaint was, however, accepted in line with the earlier case of *Tysiąc v. Poland.*[190] The Court held that:

> (...) the authorities failed to comply with their positive obligation to secure to the third applicant effective respect for her private life by reason of the absence of any implementing legislative or regulatory regime providing an accessible and effective procedure by which the third applicant could have established whether she qualified for a lawful abortion in Ireland in accordance with Article 40.3.3 of the Constitution.[191]

While the Court thus – unlike the Supreme Court in *Roe v. Wade*[192] – denied that the right to privacy incorporates a right to abortion, the Court did rule that a state that recognizes legal abortions must provide an accessible and effective procedure that does not limit real possibilities to obtain it.[193] While the European Convention does not provide substantive protection in abortion cases, it does provide procedural protection. This is in stark contrast with the approach of the U.S. Supreme Court in the case of *Webster v. Reproductive Health Services.* This case concerned *inter alia* prohibitions on the use of state employees and facilities to perform or assist abortions, except where the mother's life was in danger. The Supreme Court, in an opinion written by Justice Rehnquist, held that:

> The restrictions in §§ 188.210 and 188.215 of the Missouri statute on the use of public employees and facilities for the performance or assistance of nontherapeutic abortions do not contravene this Court's abortion decisions. The Due Process Clauses generally confer no affirmative right to governmental aid, even where such aid may be necessary to secure life, liberty, or property interests of which the government may not deprive the individual.[194]

While the Supreme Court thus recognizes a 'negative' right to abortion, unlike the European Court, it does not recognize a 'positive' right to the facilitation of such legal abortions. The European Court on the other hand allows the states a significant latitude in deciding how to weigh the different competing interests,[195] but when a state establishes a legal framework that reconciles these competing interests, this framework should at least include effective procedural protection. Strangely, thereby the European Court has developed a 'conditional' positive obligation (i.e. procedural protection) that is 'parasitical' on a non-recognized obligation to respect a woman's choice. The European Court has thus accepted that there may be procedural protection required under the ECHR in a field in which it does not require substantive protection. The Court seems to apply this strategy of

---

[190] ECtHR 20 March 2007, No. 5410/03, *Tysiąc v. Poland.*

[191] *A, B and C v. Ireland*, supra, note 153, para. 267.

[192] U.S. Supreme Court 22 January 1973, *Roe v. Wade*, 410 U.S. 113.

[193] *Tysiąc v. Poland*, supra, note 190, para. 116.

[194] U.S. Supreme Court 3 July 1989, *Webster v. Reproductive Health Services*, 492 U.S. 490.

[195] Undoubtedly, the Court thereby failed to provide sufficient substantive 'protection by the law', as external preferences such as public morals were taken into consideration. See in a similar sense, S. Smet, "A., B. and C. v. Ireland: Abortion and the Margin of Appreciation", 17 December 2010, http://strasbourgobservers.com, with references to Letsas and Dworkin.

'proceduralization' especially in controversial cases, such as abortion and euthanasia/assisted suicide.[196]

4.6.2 *Procedural Protection in the ECHR*

The European Convention explicitly recognizes some procedural rights, such as the right to a fair trial (Art. 6 ECHR), encompassing *inter alia* a right of access to court,[197] and the right to an effective remedy against violations of Convention rights (Art. 13 ECHR). These explicit procedural safeguards have resulted in a vast amount of case law in which the European Court has further developed the content of these provisions. Art 6 ECHR is applicable when a 'criminal charge' and 'civil rights and obligations' are being determined. Art. 13 ECHR, in turn, is applicable when an arguable claim has been raised that there has been a violation of another Convention right.[198] Needless to say, the right to a fair trial with all its sub-rights "discloses an extensive array of positive obligations."[199] The obligation to develop a performant justice system arguably is the most far-reaching obligation to fulfill under the ECHR, requiring the mobilization of vast amounts of state resources. For the sake of this discussion, I am, however, not particularly interested in these explicit guarantees. I am rather interested in procedural guarantees which are implicit in substantive Convention provisions, and more particularly in the way they require states to structure their legal framework in a way that recognizes and gives effect to these implicit procedural guarantees.

The Court has found implicit procedural guarantees in basically every Convention right. Firstly, the Court has recognized a positive obligation to investigate serious violations of human rights as being implicitly being part of at least the following rights: the right to life (Art. 2 ECHR),[200] the prohibition of torture and of inhuman

---

[196] The Court has rejected a positive obligation to facilitate assisted suicide in ECtHR 29 April 2002, No. 2346/02, *Pretty v. the United Kingdom*. In ECtHR 20 January 2011, No. 31322/07, *Haas v. Switzerland*, the Court, however, did not exclude the existence of *"a positive obligation on the State to take the necessary measures to permit a dignified suicide"* (para. 53), but nonetheless did not find a violation, because he had access to a procedure to obtain legal assisted suicide (i.e. the requirement for a medical prescription, issued on the basis of a full psychiatric assessment). In ECtHR 19 July 2012, No. 497/09, *Koch v. Germany*, the Court explicitly did not want to rule on the substantive claim – due to a lack of European consensus on the issue – but nonetheless did find a violation of Art. 8 ECHR, because the applicant did not have the opportunity to have the merits of her request examined by a court (see Sect. 4.6.3.1).

[197] ECtHR (GC) 21 February 1975, No. 4451/70, *Golder v. the United Kingdom*.

[198] Harris et al., supra, note 9, 560–561.

[199] Mowbray, supra, note 38, 124.

[200] E.g. ECtHR (GC) 27 September 1995, No. 18984/91, *McCann and Others v. the United Kingdom*, para. 161. The case concerned the fatal shooting of three IRA terrorists in Gibraltar. The Court recognized a positive obligation for the state to conduct "some form of effective official investigation when individuals have been killed as a result of the use of force by, inter alios, agents of the State."

and degrading treatment or punishment (Art. 3 ECHR),[201] the prohibition of slavery, servitude and forced labor (Art. 4 ECHR),[202] the right to liberty (Art. 5 ECHR),[203] the right to respect for family and private life (Art. 8 ECHR),[204] the right to freedom of religion (Art. 9 ECHR),[205] the right to freedom of expression (Art. 10 ECHR),[206] the prohibition of discrimination (Art. 14 ECHR)[207] and the right to property (Art. 1 Protocol 1).[208] The obligation to investigate concerns both violations by state agents – either by action[209] or inaction[210] – as violations by non-state agents.[211] This obligation overlaps to a high degree with the requirements of Art. 13 ECHR, the right to an effective remedy.[212] Secondly, the Court requires access to an effective

[201] E.g. ECtHR 28 October 1998, No. 24760/94, *Assenov and Others v. Bulgaria*, para. 102. The Court found a positive obligation to conduct an effective official investigation into an arguable claim that the applicant had been seriously ill-treated by the police or other state agents.

[202] *Rantsev v. Cyprus and Russia*, supra, note 150, para. 288. In this human trafficking case, the Court recognized "a procedural obligation to investigate situations of potential trafficking."

[203] E.g. ECtHR 25 May 1998, No. 24276/94, *Kurt v. Turkey*, para. 124. The case concerned the enforced disappearance of a Kurdish man. The Court required "a prompt effective investigation into an arguable claim that a person has been taken into custody and has not been seen since."

[204] *M.C. v. Bulgaria*, supra, note 145, para. 153. The Court recognized a positive obligation under both Art. 3 ECHR and Art. 8 ECHR to effectively investigate and prosecute allegations of rape. In the case of *Craxi (No. 2) v. Italy*, supra, note 110, para. 74 – concerning the publication by the press of the leaked content of intercepted phone calls of the former Italian prime minister – the Court recognized a positive obligation "to carry out inquiries in order to rectify the matter [i.e. the disclosure of a private nature] to the extent possible."

[205] ECtHR 3 May 2007, No. 71156/01, *97 Members of the Gldani Congregation of Jehovah's Witnesses and Others v. Georgia*, paras. 133–134. While not explicitly recognizing a positive obligation to investigate under Art. 9 ECHR, the Court did take into account the failures in investigating the applicants' complaints when finding a violation of Art. 9 ECHR.

[206] ECtHR 16 March 2000, No. 23144/93, *Özgür Gündem v. Turkey*, paras. 44–45. The case concerned a violent campaign against a Kurdish newspaper. According to the Court, Art. 10 ECHR required an effective investigation of "the applicant's allegations that the attacks were part of a concerted campaign which was supported, or tolerated, by the authorities."

[207] E.g. ECtHR (GC) 6 July 2005, No. 43577/98, *Nachova and Others v. Bulgaria*. The case concerned the obligation to examine a possible racist motive in the killing of two Roma deserters when they attempted to flee from military policemen.

[208] E.g. ECtHR (GC) 10 May 2001, No. 25781/94, *Cyprus v. Turkey*, para. 271. The Court examined whether there was an administrative practice by the Turkish Cypriot authorities to fail to examine acts of criminal damage to Greek Cypriots' property, when examining whether there had been a violation of Art. 1 Protocol 1.

[209] In that case, they can be considered to be 'conditional' positive obligations.

[210] E.g. ECtHR 20 March 2008, Nos. 15339/02, 21166/02, 20058/02, 11673/02 and 15343/02, *Budayeva and Others v. Russia*, para. 142, concerning the failure to investigate the failure of state authorities to protect and warn the inhabitants of a village hit by mudslides.

[211] E.g. *M.C. v Bulgaria*, supra, note 145.

[212] According to the Court, the obligation under Art. 13 ECHR is broader, in the sense that it also encompasses the obligation to provide the victim or the next-of-kin with appropriate compensation, see e.g. ECtHR 19 February 1998, No. 22729/93, *Kaya v. Turkey*, para. 107. In *Öneryildiz v. Turkey*, supra, note 140, the Court held that a violation of a procedural obligation under Art. 2

remedy – administrative, judicial or both – to allow victims to challenge violations of their human rights. This will be examined more into detail hereunder.[213] Thirdly, the Court has also recognized implicit procedural obligations in the context of careful decision-making – *inter alia* participation rights and the requirement to adequately examine the factual basis for a certain decision– particularly under the right to respect for family and private life (Art. 8 ECHR)[214]: for example, with respect to the taking into care of children,[215] custody proceedings,[216] urban planning[217] and environmental protection.[218] The Court has found similar implicit procedural obligations in the context of careful decision-making in cases concerning freedom of religion (Art. 9 ECHR),[219] freedom of expression (Art. 10 ECHR)[220] and freedom of assembly (Art. 11 ECHR)[221] and there is no reason why similar obligations cannot be recognized in the context of all Convention rights.[222] This last category of procedural obligations consists of 'conditional' positive obligations: they are dependent on whether or not the state chooses to interfere with an individual's rights (i.e. a negative obligation).[223] For the sake of this discussion, I will focus principally on the 'structural' elements of procedure rather than on the application of these procedures in practice.[224]

The idea of implicit procedural protection in substantive rights, is to a certain extent comparable with the notion of procedural due process under the U.S. Bill

---

ECHR does not automatically result in a violation of Art. 13 ECHR: "[w]hat is important is the impact the State's failure to comply with its procedural obligation under Article 2 had on the deceased's family's access to other available and effective remedies for establishing liability on the part of State officials or bodies for acts or omissions entailing the breach of their rights under Article 2 and, as appropriate, obtaining compensation" (para. 148).

[213] See Sect. 4.6.3.1.

[214] Also Brems and Lavrysen, supra, note 99, 191–193.

[215] E.g. ECtHR (GC) 8 July 1987, No. 9749/82, *W. v. the United Kingdom.*

[216] E.g. ECtHR 26 February 2004, No. 74969/01, *Görgülü v. Germany.*

[217] E.g. ECtHR 25 September 1996, No. 20348/92, *Buckley v. the United Kingdom.*

[218] E.g. *Hatton and Others v. the United Kingdom*, supra, note 14.

[219] ECtHR (GC) 10 November 2005, No. 44774/98, *Leyla Şahin v. Turkey*, para. 159.

[220] ECtHR 21 October 2010, No. 35016/03, *Saliyev v. Russia*, para. 76.

[221] ECtHR 26 July 2007, No. 10519/03, *Barankevich v. Russia*, para. 33.

[222] See, for example, also ECtHR 24 October 1986, No. 9118/80, *AGOSI v. the United Kingdom*, para. 55 (with respect to the right to property, Art. 1 Protocol 1) and ECtHR 9 April 2002, 46726/99, *Podkolzina v. Latvia*, para. 35 (with respect to the right to free elections, Art. 3 Protocol 1).

[223] In this sense, they are comparable with the 'quality of the law' condition. A finding of a failure of the 'quality of the law' condition, however, always results in a violation of the Convention right, whereas these procedural obligations are taken into account as elements in the proportionality test. Brems and I have argued that severe failures of procedural justice in the context of careful decision-making should nonetheless automatically result in a violation of the Convention right concerned (Brems and Lavrysen, supra, note 99, 199).

[224] The Court, for example, has a very rich case law on the way state authorities have to conduct an investigation under Art. 2 ECHR (the right to life), e.g. ECtHR (GC) 15 May 2007, No. 52391/99, *Ramsahai and Others v. the Netherlands.*

of Rights. The due process clauses of the Fifth and Fourteenth Amendment require the existence of procedural safeguards when the government deprives an individual of life, liberty or property. The most elaborate statement of procedural due process was made in the case *In re Gault,*[225] in which the Supreme Court held that due process entitles juvenile defendants to many of the same procedural safeguards as adults in criminal trials,[226] prior to being committed to a state industrial school: a right to adequate notice of hearing, the right to counsel, the right of confrontation and cross-examination of witnesses and the privilege against self-incrimination. In the case of *Mathews v. Elridge* – in which the Supreme Court held that the termination of social security benefits did not require a pre-termination hearing – the Court clarified how it determines the requisite extent of protection by procedural due process:

> '[D]ue process is flexible, and calls for such procedural protections as the particular situation demands.' (...) Accordingly, resolution of the issue whether the administrative procedures provided here are constitutionally sufficient, requires analysis of the governmental and private interests that are affected. (...) More precisely, our prior decisions indicate that identification of the specific dictates of due process generally requires consideration of three distinct factors: first, the private interest that will be affected by the official action; second, the risk of an erroneous deprivation of such interest through the procedures used, and the probable value, if any, of additional or substitute procedural safeguards; and, finally, the Government's interest, including the function involved and the fiscal and administrative burdens that the additional or substitute procedural requirement would entail.[227]

Procedural due process is thus highly flexible and context-dependent. Procedural due process can be considered as a 'conditional' positive obligation, similar to procedural positive obligations related to careful decision-making in the European Court's case law – the latter is, however, broader as it is required with respect to every Convention right, and not only with respect to life, liberty and property. Procedural protection under the ECHR will in some cases also be more extensive, as illustrated by the cases concerning the treatment against their will of mentally ill persons with antipsychotic drugs: the U.S. Supreme Court in *Washington v. Harper* did not accept that procedural due process required a judicial proceeding,[228] while the European Court did require access to a judicial remedy in the case of *Storck v. Germany.*[229] The approaches of both Courts are, however, in essence highly comparable.[230]

[225] U.S. Supreme Court 15 May 1967, In re Gault, 387 U.S. 1.

[226] Which are set out in the Fifth and Sixth Amendment.

[227] U.S Supreme Court 24 February 1976, *Mathews v. Elridge*, 424 U.S. 319.

[228] U.S. Supreme Court 27 February 1990, *Washington v. Harper*, 494 U.S. 210.

[229] *Storck v. Germany*, supra, note 22.

[230] Also with respect to the application of proportionality analysis in order to verify the appropriate extent of protection.

4.6.3 General Principles from the European Court's Case Law

Many principles that have been found in the context of substantive 'protection by the law' *mutatis mutandis* also apply to procedural protection.

1. As with substantive protection, the existence of knowledge by the state is of course crucial before it can be held accountable for failing to provide the requisite procedural protection.[231]
2. Procedural protection has to be applied in a non-discriminatory way in order to satisfy Art. 14 ECHR. This may also require positive measures, in the sense that procedures not simply have to be applied in the same way with respect to members of the majority and minorities. For example, if necessary, these procedures have to be adapted to facilitate effective participation[232] or to specifically take into account the discriminatory nature of a human rights violation.[233]
3. The principle of proportionality requires that, the more serious the human rights violation, the more procedural protection is required. In the context of Art. 8 ECHR, the right to respect for family life, the Court has, for example, acknowledged that more procedural protection is required in cases concerning access rights and parental authority – compared with cases concerning placement in care – as the former is a more severe interference because it entails the risk that family relations are effectively curtailed.[234] The principle of proportionality also plays an important role in determining whether effective protection requires *ex ante* remedies (see Sect. 4.6.3.4). The link between procedural protection and the principle of proportionality is obvious from the fact that the Court mostly examines the level of procedural protection in the proportionality test. The European Court has the requirement of proportionate procedural protection in common with the U.S. Supreme Court. In the Supreme Court's case law, the strength of the procedural due process safeguards depends on the importance of the issue at stake: the Supreme Court has, for example, held that procedural

---

[231] *Mutatis mutandis K.U. v. Finland*, supra, note 115.

[232] For example, the reasonable accommodation of persons with a disability to enable them to participate effectively in the procedure, e.g. ECtHR 15 June 2004, *S.C. v. the United Kingdom* (Art. 6 ECHR).

[233] The Court has, for example, recognized a positive obligation to investigate possible racist motives, e.g. *Nachova and Others v. Bulgaria*, supra, note 207.

[234] ECtHR 26 Feburary 2002, No. 46544/99, *Kutzner v. Germany*, para. 67: "(...) a stricter scrutiny is called for both of any further limitations, such as restrictions placed by those authorities on parental rights and access, and of any legal safeguards designed to secure an effective protection of the right of parents and children to respect for their family life. Such further limitations entail the danger that family relations between the parents and a young child are effectively curtailed."

protection needs to be higher in cases of the cutting of welfare benefits[235] than in cases concerning the termination of social security benefits, because the need of a social security beneficiary is likely to be less than the need of the welfare recipient.[236] The application of the principle of proportionality to procedural 'protection by the law' is compatible with Alexy's theoretical account of 'protection by the law' above.

4. As with substantive protection, providing sufficient procedural protection is particularly important in cases involving conflicting rights.[237] Xenos has argued that it is crucial to develop a 'framework of due process' in order to deal with such conflicts.[238] According to Xenos, "[a]s long as due process has been observed, it is primarily for the state's authorities to strike the fair balance of competing interests, due to their better position to evaluate in detail the plethora of *ad hoc* information of each case."[239] As with substantive protection, the European Court therefore applies light scrutiny[240] in cases where such a 'framework of due process' is in place.[241]
5. As with substantive protection, the principle of effectiveness has been the catalyzer of the Court's procedural protection case law.[242] While the choice of means to provide procedural 'protection by the law' in principle falls within the state's margin of appreciation,[243] the 'baseline' of the principle of effectiveness may in

---

[235] *Goldberg v. Kelly*, supra, note 52.

[236] *Mathews v. Elridge*, supra, note 227. While the Court required a pre-termination hearing in the case of *Goldberg v. Kelly*, this was not required in *Mathews v. Elridge*.

[237] See, for example, the case discussed above of *Calvelli and Ciglio v. Italy*, supra, note 139. For a similar argument, see Brems and Lavrysen, supra, note 99, 183–184. See also O. De Schutter and F. Tulkens, "Rights in Conflict: the European Court of Human Rights as a Pragmatic Institution" in E. Brems, *Conflicts Between Fundamental Rights* (Antwerp: Intersentia, 2008), 210–213.

[238] Xenos, supra, note 11, 137. Xenos refers to the cases of ECtHR 26 May 1994, No. 16969/90, *Keegan v. Ireland*; ECtHR (GC) 13 July 2000, Nos. 39221/98; 41963/98, *Scozzari and Giunta v. Italy*; *Kutzner v. Germany*, supra, note 234; ECtHR 26 September 2006, No. 36065/97, *H.K. v. Finland*; and ECtHR 18 December 2008, No. 39948/06, *Saviny v. Ukraine*. See, however, the case of ECtHR (GC) 13 February 2003, No. 42326/98, *Odièvre v. France*, para. 49 in which the Court rejected the need for procedural protection in a conflicting rights case, because it considered the 'constitutional' solution of a blanket preference for the right to remain anonymous of the natural mother, above the right to privacy to gain access to information about one's origins of the adopted child.

[239] Ibid., 138.

[240] By allowing the state a so-called 'wide margin of appreciation'. This concept will be addressed more elaborately in Sect. 4.7.

[241] *Mosley v. the United Kingdom*, supra, note 181, para. 124, in which the Court acknowledges "the diversity of practice among member States as to how to balance the competing interests of respect for private life and freedom of expression" and recognizes that this results in a wide margin of appreciation.

[242] See, for example, the leading case of *Airey v. Ireland*, supra, note 37, discussed infra.

[243] E.g. ibid., para. 26. See also ECtHR 13 December 2012, Nos. 3675/04 and 23264/04, *Flamenbaum and Others v. France*, para. 159, in which the Court held, in the context of procedural protection, that "si l'État est tenu de prendre dûment en considération les intérêts particuliers dont il a l'obligation d'assurer le respect en vertu de l'article 8, il y a lieu, en principe, de lui laisser le

some cases prompt the Court to require more 'detailed' protection. In the case of *Zehentner v. Austria* the Court, for example, held that "persons who lack legal capacity are particularly vulnerable and States may thus have a positive obligation under Article 8 to provide them with specific protection by the law."[244] The principle of effectiveness may in certain cases also require – besides *ex post* remedies – the development of *ex ante* remedies (see Sect. 4.6.3.4). The area in which the Court arguably has developed the most 'detailed' procedural protection is the context of secret surveillance measures. The Court *inter alia* requires the following safeguards to be in place: a definition of "the nature of the offences which may give rise to an interception order; a definition of the categories of people liable to have their communications monitored; a limit on the duration of such monitoring; the procedure to be followed for examining, using and storing the data obtained; the precautions to be taken when communicating the data to other parties; and the circumstances in which data obtained may or must be erased or the records destroyed"[245]; the provision of information to the persons concerned as soon as notification can be made without jeopardizing the purpose of the surveillance after its termination[246]; the determination of "the authorities competent to permit, carry out and supervise them, and the kind of remedy provided by the national law",[247] in particular the requirement of effective scrutiny by the courts[248] and overall control over the system of secret surveillance by an independent body.[249] The Court has provided a rationale for its firm position in its first case on secret surveillance measures, *Klass and Others v. Germany*: "being aware of the danger such a law poses of undermining or even destroying democracy on the ground of defending it, [the Court] affirms that the Contracting States may not, in the name of the struggle against espionage and terrorism, adopt whatever measures they deem appropriate."[250]

As this short overview teaches us that the general principles of procedural and substantive 'protection by the law' are thus largely the same, and in order to avoid redundancy, it is more interesting to focus on some procedurally specific issues instead: (1) the effectiveness and (2) accessibility of procedures, (3) accountability and (4) the adequate timeframe of procedural protection.

---

choix des moyens à employer pour remplir ses obligations." The applicants complained about the fact that the entire project concerning the extension of the runway of a local airport could not be examined by a single judge. The Court did not find this 'fragmentation' of procedures problematic because the applicants nonetheless enjoyed sufficient procedural protection.

[244] ECtHR 16 July 2009, No. 20082/02, *Zehentner v. Austria*, para. 63.

[245] E.g. ECtHR 28 June 2007, No. 62540/00, *Association for European Integration and Human Rights and Ekimdzhiev v. Bulgaria*, para. 76.

[246] Ibid., para. 90.

[247] Ibid., para. 77.

[248] ECtHR 8 June 2006, No. 10337/04 *Lupsa v. Romania*, para. 34.

[249] *Association for European Integration and Human Rights and Ekimdzhiev v. Bulgaria*, supra, note 245, para. 87.

[250] ECtHR (GC) 6 September 1978, No. 5029/71, *Klass and Others v. Germany*, para. 49.

4.6.3.1 Access to Procedures

As illustrated by the abortion cases, there may be a right of access to a certain procedure implicit in substantive Convention rights. In *Tysiąc v. Poland*, the Court held that:

> (…) the concepts of lawfulness and the rule of law in a democratic society command that measures affecting fundamental human rights be, in certain cases, subject to some form of procedure before an independent body competent to review the reasons for the measures and the relevant evidence (…). In ascertaining whether this condition has been satisfied, a comprehensive view must be taken of the applicable procedures (…). In circumstances such as those in issue in the instant case, such a procedure should guarantee to a pregnant woman at least the possibility to be heard in person and to have her views considered. The competent body should also issue written grounds for its decision.[251]

Art. 8 ECHR, the right to privacy, may thus encompass a right of access to a procedure before an independent – but not necessarily judicial – body that provides sufficient procedural safeguards. This clearly resembles the requirements of Art. 13 ECHR, the right to an effective remedy.[252] This overlap between the procedural requirements under Art. 8 ECHR and those under Art. 13 ECHR was acknowledged by the *Tysiąc* Court, as it did not examine the complaint under Art. 13 ECHR separately, because both complaints essentially overlapped.[253]

---

[251] *Tysiąc v. Poland*, supra, note 190, para. 117.

[252] See e.g. ECtHR 25 March 1983, Nos. 5947/72; 6205/73; 7052/75; 7061/75; 7107/75; 7113/75; 7136/75, *Silver and Others v. the United Kingdom*, para. 113: "The principles that emerge from the Court's jurisprudence on the interpretation of Article 13 (…) include the following: (a) where an individual has an arguable claim to be the victim of a violation of the rights set forth in the Convention, he should have a remedy before a national authority in order both to have his claim decided and, if appropriate, to obtain redress (…); (b) the authority referred to in Article 13 (…) may not necessarily be a judicial authority but, if it is not, its powers and the guarantees which it affords are relevant in determining whether the remedy before it is effective (…)."

[253] *Tysiąc v. Poland*, supra, note 190, para. 135. See similarly *A, B and C v. Ireland*, supra, note 153, para. 274. In the case of ECtHR 28 January 2003, No. 44647/98, *Peck v. the United Kingdom* – concerning the disclosure to the press by local authorities of a CCTV tape in which the applicant was seen attempting to commit suicide in public – the Court considered it more appropriate to consider the lack of an effective domestic remedy under Art. 13 ECHR than under Art. 8 ECHR (para. 90). Again, this illustrates the overlap of both sets of procedural requirements. In a case concerning the night flight scheme of Heathrow airport, the Court, on the other hand, found the remedy of judicial 'Wednesbury unreasonableness' review insufficient for the purposes of Art. 13 ECHR (paras. 141–142), whereas it did not find a procedural violation of Art. 8 ECHR (para. 128–129). This suggests that in some cases Art. 13 ECHR may provide more protection. On the other hand, procedural protection implicitly encompassed by a substantive Convention right may sometimes be broader than the explicit procedural protection under Art. 13 ECHR. In the case of *Redfearn* the Court found a 'procedural' violation of Art. 11 ECHR, while rejecting the complaint under Art. 13 ECHR, because this provision "does not require the law to provide an effective remedy where the alleged violation arises from primary legislation" (*Redfearn v. the United Kingdom*, supra, note 151, para. 62, with reference to ECtHR (GC) 21 February 1986, No. 8793/79, *James and Others v. the United Kingdom*, para. 85).

In some cases, a substantive Convention right may even encompass a right of access to court. The case of *Koch v. Germany* concerned the refusal to give a paralyzed woman authorization to acquire a lethal dose of medication that would allow her to commit suicide. The Court found a violation of Art. 8 ECHR because the domestic courts should have examined the merits of the applicant's claim[254] – they had declared the applicant's claim inadmissible on procedural grounds. Similarly, in *Zehentner v. Austria* concerning the applicant's eviction from her apartment, the Court considered that "[a]ny person at risk of an interference of this magnitude should in principle be able to have the proportionality of the measure determined by an independent tribunal in the light of the relevant principles under Article 8 of the Convention",[255] the right to respect for home. This 'right to judicial review'[256] overlaps with the right of access to court, as recognized under Art. 6 ECHR, the right to a fair trial.[257] Again, this overlap is acknowledged by Court as in both cases it did not consider it necessary to examine the applicant's complaint under Art. 6 ECHR separately.[258] It seems that the Court only recognized a right of access to court – i.e. a higher degree of protection – implicit in a substantive human rights provision with respect to the most serious human rights issue: this is an application of the principle of proportionality.

Another important source of procedural case law concerns access to information. The case of *Gaskin v. the United Kingdom* concerned the refusal to allow the applicant full access to confidential files on his placement in foster care as a child.

---

[254] *Koch v. Germany*, supra, note 196, paras. 71–72. In the earlier case of *Haas v. Switserland*, supra, note 196 – concerning the refusal to prescribe the applicant, who had suffered from a serious bipolar affective disorder for about 20 years, a lethal dose of medication – the Court, however, accepted that "the requirement for a medical prescription, issued on the basis of a full psychiatric assessment" was sufficient to meet the obligation under Art. 2 ECHR, the right to life, "to establish a procedure capable of ensuring that a decision to end one's life does indeed correspond to the free wish of the individual concerned" (para. 58).

[255] *Zehentner v. Austria*, supra, note 244, para. 59.

[256] *Koch v. Germany*, supra, note 196, para. 53.

[257] On procedural restrictions that restrict the right of access to court, see e.g. ECtHR (GC) 21 November 2001, No. 35763/97, *Al-Adsani v. the United Kingdom*, para. 53: "The right of access to a court is not (...) absolute, but may be subject to limitations; these are permitted by implication since the right of access by its very nature calls for regulation by the State. (...) It must be satisfied that the limitations applied do not restrict or reduce the access left to the individual in such a way or to such an extent that the very essence of the right is impaired. Furthermore, a limitation will not be compatible with Article 6 § 1 if it does not pursue a legitimate aim and if there is no reasonable relationship of proportionality between the means employed and the aim sought to be achieved (...)."

[258] *Koch v. Germany*, supra, note 196, para. 84; *Zehentner v. Austria*, supra, note 244, para. 82. See on the other hand the case of ECtHR 25 July 2002, No. 48553/99, *Sovtransavto Holding v. Ukraine* – concerning a dispute about the increase of the capital of a private company of which the applicant was a minority shareholder – in which the Court examined both the "obligation to afford judicial procedures that offer the necessary procedural guarantees", as encompassed by the right to property, Art. 1 Protocol 1 (para. 96), as well as the right of access to court under Art. 6 ECHR (para. 81).

While there was the possibility to request a waiver of confidentiality from the contributors of these files, this was not sufficient for the Court because:

> (…) under such a system the interests of the individual seeking access to records relating to his private and family life must be secured when a contributor to the records either is not available or improperly refuses consent. Such a system is only in conformity with the principle of proportionality if it provides that an independent authority finally decides whether access has to be granted in cases where a contributor fails to answer or withholds consent. No such procedure was available to the applicant in the present case.[259]

The Court thereby links procedural protection with proportionality analysis: access to a procedure before an independent authority is necessary in order to ensure that the proportionality of state action or inaction (a substantive question) is adequately assessed.[260] The *Gaskin* case as well as the *Zehentner* case above, illustrate what Sébastien Van Drooghenbroeck calls the obligation on the national authorities to employ the proportionality principle – one of the formal aspects of proportionality.[261] Procedural protection in this case thus primarily has an instrumental function: it prompts the state authorities to make an appropriate substantive decision themselves.

The case of *Roche v. the United Kingdom,* in turn, concerned an ex-serviceman who was unable to gain access to his service records in order to be able to verify whether his severe health problems were caused by his participation in mustard and nerve gas test while serving in the British army. Taking into account the credible link between the military tests and the applicant's health problems, as well as the lack of any pressing reason to withhold the information, the Court held that:

> (…) a positive obligation arose to provide an 'effective and accessible procedure' enabling the applicant to have access to 'all relevant and appropriate information' (…) which would allow him to assess any risk to which he had been exposed during his participation in the tests (…).[262]

The Court had considered a procedure for the Pensions Appeal Tribunal appropriate in the earlier case of *McGinley and Egan v. the United Kingdom.*[263] The case

---

[259] *Gaskin v. the United Kingdom*, supra, note 17, para. 49.

[260] In the case of *Odièvre v. France*, supra, note 238, paras. 43–49 – concerning an adopted child who wanted access to information, to enable her to trace her natural mother who had abandoned her at birth – the Court did not consider such a procedure necessary, essentially because it considered a blanket ban on access to such information to be proportionate in the light of the countervailing right to privacy of the mother. As the Court considered the refusal proportionate anyway, it saw no need to require a separate procedure to examine its proportionality in practice.

[261] S. Van Drooghenbroeck, *La Proportionnalité dans le Droit de la Convention Européenne des Droits de* l'Homme (Bruxelles: Facultés Universitaires Saint-Louis, 2001), 322.

[262] ECtHR (GC) 19 October 2005, No. 32555/96, *Roche v. the United Kingdom*, para. 162. In ECtHR 12 June 2012, No. 42730/05, *Savda v. Turkey*, para. 98, the Court has *mutatis mutandis* found similar procedural safeguards to be inherent in the right to freedom of religion, Art. 9 ECHR. This case concerned the absence of a procedure to verify whether the applicant met the condition for recognition as a conscientious objector.

[263] ECtHR 9 June 1998, Nos. 21825/93; 23414/94, *McGinley and Egan v. the United Kingdom.*

concerned access to health information in the context of former servicemen applying for an increased pension as a result of health damage likely sustained during participation in nuclear tests. In the case of *Roche* such a procedure was, however, not appropriate, as the applicant wished to obtain information "independently of any litigation and, in particular, of a pension application."[264] The Court held that:

> The Court's judgment in McGinley and Egan did not imply that a disclosure procedure linked to litigation could, as a matter of principle, fulfil the positive obligation of disclosure to an individual, such as the present applicant, who has consistently pursued such disclosure independently of any litigation. Consistently with judgments in Guerra and Others and Gaskin and as the applicant argued, it is an obligation of disclosure (...) not requiring the individual to litigate to obtain it.[265]

While the cases of *Koch* and *Zehentner* illustrate that procedural protection sometimes requires access to courts, the case of *Roche* on the other hand illustrates that such a general remedy may sometimes be too burdensome to provide effective protection.[266] In such a case, more specific guarantees may be necessary, such as the provision of a specific administrative procedure.

4.6.3.2 Effectiveness Procedures

The Court has always stressed that such procedures need not only be accessible, but also effective. The broad implications of the principle of effectiveness on procedural protection are probably best captured in the old case of *Airey v. Ireland*. Mrs. Airey wished to obtain a decree of judicial separation[267] from her abusive husband. In the absence of legal aid and because she was not in a financial position to pay the costs involved herself, she was unable to find a solicitor willing to act for her. The Court held that:

> Effective respect for private or family life obliges Ireland to make this means of protection effectively accessible, when appropriate, to anyone who may wish to have recourse thereto. However, it was not effectively accessible to the applicant: not having been put in a position in which she could apply to the High Court (...), she was unable to seek recognition in law of her de facto separation from her husband.[268]

---

[264] *Roche v. the United Kingdom*, supra, note 262, para. 164.

[265] Ibid., para. 165.

[266] See also *A, B and C v. Ireland*, supra, note 153, para. 263, in which the Court considered that "neither the medical consultation nor litigation options relied on by the Government constituted effective and accessible procedures which allowed the third applicant to establish her right to a lawful abortion in Ireland."

[267] At that time, a real divorce was not allowed under Irish law. After a judicial separation, a couple remained married but was discharged of the obligation to cohabit.

[268] *Airey v. Ireland*, supra, note 37, para. 33. For these reasons, the Court also found a violation of the right of access to court (paras. 26–28). For a strikingly similar case, see U.S. Supreme Court 2 March 1971, *Boddie v. Connecticut*, 401 U.S. 371. In this case, the Supreme Court found that the fact that poor women were unable to bring divorce suits due to their inability to pay high court fees and costs, was in denial of procedural due process.

In the European Convention, there generally is no right to legal aid in non-criminal cases. However, in certain non-criminal cases, if the individual does not have sufficient means and if there is a human right at stake, the principle of effectiveness does require such aid.[269] The state is therefore under a positive obligation to establish a legal aid scheme which facilitates effective access to procedures in order to effectively protect human rights.[270]

In order to be effective in practice, a remedy may also require additional procedural measures. The case of *Mikulić v. Croatia* concerned the refusal of the applicant's alleged father to undergo a DNA test in the context of paternity proceedings. While the Court did not consider the impossibility to compel the alleged father to comply with a court order for a DNA test to be incompatible as such with Art. 8 ECHR, the right to privacy, the Court did hold that:

> (…) under such a system the interests of the individual seeking the establishment of paternity must be secured when paternity cannot be established by means of DNA testing. The lack of any procedural measure to compel the alleged father to comply with the court order is only in conformity with the principle of proportionality if it provides alternative means enabling an independent authority to determine the paternity claim speedily. No such procedure was available to the applicant in the present case (…).[271]

Summarizing, the procedural guarantees implicitly encompassed by substantive Convention rights may thus require access to a procedure – administrative, judicial or both. To a certain extent, these requirements overlap with those of Art. 6 ECHR and Art. 13 ECHR. Furthermore, additional positive measures may be required in order to enhance the effectiveness of a certain procedure.

4.6.3.3 Accountability

Procedures must be designed as to ensure accountability for human rights violations. This is particularly evident from the procedural obligations inherent in Art. 2 ECHR, the right to life, and Art. 3 ECHR, the prohibition of torture and of inhuman or degrading treatment or punishment. For example, in the case of *Nachova and Others v. Bulgaria*, the Court has held that Art. 2 ECHR, the right to life, requires that:

> (…) there should be some form of effective official investigation when individuals have been killed as a result of the use of force (…). The essential purpose of such an investigation is to secure the effective implementation of the domestic laws safeguarding the right to life and, in those cases involving State agents or bodies, to ensure their accountability for deaths occurring under their responsibility (…).[272]

---

[269] See also ECtHR 15 February 2005, No. 68416/01, *Steel and Morris v. the United Kingdom*. In this case, the Court held that the provision of legal aid depends "inter alia upon the importance of what is at stake for the applicant in the proceedings, the complexity of the relevant law and procedure and the applicant's capacity to represent him or herself effectively" (para. 61).

[270] According to the Airey Court, another means to provide effective access could be the simplification of the procedure (para. 26).

[271] ECtHR 7 February 2002, No. 53176/99, *Mikulić v. Croatia*, para. 64.

[272] *Nachova and Others v. Bulgaria*, supra, note 207, para. 110.

Similarly, in the case of *Assenov and Others v. Bulgaria*, concerning the obligation to investigate violations of Art. 3 ECHR, the prohibition of torture and of inhuman or degrading treatment or punishment, the Court held that:

> This investigation (...) should be capable of leading to the identification and punishment of those responsible (...). If this were not the case, the general legal prohibition of torture and inhuman and degrading treatment and punishment, despite its fundamental importance (...), would be ineffective in practice and it would be possible in some cases for agents of the State to abuse the rights of those within their control with virtual impunity.[273]

The concern in both cases with accountability and the fight against impunity is related to the instrumental function of procedural protection. The procedural obligation is based on the need to ensure effective protection of the substantive right concerned[274]: accountability deters state agents from committing actions or inactions[275] that result in the death or ill-treatment of individuals. Accountability, however, also has another function: it allows the victims of human rights violation to understand what happened and to identify those responsible.[276] This relates to the intrinsic function of procedural protection: it is crucial that victims or their next-of-kin are provided with procedural justice.[277] This explains, for example, why the Court has recognized participation rights of victims or their next-of-kin as part of the obligation to conduct an effective official investigation.[278]

4.6.3.4 Adequate Time Frame

The effectiveness of procedural protection may depend on the time frame. This is perfectly illustrated by the abortion case of *Tysiąc v. Poland*, in which the Court held that:

> (...) the very nature of the issues involved in decisions to terminate a pregnancy is such that the time factor is of critical importance. The procedures in place should therefore ensure that such decisions are timely so as to limit or prevent damage to a woman's health which might be occasioned by a late abortion. Procedures in which decisions concerning the availability of lawful abortion are reviewed post factum cannot fulfill such a function. In the Court's view, the absence of such preventive procedures in the domestic law can be said to amount to the failure of the State to comply with its positive obligations under Article 8 of the Convention.[279]

---

[273] *Assenov and Others v. Bulgaria*, supra, note 201, para. 102.

[274] Mowbray, supra, note 38, 29.

[275] E.g. *Budayeva and Others v. Russia*, supra, note 210, para. 142.

[276] J. Van Dyke, "Promoting Accountability for Human Rights Abuses, 8 *Chapman Law Review* (2008), 156. In ECtHR (GC) 13 December 2012, No. 39630/09, *El-Masri v. "The Former Yugoslav Republic of Macedonia"*, para. 191, the Court recognized a 'right to the truth' as implicit in the procedural obligations under Art. 3 ECHR.

[277] Brems and Lavrysen, supra, note 99, 193–194.

[278] *Ramsahai and others v. the Netherlands*, supra, note 224, para. 321 (Art. 2 ECHR) and *97 Members of the Gldani Congregation of Jehovah's Witnesses and Others v. Georgia*, supra, note 206, para. 122 (Art. 3 ECHR).

[279] *Tysiąc v. Poland*, supra, note 190, para. 118.

For the applicant, it was crucial that she could challenge the refusal to allow access to a lawful abortion on health grounds in a timely way. More generally, the case illustrates that *ex post* remedies are not sufficient in cases where there is a risk of irreparable harm: an *ex ante* procedure is necessary as to allow an individual to challenge the decision concerned before the irreparable harm occurs.

Another example is the case of *Storck v. Germany*, concerning the confinement of the applicant in a private institution for 20 years, against her will and without court order authorizing her detention. While there was a criminal offence of deprivation of liberty, as well as the possibility to claim compensation for damage caused by unlawful detention, the Court ruled that the applicant did not enjoy sufficient procedural protection for the sake of Art. 5(1) ECHR, the right to liberty:

> (…) the Court, having regard to the importance of the right to liberty, does not consider that such retrospective measures alone provide effective protection for individuals in such a vulnerable position as the applicant. (…) It must be borne in mind that the applicant, once detained and treated with strong antipsychotic medication, was no longer in a position to secure independent outside help.[280]

Based on this finding, the Court considered that no separate issue arose under Art. 5(4) ECHR, that generally requires the provision of a remedy to challenge the legality of detention.[281] Again an *ex post* remedy was not considered sufficient in the light of the importance of the right to liberty and the possibility of irreparable harm, as the applicant would be unable to secure independent outside help. Another reason may be that by 'privatizing' the power to detain a mentally ill person, the state had deprived the applicant from existing *ex ante* remedies that would have applied in the case of state organized detention. In a similar sense, the Court found a violation of Art. 8 ECHR, the right to privacy, regarding the applicant's complaint about administration of drugs against her will, because the possibility of prosecution on the basis of the criminal offence of assault was not considered sufficient:

> (…) just as in cases of deprivation of liberty, the Court finds that such retrospective measures alone are not sufficient to provide appropriate protection of the physical integrity of individuals in such a vulnerable position as the applicant.[282]

The Court has, however, refrained from generally obliging states to develop *ex ante* remedies against all kinds of human rights violations. The case of *Mosley v. the United Kingdom,* for example, concerned a complaint by the former International Automobile Federation president about the publication in *News of the World* of an article entitled "F1 boss has sick Nazi orgy with 5 hookers", containing photographs of him engaged in sexual activities. The magazine was convicted by a domestic court for breaching the applicant's privacy, holding *inter alia* that there had not been a Nazi element to his sexual activities. In Strasbourg, the applicant argued that effective protection against violations of Art. 8 ECHR, the right to privacy, required the existence of a legally binding pre-notification rule, obliging the press to give

---

[280] *Storck v. Germany*, supra, note 22, para. 105.

[281] Ibid., para. 118.

[282] Ibid., para. 150.

prior notification before the publication of an article which interfered with an individual's privacy, enabling him or her to apply for an injunction in time. The Court started its examination by recapitulating its prior case law:

> The Court further observes that, in its examination to date of the measures in place at domestic level to protect Article 8 rights in the context of freedom of expression, it has implicitly accepted that ex post facto damages provide an adequate remedy for violations of Article 8 rights arising from the publication by a newspaper of private information.[283]

The Court did not consider it necessary to change the approach in the case at hand, taking into account the state's wide margin of appreciation, the doubts about the clarity and potential effectiveness of such a pre-notification rule, and most importantly, the countervailing principle of press freedom.[284]

The fact that the *Mosley* Court, despite its prior case law, continued to examine whether an *ex ante* remedy may have be required in the case at hand, teaches us that the need for *ex ante* remedies to provide effective protection of human rights cannot be *a priori* excluded. An *ex ante* remedy will be required, taking into account the state's margin of appreciation, when (1) the effectiveness of that remedy is established, and (2) when imposing such a remedy respects the principle of proportionality, taking into account countervailing principles – the risk of irreparable harm will be a weighty element in the proportionality analysis. Such an interpretation appears to be fully in line with Alexy's above discussed theoretical conception of procedural protection.

4.7 Margin of Appreciation

Substantive and procedural 'protection by the law' may be the key to a better application of the so-called margin of appreciation doctrine – one of the European Court's most important but nonetheless controversial adjudication tools. The Court uses the margin of appreciation as an instrument of judicial deference to the decisions of domestic authorities. The doctrine is based on the premise that the power of the Court, as a supranational institution, "to review decisions taken by domestic authorities should be more limited than the powers of a national constitutional court or other national bodies that monitor or review compliance with an entrenched bill of rights."[285] If the margin of appreciation is wide, the Court applies light scrutiny, whereas if the margin of appreciation is narrow, it applies strict scrutiny. The Court

---

[283] *Mosley v. the United Kingdom*, supra, note 181, para. 120.

[284] Ibid., paras. 118–132.

[285] Letsas, supra, note 8, 721. Letsas calls this the 'structural concept of the margin of appreciation'. Sometimes, the Court also applies the margin of appreciation in order to examine whether a fair balance was struck between individual rights and the public interest (706). According to Letsas, this 'substantive concept of the margin of appreciation', however, is not really useful as it "lacks any normative force that can help us strike a balance between individual rights and public interest" (711).

uses a set of criteria in order to establish whether the margin is wide or narrow, or something in between. The margin is, for example, wide in socio-economic matters when there is no consensus between the European states as to whether a certain interest is worthy of protection or on how to protect it, or when public morals are at stake. The margin is, for example, narrow when a particularly important facet of an individual's existence or identity is at stake.[286] The Court, moreover, generally allows a wider margin of appreciation in cases concerning positive obligations than in negative obligation cases.[287]

The case of *Aksu v. Turkey* concerned a complaint by a Turkish man of Roma origin, that certain government-funded publications included stereotypes about Roma which were offensive and discriminatory. According to the Court, "any negative stereotyping of a group, when it reaches a certain level, is capable of impacting on the group's sense of identity and the feelings of self-worth and self-confidence of members of the group."[288] The Court therefore held that the issue came within the scope of Art. 8 ECHR, the right to respect for private life, and went on to examine whether the state had complied with its positive obligation to protect the applicant's private life. The Court then turned to the discussion on the extent of the margin of appreciation. It tended to granting a wide margin of appreciation on the basis that conflicting rights were at stake. However, the Court then remarked that:

> All of this presupposes that an effective legal system was in place and operating for the protection of the rights falling within the notion of 'private life', and was available to the applicant.[289]

Because of the importance of freedom of expression (Art. 10 ECHR), the Court found that there had not been a violation of Art. 8 ECHR. What, however, is interesting from the perspective of this contribution, is that the Court has clearly linked the margin of appreciation to the extent that 'protection by the law', both substantive and procedural, was provided.[290] In the absence of such a legal framework, the Court will apply strict scrutiny. If the state has, however, developed a legal framework that

---

[286] For an elaborate discussion on the margin of appreciation in the Court's case law, see Y. Arai-Takahasi, *The margin of appreciation doctrine and the principle of proportionality in the jurisprudence of the ECHR* (Oxford: Intersentia, 2000).

[287] *Women on Waves and others v. Portugal*, supra, note 31, para. 40.

[288] *Aksu v. Turkey*, supra, note 122, para. 58.

[289] Ibid., para. 68. See similarly ECtHR 27 April 2009, No. 39311/05, *Karako v. Hungary*, para. 19: "(...) the choice of measures designed to secure compliance with that obligation falls within the Contracting States' margin of appreciation. The Court considers, as a minimum requirement, that an effective legal system must be in place and operating for the protection of the rights falling within the notion of "private life", and it is satisfied that such a system was indeed available to the applicant in the present case." With respect to procedural protection, see *Zehentner v. Austria*, supra, note 244, para. 58: "The procedural safeguards available to the individual will be especially material in determining whether the respondent State has, when fixing the regulatory framework, remained within its margin of appreciation."

[290] As noted in Sect. 4.5.1.2, such a legal framework is particularly important in cases such as Aksu, that involve conflicting rights.

duly takes into account the Convention rights concerned, then the Court will only apply light scrutiny to the examination of the facts at hand.[291]

Such an approach is in line with some calls in legal doctrine that the Court should focus more on procedural review and less on substantive review.[292] In any event, such procedural review can never entirely be a substitute for substantive review, even when the margin of appreciation is wide. In this sense, the Court itself has repeatedly acknowledged that "[the] margin of appreciation goes hand in hand with a European supervision embracing both the law and the decisions applying it."[293] The advantage of the *Aksu* approach is that, in most cases, the Court does not have to fully engage with the sometimes very complex factual circumstances of the case. Arguably, engagement with the facts of the case is a very burdensome challenge for a supranational court, and the Court may therefore not be best placed to make a sound factual analysis. However, this does not necessarily go at the cost of human rights protection, as extended 'protection by the law', both substantive and procedural, is required at the domestic level. In this sense, such an approach encourages member states to act in line with the principle of subsidiarity. This principle, which has been stressed over and over again in the recent Brighton Declaration on the future of the Court,[294] lays the primary responsibility for human rights protection with the member states, and confines the role of the Court to those cases in which the domestic system fails to provide effective protection.[295] 'Protection by the law', arguably the most effective way to prevent human rights violations, lies at the heart of such a true subsidiary approach.

4.8 Conclusion

In the case of *McCann and Others v. the United Kingdom*, the European Court of Human Rights has elucidated its general policy that "it is not the role of the Convention institutions to examine in abstracto the compatibility of national

[291] For a similar argument that the Court should only provide a wide margin of appreciation when procedural justice is delivered at the domestic level, see: Brems and Lavrysen, supra, note 99, 195–198, with reference to e.g. ECtHR 27 March 2008, No. 44009/05, *Shtukaturov v. Russia*, para. 89.

[292] E.g. J. Gerards, "The Prism of Fundamental Rights", 8 *European Constitutional Law* Review (2012), 197–201.

[293] *Leyla Şahin v. Turkey*, supra, note 219, para. 110.

[294] Declaration adopted at the High Level Conference on the Future of the European Court of Human Rights, Brighton, 19–20 April 2012. The Court has linked the principle of subsidiarity with procedural 'protection by the law' in the case of *Koch v. Germany*, supra, note 196, para. 71: "Having regard to the principle of subsidiarity, the Court considers that it is primarily up to the domestic courts to examine the merits of the applicant's claim. The Court has found above that the domestic authorities are under an obligation to examine the merits of the applicant's claim (...)."

[295] In this sense, subsidiarity has two dimensions: a domestic and a supranational. Governments too often abuse the concept of subsidiarity to blame the Court for being too 'activist', and to call upon the Court to show more judicial restraint, while ignoring the domestic dimension of the concept.

legislative or constitutional provisions with the requirements of the Convention."[296] The Court's general policy is to provide 'individual' rather than 'constitutional justice'.[297] According to Steven Greer, 'individual justice' focuses on "[providing] every deserving applicant with a remedy for a Convention violation", while 'constitutional justice' focuses on "[ensuring] that administrative and judicial processes in member states effectively conform to pan-European Convention standards."[298] According to Fyrnys, 'constitutional justice' relates to the Court's lawmaking role, i.e. "the generation and stabilization of normative expectations beyond an individual case by providing legal arguments for later disputes."[299] Especially because of the overburdening of the Court due to the enormous increase of the amount of applications,[300] Greer and others have argued that the Court should focus more on delivering 'constitutional justice' rather than on delivering 'individual justice' in every single case.[301]

Through its emerging case law on the positive obligation to adequately protect human rights – or 'protection by the law' – the European Court has put a step in the direction of a more 'constitutionalized' jurisprudence. The 'protection by the law' case law illustrates the adoption by the Court of a broader perspective than simply the individual circumstances of the applicant at hand, in order to scrutinize the systemic failures in the domestic state's legal system that have caused the applicant's human rights violation or at least allowed it to take place. Whenever the Court identifies such a failure, the importance of its findings extends far beyond the individual circumstances of the applicant at hand: the respondent state – as well as other states with similar problems – will have to provide adequate 'protection by the law' in line with Convention standards. In Cesare Pitea's words, "the 'particular' (a violation in a specific case) is the hook for reaching the 'general' (shortcomings in the legal framework) through the causal link established between the latter and the former."[302] Thereby the Court provides 'constitutional justice', without, however, abandoning its 'individual justice' function. This is in line with the recent Brighton Declaration, in which the right of individual application was reaffirmed as the cornerstone of the

[296] McCann and Others v. the United Kingdom, supra, note 200, para. 153. Reference by C. Pitea, "Scoppola v. Italy (no. 3): The Grand Chamber faces the 'constitutional justice vs. individual justice' dilemma (but it doesn't tell)", 20 June 2012, strasbourgobservers.com.

[297] Pitea, supra, note 296.

[298] S. Greer, "Constitutionalizing Adjudication under the European Convention on Human Rights", 23 *Oxford Journal of Legal Studies* (2003), 405.

[299] M. Fyrnys, "Expanding Competences by Judicial Lawmaking: The Pilot Judgment Procedure of the European Court of Human Rights", 12 *German Law Journal* (2011), 1232.

[300] While the Court only received 8,400 applications in 1999 this exponentially increased to 57,100 in 2009 (ECtHR, "50 YEARS OF ACTIVITY – The European Court of Human Rights: Some Facts and Figures", echr.coe.int) and further to 64,500 in 2011 (ECtHR, "Analysis of statistics 2011", January 2012, echr.coe.int).

[301] E.g. Greer, supra, note 298, 405–433; S. Greer "What's Wrong with the European Convention on Human Rights?", 30 *Human Rights Quarterly* (2008) 680–702; L. Wildhaber, "A Constitutional Future for the European Court of Human Rights", 23 *Human Rights Law Journal* (2002), 161–165.

[302] Pitea, supra, note 296.

Convention system, while at the same time the Court was called to focus in particular on systemic and structural problems.[303]

As is apparent from the discussion above, the European Court has developed an impressive 'constitutional' jurisprudence on substantive as well as procedural 'protection by the law'. Where possible, this article has provided a comparison of the European Court's approach with the approach of the U.S. Supreme Court. While there is some similarity between 'procedural' protection by the law and the doctrine of procedural due process, the differences are remarkable. This is principally explained by the rejection of positive obligations by the Supreme Court, with the notable exception of so-called 'conditional' positive obligations.

This article has tried to identify certain general principles from the Court's 'protection by the law' case law. Three important conclusions can be drawn from this discussion. (1) 'Protection by the law' largely depends on the 'conceptual proximity' between the human rights violation on the one hand and the positive obligation to respect/protect/fulfill on the other. (2) Two principles are crucial in the development of the Court's 'protection by the law' jurisprudence: the principle of effectiveness and the principle of proportionality. Combined, these principles operate in a similar way as the theoretical account of 'protection by the law' provided by German constitutional law theorist Robert Alexy. However, there is an important limit to such an 'optimization' conception of 'protection by the law': the nature of Convention rights as minimum guarantees, which is reflected in the state's margin of appreciation to choose the means as to how to provide protection. (3) 'Protection by the law' is the key to the proper application of the margin of appreciation doctrine. The adequacy of 'protection by the law' must always be a proxy in the determination of the width of the state's margin of appreciation. There are some promising examples of cases in which the Court acknowledged the link between 'protection by the law' and the margin of appreciation doctrine – generalizing these examples would be a good step in the direction of 'true' respect for the subsidiarity principle.

---

[303] Brighton Declaration, supra, note 294, paras. 31 and 33. Another way of focusing on systemic and structural problems is through the application of the so-called 'pilot judgment procedure', see e.g. Fyrnys, supra, note 299, 1231–1260.

Chapter 5
The Adjudication Process and Reasoning at the International Criminal Court: The *Lubanga* Trial Chamber Judgment, Sentencing and Reparations

Susana SáCouto and Katherine Cleary

Abstract The article analyzes certain aspects of the first judgment issued by the International Criminal Court, as well as the accompanying decisions relating to sentencing and the principles according to which reparations will be awarded to victims of the convicted individual, Thomas Lubanga Dyilo. Specifically, the article addresses: (i) the considerable amount of time that elapsed between the close of trial and the issuance of the judgment in the *Lubanga Case*; (ii) the Trial Chamber's failure to adequately clarify in its judgment certain aspects of the crimes with which Mr. Lubanga was charged; (iii) the lack of clarification in the sentencing decision regarding the relationship among factors relevant to the sentence and the means by which the majority of the Chamber reached its conclusion that 14 years was the appropriate length of the sentence; and (iv) the purpose and timing of the Chamber's decision relating to reparations. In sum, the article finds that, while the overall approach of Trial Chamber I in presiding over the Court's first trial is to be commended, and the judgment is largely sound, the Court and its constituents – including the parties, affected communities and the broader public – may be better served if future Trial Chambers strive to deliver judgments within a shorter period of time, while also ensuring that their reasoning on the crimes charged is fully explained. Furthermore, future decisions on sentencing will benefit from greater clarity. Finally, Trial Chambers in other cases should reconsider whether it is wise to issue any decisions on reparations prior to a final judgment on the guilt of the accused.

S. SáCouto (✉) • K. Cleary
War Crimes Research Office, American University Washington College of Law, Washington, DC, USA
e-mail: ssacouto@wcl.american.edu; kcleary@wcl.american.edu

Y. Haeck and E. Brems (eds.), *Human Rights and Civil Liberties in the 21st Century*, Ius Gentium: Comparative Perspectives on Law and Justice 30,
DOI 10.1007/978-94-007-7599-2_5,

5.1 Introduction

On 14 March 2012, the International Criminal Court (ICC) issued its first judgment, convicting Congolese rebel leader Thomas Lubanga Dyilo of conscripting, enlisting, and using children under the age of 15 to participate in an armed conflict not of an international character.[1] Several months later, on 10 July 2012, the Chamber issued a decision sentencing Mr. Lubanga to 14 years in prison, with credit for time served.[2] Finally, on 7 August 2012, the Chamber issued a document entitled "Decision Establishing Principles and Procedures to be Applied to Reparations," by which it set forth "certain principles relating to reparations and the approach to be taken to their implementation,"[3] but declined to rule on any individual application for reparations or issue any specific order regarding the award of reparations to Mr. Lubanga's victims.[4] While this jurisprudence is notable in a number of respects, in light of the focus of this conference on the adjudication process and the reasoning of decisions dealing with human rights issues, this article will examine four limited aspects of the Trial Chamber's decisions. Specifically, the article analyzes: (i) the considerable amount of time that elapsed between the close of trial and the issuance of the judgment in the *Lubanga Case*; (ii) the Trial Chamber's failure to adequately clarify in its judgment certain aspects of the crimes with which Mr. Lubanga was charged; (iii) the lack of clarification in the sentencing decision regarding the relationship among factors relevant to the sentence and the means by which the majority of the Chamber reached its conclusion that 14 years was the appropriate length of the sentence; and (iv) the purpose and timing of the Chamber's decision relating to reparations.

5.2 Length of Time to Issue Judgment

Before turning to any of the substantive aspects of the Trial Chamber's judgment, it must be pointed out that the judgment was not delivered until well over 6 months after the closing arguments of the parties in the case,[5] and just under 6 years after Mr. Lubanga's initial transfer to the custody of the Court.[6] Admittedly, this was the ICC's first judgment. Moreover, the judgment is commendable in many respects: not only is it extremely well-organized, with a detailed table of contents at the

[1] See generally ICC (Trial Chamber Judgment), 14 March 2012, No. 01/04-01/06-2842, *The Prosecutor v. Thomas Lubanga Dyilo*, Judgment pursuant to Article 74 of the Statute.

[2] See generally ICC (Trial Chamber Decision), 10 July 2012, No. 01/04-01/06-2901, *The Prosecutor v. Thomas Lubanga Dyilo*, Decision on Sentence Pursuant to Article 76 of the Statute.

[3] ICC (Trial Chamber Decision) 7 August 2012, No. 01/04-01/06-2904, *The Prosecutor v. Thomas Lubanga Dyilo*, Decision Establishing Principles and Procedures to be Applied to Reparations, para. 181.

[4] Ibid.

[5] Ibid., para. 11 (noting that the parties' closing arguments were delivered 25 and 26 August 2011).

[6] See ICC (Pre-Trial Chamber), 17 March 2006, No. 01/04-01/06-38, *The Prosecutor v. Thomas Lubanga Dyilo*, Order Scheduling the First Appearance of Mr. Thomas Lubanga Dyilo, at 2 (noting that Mr. Lubanga was in the custody of the ICC as of 17 March 2006).

beginning,[7] but it also clearly and meticulously explains the Chamber's views on various issues that were before the court for the first time, including the Prosecution's use of intermediaries in its investigations.[8] In addition, the detail and clarity of the Chamber's explanations is consistent with an important goal of international criminal proceedings, namely contributing to the establishment of an accurate historical record of the circumstances surrounding the crimes with which an accused is charged.[9] Nevertheless, the timing of the *Lubanga* judgment is disappointing for a number of reasons. The first is that the judgment involves a single accused who was charged with a single war crime, although the same crime was charged in the context of both international and non-international armed conflict.[10] If the *Lubanga* Trial Chamber took well over 6 months to issue its judgment, it is unclear how the Court will deal with other cases involving multiple accused charged with multiple crimes.[11] Second, although the trend in international criminal law has been towards lengthy judgments issued months after the close of trial,[12] international criminal bodies have often been criticized for issuing judgments long after the end of trial.[13] Third, untimely judgments are obviously not in the interest of the accused, who, like

[7] See generally *Lubanga* Trial Judgment, supra, note 1.

[8] See generally *Lubanga* Trial Judgment, supra, note 1, paras. 178–484.

[9] See, e.g., Mark Ellis, "Combating Impunity and Enforcing Accountability as a Way to Promote Peace and Stability – The Role of International war Crimes Tribunals", 2 Journal of National Security Law And Policy (2008), 111, 112.

[10] As discussed below, while the Prosecutor only charged Mr. Lubanga with the crime of conscripting, enlisting, or using children to participate actively in *non-international* armed conflict, the Court's Pre-Trial Chamber expanded the scope of the charges and the Trial Chamber considered evidence regarding Mr. Lubanga's responsibility for the crime in both non-international and international armed conflict. See *infra* note 75 ff. and accompanying text.

[11] See, e.g., ICC (Pre-Trial Chamber), 1 October 2008, No. 01/04-01/07-717, 01/04-01/07-611, *The Prosecutor v. Germain Katanga and Mathieu Ngudjolo Chui*, Decision on the Confirmation of Chargesat 209–212 (involving two accused charged with seven counts of war crimes and three counts of crimes against humanity). In addition, other international criminal bodies have repeatedly dealt with cases involving upwards of four accused charged with multiple acts allegedly constituting war crimes, crimes against humanity and genocide. See, e.g., ICTY (Trial Chamber Judgment), 10 June 2010, No. IT-05-88-T, *The Prosecutor v. Vujadin Popović*, et al., at 832–888 (detailing the Chamber's holdings on multiple charges of genocide, war crimes and crimes against humanity against seven accused); ICTR (Trial Chamber Judgment), 24 June 2011, No. ICTR-97-21-T, *The Prosecutor v. Pauline Nyiramasuhuko* et al., at 1449–1452 (detailing the Chamber's holdings on multiple charges of genocide, war crimes and crimes against humanity against six accused).

[12] Indeed, the trial judgment of the Special Court for Sierra Leone in the case against Charles Taylor was issued 14 months after the parties delivered their closing arguments and is over 2,500 pages in length. See SCSL (Trial Chamber Judgement), 18 May 2012), No. SCSL-03-01-T, *The Prosecutor v. Charles Ghankay Taylor*, paras. 7067, 7070 (noting that the Prosecution delivered its closing argument on 8 and 9 February 2011, the Defense gave its closing argument on 9 and 10 March 2011, and that both parties made rebuttal arguments on 11 March 2011).

[13] See, e.g., Anna Bonini, *SCSL: Delayed Justice*, iLawyer: A Blog on International Justice (2 May 2012), available at: http://ilawyerblog.com/scsl-delayed-justice; Geoffrey Robertson, "Awaiting a Verdict In Charles Taylor's War Crimes Trial", *Newsweek*, 16 April 2012, available at: http://www.thedailybeast.com/newsweek/2012/04/15/awaiting-a-verdict-in-charles-taylor-s-war-crimes-trial.html (noting that "[o]ne disquieting feature of the case is the time the court has taken to deliver this judgment" and that "the issues are complicated but it should not take over a year to give reasons for a verdict.").

Mr. Lubanga, often remain in detention pending the issuance of the judgment and who cannot begin to prepare to exercise his or her right to appeal the judgment until after it has been issued, thereby delaying the ultimate conclusion of the case. Finally, long delays between the end of trial and the judgment are also not in the interests of victims, whose "overriding interest" in international criminal trials has been described as "the interest in seeing that crimes are effectively investigated and *that justice is done*."[14] Indeed, victims at the ICC have a particular interest in the speedy conclusion of a case because the ability of victims to obtain reparations depends on a judgment on the guilt of the accused.[15]

5.3 Failure to Adequately Explore in the Judgment the Crime of Conscripting, Enlisting, or Using Children to Participate Actively in Hostilities

Given the length of time it took to issue the *Lubanga* judgment, it is surprising that the majority opinion fails to clarify certain critical aspects of the war crime with which Mr. Lubanga was charged. In particular, the majority opinion leaves open questions about the aspect of the crime relating to the use of children "to participate actively in hostilities", and the scope of the crime when charged in the context of international armed conflict. The failure of the Chamber to clarify the law on these issues is regrettable given the fact that the crime is a relatively new crime in international criminal law, and has only been prosecuted in one other international criminal body, the Special Court for Sierra Leone, which focused solely on the crime when committed in the context of non-international armed conflict.[16]

5.3.1 Use of Children to Participate Actively in Hostilities

5.3.1.1 Trial Chamber Judgment

Articles 8(2)(b)(xxvi) and 8(2)(e)(vii) of the Rome Statute prohibit not only the conscription and enlistment of children under the age of 15, but also the use of such children "to participate actively in hostilities."[17] The concept of "active participation"

---

[14] Human Rights Watch, *Commentary to the Second Preparatory Commission Meeting on the International Criminal Court*, July 1999, at 26 (emphasis added).

[15] See *infra* note 123 ff. and accompanying text.

[16] See Statute of the Special Court for Sierra Leone, Art. 3, *annexed to* United Nations Security Council Doc. 246, S/2002/246 (2002).

[17] Rome Statute of the International Criminal Court, 2187 U.N.T.S. 90, *adopted on* 17 July 1998, *entered into force* 1 July 2002, Art. 8(2)(b)(xxvi); Ibid. Art. 8(2)(e)(vii).

is not defined in the documents governing the ICC, leaving it to the *Lubanga* Trial Chamber to define the scope of activities that are proscribed by the relevant articles of the Statute. The Chamber began by noting that the Court's Elements of Crimes require that "the conduct took place in the context of and was associated with an armed conflict",[18] and that the "*travaux préparatoires* of the Statute suggest that although direct participation is not necessary, a link [with combat] is nonetheless required."[19] The Chamber also determined that the drafters of the Rome Statute "clearly intended to import a wide interpretation to the activities and roles that are covered by the offence of using children under the age of [15] actively to participate in hostilities."[20] It then explained:

> The extent of the potential danger faced by a child soldier will often be unrelated to the precise nature of the role he or she is given. Those who participate actively in hostilities include a wide range of individuals, from those on the front line (who participate directly) through to the boys or girls who are involved in a myriad of roles that support the combatants. All of these activities, which cover either direct or indirect participation, have an underlying common feature: the child concerned is, at the very least, a potential target. *The decisive factor, therefore, in deciding if an "indirect" role is to be treated as active participation in hostilities is whether the support provided by the child to the combatants exposed him or her to real danger as a potential target.* In the judgment of the Chamber these combined factors – the child's support and this level of consequential risk – mean that although absent from the immediate scene of the hostilities, the individual was nonetheless actively involved in them.[21]

However, unlike the *Lubanga* Pre-Trial Chamber, which provided examples in its decision confirming the charges against Mr. Lubanga[22] of activities that would fall within the scope "active participation" and those that would not,[23] the majority

---

[18] International Criminal Court, *Elements of Crimes*, U.N. Doc. PCNICC/2000/1/Add.2 (2000), Art. 8(2)(b)(xxvi); ibid. Art. 8(2)(e)(vii).

[19] *Lubanga* Trial Judgment, supra, note 1, para. 621.

[20] Ibid. para. 627.

[21] Ibid. para. 628 (emphasis added).

[22] For more on the confirmation of charges process, see *infra,* note 74 and accompanying text.

[23] See ICC (Pre-Trial Chamber I Decision on the Confirmation of Charges), 29 January 2007, No. ICC-01/04-01/06-803, *The Prosecutor v. Thomas Lubanga Dyilo*, paras. 261–263. Specifically, the Pre-Trial Chamber held that "'[a]ctive participation' in hostilities means not only direct participation in hostilities, combat in other words, but also covers active participation in combat-related activities such as scouting, spying, sabotage and the use of children as decoys, couriers or at military check-points," and that guarding military objectives or acting as a bodyguard may also constitute active participation where such activities "have a direct impact on the level of logistic resources and on the organisation of operations required by the other party to the conflict." Ibid. paras. 261, 263. By contrast, according to the Pre-Trial Chamber, active participation does not encompass activities that are "clearly unrelated to hostilities," such as "food deliveries to an airbase or the use of domestic staff in married officers' quarters." Ibid. para. 262. The Special Court for Sierra Leone has also provided examples of activities falling within the scope of "active participation" in hostilities in interpreting the provision in that Court's statute prohibiting the use of children soldiers in armed conflict, which is identical to Article 8(2)(e)(vii) of the Rome Statute. See SCSL (Trial Chamber Judgment) 20 June 2007, No. SCSL-04-16-T, *The Prosecutor v. Alex Tamba Brima*, et al., para. 737 ("Any labour or support that gives effect to, or helps maintain, operations

of the Trial Chamber concluded that, "[g]iven the different types of roles that may be performed by children used by armed groups, the Chamber's determination of whether a particular activity constitutes 'active participation' can only be made on a case-by-case basis."[24]

The Trial Chamber then turned to the issue of whether evidence that sexual violence was committed against children by members of Mr. Lubanga's armed forces could be considered under the charge of using children to participate actively in armed conflict.[25] As has been well-documented elsewhere,[26] the failure of the ICC Prosecutor to include charges relating to sexual violence in the case against Mr. Lubanga has been a contentious issue throughout the proceedings. Despite early calls from human rights groups that the Prosecutor add charges reflecting evidence that members of Mr. Lubanga's militia were responsible for acts of sexual violence,[27] the Prosecution included no reference to sexual violence in its Document Containing the Charges,[28] which sets forth "the charges on which the Prosecutor intends to bring the person to trial."[29] Furthermore, while the Prosecution did allude to evidence of sexual violence in its opening statement at trial,[30] it subsequently opposed a motion[31] filed by victims participating in the *Lubanga* trial seeking to

---

in a conflict constitutes active participation. Hence carrying loads for the fighting faction, finding and/or acquiring food, ammunition or equipment, acting as decoys, carrying messages, making trails or finding routes, manning checkpoints or acting as human shields are some examples of active participation as much as actual fighting and combat.").

[24] *Lubanga* Trial Judgment, supra, note 1, para. 628.

[25] Ibid. paras. 620–630.

[26] See, e.g., Brigid Inder, *Reflection: Gender Issues and Child Soldiers – The Case of Prosecutor v Thomas Lubanga Dyilo* (25 August 2011), available at: http://www.iccwomen.org/documents/Gender-Issues-and-Child-Soldiers.pdf.

[27] See, e.g., Joint Letter from Avocats Sans Frontières et al. to the Chief Prosecutor of the International Criminal Court, D.R. Congo: ICC Charges Raise Concern (31 July 2006), available at: http://hrw.org/english/docs/2006/08/01/congo13891_txt.htm; Letter from Women's Initiatives for Gender Justice to Mr. Luis Moreno Ocampo, Chief Prosecutor, International Criminal Court (August 2006), available at: http://www.iccwomen.org/documents/Prosecutor_Letter_August_2006_Redacted.pdf.

[28] ICC (Office of the Prosecutor) 28 August 2006, No. ICC-01/04-01/06, *The Prosecutor v. Thomas Lubanga Dyilo*, Submission of the Document Containing the Charges Pursuant to Article 61(3)(a) and of the List of Evidence Pursuant to Rule 121(3).

[29] Rome Statute, supra, note 17, Art. 61(3)(a).

[30] *The Prosecutor v. Thomas Lubanga Dyilo*, Transcript, ICC-01/04-01/06-T-107-ENG, at 11:17–12:22 (26 January 2009) (explaining that child soldiers in Mr. Lubanga's camps were subject to rape and sexual slavery).

[31] See, e.g., *The Prosecutor v. Thomas Lubanga Dyilo*, Prosecution's Further Observations Regarding the Legal Representatives' Joint Request Made Pursuant to Regulation 55, ICC-01/04-01/06-1966 (ICC Office of the Prosecutor, 12 June 2009); *The Prosecutor v. Thomas Lubanga Dyilo*, Prosecution's Application for Leave to Appeal the "Decision giving notice to the parties and participants that the legal characterisation of the facts may be subject to change in accordance with Regulation 55(2) of the Regulations of the Court," ICC-01/04-01/06-2074 (ICC Office of the Prosecutor, 12 August 2009).

have the Trial Chamber "recharacterize" the charges against Mr. Lubanga to include the crime against humanity of sexual slavery and the war crimes of sexual slavery and cruel and/or inhuman treatment.[32] The Chamber ultimately held that it could not recharacterize the charges as requested by the victims after an Appeals Chamber decision confirmed that, under Article 74(2) of the Rome Statute, the Trial Chamber's judgment "shall not exceed the facts and circumstances (i.e. the factual allegations) described in the charges and any amendments to them."[33] As mentioned above, the Prosecution did not include factual allegations supporting charges of sexual slavery in its Document Containing the Charges,[34] nor were allegations of sexual violence included in the Pre-Trial Chamber's decision confirming the charges against Mr. Lubanga.[35] Nevertheless, testimony emerged during the trial regarding sexual violence against children serving in Mr. Lubanga's militia.[36] In addition, United Nations Under-Secretary General for Children and Armed Conflict, Radhika Coomaraswamy, submitted to the Chamber that "active participation" under the provisions of the Rome Statute relating to use of children in armed conflict should encompass "children who serve essential support functions for armed forces and armed groups during the period of hostilities," including "girls or boys used for sexual exploitation."[37] Finally, the Prosecution referred to sexual violence several times in its closing statement at trial[38] and argued that active participation in hostilities includes sending out soldiers to "procure" girls

[32] See generally *The Prosecutor v. Thomas Lubanga Dyilo*, Joint Application of the Legal Representatives of the Victims for the Implementation of the Procedure Under Regulation 55 of the *Regulations of the Court*, No. ICC-01/04-01/06-1891-tEng (ICC Trial Chamber, 22 May 2009). For a detailed discussion of the victims' application for recharacterization of the charges and the Trial Chamber's response, See War Crimes Research Office, *Defining the Case Against an Accused Before the International Criminal Court: Whose Responsibility Is It?* (December 2009), available at: http://www.wcl.american.edu/warcrimes/icc/documents/WCRO_Report_on_Defining_Case_Nov2009.pdf?rd=1

[33] *Lubanga* Trial Judgment, supra, note 1, para. 630 (referring to the relevant decisions of the Trial Chamber and the Appeals Chamber on the victims' motion for recharacterization of the charges).

[34] See supra, note 28 ff. and accompanying text.

[35] See generally *Lubanga* Decision on the Confirmation of Charges, supra, note 23.

[36] See Women's Initiatives for Gender Justice, *Gender Report Card 2009*, at 71–85, available at: http://www.iccwomen.org/news/docs/GRC09_web-2-10.pdf (summarizing the testimony on sexual violence that emerged during the *Lubanga* trial in 2009); Women's Initiatives for Gender Justice, *Gender Report Card 2010*, at 135–138, available at: http://www.iccwomen.org/news/docs/GRC10-WEB-11-10-v4_Final-version-Dec.pdf (summarizing the testimony on sexual violence that emerged during the *Lubanga* trial in 2010).

[37] *The Prosecutor v. Thomas Lubanga Dyilo*, Written Submissions of the United Nations Special Representative of the Secretary-General on Children and Armed Conflict, ICC-01/04-01/06-1229-AnxA, para. 23 (18 March 2008). See *also The Prosecutor v. Thomas Lubanga Dyilo*, Transcript, ICC-01/04-01/06-T-223-ENG, at 14:4–16:5 (7 January 2010).

[38] *The Prosecutor v. Thomas Lubanga Dyilo*, Transcript, ICC-01/04-01/06-T-356-ENG, at 9:9–25 (25 August 2011); ibid. at 52:16.

"so that the commander could sleep with them."[39] Thus, the Trial Chamber was faced with the question whether evidence of sexual violence could be considered in support of the limited charges against Mr. Lubanga. In response, the majority held that, "[r]egardless of whether sexual violence may properly be included within the scope of 'using [children under the age of 15] to participate actively in hostilities' *as a matter of law*, because *facts relating to sexual violence* were not included in the Decision on the Confirmation of Charges, it would be impermissible for the Chamber to base its [judgment] on the evidence introduced during the trial that is relevant to this issue."[40]

5.3.1.2 "Active" Versus "Direct" Participation in Hostilities

One problem with the Trial Chamber's analysis is that it fails to clarify the distinction between the war crime under *international criminal law* of using children to "participate actively in hostilities"[41] and the concept under *international humanitarian law* (IHL) of "active" or "direct" participation in hostilities.[42] IHL treaties use both terms to delineate the category of persons, including civilians, who are immune from attack during an armed conflict. For instance, Article 3 common to the four Geneva Conventions extends its minimum protections to all "[p]ersons taking no *active* part in the hostilities."[43] Similarly, Additional Protocol I (AP I) guarantees certain rights to civilians "unless and for such time as they take a *direct* part in hostilities,"[44] including the right to be free from attack,[45] and Additional Protocol II (AP II) makes clear that those "who do not take a *direct* part or who have ceased to take part in hostilities," shall be treated humanely.[46] Importantly, the terms "active" and "direct" have been treated synonymously under international humanitarian law.[47] Indeed, as IHL scholar Nicole Urban has summarized:

---

[39] Ibid. at 15:17–16:4; ibid. at 55:15–17.

[40] *Lubanga* Trial Judgment, supra, note 1, para. 630 (emphasis added).

[41] Rome Statute, supra, note 17, Art. 8(2)(e)(vii).

[42] See, e.g., Convention (III) relative to the Treatment of Prisoners of War, Geneva, 12 August 1949, Art. 3; Protocol Additional to the Geneva Conventions of 12 August 1949, and relating to the Protection of Victims of International Armed Conflicts (Protocol I), 8 June 1977, Art. 51(3); Protocol Additional to the Geneva Conventions of 12 August 1949, and relating to the Protection of Victims of Non-International Armed Conflicts (Protocol II), 8 June 1977, Art. 4(2).

[43] See, e.g., Third Geneva Convention, supra, note 42, Art. 3(emphasis added).

[44] Protocol Additional to the Geneva Conventions of 12 August 1949, and relating to the Protection of Victims of International Armed Conflicts (Protocol I), 8 June 1977, Art. 51(3) (emphasis added).

[45] Ibid. Art. 51(2).

[46] Protocol Additional to the Geneva Conventions of 12 August 1949, and relating to the Protection of Victims of Non-International Armed Conflicts (Protocol II), 8 June 1977, Art. 4(2) (emphasis added).

[47] See, e.g., International Committee of the Red Cross, *Interpretive Guidance on the Notion of Direct Participation in Hostilities under IHL*, at 43–44 (2009) ("The notion of direct participation

> In the [International Committee of the Red Cross's (ICRC)] Interpretive Guidelines on the Notion of Direct Participation in Hostilities it was noted that although the Additional Protocols and the Geneva Conventions use different words, the phrase "*participent directement*" is used consistently throughout French texts of each treaty: a fact that strongly suggests a uniform meaning across IHL. Further, the ICRC found that the concept of participation in hostiles [sic] should be interpreted consistently across both international and non-international armed conflicts. Similarly, the Trial Chamber of the [International Criminal Tribunal for Rwanda] in the *Akayesu Decision* was called upon to interpret the meaning of the term 'active' in the concept of Common Article 3 and held that "direct" and "active" "are so similar that, for the Chamber's purposes, they may be treated as synonymous.[48]

By contrast, the *Lubanga* Trial Chamber distinguishes between the terms "active" and "direct," saying that the "use of the expression 'to participate actively in hostilities' [under the Rome Statute], as opposed to the expression 'direct participation' (as found in Additional Protocol I to the Geneva Conventions) was clearly intended to import a wide interpretation to the activities and roles that are covered by the offence ..."[49] Furthermore, as explained above, the Trial Chamber adopted a broad interpretation of "active" participation in hostilities, holding that it "include[s] a wide range of individuals, from those on the front line (who participate directly) through to the boys or girls who are involved in a myriad of roles that support the combatants,"[50] whereas the tendency under IHL has been to narrowly interpret both "active" and "direct" participation in order to maximize the scope of protection afforded to civilians.[51]

---

in hostilities has evolved from the phrase 'taking no active part in the hostilities' used in Article 3 [of the four Geneva Conventions]. Although the English texts of the Geneva Conventions and Additional Protocols use the words 'active' and 'direct', respectively, the consistent use of the phrase '*participent directement*' in the equally authentic French texts demonstrate that the terms 'direct' and 'active' refer to the same quality and degree of individual participation in hostilities. Furthermore, as the notion of taking a direct part in hostilities is used synonymously in the Additional Protocols I and II, it should be interpreted in the same manner in international and non-international armed conflict.").

[48] Nicole Urban, *Direct and Active Participation in Hostilities: The Unintended Consequences of the ICC's decision in* Lubanga, EJIL Talk, 11 April 2012, available at: http://www.ejiltalk.org/direct-and-active-participation-in-hostilities-the-unintended-consequences-of-the-iccs-decision-in-lubanga/ (internal citations omitted).

[49] *Lubanga* Trial Judgment, supra, note 1, para. 627.

[50] Ibid. para. 628.

[51] See, e.g., Commentary to Protocol Additional to the Geneva Conventions of 12 August 1949, and relating to the Protection of Victims of International Armed Conflicts (Protocol I), 8 June 1977, Art. 51(3), available at: http://www.icrc.org/ihl.nsf/1a13044f3bbb5b8ec12563fb0066f226/5e5142b6ba102b45c12563cd00434741!OpenDocument ("In general the immunity afforded civilians is subject to a very stringent condition: that they do not participate directly in hostilities, *i.e.*, that they do not become combatants, on pain of losing their protection. Thus 'direct' participation means acts of war which by their nature or purpose *are likely to cause actual harm to the personnel and equipment of the enemy armed forces*.") (emphasis added); International Committee of the Red Cross, *Interpretive Guidance on the Notion of Direct Participation in Hostilities under IHL*, at 45 (2009) (explaining that the "notion of direct participation in hostilities refers to *specific hostile acts*

The Trial Chamber's reasoning on this point is potentially problematic in two ways. First, it could be interpreted to suggest that, contrary to the tendency explained directly above to treat the concepts of "active" and "direct" participation synonymously under IHL, the term "active" as used in Common Article 3 in fact covers a wider array of activity for purposes of IHL than does the term "direct" as used in AP I and APII. This would suggest that it is easier for an individual to lose his or her civilian immunity, and thus become a legitimate target of attack, in non-international armed conflicts to which AP II does not apply[52] than it would be for the same individual to lose his or her civilian immunity in international armed conflict or non-international armed conflicts covered by AP II. Second, the *Lubanga* Trial Chamber's approach could be read to suggest that, although the terms "active" participation and "direct" participation remain synonymous under international humanitarian law, *both* should be interpreted broadly, thereby making it more likely that an individual could lose civilian immunity in either non-international or international armed conflict. Under this reading, the Trial Chamber's approach effectively blurs the distinction in IHL between "direct" participation in hostilities by civilians, which entails loss of immunity from attack, and "indirect" participation, which does not. As Urban has written:

> By seeking to give a broad interpretation to 'active participation', the Court is, laudably, ensuring that the protection contained in Article 8(2)(e)(vii) has a long reach and does not exclude many children who do not participate in front line combat but who, nevertheless, are essential to combat. But caution must be exercised, as what the Court is seeking to give with one hand, it is taking away with the other … . The broader the Court's understanding of the term 'active' under Article 8(2)(e)(vii), the narrower the protection available under Common Article 3 … . Should the sexual exploitation of and violence against child soldiers render them 'active' participants in hostilities under one Article, there is a real risk that they will also be considered as active participants in hostilities under the others … . This results in an overall net reduction in protection for those children that the Court is seeking to protect.[53]

Indeed, as commentator Cecile Aptel explains, the *Lubanga* Trial Chamber's approach is dangerous because it fails to make clear "that there is no contradiction between, on the one hand, broadening the human rights protection afforded to all

carried out by individuals *as part of the conduct of hostilities* between parties to an armed conflict" and that the "treaty terms of 'direct' and 'active' indicate the same quality and degree of individual participation in hostilities") (emphasis added).

[52] While Common Article 3 of the Geneva Conventions applies to all cases of "armed conflict not of an international character," see, e.g., Third Geneva Convention, supra, note 42, Art. 3, Additional Protocol II applies only to non-international armed conflicts "which take place in the territory of a High Contracting Party between its armed forces and dissident armed forces or other organized armed groups which, under responsible command, exercise such control over a part of its territory as to enable them to carry out sustained and concerted military operations and to implement [AP II]." AP II, supra, note 46, Art. 1(1).

[53] Urban, supra, note 48.

children associated with armed groups/forces to better protect them from recruitment and use by armed groups and forces, and, on the other hand, restrictively construing the category of those children 'directly participating in hostilities' so that only those most directly involved in combat lose their protection as civilians under international humanitarian law."[54] Arguably, this problem could have been avoided if the *Lubanga* Trial Chamber had explicitly acknowledged this issue and limited its analysis of the term "active" to the context of this case, either because it understood its unique interpretation of the term as restricted to the ICL context, or because it viewed the different interpretations of the term under ICL and IHL as necessary to give effect to the "child-protective" purpose of the provisions under each body of law.

Notably, in another context, international criminal bodies have distinguished between the interpretation of a *human rights* concept and a seemingly analogous concept under *international criminal law*, and in doing so, made clear the basis for the distinction, thereby indicating that the interpretation of one does not affect the interpretation of the other. Specifically, both the International Criminal Tribunal for the former Yugoslavia (ICTY) and the International Criminal Tribunal for Rwanda (ICTR) have held that the elements of the crime against humanity of torture differs from the definition of torture under the Convention against Torture in that the former does not require "that the perpetrator of the crime of torture be a public official, nor does the torture need to have been committed in the presence of such an official."[55] The reason for this difference was set forth by the ICTY in the *Brđanin* case, which explained:

> [T]he definition of the [Convention Against Torture] *relies on the notion of human rights*, which is largely built on the premises that human rights are violated by States or Governments. *For the purposes of international criminal law*, which deals with the criminal responsibility of an individual, this Trial Chamber agrees ... that "the characteristic trait of the offence [under the Tribunal's jurisdiction] is to be found in the nature of the act committed rather than in the status of the person who committed it."[56]

A similar approach – that is, explicitly adopting and explaining different interpretations of concepts that appear under both ICL and IHL – could have been taken by the Trial Chamber in the *Lubanga* case.

---

[54] Cecile Aptel, *Lubanga Decision Roundtable: The Participation of Children in Hostilities*, Opinion Juris (18 March 2012), available at: http://opiniojuris.org/2012/03/18/lubanga-decision-roundtable-the-participation-of-children-in-hostilities/?utm_source=feedburner&utm_medium=feed&utm_campaign=Feed%3A+opiniojurisfeed+%28Opinio+Juris%29.

[55] ICTY (Trial Chamber Judgment), 1 September 2004, IT-99-36-T, *The Prosecutor v. Radoslav Brđanin*, para. 488. See also ICTR (Trial Chamber Judgment), 15 May 2003; ICTR-97-20-T, *The Prosecutor v. Laurent Semanza*, Judgement, paras. 342–43.

[56] *Brđanin* Trial Judgement, supra, note 55, para. 489 (emphasis added).

5.3.1.3 Scope of the Crime of Using Children to "Participate Actively in Hostilities"

Another issue raised by the majority's approach to analyzing the use of children to "participate actively in hostilities" is the ambiguity in the scope of the crime with which the accused was charged. As Judge Odio Benito summarized in her Separate and Dissenting Opinion, the majority's decision leaves the "legal definition of the concept of 'use to participate actively in the hostilities' … to a case-by-case determination" that will "ultimately be evidence-based and thus limited by the charges and evidence brought by the prosecution against the accused."[57] According to Judge Odio Benito, such a case-by-case approach is misguided because it "can produce a limited and potentially discriminatory assessment of the risks and harms suffered by the child."[58] In particular, the judge argued, "[b]y failing to deliberately include within the legal concept of 'use to participate actively in the hostilities' the sexual violence and other ill [-]treatment suffered by girls and boys, the Majority of the Chamber is making this critical aspect of the crime invisible."[59] Furthermore, Judge Odio Benito criticized the majority's approach on the ground that the "Chamber has the responsibility to define the crimes based on the applicable law, and not limited to the charges brought by the prosecution against the accused."[60] Indeed, Judge Odio Benito considers "it necessary and a duty of the Chamber to include sexual violence within the legal concept of 'use to participate actively in the hostilities,'" regardless of the majority's finding that its decision on the guilt of the accused was limited to the facts and circumstances described in the charges.[61]

As discussed above, the failure of the Prosecution to charge Mr. Lubanga directly with crimes involving sexual violence was a contentious issue throughout the case,[62] and Judge Odio Benito's approach appears to constitute a final attempt to ensure that the ICC's judgment reflect the evidence that emerged at trial regarding the harm caused to child victims of such violence.[63] However, it is questionable whether "subsuming sexual crimes under the category of '… use[d] to participate actively in

---

[57] *Lubanga* Trial Judgment, supra, note 1, Separate and Dissenting Opinion of Judge Odio Benito, para. 15.

[58] Ibid.

[59] Ibid. para. 16.

[60] Ibid. para. 15.

[61] Ibid. para. 17.

[62] See supra, note. 26 ff. and accompanying text.

[63] See, e.g., *Lubanga* Trial Judgment, supra, note 1, Separate and Dissenting Opinion of Judge Odio Benito, para. 8 ("However, ICC trial proceedings should also attend to the harm suffered by the victims as a result of the crimes within the jurisdiction of the Court. It becomes irrelevant, therefore, if the prosecutor submitted the charges as separate crimes or rightfully include[ed] them as embedded in the crimes of which Mr. Lubanga is accused."). See also Aptel, supra, note 54 ("Judge Odio-Benito's concern appears to stem notably from the failure of the prosecution to charge Lubanga for the sexual crimes committed against some of the child-soldiers.").

hostilities' [is] the optimal solution to highlight the plight of the children victims of these crimes."[64] As Aptel has asked:

> Is this the best manner to demonstrate the tragic and long-lasting suffering caused to the victims of sexual violence, rape, sexual slavery and forced pregnancies, too often suffered by the girls associated with armed groups? As all and each [of] the above crimes constitute separate offences, duly recognized and criminalized under the Rome Statute, are they not worthy of separate consideration, as a way to fully acknowledge their existence and the particular harm suffered by the victims, *in addition to* the harm caused by their recruitment or use by armed groups/forces?[65]

Nevertheless, Judge Odio Benito's point is well-taken that it was incumbent on the Chamber, as the first Chamber of the ICC, to define the scope of the crime of using children to participate actively in armed conflict, rather than adopting a case-by-case approach. One solution may be for future Chambers to adopt a broader conceptual view of the crime. As explained above, the Trial Chamber chose to focus on whether the "support provided by the child to the combatants exposed him or her to real danger by becoming a potential target."[66] Yet, as Mark Drumbl, the author of a recent book examining the ways in which the problem of child soldiering has been dealt with under international law, has written:

> This approach obscures the reality that some child soldiers may face the prospect of greater harm from members of their own forces (whether adult leaders, mid-level officials or fellow children) than from "enemy" forces. Sexual slavery and abusive punishment come to mind.[67]

A better approach may be that advocated by UN Under-Secretary General for Children and Armed Conflict, Coomaraswamy, who argued to the *Lubanga* Chamber that the crime of using children under the age of 15 to "participate actively in hostilities" should cover any activity of the child that is used to "support conflict."[68] As Coomaraswamy pointed out in her *amicus* submission in the *Lubanga Case*, this approach is consistent with the United Nations policy for disarmament, demobilization, and reintegration (DDR), which states: "No distinction should be made between combatants and non-combatants when [DDR] eligibility criteria are determined, as these roles are blurred in armed forces and groups, where children, and girls in particular, perform numerous combat support and non-combat roles that are essential to the functioning of the armed force or group."[69] It also conforms with the approach adopted by the Special Court for Sierra Leone, which interpreted a provision

---

[64] Aptel, supra, note 54.

[65] Ibid. (emphasis in original).

[66] *Lubanga* Trial Judgment, supra, note 1, para. 820.

[67] Mark Drumbl, *Lubanga Decision Roundtable: Lubanga Legacies?*, Opinion Juris (19 March 2012), available at: http://opiniojuris.org/2012/03/19/lubanga-decision-roundtable-legacies/?utm_source=feedburner&utm_medium=feed&utm_campaign=Feed%3A+opiniojurisfeed+%28Opinio+Juris%29.

[68] *Lubanga* Coomaraswamy *Amicus* Submission, supra, note 37, para. 17 (emphasis added).

[69] Ibid. para. 18 (citing United Nations, Operational Guide to the Integrated Disarmament, Demobilization, and Reintegration Standards, § 5.30, 218 (1 August 2006)).

identical to that found at Article 8(2)(e)(vii) of the Rome Statute as prohibiting using children for "[a]ny labour or support that gives effect to, or helps maintain, operations in a conflict."[70] While this approach will still be somewhat fact-specific, it follows as a general matter that "children who serve essential support functions for armed forces and armed groups during the period of hostilities may function in any of the following roles over the course of their use, including but not limited to: cooks, porters, nurses, spies, messengers, administrators, translators, radio operators, medical assistants, public information workers, youth camp leaders *and girls or boys used for sexual exploitation*."[71] Of course, as discussed above,[72] the adoption of any such approach by the International Criminal Court must clearly be limited to the context of the *international criminal law* prohibition against using children to participate actively in hostilities.

5.3.2 *Scope of the Crime in International Armed Conflict*

As discussed above, Mr. Lubanga was charged solely with criminal responsibility in relation to the conscription, enlistment or use of children in armed conflict. In particular, the ICC Prosecutor charged Mr. Lubanga under Article 8(2)(e)(vii) of the Rome Statute, which criminalizes "[c]onscripting or enlisting children under the age of 15 years into armed forces or groups or using them to participate actively in hostilities" as a serious violation of "the laws and customs applicable in armed conflicts not of an international character."[73] However, following the confirmation of charges hearing in the *Lubanga Case*,[74] the Pre-Trial Chamber issued a decision committing Mr. Lubanga to trial not only for the crime charged but also for the crime of conscripting, enlisting or using children to participate actively in international armed conflict under Article 8(2)(b)(xxvi).[75] Notably, Article 8(2)(b)(xxvi)

[70] *Brima*, et al. Trial Judgment, supra, note 23, paras. 736–737.

[71] *Lubanga*, Coomaraswamy *Amicus* Submission, supra, note 37, para. 23 (emphasis added).

[72] See supra, note 41 ff. and accompanying text.

[73] *The Prosecutor v. Thomas Lubanga Dyilo*, Submission of the Document Containing the Charges Pursuant to Article 61(3)(a) and of the List of Evidence Pursuant to Rule 121(3), ICC-01/04-01/06-356 (ICC Office of the Prosecutor, 28 August 2006). Article 61(3) of the Rome Statute provides as follows: "Within a reasonable time before the hearing, the person shall: (a) Be provided with a copy of the document containing the charges on which the Prosecutor intends to bring the person to trial; and (b) Be informed of the evidence on which the Prosecutor intends to rely at the hearing." Rome Statute, supra, note 17, Art. 61(3).

[74] The confirmation of charges is a process unique to the International Criminal Court under which the Pre-Trial Chamber holds a hearing, within a reasonable time after an accused is transferred to or surrenders to the Court, to confirm that there is sufficient evidence to establish substantial grounds to believe that the accused committed the crimes charged by the Prosecutor. See Rome Statute, supra, note 17, Art. 61.

[75] *Lubanga* Decision on the Confirmation of Charges, supra, note 23, at 156. For an analysis of the Pre-Trial Chamber's authority to confirm charges not contained in the Prosecutor's Document

differs in a significant respect from Article 8(2)(e)(vii) in that the former requires not only that the crime be committed in international armed conflict, but also that the children be conscripted or enlisted into "the national armed forces,"[76] suggesting that, in a conflict that is characterized as international but nevertheless involves non-state actors, *only* the state actors could be prosecuted for the crime of conscripting or enlisting child soldiers.

When the *Lubanga* case reached the trial stage, the Prosecutor requested that the Trial Chamber restore the charges to the form initially alleged by the Prosecution, i.e., to include charges only of war crimes occurring in the context of a non-international armed conflict.[77] However, the Trial Chamber concluded that it had "no authority to ignore, strike down or declare null and void the charges as confirmed by the Pre-Trial Chamber,"[78] meaning the Trial Chamber considered charges under both Article 8(2)(b)(xxvi) and Article 8(2)(e)(vii) in its judgment. With regard to the former, the Chamber concluded that the evidence failed to establish that the crimes alleged against Mr. Lubanga were committed in the context of an international armed conflict.[79] In light of this conclusion, the majority of the Trial Chamber went on to hold that "it is unnecessary to interpret or discuss Article 8(2)(b)(xxvi)" of the Statute.[80] Judge Odio Benito took issue with this paragraph in her Separate and Dissenting Opinion, arguing:

Containing the Charges, See War Crimes Research Office, *Defining the Case Against an Accused Before the International Criminal Court: Whose Responsibility Is It?* (December 2009), available at: https://www.wcl.american.edu/warcrimes/icc/documents/WCRO_Report_on_Defining_Case_Nov2009.pdf?rd=1.

[76] Rome Statute, supra, note 17, Art. 8(2)(b)(xxvi).

[77] See *The Prosecutor v. Thomas Lubanga Dyilo*, Decision on the Status Before the Trial Chamber of the Evidence Heard by the Pre-Trial Chamber and the Decisions of the Pre-Trial Chamber in Trial Proceedings, and the Manner in Which Evidence Shall Be Submitted, ICC-01/04-01/06-1084 (ICC Trial Chamber, 13 December 2007).

[78] Ibid. para. 39.

[79] *Lubanga* Trial Judgment, supra, note 1, paras. 563–565. Specifically, the Chamber concluded: "[A]lthough there is evidence of direct intervention on the part of Uganda, this intervention would only have internationalised the conflict between the two states concerned (viz. the DRC and Uganda). Since the conflict to which the UPC/FPLC [Lubanga's militia] was a party was not "a difference arising between two states" but rather protracted violence carried out by multiple non-state armed groups, it remained a non-international conflict notwithstanding any concurrent international armed conflict between Uganda and the DRC .... Focussing [*sic*]solely on the parties and the conflict relevant to the charges in this case, the Ugandan military occupation of Bunia airport does not change the legal nature of the conflict between the UPC/FPLC [and other rebel groups] since this conflict, as analysed above, did not result in two states opposing each other, whether directly or indirectly, during the time period relevant to the charges. In any event, the existence of a possible conflict that was 'international in character' between the DRC and Uganda does not affect the legal characterisation of the UPC/FPLC's concurrent noninternational armed conflict with [other] militias, which formed part of the internal armed conflict between the rebel groups." Ibid.

[80] Ibid. para. 568.

> Although the Chamber has concluded that the crimes were committed in the context of a non-international armed conflict, this case has been argued by the parties and participants pursuant to the decision on the confirmation of the charges, which encompasses both Article 8(2)(b)(xxvi) and Article 8(2)(e)(vii) of the Statute. In fact, the defence has from start to finish argued that the armed conflict in question is an international armed conflict, and thus, it is foreseeable that this aspect could be the subject matter of an eventual appeal.

Thus, the discussion on the concept of "national armed forces" is required as this is a live issue in the present case.[81]

While the majority is correct that it was not *required* to address the requirements of Article 8(2)(b)(xxvi) in its judgment, the fact that the Pre-Trial Chamber in the case addressed the issue in its confirmation of charges decision, and that the parties presented evidence and arguments on the scope of the crime to the Trial Chamber, meant that the Chamber was well-positioned to opine on the interpretation of the charge in an effort to provide clarity on the law for future litigants. Although the Trial Chamber's views on the issue would be viewed as *dicta*, its interpretation of the provision would have nevertheless been useful in terms of advancing the state of this new crime under the Rome Statute.[82]

5.4 Lack of Clarity in the Sentencing Decision

As explained in the Introduction, the Trial Chamber issued a decision on 10 July 2012 sentencing Mr. Lubanga to 14 years in prison, with credit for time served.[83] Once again, Judge Odio Benito issued a dissenting opinion, arguing that the majority inappropriately "disregarded factors such as 'punishment' and 'sexual violence' in the determination of the sentence" and that Mr. Lubanga deserved a sentence of 15 years.[84] Unfortunately, while the majority decision carefully steps out its reasoning with respect to various factors it considers relevant to its determination of the sentence, two things are left unclear by the decision. First, the Chamber fails to explain the *relationship among* these factors, an ambiguity that is highlighted by Judge Odio Benito's dissent, as explained below. Second, neither the majority nor the dissent explains how the various factors considered relevant to sentencing lead the judges to the length of sentence ultimately considered appropriate.

---

[81] *Lubanga* Trial Judgment, supra, note 1, Separate and Dissenting Opinion of Judge Odio Benito, para. 12.

[82] As noted above, while the Statute of Special Court for Sierra Leone also criminalized the conscription, enlistment or use of children in armed conflict, that Court's jurisdiction was limited to crimes committed in non-international armed conflict, meaning that the jurisprudence of the Special Court in no way addresses the unique elements of the specific crime captured by Article 8(2)(b)(xxvi) of the Rome Statute. See supra, note 23 and accompanying text.

[83] See generally *Lubanga* Decision on Sentence Pursuant to Article 76 of the Statute, supra, note 2.

[84] Ibid. Dissenting Opinion of Judge Odio Benito, paras. 22, 27.

5.4.1 Trial Chamber's Decision on Sentencing

The majority begins its decision by reviewing the legal framework for sentencing at the ICC. This includes the following provisions:

- Article 78(1) of the Rome Statute, which states: "In determining the sentence, the Court shall, in accordance with the Rules of Procedure and Evidence, take into account such factors as the gravity of the crime and the individual circumstances of the convicted person."[85]
- Rule 145(1)(c), which provides: "In its determination of the sentence pursuant to Article 78, Paragraph 1, the Court shall: ... In addition to the factors mentioned in Article 78, Paragraph 1, give consideration, *inter alia*, to the extent of the damage caused, in particular the harm caused to the victims and their families, the nature of the unlawful behaviour and the means employed to execute the crime; the degree of participation of the convicted person; the degree of intent; the circumstances of manner, time and location; and the age, education, social and economic condition of the convicted person."[86]
- Rule 145(2), which states: "In addition to the factors mentioned above, the Court shall take into account, as appropriate:

  (a) Mitigating circumstances such as: (i) The circumstances falling short of constituting grounds for exclusion of criminal responsibility, such as substantially diminished mental capacity or duress; (ii) The convicted person's conduct after the act, including any efforts by the person to compensate the victims and any cooperation with the Court;

  (b) As aggravating circumstances: (i) Any relevant prior criminal convictions for crimes under the jurisdiction of the Court or of a similar nature; (ii) Abuse of power or official capacity; (iii) Commission of the crime where the victim is particularly defenceless; (iv) Commission of the crime with particular cruelty or where there were multiple victims; (v) Commission of the crime for any motive involving discrimination on any of the grounds referred to in Article 21, Paragraph 3; (vi) Other circumstances which, although not enumerated above, by virtue of their nature are similar to those mentioned."[87]

The majority then goes on to analyze a number of these factors. For instance, in relation to the gravity of the crime, the majority notes that the "crimes of conscripting and enlisting children under the age of 15 and using them to participate actively in hostilities are undoubtedly very serious crimes that affect the international community as a whole," explaining that using children to participate in hostilities exposed them to "real danger as potential targets" and stressing the vulnerability

---

[85] Rome Statute, supra, note 17, Art. 78(1).

[86] International Criminal Court, Rules of Procedure and Evidence, U.N. Doc. PCNICC/2000/1/Add.1, R. 145(1)(c) (2000).

[87] Ibid. R. 145(2).

of children.[88] The majority also considers: the scale of the crimes, recalling its finding in the *Lubanga* judgment that the recruitment and use of child soldiers by Mr. Lubanga's militia was "widespread;"[89] the degree of the participation of the convicted person, noting its finding that Mr. Lubanga acted as a co-perpetrator in the crimes[90]; and the individual circumstances of the convicted person, including the fact that he is "clearly an intelligent and well-educated individual, who would have understood the seriousness of the crimes of which he has been found guilty."[91] Turning to aggravating circumstances, the majority first explains that the Prosecution argued that, *inter alia*, "the harsh conditions in the camps and the brutal treatment of children" and the infliction of sexual violence upon female child solders should be treated as aggravating factors.[92] The majority also makes clear that the Prosecution must prove any aggravating factors "beyond a reasonable doubt."[93] Applying this standard, the majority concludes that the Prosecution failed to adequately establish that Mr. Lubanga was responsible for the harsh treatment of or sexual violence against child soldiers, and thus it does not count these, or any other circumstances, as aggravating factors.[94] As for mitigating factors, which must be established by the Defense "on a balance of probabilities,"[95] the majority holds that it will take into account the fact that Mr. Lubanga was "respectful and cooperative throughout the proceedings, notwithstanding some particularly onerous circumstances."[96] After consideration of each of these factors, the majority concludes that Mr. Lubanga should receive a 13 year sentence for the crime of conscripting children, 12 years for the crime of enlisting children, and 14 years for using children to actively participate in hostilities.[97] Thus, the total term of appropriate imprisonment, according to the majority, is a joint sentence of 14 years.[98]

In her dissenting opinion, Judge Odio Benito begins by stating that she agrees with the majority that, "in the determination of the sentence against the convicted

[88] *Lubanga* Decision on Sentence Pursuant to Article 76 of the Statute, supra, note 2, para. 37.

[89] Ibid. paras. 49–50.

[90] Ibid. paras. 51–53.

[91] Ibid. paras. 54–56.

[92] Ibid. paras. 57, 62.

[93] Ibid. para. 33.

[94] Ibid. paras. 57–81. The majority also rejects the Prosecution's argument that the commission of the crime when the victims are particularly defenseless should be an aggravating factor, noting that it had already taken into account the age of the children in assessing the gravity of the crime. Ibid. paras. 77–78. Finally, the majority rejects the Prosecution's argument that Mr. Lubanga acted with discriminatory motive in that "the female recruits were subjected to sexual violence, rape and 'conjugal subservience' on the basis of their gender," concluding that there was no evidence that Mr. Lubanga "deliberately discriminated against women" in the commission of the offenses for which he was convicted. Ibid. paras.79–81.

[95] Ibid. para. 34.

[96] Ibid. para. 91.

[97] Ibid. para. 98.

[98] Ibid. para. 99.

person, the Chamber should take into account the widespread use of child soldiers ...; the significant position of authority held by Mr Lubanga within [his militia] and his ability through the relevant period to prevent the commission of the offenses."[99] Moreover, she agrees with the majority "that no aggravating circumstances are to be considered" and that Mr. Lubanga's cooperation with the Court should be taken into account as a mitigating factor.[100] However, Judge Odio Benito "strongly disagree[s]" with the fact that the majority, as she writes, "disregards the damage caused to the victims and their families, particularly as a result of the harsh punishments and sexual violence suffered by the victims of these crimes pursuant to Rule 145(c)."[101] She explains:

> the Chamber received ample evidence during the trial related to the conditions in which boys and girls were recruited and the harms they suffered as a result of their involvement with [Mr. Lubanga's militia]. The evidence received as regards the punishments and harsh conditions of children in the recruitment camps and the sexual violence they suffered (mainly but not exclusively the girls) at their young age should be taken into consideration when determining the sentence against the convicted person as it touches upon the gravity of the crimes of enlistment, conscription and use of children under the age of 15 to participate actively in the hostilities, and particularly the damage caused to the child victims and their families as a result of these crimes.[102]

Judge Odio Benito also makes clear that she finds that the harm caused to victims and their families has been proven beyond reasonable doubt.[103] Based on these findings, Judge Odio Benito concludes that the appropriate sentence for Mr. Lubanga is 15 years imprisonment.[104]

5.4.2 *Relationship Among Various Factors Relevant to Sentencing*

As noted above, the Rome Statute and Rules of Procedure and Evidence require the Chamber to consider a number of factors in determining its sentence, including the gravity of the crime, the individual circumstances of the convicted person, the extent of the damage caused, the degree of participation of the convicted person, the degree

---

[99] *Lubanga* Decision on Sentence Pursuant to Article 76 of the Statute, supra, note 2, Dissenting Opinion of Judge Odio Benito, para. 1.

[100] Ibid.

[101] Ibid. para. 2. Judge Odio Benito also disagrees with the majority's "decision to impose a differentiated sentence to the convicted person as regards the crimes of enlistment, conscription and use to participate actively in the hostilities." Ibid. para. 3.

[102] Ibid. para. 6.

[103] Ibid. paras. 19–23. Indeed, Subheading "E" of Judge Odio Benito's dissent reads: "The harm caused to victims and their families has been proven beyond reasonable doubt as a factor pursuant to Rule 145(l)(c) of the Rules." Ibid. at 49.

[104] Ibid. para. 27.

of intent, and aggravating and mitigating circumstances. However, neither the Rome Statute nor the Rules of Procedure and Evidence establish whether each of the factors must be proven according to the same standard or otherwise indicate the relationship among the factors. The *Lubanga* majority makes clear, following the jurisprudence of the ICTY, that factors should not be double counted, saying that "[a]ny factors that are to be taken into account when assessing the gravity of the crime will not additionally be taken into account as aggravating circumstances, and *vice versa*."[105] Furthermore, as explained above, the Chamber also establishes that, "[s]ince any aggravating factors established by the Chamber may have a significant effect on the overall length of the sentence Mr. Lubanga will serve, it is necessary that they are established to the criminal standard of proof, namely 'beyond a reasonable doubt.'"[106] Yet the majority of the Trial Chamber does not explain why it considers some factors, including the alleged brutal treatment of child soldiers and acts of sexual violence, as aggravating circumstances, as opposed to as factors relating to the gravity of the crime or extent of the damage caused, as Judge Odio Benito does in her dissent. Nor does Judge Odio Benito explain why she considers the harsh treatment of children and sexual violence as factors going to the gravity of the crime, rather than as aggravating circumstances, as urged by the Prosecution. Perhaps the explanation is that she agrees with the majority that the harsh treatment and sexual violence cannot be attributed to Mr. Lubanga in a manner sufficient to warrant treating these factors as aggravating circumstances, but she does not state this, and it is not clear that factors affecting the gravity of the crime for purposes of sentencing need not be attributable to the convicted person. Otherwise, presumably any factor that does not amount to an aggravating circumstance due to attribution problems could be counted as going to the gravity of the crime. Clarity on these issues, in both the majority and dissenting opinions, would have been helpful both in this case and for future sentencing decisions by the Court.

5.4.3 Determination of the Appropriate Length of Prison Sentence

A second problem with both the majority's and the dissent's opinions on sentencing is that neither indicates how the factors they considered relevant to sentencing led them to determine the appropriate sentence for the accused. The Prosecution requested a 30-year sentence,[107] which the Chamber obviously rejects, but without explanation. The majority does observe that a life sentence "would be inappropriate," citing Rule 145(3) of the ICC Rules, which states that such a sentence must be "justified by the extreme gravity of the crime and the individual circumstances of

[105] *Lubanga* Decision on Sentence Pursuant to Article 76 of the Statute, supra, note 2, para. 35.
[106] Ibid. para. 33.
[107] *Lubanga* Decision on Sentence Pursuant to Article 76 of the Statute, supra, note 2, para. 95.

the convicted person, as evidenced by the existence of one or more aggravating circumstances,"[108] and noting that it did not find any aggravating circumstances in the present case.[109] The majority also makes reference to the sentencing practices of the Special Court for Sierra Leone (SCSL), the only other international criminal body that has handed down convictions for war crimes involving child soldiers, explaining that, "[a]lthough the decisions of other international courts and tribunals are not part of the directly applicable law under Article 21 of the [Rome] Statute," these bodies "are in a comparable position to the Court in the context of sentencing."[110] However, the practice of the SCSL is not particularly instructive, as the sentences imposed by that court for the relevant crimes range from 7 to 50 years.[111] Finally, as explained above, the majority discusses a number of factors relevant to sentencing, but it does not explain how these factors together led it to determine that Mr. Lubanga should receive a 13 year sentence for the crime of conscripting children, 12 years for the crime of enlisting children, and 14 years for using children to actively participate in hostilities. For instance, it is not clear whether the majority determined an appropriate sentence for each of the relevant crimes, and then added time based on the gravity of the crime, the degree of Mr. Lubanga's participation and the individual circumstances of Mr. Lubanga, while subtracting time based on the mitigating circumstance, or whether it took a totality of the circumstances approach. As commentator Dov Jacobs has observed: "[A]fter 25 pages of factors that were or were not considered, the result, 14 years, falls from the sky without the reader being any more enlightened, despite the appearance of explanation. The Judge[s] might as well have thrown dice and rendered a one-page decision."[112] Similarly, while Judge Odio Benito states in her dissent that she believes the appropriate prison sentence for Mr. Lubanga is 14 years, presumably adding 1 year based on her findings regarding the harm caused to victims and their families, she is also silent as to why 14 years was an appropriate base to which to add the additional year. It is also notable that neither decision makes any reference to the goals of sentencing in international criminal law or how the judges' determinations are consistent with those goals.

[108] ICC Rules, supra, note 86, R. 145(3).

[109] *Lubanga* Decision on Sentence Pursuant to Article 76 of the Statute, supra, note 2, para. 96.

[110] Ibid. para. 12.

[111] Specifically, as the *Lubanga* majority explains in the RUF case, the SCSL sentenced Issa Hassan Sesay to 50 years for using children actively in hostilities and Morris Kallon to 35 years for his involvement in use of child soldiers. Ibid. para. 13. In the CDF case, the SCSL sentenced Allieu Kondewa to 7 years for conscripting child soldiers in order to participate actively in hostilities, although this conviction was later overturned on appeal. Ibid. para. 15. The *Lubanga* majority also explains that, although the defendants in the AFRC and Taylor cases were also convicted for the use of child soldiers, in those cases, the SCSL imposed a global sentence for all crimes without breaking down how many years imposed on defendants for each crimes. Ibid. para. 12.

[112] Dov Jacobs, *Some thoughts on the Lubanga Sentence: A Throw of the Dice*, Spreading the Jam, 10 July 2012, available at: http://dovjacobs.blogspot.com/2012/07/some-thoughts-on-lubanga-sentence-throw.html.

5.5 Purpose and Timing of the Trial Chamber's Decision Relating to Reparations

As explained above, the Trial Chamber's decision relating to reparations consists of "certain principles relating to reparations and the approach to be taken to their implementation,"[113] but does not include a ruling on any individual application for reparations nor any specific order regarding the award of reparations to Mr. Lubanga's victims.[114] According to the Chamber, the decision was issued pursuant to Article 75(1) of the Rome Statute, which states that "[t]he Court *shall establish principles* relating to reparation to, or in respect of, victims, including restitution, compensation and rehabilitation."[115] However, the Chamber also makes clear that the principles set forth in its decision "are limited to the circumstances of the present case,"[116] calling into question whether the decision fulfills the aim of Article 75(1). Indeed, as the War Crimes Research Office argued in a report published in June 2010, although none of the texts governing the ICC establish specific procedures for the adoption of the "principles" referred to in Article 75(1), there is strong support for the notion that the provision creates an obligation on the judges of the Court's Trial Division to collectively and proactively develop the principles referred to in the provision *outside of the context of any single case*.[117] Specifically, the report notes that, absent the issuance of general guidelines, the significant ambiguity regarding both procedural and substantive aspects of the Court's reparations scheme is likely to breed frustration on the part of victims and intermediaries seeking to conduct outreach with respect to the scheme.[118] Furthermore, the report contends that the lack of guidance on a variety of issues related to the reparation

[113] *Lubanga* Decision Establishing Principles and Procedures to be Applied to Reparations, supra, note 3, para. 181.

[114] See generally Ibid.

[115] Rome Statute, supra, note 17, Art. 75(1) (emphasis added).

[116] *Lubanga* Decision Establishing Principles and Procedures to be Applied to Reparations, supra, note 3, para. 181.

[117] See War Crimes Research Office, *The Case-Based Reparations Scheme at the International Criminal Court*, at 28–32 (June 2010), available at: https://www.wcl.american.edu/warcrimes/icc/documents/report12.pdf.

[118] See, e.g., Carla Ferstman and Mariana Goetz, Reparations before the International Criminal Court: The Early Jurisprudence on Victim Participation and Its Impact on Future Reparations Proceedings, in Carla Ferstman, Mariana Goetz and Alan Stephens (eds.) *Reparations for Victims of Genocide, War Crimes and Crimes against Humanity* (Leiden: Brill, 2009) 313, 350 ("If [certain] very basic considerations about the nature and forms of reparations will only be considered after the trial, the application forms for reparations which are currently available for victims to complete and submit to the Court[] are like a 'shot in the dark' – victims have no idea what they are aiming at, nor is it clear whether the detailed information they provide would serve any utility whatsoever in the determination of the award.").

scheme, combined with the fact that the judges of the ICC hail from diverse backgrounds, leaves open the possibility for wide discrepancies in the approach to reparations across cases.[119] Importantly, discrepancies in the Court's approach to reparations may not only result in unfairness to individual victims in particular cases, but may also lead to perceptions that the overall scheme is unfair or arbitrary. In fact, the Inter-American Court of Human Rights, despite being one of the most progressive mechanisms with respect to ordering reparations, has been criticized for providing inconsistent awards to similarly situated victims, particularly because there is no comparative analysis between cases to show how the Court makes its determinations given the differing circumstances in each case.[120] The establishment of principles guiding the ICC reparations scheme from the outset would likely help the Court avoid similar criticisms by establishing consistent and transparent standards and procedures to apply across cases. The issuing of principles specific to a single case, by contrast, does nothing to ensure that like victims will be treated similarly by the Court.

---

[119] This, in fact, occurred in the early jurisprudence of the Court with respect to the requirements set forth by different Chambers regarding participation of victims under Article 68(3) of the Statute, which permits victims to present their "views and concerns" to the Court at appropriate stages of proceedings. Rome Statute, supra, note 17, Art. 68(3). For instance, Pre-Trial Chamber I, presiding over the Situation in the Democratic Republic of Congo, and Pre-Trial Chamber II, presiding over the Situation in Uganda, adopted different approaches to the requirement in Rule 85(a) that victims be "natural persons." Pre-Trial Chamber I, the first Chamber to rule on the issue, held that a "natural person" is "any person who is not a legal person," and that therefore victims will satisfy the "natural persons" requirement simply by virtue of being "human beings." *Situation in the Democratic Republic of Congo*, Decision on the Applications for Participation in the Proceedings VPRS 1, VPRS 2, VPRS 3, VPRS 4, VPRS 5 and VPRS 6, ICC-01/04-101-tEN-Corr, para. 80 (ICC Pre-Trial Chamber I, 17 January 2006). Over a year and a half later, however, Pre-Trial Chamber II held that the term "natural persons" requires that the "identity of the applicant" be "duly established." *Situation in Uganda*, Decision on Victims' Applications for Participation a/0010/06, a/0064/06 to a/0070/06, a/0081/06 to a/0104/06 and a/0111/06 to a/0127/06, ICC-02/04-101, para. 12 (10 August 2007). Moreover, Pre-Trial Chamber II held that such identity could only be established by a document "(i) issued by a recognized public authority; (ii) stating the name and the date of birth of the holder; and (iii) showing a photograph of the holder," Ibid. para. 16, whereas Pre-Trial Chamber I permitted victims to establish their identity through a wide range of documents. See *Situation in Democratic Republic of the Congo*, Decision on the Requests of the Legal Representative of Applicants on Application Process for Victims' Participation and Legal Representation, ICC-01/04-374, paras. 13–15 (ICC Pre-Trial Chamber I, 17 August 2007). While Pre-Trial Chamber II subsequently relaxed its identification requirements for applications to participate in proceedings, See *Situation in Uganda*, Decision on Victims' Applications for Participation a/0010/06, a/0064/06 to a/0070/06, a/0081/06, a/0082/06, a/0084/06 to a/0089/06, a/0091/06 to a/0097/06, a/0099/06, a/0100/06, a/0102/06 to a/0104/06, a/0111/06, a/0113/06 to a/0117/06, a/0120/06, a/0121/06 and a/0123/06 to a/0128/06, ICC-02/04-125 (ICC Pre-Trial Chamber II, 14 March 2008), it would be much more difficult to retroactively standardize requirements for reparations awards *after* one or more awards have been ordered.

[120] See, e.g., Arturo J. Carrillo, "Justice in Context: The Relevance of Inter-American Human Rights Law and Practice to Repairing the Past" in Pablo de Greiff (ed.) *The Handbook of Reparations* (Oxford: Oxford University Press, 2006) 504, 529–530.

The timing of the Trial Chamber's decision is also questionable in that it authorizes the Trust Fund for Victims (TFV)[121] to commence implementation of a five-step plan that involves consulting with victims in order to assess the harm caused by Mr. Lubanga and devise an appropriate reparations program, despite the fact that the Defense for Mr. Lubanga has filed an appeal challenging his conviction.[122] While it is understandable that the Chamber would want to expedite any reparations ultimately awarded to victims of Mr. Lubanga, the Rome Statute makes clear that reparations may only be awarded against persons convicted by the Court,[123] meaning that no reparations are due if the Appeals Chamber vacates the Trial Chamber's conviction of Mr. Lubanga. Hence, initiating the process prior to a final judgment from the Appeals Chamber not only risks wasting the resources of the TFV, but also of the judges, the parties and the participating victims, as multiple appeals have already been filed against the Trial Chamber's 7 August 2012 decision.[124] Moreover, the decision risks unduly raising the expectations of victims consulted by the TFV in the event that the conviction is ultimately overturned. Indeed, much concern has been expressed about the potential for unmet expectations of victims in the context of the ICC repara-

---

[121] The TFV is an independent body, as opposed to an organ of the Court, established pursuant to Article 79 of the Rome Statute "for the benefit of victims of crimes within the jurisdiction of the Court, and of the families of such victims." Rome Statute, supra, note 17, Art. 79(1). According to the TFV's website, the Fund "fulfils two mandates for victims of crimes under jurisdiction of the ICC: (1) Reparations: implementing Court-ordered reparations awards against a convicted person when directed by the Court to do so. (2) General Assistance: using voluntary contributions from donors to provide victims and their families in situations where the Court is active with physical rehabilitation, material support, and/or psychological rehabilitation." Trust Fund for Victims Website, *The Two Roles Of The TFV*, available at: http://www.trustfundforvictims.org/two-roles-tfv. The website further explains: "In relation to its first role, the Court may order money and other property collected through fines or forfeiture from a convicted person to be transferred to the TFV for the implementation of reparations awards. However, the TFV has also been established to complement such resources through voluntary contributions from donors. The Board of Directors may determine the extent to which the TFV will complement court-ordered reparations, in accordance with Regulation 56 of the Regulations of the TFV. The TFV general assistance is supported by voluntary contributions solely." Ibid.

[122] See *The Prosecutor v. Thomas Lubanga Dyilo*, Acte d'appel de la Défense de M. Thomas Lubanga à l'encontre du "Jugement rendu en application de l'article 74 du Statut" rendu par la Chambre de première instance I le 14 mars 2012, ICC-01/04-01/06-2934 (Defense for Thomas Lubanga Dyilo, 3 October 2012).

[123] Specifically, Article 75(2) states: "The Court may make an order directly against *a convicted person* specifying appropriate reparations to, or in respect of, victims, including restitution, compensation and rehabilitation." Rome Statute, supra, note 17, Art. 75(2) (emphasis added).

[124] See, e.g., *The Prosecutor v. Thomas Lubanga Dyilo*, Appeal of the Defence for Mr Thomas Lubanga against Trial Chamber I's Decision establishing the principles and procedures to be applied to reparation rendered on 7 August 2012, ICC-01/04-01/06-2917 (Defense for Thomas Lubanga Dyilo, 6 September 2012); *The Prosecutor v. Thomas Lubanga Dyilo*, Appeal against Trial Chamber I's Decision establishing the principles and procedures to be applied to reparation of 7 August 2012, ICC-01/04-01/06-2914 (Legal Representatives of Victims, 3 September 2012); *The Prosecutor v. Thomas Lubanga Dyilo*, Appeal against Trial Chamber I's Decision establishing the principles and procedures to be applied to reparations of 7 August 2012, ICC-01/04-01/06-2909 (Office of Public Counsel for Victims and Legal Representatives of Victims, 24 August 2012).

tions process generally,[125] and a decision authorizing consultations with victims regarding reparations that may not ultimately be forthcoming exacerbates this potential. Notably, the timing of the Trial Chamber's decision cannot be justified on the ground that it is efficient to ensure that the same three judges that presided over Mr. Lubanga's trial also preside over the reparations proceedings, as the decision holds that the reparations will be "monitored and overseen by a *differently composed Chamber*," which will be "in a position to resolve any contested issues arising out of the work and the decisions of the TFV."[126] This fact, coupled with concerns of efficiency and the expectations of victims, strongly suggests that no decision on reparations should have been issued until after the Appeals Chamber has ruled on the Defense's appeal against Mr. Lubanga's conviction.

5.6 Conclusion

The delivery of the first judgment of the ICC is an historic occasion and critical accomplishment for the world's first permanent international criminal court. While the overall approach of Trial Chamber I in presiding over the Court's first trial is to be commended, and the judgment is largely sound, the Court and its constituents – including the parties, affected communities and the broader public – may be better served if future Trial Chambers strive to deliver judgments within a shorter period of time, while also ensuring that their reasoning on the crimes charged is fully explained. Furthermore, future decisions on sentencing will benefit from greater clarity. Finally, Trial Chambers in other cases should reconsider whether it is wise to issue any decisions on reparations prior to a final judgment on the guilt of the accused.

---

[125] See, e.g., Marc Henzelin, Veijo Heiskanen, and Guénaël Mettraux, "Reparations to Victims before the International Criminal Court: Lessons from International Mass Claims Processes", 17 *Criminal Law Forum* (2006) 317, 343 ("Considering the hopes that have been invested in the ability of the Court to provide a meaningful remedy to victims of the crimes falling under its jurisdiction, and the legal and practical difficulties which reparation claims potentially stimulate, there is a real risk of procedural impotency on the part of the Court and unfulfilled expectations on the part of the victims.").

[126] *Lubanga* Decision Establishing Principles and Procedures to be Applied to Reparations, supra, note 3, paras. 261–262 (emphasis added).

Chapter 6
Interim Measures Before the Inter-American and African Human Rights Commissions: Strengths and Weaknesses

Clara Burbano-Herrera and Frans Viljoen

Abstract Interim measures in international human rights law may be defined as a tool, the purpose of which is to prevent irreparable harm to persons who are in a situation of extreme gravity and urgency. Interim measures result in an immediate protection offered by the member State to the beneficiaries in compliance with the order issued by an international body. This article aims to illustrate that although interim measures in the African and the Inter-American system have been a useful legal tool to avoid (further) human rights violations in difficult situations, there are still some obstacles that may lead to the interim measures not functioning as one would wish. We begin by mentioning three aspects of interim measures that lend themselves to a comparison between the two regional systems: the admissibility requirements; the frequency of their use; and the rights and beneficiaries protected through these interim measures. Taking into account the aforementioned comparison, the merits and deficiencies of interim measures in regional human rights systems will be highlighted, and recommendations will be advanced for improving their functioning and impact.

C. Burbano-Herrera (✉)
Co-Lecturer at the Human Rights Centre of Ghent University, Ghent, Belgium

Postdoctoral Research Fellow at the Research Foundation Flanders, Brussels, Belgium
e-mail: Clara.BurbanoHerrera@UGent.be

F. Viljoen
Director of the Centre for Human Rights, University of Pretoria,
Pretoria, Republic of South Africa
e-mail: frans.viljoen@up.ac.za

Y. Haeck and E. Brems (eds.), *Human Rights and Civil Liberties in the 21st Century*, Ius Gentium: Comparative Perspectives on Law and Justice 30,
DOI 10.1007/978-94-007-7599-2_6,

6.1 Introduction

In international human rights law, provisional,[1] precautionary[2] or interim measures[3] have been developed as an instrument for preventing human rights violations.[4] At the regional level, in Africa and the Americas, both the African Commission on Human and Peoples' Rights (hereinafter the 'African Commission') and the Inter-American Commission on Human Rights (hereinafter the 'Inter-American Commission' or 'IACHR') are competent in cases of extreme gravity and urgency to issue interim measures in order to prevent irreparable damage to the rights of victim(s) and person(s) protected under the African Charter on Human and Peoples' Rights (hereinafter the 'African Charter'),[5] the American Declaration of the Rights and Duties of Man (hereinafter the 'American Declaration' or 'Declaration')[6] and the American Convention on Human Rights (hereinafter the 'American Convention').[7]

Interim measures have two key characteristics. First, they are precautionary (or preventive), in that they ensure that human rights violations are not committed during the time a matter is under examination before one of the above-mentioned quasi-judicial supervisory organs. In this sense, interim measures that are complied with by States also give the latter the opportunity not to be held internationally responsible, because they have corrected in time situations in which violations of human

[1] Under the African system, the measures adopted by the African Commission and the African Court are called 'provisional measures'.

[2] Under the Inter-American system, the measures adopted by the Inter-American Commission are called 'precautionary measures' and the measures adopted by the Inter-American Court are called 'provisional measures'.

[3] In this article we will refer to them as 'interim measures'.

[4] See C. Burbano-Herrera and F. Viljoen, "Provisional Measures Issued by the African Commission and African Court on Human and People's Rights", in Y. Haeck and C. Burbano-Herrera (eds.) *Interim Measures in International Human Rights Law* (Oxford: Oxford University Press, forthcoming 2013).

[5] The African Charter on Human and Peoples' Rights (also called the 'Banjul Charter') was adopted in Nairobi, Kenya, by the Organisation of African Unity on 27 June 1981 and entered into force on 21 October 1986. The substance of the Charter has been extended by the adoption of the Protocol to the African Charter on the Rights of Women in Africa in 2003, over which the African Commission and Court also have jurisdiction, including the competence to issue provisional measures. In the African system, the African Charter on the Rights and Welfare of the Child (African Children's Charter) was also adopted in Addis Ababa, Ethiopia on 11 July 1990, and it entered into force on 29 November 1999. The African Children's Committee is the supervisory bodies. By ratifying the African Children's Charter, states automatically accept the competence of the African Children's Committee to 'receive' individual and inter-state communications. This body held its first meeting in 2002. See, African Children's Charter, arts. 32, 43 and 44. However, this body does not have an explicit competence to adopt provisional measures.

[6] The American Declaration was adopted in 1948 in Bogota, Colombia, by the OAS General Assembly. The American Declaration and other Inter-American human rights documents can be viewed on the website of the OAS, http://www.oas.org

[7] The American Convention on Human Rights was adopted in San José, Costa Rica, by the Organization of American States on 22 November 1969, and entered into force on 18 July 1978. As of 2012, only 23 of the 35 States have ratified the American Convention.

rights could have occurred or they have prevented further violation of these rights. Second, interim measures serve a protective purpose, because their objective is to protect the rights contemplated in the African Charter, the American Convention and the American Declaration, and the other human rights treaties ratified by African and American States (hereinafter 'the States'). By complying with interim measures States also show respect for the quasi-judicial bodies issuing those measures, and for the human rights themselves.[8]

This contribution aims to illustrate that, although interim measures in the African and the Inter-American system have been a useful legal tool to avoid (further) human rights violations in difficult situations, there are still some obstacles that may lead to the interim measures not functioning as one would wish. We begin by mentioning three aspects of interim measures that lend themselves to a comparison between the two regional systems: (1) the admissibility requirements; (2) the frequency of their use; and (3) the rights and beneficiaries protected through these interim measures. Taking into account the aforementioned comparison, (4) the merits and deficiencies of interim measures in regional human rights systems will be highlighted, and recommendations will be advanced for improving their functioning and impact.

6.2 Legal Basis

None of the universal or regional human rights treaties establishing quasi-judicial bodies bestows an explicit mandate on these bodies to issue interim measures.[9] However, the Rules of Procedure of these bodies have, for decades, served as the basis for institutionalizing practices of issuing interim measures. The African Commission and the Inter-American Commission (herein after 'the Commissions') are prime examples of long-standing practices in this regard. In 1988, the African Commission incorporated the competence to adopt such measures in its first set of Rules of Procedure, more specifically in Rule 109. When it amended its Rules of Procedure in 1995, the Commission elaborated upon its competence to adopt interim measures in Rule 111.[10] Since 2010, the restated competence to adopt provisional

[8] See F. Viljoen, *International Human Rights Law in Africa,* (Oxford: Oxford University Press, 2012) 306.

[9] See e.g., Human Rights Committee, Rules of Procedure, r. 92; the Committee Against Torture, Rules of Procedure r. 114(1); African Commission on Human and Peoples' Rights, Rules of Procedure, r. 98; the extinct European Commission of Human Rights, Rules of Procedure, r. 36; the Committee on the Elimination of Racial Discrimination, Rules of Procedure, r. 94 (3) and the Committee on the Elimination of Discrimination against women, Rules of Procedure, r. 63 (1).

[10] The Rules of Procedure were adopted by the African Commission during its 2nd ordinary session held in Dakar (Senegal), from 2 to 13 February 1988 and were revised by the Commission during its 18th ordinary session held in Praia (Cabo-Verde), from 2 to 11 October 1995. The Rules were also revised during its 47th ordinary session held in Banjul (The Gambia), from 12 to 26 May 2010 and entered into force 18 August 2010.

measures is contained in Rule 98 of the Commissions' current Rules of Procedure, which state that '[...] the Commission may, on its initiative or at the request of a party to the Communication, request that the State concerned adopt Provisional Measures to prevent irreparable harm to the victim or victims of the alleged violation, as urgently as the situation demands'.[11] In the Inter-American system, interim measures were also expressly incorporated in the first Commission's Rules of Procedure in 1980.[12] Since 2009, the restated competence to adopt interim measures is contained in Rule 25 of the Commission's Rules of Procedure, which state that '[i]n serious and urgent situations, the Commission may, on its own initiative or at the request of a party, request that a State adopt precautionary measures'.[13] The faculty to grant precautionary measures has also been recognized in Article XIII of the Inter-American Convention on Forced Disappearance of Persons.[14]

The adoption of interim measures by the Inter-American Commission requires the existence of a 'serious' and 'urgent situation' that may cause 'irreparable harm' to persons, if action is not taken. The competence of the African Commission is formulated slightly differently, in that it may adopt provisional measures in order 'to prevent irreparable harm' to the victim or the victims of the alleged violation, as 'urgently' as the situation demands.[15] There is no specific mention that the African Commission may act in 'serious' situations. Although the preconditions for the adoption of interim measures by the two quasi-judicial organs are not exactly similar, the provisions are not necessarily mutually exclusive.

---

[11] Rule 98 also provides that: "2. If the Commission is not in session at the time that a request for Provisional Measures is received, the Chairperson, or in his or her absence, the Vice-Chairperson, shall take the decision on the Commission's behalf and shall so inform members of the Commission; 3. After the request for Provisional Measures has been transmitted to the State Party, the Commission shall send a copy of the letter requesting Provisional Measures to the victim, the Assembly, the Peace and Security Council, and the African Union Commission. 4. The Commission shall request the State Party concerned to report back on the implementation of the Provisional Measures requested. Such information shall be submitted within fifteen (15) days of the receipt of the request for Provisional Measures; 5. The granting of such measures and their adoption by the State Party concerned shall not constitute a prejudgment on the merits of a Communication."

[12] During its existence, the Commission has in total drafted four sets of Rules of Procedure: in 1966, 1980, 2001 (amended in 2002, 2003, 2006 and 2008) and 2009 (amended in 2011 and 2013). The 1980 Commission's Rules of Procedure, approved by the Commission at its 49th period of sessions, held on 8 April (r. 26); 2000 Commission's Rules of Procedure, approved by the Commission at its 109th period of sessions, held from 4 to 8 December 2000, and modified at its 116th period of sessions, held from the 7 to 25 October 2002, at its 118th period of sessions, held from 6 to 24 October 2003, at its 126th period of sessions, held from 16 to 27 October 2006 and at its 132th period of sessions, held from 17 to 25 July 2008 (r. 25) 2009; Commission's Rules of Procedure, approved by the Commission at its 137th regular period of sessions, held from 28 October to 13 November 2009, entered into force on 31 December 2009 (r. 25), and amended on 2 September 2011 and by Resolution 1-2013. It will enter into force on 1 August 2013.

[13] See Article 25.

[14] The Inter-American Convention on Forced Disappearance of Persons was adopted in Belem Do Para, Brazil, by the Organisation of American States on 6 September 1994, and entered into force on 28 March 1996. This Convention has been ratified by 14 States.

[15] 2010 Rules of Procedure, r. 98 (1).

The Rules of Procedure of the Inter-American Commission which were recently amended, indicate that the term "serious situation" refers to a grave impact that an action or omission can have on a protected right, or on the eventual effect of a pending decision in a case or petition before the organs of the Inter-American system; and an "urgent situation" refers to a risk or threat that is imminent and can materialize, thus requiring immediate preventive or protective action'.[16] Taking into consideration that, until now, the Commissions in both systems have not adopted reasoned decisions on interim measures, it is virtually impossible to conduct a rigorous analysis of the circumstances giving rise to interim measures, or to shed further light on the difference between the terms 'urgent' and 'serious'.

Most probably, decisions by the Commissions to adopt or reject interim measures or to request more information from the State involved is preceded by an analysis of the situation in order to assess whether such a measure may be necessary. In both human rights systems, serious and urgent situations are clearly present when there is an imminent risk to life and personal integrity, involving, for example, unlawful death sentences, death threats, the risk of torture, in human or degrading punishment or treatment, or serious danger arising from conditions of detention.

The fact that interim measures are not included in the African Charter or in the American Convention, has resulted in a debate in the respective human rights systems as to their binding character. On the one hand, some States on the American continent, most pertinently the United States,[17] recently joined by Ecuador,[18] argue that interim measures issued by the Inter-American Commission are not true or legally binding orders that must be complied with by the States parties. On the other hand, most legal scholars deduce the binding character of these measures from a teleological interpretation of the American Declaration and Convention, the Rules of Procedure of the Inter-American Commission in the case of the Americas, and the African Charter with respect to the African system.[19]

We are of the view that interim measures adopted by the Commissions are not merely recommendatory requests. States parties cannot simply reject their implementation. Both systems give their respective Commissions the function to promote and protect human rights. In exercising such generic function, the Commissions have determined that this function included the power to grant interim measures.

---

[16] Rules of Procedure, art. 25 (2).

[17] See, U.S. Additional Response to the request for precautionary measures detention of enemy combatants at Guantanamo Bay, Cuba, IACHR (15 July 2002), available at: http://www.state.gov/s/l/38642.htm. The United States has not ratified the Inter-American Convention on forced Disappearance of Persons.

[18] In March 2013, in a meeting of States, the President of Ecuador, Rafael Correa indicated that '[...] the Commission does not have competence to adopt precautionary measures [...]'. See http://www.elcomercio.com/politica/Polemico-debate-medidas-cautelares-Guayaquil-CIDH-Derechos_Humanos_0_881311902.html. (Accessed on 12 March 2013). The Inter-American Convention on Forced Disappearance of Persons has been ratified by Ecuador.

[19] See e.g. H. Faúndez Ledesma, *The Inter-American System for the Protection of Human Rights*, 2nd ed., (San José: Inter-American Institute for Human Rights, 2007) 361–362; and F. Gonzales, "Urgent Measures in the Inter-American Human Rights System" 7 *Revista Sur* (2010) 13, 52–53.

In the case of the African system, according to Article 30 of the African Charter, 'the Commission shall be established within the Organization of African Unity, to promote human and peoples' rights and ensure their protection in Africa'. Article 45 indicates that the Commission is mandated to 'promote' and 'ensure the protection of human and peoples' rights'. In the Inter-American system, Article 106 of the OAS Charter recognizes that the principal function of the Inter-American Commission is to promote the 'observance' and 'protection' of human rights, and to serve as a consultative organ of the Organization in these matters. Even though the American Convention does not expressly provide for precautionary measures, the Inter-American Convention on Forced Disappearance of Persons recognizes the binding force of precautionary measures when it stipulates in Article XIII that '[f] or the purposes of this Convention, the processing of petitions or communications presented to the Inter-American Commission on Human Rights alleging the forced disappearance of persons, shall be subject to the procedures established in the American Convention on Human Rights and to the Statute and Regulations of the Inter-American Commission on Human Rights and to the Statute and Rules of Procedure of the Inter-American Court of Human Rights, including the provisions on precautionary measures'.[20]

Article 33 of the American Convention indicates that the Commission is one of the main organs of the Inter-American system with the competence to evaluate the compliance of the obligations assumed by the States, and Article 41(b) of the American Convention gives the Commission competence to recommend to States the adoption of certain actions to improve the human rights situation. Furthermore, Article 18(b) of its Statute basically reproduces Article 41(b). In this regard, it is sufficient that a State has ratified the African Charter or the OAS Charter (hereinafter 'the Charters' or 'Regional Charters') to be obligated by the recommendations or 'requests' of the Commissions. Otherwise, it would not make sense to give functions and responsibilities to the respective Commissions which, when exercised, do not have any effect in reality, because States may negate them. Some OAS States, especially Colombia since 2003, have even expressly recognized that interim measures are mandatory and binding. According to the Colombian Constitutional Court's jurisprudence, interim measures issued by the Inter-American Commission are "a judicial act adopted by an international body for the protection of human rights",[21] and the Constitutional Court held that non-compliance with the Commission's interim measures "[…] would amount to a disregard for the international obligations to respect and ensure enshrinement in Articles 1 and 2 of the American Convention".[22] The Judicial Committee of the Privy Council, in a case related to Trinidad and Tobago,[23] also gave domestic legal effect to the interim measures requested by the

[20] Inter-American Convention on Forced Disappearance of Persons, supra, note 14.

[21] Colombian Constitutional Court, Judgment T-558 of 2003.

[22] Colombian Constitutional Court, Judgment T-786 of 2003; T-327 of 2004, T-385 of 2005; T-524 of 2005; T435 of 2009 and T-367 of 2010.

[23] It is the highest court of appeal (or court of last resort) for several independent Commonwealth countries. It is one of the highest courts in the United Kingdom.

Inter-American Commission, by preventing the State from executing condemned prisoners while their complaints were pending before the Inter-American system on human rights.[24] The Privy Council judgment expressly indicated that '[for] the Government to carry out the sentences of death before the [inter-American] petitions have been heard, would deny the appellants their constitutional right to due process.'[25] In addition, the Inter-American Court, referring to the non-compliance of Trinidad and Tobago with a request of interim measures issued by the Commission, pointed out that, based on the principles of effectiveness and good faith, the States Parties to the Convention should comply in good faith (*pacta sunt servanda*) with the provisions of the Convention, including those relative to the operation of the two supervisory organs of the American Convention. '[...] States Parties must refrain from taking actions that may cause irreparable harm to persons by reason of the gravity of the possible consequences of said acts.'[26] In turn, the General Assembly of the OAS has encouraged State parties to '[f]ollow up on the recommendations of the IACHR, including, *inter alia,* precautionary measures'.[27]

In that regard, State parties to the Regional Charters do not have any justification to indiscriminately ignore requests for interim measures adopted by the regional quasi-judicial supervisory bodies. Denying the obligation to comply with orders of interim measures would go against the core of the Regional Charters and the obligation of the States to give effect and guarantee the rights and freedoms enshrined in those instruments.[28] It must be mentioned that, although it is true that the legal instrument of interim measures issued by the respective Commissions were not provided for in the Regional Charters or other human right instruments – with the exception of the mention in Article XIII of the Inter-American Convention on Forced Disappearance of Persons – the silence on its exclusion in the *travaux préparatoires* cannot be interpreted as a clear intention to wrest from them their binding character, because there was simply no discussion on the topic. Finally, as already mentioned, interim measures adopted by the Commissions often do benefit from State adherence to the principle of *pacta sunt servanda*, which derives from international treaties.[29] According to this principle, every treaty in force is binding upon the parties to it,

[24] B. Tittemore, "The Mandatory Death Penalty in the Commonwealth Caribbean and the Inter-American Human Rights System: An Evolution in the Development and Implementation of International Human Rights Protections" (2004) 13 *William and Mary Bill of Rights Journal* 445. See also Case 11.816, *Haniff Hilaire v. Trinidad and Tobago,* Precautionary measures, Inter-Am. Comm. HR, Order of 16 October 1997 (1997 Annual Report) ('*Haniff Hilaire* case').

[25] *Thomas & Hilarie v. Baptiste*, [1999] 3 W. L. R. 249, 2 A.C.1. p 12 and 19. The judgment is available at: http://www.internationaljusticeproject.org/pdfs/Hilaire.pdf. (Accessed on 21 March 2013). See also Tittemore, supra, note 24, 467.

[26] *James et al. v. Trinidad and Tobago*, Provisional Measure, Inter-Am.Ct.HR, Order of 26 November 2001, para. 10.

[27] Gonzales, supra, note 19, 53.

[28] Burbano-Herrera and Viljoen, supra, note 4.

[29] Vienna Convention on the Law of Treaties of 1969, art. 27.

and must be performed by them in good faith. This good faith basis of treaties implies that a party to the treaty cannot invoke provisions of its domestic law as a justification for a failure to perform.[30]

6.3 Frequency of the Use of Precautionary Measures

In the Inter-American system, interim measures before the Commission may be requested with respect to all 35 member states of the OAS, and their adoption does not require a case to be pending before the Commission, nor do the measures need to be prompted by a complaint/communication of human rights violations.[31] These practices have permitted the Commission to grant interim measures in a high amount of cases and in a great variety of circumstances. The available annual reports[32] of the Inter-American Commission show that, between 1994[33] and 2012,[34] 771 interim

---

[30] In the African system, the following rights could be limited by the 'claw-back' clauses: the right to liberty and security (Article 6); the freedom of conscience (Article 8); the freedom of expression (Article 9); the freedom of association (Article 10); and the freedom of movement (Article 12). However, the Commission has established that in case of limitations, it should be conformed to international human rights standards. See Communication 101/93, *Civil Liberties Organization (in respect of Bar Association) v. Nigeria* (2000) AHRLR 186 (ACHPR 1995) para. 15. In the Inter-American system, Article 27 (2) of the American Convention indicates explicitly which provision does not authorize any suspension: Article 3 (Right to Juridical Personality), Article 4 (Right to Life), Article 5 (Right to Humane Treatment), Article 6 (Freedom from Slavery), Article 9 (Freedom from Ex Post Facto Laws), Article 12 (Freedom of Conscience and Religion), Article 17 (Rights of the Family), Article 18 (Right to a Name), Article 19 (Rights of the Child), Article 20 (Right to Nationality), and Article 23 (Right to Participate in Government), or of the judicial guarantees essential for the protection of such rights. With regard to the rights which could be limited, the Court has indicated that it is not a question of a suspension of guarantees in an absolute sense, nor of a suspension of rights. See I/A Court H.R. *Habeas Corpus in Emergency Situations* (Arts. 27(2), 25(1) and 7 (6) American Convention on Human Rights). Advisory Opinion OC-8/87 of 30 January 1987.

[31] Inter-American Commission, Rules of Procedure, art 25(2). "In serious and urgent situations, the Commission may, on its own initiative or at the request of a party, request that a State adopt precautionary measures to prevent irreparable harm to persons under the jurisdiction of the State concerned, independently of any pending petition or case."

[32] The Annual Reports have been published since 1970 and precautionary measures have been adopted since 1980. However, it is only since 1996 that the Commission includes in its Report a specific section with information about precautionary measures. Official information on the Commission's early use of precautionary measures is not available.

[33] In the Annual Reports of 1996 and 1997, there are references of precautionary measures adopted in 1994 and 1995. See e.g. *Hernando Valencia Villa v. Colombia,* Precautionary measures, Inter-Am. Comm. HR, Order of 28 September 1994 (1997 Annual Report) ('*Hernando Valencia Villa* matter'); and Case 11.458, *Jorge Vásquez Durand v. Ecuador,* Precautionary measures, Inter-Am. Comm. HR, Order of 1 June 1995 (1996 Annual Report) ('*Jorge Vásquez Durand* case').

[34] In 2012, 25 PM have been examined.

measures were granted.[35] This means that almost 43 measures were adopted every year.[36] If we compare this rate to the activity of the African Commission, which in 24 years has adopted only some 21 interim measures, we can conclude without fear of contradiction that the Inter-American Commission has been much more active. However, the lack of data on the interim measures that were rejected or not answered by the Inter-American Commission is problematic. With regard to this subject, the information available on the OAS homepage,[37] points to 3,009 requests of interim measures that were received from 1 January 2002 until 31 December 2011.[38] During the same period, 474 measures were adopted, which means that only about 15 % of the requests were granted. The other requests were rejected or remained unanswered: there is little solid information on the subject. This lack of information is unfortunate. It appears that the widely held belief that the Inter-American Commission almost always grants interim measures, is unfounded.

The African Commission may adopt interim measures with respect to all AU member States, with the exception of newcomer South Sudan.[39] During the period 1 January 1993 to 31 December 2012,[40] according to information available to us, twenty one of 28 interim[41] measure requests were granted,[42] which means less than

[35] A manual count of the precautionary measures adopted by the Commission shows that measures were granted as follows: 1994 (1 PM); 1995(6 PM); 1996 (26 PM); 1997(48 PM); 1998 (47 PM); 1999 (50 PM); 2000 (44 PM); 2001 (61 PM); 2002 (81 PM); 2003 (60 PM); 2004 (45 PM); 2005 (61 PM); 2006 (24 PM); 2007 (34 PM); 2008 (27 PM); 2009 (35 PM); 2010 (53 PM); 2011 (57 PM). These numbers, in some occasions, are different from the statistics included by the Commission in its Annual Reports.

[36] There is no official information on the precautionary measures that were rejected and not responded to. With respect to this, the Commission only provided statistics.

[37] The website of the OAS is: http:/www.oas.org

[38] In 2005, (265 PM); 2006 (314 PM); 2007 (250 PM); 2008 (301 PM); 2009 (324 PM); 2010 (375 PM) and 2011 (422 PM). There is no official information on the interim measures requested in 2002, 2003 and 2004. See 2011 Commission Annual Report, p 64. The Inter-American Commission publishes the decisions on interim measures and Annual Reports on its website. It may be accessed on: http://www.oas.org/en/iachr/consultation/2_measures.asp

[39] The African Union (AU) is an international organization, since South Sudan joined it last year, consisting of 54 African states. Today, 54 of the 55 states on the African continent are a member of the African Union. The exception is Morocco, which has withdrawn from the Organization of Africa Unity (OAU) in 1984, after the African Union recognised the Western Sahara as a sovereign state.

[40] Although the African Commission has the competence to adopt interim measures since 1988, the first time that the Commission adopted an interim measure was in 1993.

[41] The Institute for Human Rights and Development in Africa (IHRDA), an NGO based in Banjul, publishes the decisions of interim measures of the African Commission and the African Court. It may be accessed on its website: http://caselaw.ihrda.org. The Centre for Human Rights of the University of Pretoria also publishes the decisions of provisional measures on its website: http://www.chr.up.ac.za/index.php/browse-by-subject/538-interimprovisional-measures.html, and it also publishes the African Human Rights Law Reports (AHRLR), see: www.chr.up.ac.za/index.php/publications/ahrlr.html. See also the Commission's website: www.achpr.org.

[42] In total, 26 cases were examined. In the communications 137/94, 139/94, 154/96 and 161/97, *International Pen, Constitutional Rights Project, Interights (in respect of Ken Saro-Wiwa Jr and Civil Liberties Organisation) v. Nigeria ('Saro-Wiwa* case'*)* and in the application 6/12, *African Commission v. Kenya (concerning the Ogiek of Mau Forest Area) ('Ogiek of Mau Forest Area* case'*)*, two different decisions of interim measures were adopted in each case.

one interim measure granted annually. As to the small number of requests for interim measures by the African Commission, one of the contributing factors could be that some cases are not publicly accessible, because the Commission does not keep a record or list of such requests. It is also not certain how many interim measures the Commission has not been allowed to publish on the basis of the application of Article 59 of the Charter.[43] The Commission is required to submit to each regular session of the Assembly of the Heads of State and Government ('Assembly') a report on its work during the previous year. Unlike the Inter-American Commission, the African Commission has an obligation under Article 59 of the African Charter to keep its protective activities (including requests for provisional measures) confidential. Consequently, the public has only access to the decisions of the cases that are published in the Annual Report of the African Commission, following the Assembly's decision to authorise their publication. Finally, it is also possible that the small number of requests for interim measures may be the result of a lack of institutional competence and prioritisation of these measures by the Commission and its Secretariat. It seems to be a good idea that in the future, Commissioners and staff of both Commissions should meet to share experiences with regard to their work on interim measures.

6.4 Rights Protected and Beneficiaries

Although the provisions in the Inter-American and the African systems do not restrict the use of interim measures to protect any particular category of rights, such measures have almost exclusively been requested and granted in order to protect civil and political rights, most frequently the right to life, the right to humane treatment, the right to a fair trial and judicial protection. Only on a few occasions, have the right to freedom of expression and the right to property received protection. Despite the absence of a clear substantive basis providing protection of social and economic rights, the Inter-American Commission granted interim measures with the aim of ordering medical treatment in a number of instances. From a comparative perspective, it is a matter of concern that although the African Charter makes some social and economic rights unequivocally justiciable,[44] – in particular the right to education[45] and the right to health[46] – the case law on interim measures seems biased, in that interim measures are, with very rare exceptions, adopted in order to

[43] According to Article 59(1), all measures taken within the provisions of Chapter III 'Procedure of the Commission' of the African Charter shall remain confidential until such a time as the Assembly of Heads of State and Government shall otherwise decide.

[44] African Charter, art. 22.

[45] Ibid., art. 17.

[46] Ibid., art. 16.

protect traditional civil and political rights. Until now, interim measures adopted by the African Commission have protected the right to health in only a single matter.[47] It is therefore ironic that the African Commission has made more sparing use of these seemingly more generous legal standards. It remains to be seen if in future cases interim measures will be adopted by the African Commission, in respect of serious situations related to the violation of socio-economic rights, for example, resulting from the lack of medicines or adequate medical treatment of persons who are very ill and lacking financial resources, or who are at risk due to manifestly inadequate housing or basic education. A possible example where the requirements of imminent risk to life may be prevented, and where interim measures may be useful, is the failure of a state to put measures in place to effectively prevent mother-to-child-transmission of HIV.

With regard to the people protected, the case law reveals that the beneficiaries in the Inter-American and the African systems are usually nationals who are in a situation of serious risk and find themselves in the midst of an armed conflict, who are sentenced to death, who are arbitrarily detained, who fear practicing their profession (whether they are human rights defenders or journalists), or who are politicians. Given the special situations of danger in the Americas and Africa, the Commissions have adopted interim measures in order to protect persons in an individual and in a collective way. In this sense, interim measures in the Inter-American system have protected groups of very significant sizes, for example, *all* inmates in certain prisons,[48] *entire* communities of an indigenous people[49] and *all* members of human rights NGOs.[50] The African Commission adopted interim

[47] The African Commission case in *Nigerian Newspapers Proscription* required the state to ensure that the health of the victims was not endangered. See Communication 140/94, 141/94 and 145/95, *Constitutional Rights Project, Civil Liberties Organisation and Media Rights Agenda v. Nigeria* (*'Nigerian Newspapers Proscription* case'*)*.

[48] The approximately 254 detainees held at Guantanamo Bay, Cuba, are included in this category. These detainees were transported by the United States following their capture in Afghanistan on 12 January 2002.The United States refused to consider the detainees to be prisoners of war, until a competent tribunal determined otherwise, which means that the detainees were held arbitrarily and incommunicado for a prolonged period of time, and they had been interrogated without legal counsel. *Detainees being held by the United States at Guantanamo Bay, Cuba v. United States of America,* Precautionary measures, Inter-Am. Comm. HR, Order of 12 March 2002 (2002 Annual Report) ('*Detainees being held by the United States at Guantanamo Bay, Cuba* matter').

[49] See e.g. PM 395/09, *Maho Indigenous Community v. Suriname,* Precautionary measures, Inter-Am. Comm. HR, Order of 27 October 2010 (2010 Annual Report) ('*Maho Indigenous Community* matter') and PM 382/10, *Indigenous Communities of the Xingu River Basin, Pará v. Brazil.* Precautionary measures, Inter-Am. Comm. HR, Order of 1 April, 2011 (2011 Annual Report) ('*Indigenous Communities of the Xingu River Basin, Pará* matter').

[50] See e.g. PM 319/09, *League of Displaced Women v. Colombia,* Precautionary measures, Inter-Am. Comm. HR, Order of 18 November 2009 (2009 Annual Report) ('*League of Displaced Women* matter') and PM 13/12, *Members of the Human Rights Lawyers Group v. Guatemala,* Precautionary measures Inter-Am. Comm. HR, Order of 2 May, 2012 ('*Members of the Human Rights Lawyers Group* matter').

measures in two matters of a collective nature. In one case, interim measures were granted in order to protect some victims of the armed conflict in Djibouti, and in another case, interim measures were awarded in order to protect approximately 15,000 indigenous members of the Ogiek Community of the Mau Forest in Kenya.[51]

Recently, the Inter-American Commission has demonstrated the ability to respond quickly under urgent circumstances – even when a matter is surrounded by heightened public controversy – in which many people were in an extreme situation of danger. Examples of such rapid response and urgent action are the following: all persons transferred to the United States naval base in Guantanamo, who were captured in connection with the US-led military operation against terrorism in 2001[52]; the persons in danger after the *coup d'état* in Honduras in 2009[53]; and the persons endangered in Haiti – mainly children and women – after the earthquake in 2010.[54] This type of rapid response is important when responding to crises that threaten human rights. The ability of the Inter-American system to respond speedily is one of its strengths; this approach should be adopted by the African Commission wherever possible.

Most of the requests for interim measures received and measures adopted by the Commissions in both systems concern the protection of clearly identified persons. The vast majority of the beneficiaries have been people in detention. Interim measures granted to detainees represent 27 % (210 out of a total of 771 adopted interim

[51] Communication 133/94, *Association pour la Défense des Droits de l'Homme et des Libertés v. Djibouti* (2000) AHRLR 80 (ACHPR 2000) ('*Afar* case') and Application 6/2012, *African Commission (in respect of the Ogiek Community of the May Forest) v. Kenya* ('*Ogiek Community of the May Forest* case').

[52] The Commission requested the United States, 2 months after the United States began transferring persons captured in connection with the US-led military operation against terrorism to its Guantanamo naval base, to take 'urgent measures necessary to determine the legal status of the detainees at Guantanamo Bay'. There quest concerned 254 male prisoners of 25 different nationalities. See *Detainees being held by the United States at Guantanamo Bay, Cuba* matter, supra, note 48.

[53] PM 196/09, (*Patricia Rodas and others v. Honduras*) Precautionary measures, Inter-Am. Comm. HR, Order of 28 June 2009 (2009 Annual Report) ('*Patricia Rodas and others* matter').

[54] According to information presented by the inter-American Commission, the precarious conditions and lack of security in the camps for internally displaced persons (IDP camps) was generating a situation of extreme danger for the women and girls who lived there. Apparently, there was an increasing number of acts of sexual violence committed in the camps: the raping of girls as young as 5 years old has been reported. See PM 340/10, *Women and girls residing in 22 Camps for internally displaced persons in Port-au-Prince v. Haiti,* Precautionary measures, Inter-Am. Comm. HR, Order of 22 December 2010 (2010 Annual Report) ('*Women and girls residing in 22 Camps for internally displaced persons in Port-au-Prince* matter')and Inter-American Commission, Press Release N° 114/10, 'IACHR expresses concern over situation in camps for displaced persons in Haiti' 18 November 2010, available at: http://www.cidh.oas.org/Comunicados/English/2010/115-10eng.htm.

measures) of the total of measures adopted in the Inter-American system and 28.5 % (8 out of a total of 21 interim measures adopted) in the African system.[55]

Beneficiaries of interim measures in the Inter-American system have been persons sentenced to death in the United States,[56] Trinidad and Tobago,[57] Jamaica[58] and the Bahamas[59]; prisoners with health problems and without access to medical care mainly in Cuba[60] and Peru[61]; and detainees in deplorable prison conditions in Argentina,[62] Brazil,[63] Colombia[64] and Haiti.[65] Conditions of detention in the Americas have been an issue of great concern, in part due to the joint detention of

---

[55] *Saro-Wiwa* case, supra, note, supra, note 42; Communication 256/2002, *Woods and Another v. Liberia*, (2003) AHRLR 125 (ACHPR 2003) ('*Woods and Another* case'); Communication 250/2002, *Zegveld and Another v. Eritrea*, (2003) AHRLR 84 (ACHPR 2003) ('*Eritrean Detention* case'); Communication 258/2002, *Miss A v. Cameroon*, (2004), AHRLR 39 (ACHPR 2004) ('*Miss A* case'); Communication 269/03, *Interights (in respect of Safia Yakubu Husaini et al.) v. Nigeria* ('*Safia Yakubu Husaini* case'); Communication 322/06, *Tsatsu Tsikata v. Ghana* ('*Tsatsu Tsikata* case'); Communication 334/06, *Egyptian Initiative for Personal Rights and Interights v. Arab Republic of Egypt ('Egypt Death Penalty* case'*)* and Application 2/2013, *African Commission (in respect of Saif Al-Islam Gaddafi) v. Libya* ('*Gaddafi's son* case').

[56] See e.g., Petition P607/04, *Troy Albert Kunkle v. United States of America*, Precautionary measures, Inter-Am. Comm. HR, Order of 7 July 2004 (2004 Annual Report) ('*Troy Albert Kunkle* matter').

[57] See e.g., Case 12.073, *Gangadeen Tahaloo v. Trinidad and Tobago*, Precautionary measures, Inter-Am. Comm. HR, Order of 21 December 1998 (1998 Annual Report) ('*Gangadeen Tahaloo* case').

[58] See e.g., Case 12.347, *Dave Sewell v. Jamaica*, Precautionary measures, Inter-Am. Comm. HR, Order of 4 December 2000 (2000 Annual Report) ('*Dave Sewell* case').

[59] See e.g., Case 11.643, *Trevor Fisher v. Bahamas*, Precautionary measures, Inter-Am. Comm. HR, Order of 1 April 1998 (1998 Annual Report) ('*Trevor Fisher* case').

[60] See e.g., PM 50/09, *Alejandro Jiménez Blanco v. Cuba*, Precautionary measures, Inter-Am. Comm. HR, Order of 18 March 2009 (2009 Annual Report) ('*Alejandro Jiménez Blanco* matter'); and PM 484/11, *José Daniel Ferrer García v. Cuba*, Precautionary measures, Inter-Am. Comm. HR, Order of 5 November 2012 ('*José Daniel Ferrer García* matter').

[61] See e.g., *Wilson García Asto v. Peru*, Precautionary measures, Inter-Am. Comm. HR, Order of 4 April 2002 (2002 Annual Report) ('*Wilson García Asto* matter').

[62] See e.g., *Convicted and tried inmates committed to the Penitentiary of Mendoza and its offices v. Argentina*, Precautionary measures, Inter-Am. Comm. HR, Order of 3 August 2004 (2004 Annual Report) ('*Convicted and tried inmates committed to the Penitentiary of Mendoza and its offices* matter').

[63] See *Men deprived of freedom in the cells located in the basement of POLINTER Police District in Rio de Janeiro v. Brazil*, Precautionary measures, Inter-Am. Comm. HR, Order of 11 November 2005 (2005 Annual Report) ('*Men deprived of freedom in the cells located in the basement of POLINTER Police District in Rio de Janeiro* matter').

[64] See e.g., *108 inmates in the Maximum Security Prison at Kilometer 14 v. Colombia*, Precautionary measures, Inter-Am. Comm. HR, Order of 18 March 2004 (2004 Annual Report) ('*108 inmates in the Maximum Security Prison at Kilometer 14* matter').

[65] See e.g., PM 144/07, *Detainees at Toussaint Louverture Police Station in Gonaïves v. Haiti*, Precautionary measures, Inter-Am. Comm. HR, Order of 16 June 2008 (2008 Annual Report) ('*Detainees at Toussaint Louverture Police Station in Gonaïves* matter').

convicted and pre-trial in mates,[66] members of armed groups and common prisoners,[67] members of different armed groups (guerrilla and paramilitary)[68] and of minors and adults.[69] Prisoners who are mistreated by staff members of their prisons have also been in serious danger.[70] In these cases, the right to life, the right to personal integrity and the right to a fair trial have been identified as being at risk.

Interim measures adopted by the African Commission with regard to detainees in some cases concerned political prisoners and human rights defenders in Togo,[71] Nigeria,[72] Libya[73] and presumed terrorists condemned to death in Egypt.[74] Detainees have been protected in a number of instances, including those alleging unlawful arrest and condemnation to death,[75] being kept in appalling health conditions,[76] or being detained with no charges brought against them.[77] Interim measures in the African system have also been requested in order to protect non-nationals and politicians, while equipment of broadcasters has also received protection, either through the protection of the right to property or freedom of expression of the owners of media outlets. Information about the Commission's granting of provisional

---

[66] See e.g., PM 364/09, *Carlos Amilcar Orellana Donis v. Guatemala,* Precautionary measures, Inter-Am. Comm. HR, Order of 19 January 2010 (2010 Annual Report) ('*Carlos Amilcar Orellana Donis* matter').

[67] See e.g., *108 inmates in the Maximum Security Prison at Kilometer 14 v. Colombia,* Precautionary measures, Inter-Am. Comm. HR, Order of 18 March 2004 (2004 Annual Report) ('*108 inmates in the Maximum Security Prison at Kilometer 14* matter').

[68] In *Political prisoners in buildings 1 and 2 of the National Model Prison in Bogotá* matter it was mentioned that: "On April 27, 2000, prisoners belonging to paramilitary groups detained in cellblock 5 launched a violent attack on prisoners in cellblock 4, killing 47 inmates and injuring 17 others. The petitioners alleged that several prisoners from cellblocks 3 and 5, with Auto defensas Unidas de Colombia bracelets, carried long-range weapons when patrolling the facilities, making threats against political prisoners". See *Political prisoners in buildings 1 and 2 of the National Model Prison in Bogotá v. Colombia,* Precautionary measures, Inter-Am. Comm. HR, Order of 11 May 2000 (2000 Annual Report) ('*Political prisoners in buildings 1 and 2 of the National Model Prison in Bogotá* matter').

[69] See e.g., *Adolescents in the Public Prison of Guarujá v. Brazil,* Precautionary measures, Inter-Am. Comm. HR, Order of 26 October 2007 (2007 Annual Report) ('*Adolescents in the Public Prison of Guarujá* matter').

[70] See e.g., PM 104/12, *Penitenciary Services Buenos Aires Province v. Argentina,* Precautionary measures Inter-Am. Comm. HR, Order of 13 April, 2012 ('*Penitenciary Services Buenos Aires Province* matter').

[71] Communication 83/92, *Jean Yakovi Degli v. Togo* ('*Togo Detention* case').

[72] *Saro-Wiwa* case, supra, note 42 and *Nigerian Newspapers Proscription* case, supra, note, 47.

[73] *Gaddafi's son* case, supra, note 55, para. 15.

[74] *Saro-Wiwa* case, supra, note 42 and *Egypt Death Penalty* case, supra, note 55.

[75] *Egypt Death Penalty* case, supra, note 55.

[76] *Saro-Wiwa* case, supra, note 42; *Nigerian Newspapers Proscription* case, supra, note 47; and *Gaddafi's son* case, supra, note 55.

[77] *Nigerian Newspapers Proscription* case, supra, note 47 paras. 2 and 49; and *Gaddafi's son* case, supra, note 55.

measures may also be revealed from the decision of the African Court on Human and Peoples' Rights, if the Commission subsequently refers the matter to the Court. In one such case, *African Commission v. Lybia, Order for Provisional Measures*,[78] it became apparent that the Commission had, on 18 April 2012, issued interim measures, requesting Lybia to ensure that a detainee, Saif Al-Islam Gaddafi, be provided access to a lawyer, be allowed to receive visits, and that his personal integrity be guaranteed.[79] In the Inter-American system, people suffering from harassment as a consequence of their connection with a legal case pending at the international[80] or national level before human rights monitoring bodies,[81] have been protected through interim measures, as well as human rights defenders,[82] journalists[83] and people with health problems. The 19 instances in which interim measures were granted by the Commission to protect persons with health problems, deserve special attention.[84] More than half of these interim measures adopted between 1999 and 2002, were aimed at the protection of persons who suffered from HIV/AIDS, and faced a lack of access to the treatment and drugs needed to fight the disease. The measures, in most of these cases, had a collective character. In total, 475 persons living with HIV/AIDS received protection.[85]

6.5 Impact, Deficiencies and Recommendations

This short contribution could not conclude without indicating the impact and identifying some deficiencies of the existing systems of considering and granting interim measures before the inter-American and the African Commission, and

[78] *Gaddafi's son* case, supra, note 55, ordered on 15 March 2013.

[79] Ibid., para. 15.

[80] See e.g., Case 11.324, *Virgilio Almanzar and others v. Dominican Republic*, Precautionary measures, Inter-Am. Comm. HR, Order of 8 November 1996 (1996 Annual Report) ('*Virgilio Almanzar and others* case').

[81] See e.g., PM 388/12, *Edgar Ismael Solorio Solís and others v. Mexico*, Inter-Am. Comm. HR, Order of 6 November 2012 ('*Edgar Ismael Solorio Solís and others* matter').

[82] With 47 precautionary measures, Colombia has the highest number of requests. It is followed by Guatemala with 27 requests and Mexico with 26 requests. See e.g., *Anselmo Roldán Aguilar v. Guatemala*, Precautionary measures, Inter-Am. Comm. HR, Order of 31 July 2001 (2001 Annual Report) ('*Anselmo Roldán Aguilar* matter').

[83] See e.g., *Carlos A. Singares Campbell v. Panama*, Precautionary measures, Inter-Am. Comm. HR, Order of 7 July 2000 (2000 Annual Report) ('*Carlos A. Singares Campbell* matter') and *Journalists working at the newspaper El Nacional v. Venezuela*, Precautionary measures, Inter-Am. Comm. HR, Order of 11 January 2002 (2002 Annual Report) ('*Journalists working at the newspaper El Nacional* matter').

[84] See Burbano-Herrera and D. Rodríguez-Pinzón, "Provisional Measures Issued by the Inter-American Commission on Human Rights", in supra, note 4.

[85] See e.g., *Odir Miranda and others v. El Salvador*, Precautionary measures, Inter-Am. Comm. HR, Order of 29 February 2000 (1999 Annual Report) ('*Odir Miranda and others* matter').

proposing some concise suggestions and recommendations to improve both these systems with regard to interim measures.

6.5.1 Impact

In general, the Inter-American Commission has shown that it is highly responsive when vulnerable people such as prisoners, indigenous peoples, human rights defenders, journalists, women, children, people in bad health and internally displaced persons are at risk. In the area of the right to life, the right to humane treatment, the right to due process and the right to health, there have been several cases where interim measures were granted and complied with. This was the case with regard to inmates who have received medical treatment[86] or whose death sentences were suspended,[87] and cases of persons living with HIV/AIDS who have started to receive specialized care.[88] An interim measure has also been issued in a case concerning a pregnant young woman with cancer, where the problem was not related to the lack of economic resources to receive treatment, but the religious belief of the medical personnel of the hospital which impeded treatment. The beneficiary was a mother of a 10-year-old girl, who had not been receiving the necessary medical attention to treat her cancer because of her pregnancy. In this case, despite the doctors' recommendation to urgently initiate chemotherapy or radiotherapy, the hospital informed the woman and her representatives that the treatment would not be given, due to the high risk that it could provoke an abortion.[89] Only after an interim measure was granted, was the mother given access to the treatment she needed. In the area of fair trial, several beneficiaries were also guaranteed a trial with the necessary judicial guarantees.[90] Human rights defenders,[91] journalists,[92]

[86] See e.g., *Wilson García Asto* matter, supra, note 61.

[87] See e.g., Petition P0353.2001, *Gerardo Valdez Maltos v. United States of America,* Precautionary measures, Inter-Am. Comm. HR, Order of 14 June 2001 (2001 Annual Report) ('*Gerardo Valdez Maltos* matter').

[88] See e.g., *15 carriers of the HIV/AIDS virus v. Peru,* Precautionary measures, Inter-Am. Comm. HR, Order of 23 September 2002 (2002 Annual Report) ('*15 carriers of the HIV/AIDS virus* matter').

[89] PM 43/10, *Amelia v. Nicaragua,* Precautionary measures, Inter-Am. Comm. HR, Order of 26 February 2010 (2010 Annual Report) ('*Amelia* matter').

[90] See e.g., Petition 12.381, *Robert Bacon Jr. v. United States of America,* Precautionary measures, Inter-Am. Comm. HR, Order of 25 April 2001 (2001 Annual Report) ('*Robert Bacon Jr.* matter').

[91] See e.g., *COFAVIC v. Venezuela,* Precautionary measures, Inter-Am. Comm. HR, Order of 19 April 2002 (2002 Annual Report) ('*COFAVIC* matter').

[92] Case 11.791, *Gustavo Gorriti Ellenbogen v. Panama,* Precautionary measures, Inter-Am. Comm. HR, Order of 18 August 1997 (1997 Annual Report) ('*Gustavo Gorriti Ellenbogen* case').

children,[93] indigenous communities,[94] witnesses[95] and politicians[96] have received personal security.

In the African system, interim measures have been adopted on some 21 occasions. While in many cases it is (virtually) impossible to establish whether the state concerned complied with the order, those that allow for an assessment of state compliance reveal erratic and limited compliance. At the same time, States have complied with these orders in at least some instances. There are thus quite a number of important cases where the presumed victims did, in fact, receive the protection they needed. Two such cases were related to people in detention in Togo[97] and Egypt[98]; one related to the protection of equipment of a radio station in Cameroon,[99] the other to the victims of an armed conflict in Djibouti.[100] In some instances, death penalty orders have been suspended pending the final decision by the African Commission. In this regard, Burundi,[101] Egypt[102] and Nigeria[103] suspended the death penalty of persons who had been sentenced to death in a way which was violating the due process. Special mention should also be made of a communication which concerns Ms Safiya Hussaini, and thus relates to the only case where the beneficiary is a woman.[104] The victim was a Nigerian nursing mother sentenced to death by stoning by a *sharia* court, for the alleged crime of adultery.[105] On February 2002, 3 months after the request of the 'urgent appeal' was notified by the Chairman of the African Commission to Nigeria, the Federal Court of Appeal in Nigeria overturned the death sentence imposed on Safiya by the lower *sharia* court in Sokoto State.[106]

---

[93] See e.g., *Women and girls residing in 22 Camps for internally displaced persons in Port-au-Prince* matter, supra, note 54.

[94] See e.g., *40 Embera Chamí indigenous persons v. Colombia,* Precautionary measures, Inter-Am. Comm. HR, Order of 15 March 2002 (2002 Annual Report) ('*40 Embera Chamí indigenous persons* matter').

[95] See e.g., *Mauricio Garcia Prieto Hillerman and others v. El Salvator,* Precautionary measures, Inter-Am. Comm. HR, Order of 20 June 1997 (1997 Annual Report) and Order of 20 November 2001 (2001 Annual Report) ('*Mauricio Garcia Prieto Hillerman and others* matter').

[96] *Agustín Jarquín Anaya and others v. Nicaragua,* Precautionary measures, Inter-Am. Comm. HR, Order of 12 February 1999 (1999 Annual Report) ('*Agustín Jarquín Anaya and others* matter').

[97] *Togo Detention* case, supra, note 71.

[98] *Egypt Death Penalty* case, supra, note 55.

[99] Communication 290/2004, *Open Society Justice Initiative (in respect of Njawe Noumeni) v. Cameroon* (2006) AHRLR 75 (ACHPR 2006) ('*Radio Freedom FM* case') para. 12.

[100] *Afar* case, supra, note 51.

[101] Communication 231/99, *Avocats Sans Frontières (in respect of Bwampamye) v. Burundi,* (2000) AHRLR 48 (ACHPR 2000) ('*Bwampamye* case') paras. 15 and 17.

[102] *Egypt Death Penalty* case, supra, note 55.

[103] *Safia Yakubu Husaini* case, supra, note 55.

[104] *Safia Yakubu Husaini* case, supra, note 55 paras. 2 and 14–16.

[105] Ibid, paras. 2 and 3.

[106] Ibid, paras. 14, 15, 20 and 22. The communication ended with a request of the complainants to withdraw the case. They could not obtain the information to prepare their written submissions on admissibility. The Commission decided to close the file.

6.5.2 Deficiencies and Recommendations

Interim measures have been an important mechanism of protection used by the quasi-judicial organs in the Inter-American and the African systems, and while they have led to results in certain instances, they still cannot be regarded as being complete and effective in every sense of the word.

Lack of a clear legal basis for interim measures: The lack of the incorporation of the interim measures in the Statute of the Commissions, the American Convention and the African Charter, has caused some States, especially on the American continent, to argue that interim measures issued by the Commission are simple recommendations, and are certainly no binding orders. Although most States have not denied the power of both Commissions to issue interim measures, it would be good if in the future, interim measures are included in the Statute of the Commissions or in the respective human rights treaties. Especially in the Inter-American system, which since 2012 has been in a reform process with the aim to strengthen the human rights system, some recommendations should be presented in this regard. However, at this point it is relevant to emphasize that in the Inter-American system, interim measures are explicitly mentioned in the Inter-American Convention on Forced Disappearance of Persons.

Lack of information and lack of reasoning in decisions on interim measures: The lack of reasoning in the decisions dealing with interim measures and the lack of publication of all requests for interim measures is problematic in both systems. Until now, in the Inter-American system, interim measures issued by the Commission have been adopted on 771 occasions, but there is a lack of publicly accessible reasoning. There is also no information about the measures which have been rejected or not yet decided. This practice will change by August 2013, when the reform of the Commission's Rules of Procedure enters into force. According to Article 25(7) of the amended Commission's Rules of Procedure, the decisions granting, extending, modifying or lifting precautionary measures shall be adopted through reasoned resolutions.

In the African system, it is (virtually) impossible to establish exactly how many interim measures have been adopted by the Commission, and whether the state concerned complied with the request or 'order'. The lack of exact numbers is due to the fact that the African Commission does not keep a register of the interim measures it has adopted or rejected, a factor further exacerbated by the requirement that the Commission's findings remain confidential until their publication has been approved by the AU Assembly (or, in practice, the Executive Council). In this regard, it should be recalled that, although the African Commission has an obligation of confidentiality with respect to its protective mandate, this principle only applies to the Commission and not to the applicants. Under the Commission's 2010 Rules of Procedure,[107] decisions on the merits are not transmitted to the parties until

[107] Rule 110(3).

the AU has authorised the publication of these decisions. Even if findings on interim measures are not findings on the merits, information on interim measures is usually only made public as part of the merits decision. Still, it appears that the outcomes of request on interim measures are mostly communicated to the parties, including the applicants (petitioners). It would be good that petitioners – who in the African system are usually NGO's – develop ways to communicate with and inform each other and the international community about their requests for interim measures. A free flow of information on the issue of interim measures is important in order to permit individual and social accountability in time, as currently it is made virtually impossible to criticise or condemn contemporaneous regimes acting in blatant violation of human rights. A timely condemnation before the violations of human rights have happened could be useful, in order to oblige compliance with the interim measures, or to shame states which do not implement them.[108]

With regard to the lack of reasoning of the decisions of interim measures, it is necessary to develop rules and criteria which are objective references, in order to respond to the diversity of cases that will surely continue to enrich the jurisprudence of interim measures in the human rights field. Although written explanations and the development of clear rules will not cause the discretion of the organs to disappear, at least they will limit it to a certain extent. Furthermore, to the extent that there is more knowledge of the arguments for adopting or rejecting the measures, this will most probably lead to greater responsibility on the part of the Commissioners and to more coherent and rational decisions. Overcoming this factor is important to strengthen the relevance of the legal instrument of interim measures, and will encourage and enhance the analysis of the relevant jurisprudence.

Inadequate use of interim measures for the protection of social and economic rights: On the American and the African continent, many people, especially children and women, suffer from a lack of access to education, health and housing. The respective Commissions could and should prevent violations of these rights through the use of interim measures, when the persons concerned are in a situation of danger and risk irreparable damage. It is of great concern that the African Commission has protected the right to health only on two occasions through interim measures, and the Inter-American Commission has since 2002 stopped protecting this right through interim measures.

Lack of will to comply with interim measures: With regard to non-compliance, there are numerous instances in both the Inter-American and the African systems, in which the respondent States have refused to comply with interim measures.[109] If States do not implement interim measures, the effectiveness of these measures leaves much to be desired. With regard to the suspension of orders of execution, the

[108] Burbano-Herrera and Viljoen, supra, note 4.

[109] *Saro-Wiwa* case, supra, note 42 in regard to Nigeria; Communication 212/98, *Amnesty International v. Zambia* (2000) AHRLR 325 (ACHPR 1999) *('Banda* case'), in regard to Zambia and Communication 284/03, *Zimbabwe Lawyers for Human Rights & Associated Newspapers of Zimbabwe v. Republic of Zimbabwe ('Zimbabwean Daily News* case'*)* in regard to Zimbabwe.

Inter-American Commission has published information of 43 interim measures. This figure corresponds to one third of the measures adopted. According to this information, 14 orders of execution were suspended, in three cases the sentence was commuted, on two occasions the inmates were released, and in 24 cases the beneficiaries were executed. That means that less than half of the measures were complied with.[110] Cases of non-compliance with regard to people whose health condition were seriously compromised, were also reported. In a case of eight beneficiaries from Honduras living with HIV/AIDS, 4 months after the measures were granted, the complainants indicated that the State had not yet provided the necessary treatment, and that four of the beneficiaries had died.[111] Likewise, it has been reported that human rights defenders,[112] workers,[113] petitioners at the national level[114] and, in general, beneficiaries of interim measures who were victims of death threats have nevertheless been killed.[115]

The rate of compliance with orders for interim measures under the African system is and remains a problem. For example, in cases related to the death penalty, the government of Nigeria executed nine persons condemned to death, despite the interim measures issued by the African Commission to suspend their execution.[116] In a case concerning Eritrea, although the Commission on several occasions had drawn the attention of the Eritrean President to the dimension of the violation of human rights, and the deplorable attitude of the authorities towards 11 former Eritrean government officials who had been illegally arrested without charge and held incommunicado in Asmara since September 2001,[117] the interim measures adopted did not result in any action being taken on the part of the Eritrean authorities.[118] The 2010 Rules require a State in respect of which the Commission has issues interim measures to report back, within 15 days of being informed of these measures, about their implementation.[119] The Commission's vigorous and

[110] Burbano-Herrera and Viljoen, supra, note 4.

[111] *Four carriers of the HIV/AIDS virus v. Honduras*, Precautionary measures, Inter-Am. Comm. HR, Order of 16 August 2002 (2002 Annual Report) ('*Four carriers of the HIV/AIDS virus* matter').

[112] *Fourteen social leaders from the department of Arauca v. Colombia,* Precautionary measures, Inter-Am. Comm. HR, Order of 29 July 2002 (2002 Annual Report) ('*14 social leaders from the department of Arauca* matter').

[113] *Thirty four workers of the Empresa Comunitaria de Acueducto y Alcantarillado de Saravena v. Colombia,* Precautionary measures, Inter-Am. Comm. HR, Order of 22 September 2003 (2003 Annual Report) ('*34 workers of the Empresa Comunitaria de Acueducto y Alcantarillado de Saravena* matter'), two beneficiaries were killed.

[114] *Eloisa Barrios and others v. Venezuela,* Precautionary measures, Inter-Am. Comm. HR, Order of 22 June 2004 (2004 Annual Report) ('*Eloisa Barrios and others* matter').

[115] *Manoel Bezerra and others v. Brazil,* Precautionary measures, Inter-Am. Comm. HR, Order of 23 September 2002 (2002 Annual Report) ('*Manoel Bezerra and others* matter').

[116] *Saro-Wiwa* case, supra, note 42 paras. 29, 103, 114 and 115.

[117] *Eritrean Detention* case, supra, note 55 para 2.

[118] Ibid.

[119] Rule 98(4).

consistent follow up of non-compliance with this requirement may play an important role to improve State compliance. It should also be borne in mind that non-compliance with the Commission's interim measures may result in a referral to the African Court on Human and Peoples' Rights.[120]

6.6 Final Considerations

The political will of States to abide by interim measures and to provide solutions that terminate situations of danger, is essential for the effective protection of persons. Although progress has been made and authorities are acting, especially in the Inter-American system, new applications that reflect situations similar to those already treated are constantly being received, including from prisoners requesting protection, new members of indigenous communities in a position of danger, relatives and witnesses being threatened and petitions from persons sentenced to death alleging violations of due process. This steady flow of requests leads us to conclude that the situation within the States has not improved a great deal and that, therefore, it is urgent to work in this regard.

It is not only necessary that States ratify international treaties and have laws that include rights and freedoms, the domestic judicial and other public authorities must also effectively apply these human rights standards. Indeed, action by national authorities is fundamental for the protection of rights; international protection is only a form of supplementary recourse, and cannot replace the primary requirement of domestic protection. Therefore, there is work to be done at the local level so that these situations of emergency do not continue to be presented with the current regularity. It is essential that solutions to the problems in States be found, because, until these problems are adequately addressed, the volume of petitions for interim measures (and petitions altogether) will continue to increase. Attention should, therefore, in particular be paid to the design of public policies to combat the problems that afflict the countries from which high requests for interim measures have emanated. Specifically, more attention should be paid to social justice, access to education, the development of a tolerant society to put an end to violence caused by political differences, by racial and ethnic origin, gender or sexual orientation. Basic reforms to the penal system and administration of justice would contribute to far less people finding themselves in a situation of danger, compelling them to approach international bodies to request protection. In the end, the adoption of interim measures reminds us that the grim realities of discrimination, social inequality, poverty, armed conflict, corruption, prison crises and impunity still exist in the Americas and Africa.

[120] Rule 118(2).

Chapter 7
The Law of the Sea and Human Rights in the *Hirsi Jamaa and Others v. Italy* Judgment of the European Court of Human Rights

Jasmine Coppens

Abstract The question of extraterritorial applicability of the principle of non-refoulement – as implicitly present in Article 3 ECHR – on the high seas was decided by the European Court of Human Rights (ECtHR) on 23 February 2012 in *Hirsi Jamaa and Others v. Italy*. The ECtHR found that the applicants had fallen within the jurisdiction of Italy as in the period between boarding onto the Italian ships on the high seas and being handed over to the Libyan authorities, the applicants had been under the continuous and exclusive *de jure* and *de facto* control of the Italian authorities. This chapter will deal with the impact of this judgment on the law of the sea rules concerning search and rescue at sea.

7.1 Introduction

Nowadays, it seems that the age of the generalist is passing in international law. The teaching as well as the practice of international law is often broken down into specialist sub-fields such as the law of the sea and international human rights law. The fact that they have their own sources, their own mechanisms to apply in cases of non-compliance and their own courts and tribunals, creates the idea that these 'self-contained' regimes are separate from general international law.[1] As indicated by a study of the International Law Commission (ILC), this 'fragmentation' of international law generates the possibility of conflicting norms and regimes.[2] For

[1] M. Koskenniemi and P. Leino, "Fragmentation of International Law: Postmodern Anxieties?", 15 *Leiden Journal of International Law* (2002), 553-579; T. Treves, "Fragmentation of International Law: the Judicial Perspective", 23 *Comunicazione e Studi* (2007) 821-875.

[2] ILC (2006), "Fragmentation of International Law: Difficulties Arising from the Diversification and Expansion of International Law. Report of the Study Group of the International Law

J. Coppens (✉)
Department of Public International Law, Ghent University, Ghent, Belgium
e-mail: Jasmine.Coppens@UGent.be

Y. Haeck and E. Brems (eds.), *Human Rights and Civil Liberties in the 21st Century*, Ius Gentium: Comparative Perspectives on Law and Justice 30,
DOI 10.1007/978-94-007-7599-2_7, © Springer Science+Business Media Dordrecht 2014

example, it is sometimes suggested that the issue of how best to regulate migration by sea bears scars of a fragmentary approach to law-making. It has been submitted that the substantive content of the law of the sea has been isolated from potentially important humanitarian considerations. The law of the sea would therefore not be very susceptible to developments in international human rights.[3]

It is true that the law of the sea encounters many of the problems that arise when specialized sets of rules overlap, especially within the framework of the 1982 Law of the Sea Convention (LOSC). However, although it is unlikely that the LOSC – or the law of the sea more generally – will be accorded a central role in the history of the international human rights law, it may be deserving of more than just a footnote.[4] Indeed, the law of the sea, its instruments and institutions have not only a direct contribution to make to human rights law, but in some instances even prove to be sufficient to protect individual human rights.[5] This idea will be the research question of this contribution: would the law of the sea provide sufficient humanitarian guarantees to deal with *Hirsi Jamaa and Others v. Italy* in 2012 (*Hirsi Case*) in a way that would have protected the rights of the migrants?

In this case before the European Court of Human Rights (ECtHR), the applicants – 11 Somali and 13 Eritrean nationals – were part of a group of about 200 individuals who left Libya aboard three vessels with the aim of reaching the Italian coast. However, after they were noticed on the high seas by ships of the Italian Revenue Police (*Guardia di finanza*) and the Coastguard, the persons on board were transferred onto Italian military ships and returned to Tripoli. This return was carried out based on a bilateral agreement between Italy and Libya.[6] The applicants relied on Article 3 ECHR to argue that the decision of the Italian authorities to intercept the vessels on the high seas – and send the applicants straight back to Libya – exposed them to the risk of ill-treatment there, as well as to the serious threat of being sent back to their countries of origin (Somalia and Eritrea), where they might also face ill-treatment.

This contribution consists of two main parts. The first part will deal with the law of the sea and the human rights considerations that it contains, both in the LOSC and in the judgments of the International Tribunal for the Law of the Sea (ITLOS). The article will pay special attention to the duty to render assistance to

---

Commission. Finalized by Martti Koskenniemi", UN Doc. A/CN.4/L.682, available at: http://untreaty.un.org/ilc/guide/1_9.htm

[3] R. Barnes, "The International Law of the Sea and Migration Control" in B. Ryan and V. Mitsilegas (eds.), *Extraterritorial Immigration Control*, (Leiden: Martinus Nijhoff Publishers, 2010) 100–146, 104–106.

[4] B. Oxman, "Human Rights and the Law of the Sea" in J. Charney, D. Anton and M. O'Connell (eds.), *Politics, Values and Functions: International Law in the 21st Century – Essays in Honor of Professor Louis Henkin*, (The Hague: Kluwer Law International, 1997), 404; B. Oxman, "Human Rights and the United Nations Convention on the Law of the Sea", 36 *Columbia Journal of Transnational Law* (1998), 399–429, 429.

[5] S. Cacciaguidi-Fahy, "The Law of the Sea and Human Rights", 9 *Panoptica* (2007), 1–21, 1.

[6] ECtHR 23 February 2012, No. 27765/09 (2012), *Hirsi Jamaa and Others v. Italy*, paras. 9–13.

persons lost or in distress at sea, as this will be the most relevant provision when dealing with the *Hirsi Case*. Indeed, Italy submitted that it intercepted the migrant vessel in the context of a rescue on the high seas.[7] The second part of the article will first deal with how the ECtHR has applied the law of the sea in several cases. Secondly, it will focus on the judgment of the *Hirsi Case*. After describing how the ECtHR reached its decision, it is interesting to take a look at this case from a law of the sea perspective. How would a lawyer specializing in the law of the sea interpret the facts and how would he or she apply the relevant law of the sea provisions? Lastly, the article will highlight some remaining questions concerning the *Hirsi* judgment.

7.2 Human Rights Considerations in the Law of the Sea

7.2.1 The Law of the Sea Convention

The law of the sea is one of the oldest branches of international law, maintaining a doctrinal framework from Hugo Grotius. His essay "Mare Liberum" was the first of its kind for international law as a whole. In 1982, after 10 years of negotiations, the Law of the Sea Convention (LOSC) was adopted. It must be viewed as forming part of the codification process of the law of the sea in the twentieth century that started with the Hague Codification Conference of 1930 on territorial waters, continued with the 1958 and 1960 Geneva Conferences on the Law of the Sea, and reached its apogee in the monumental Third United Nations Conference on the Law of the Sea from 1973 to 1982.[8] The LOSC provides a framework for the regulation of ocean spaces, primarily through the allocation of competences to coastal States and flag States. It has been described as 'the constitution for the oceans'.[9]

Until now, little attention has been given to the humanitarian principles within the law of the sea. Although the LOSC is not a human rights instrument per se, several provisions of the Convention articulate human rights principles which are to date still not used effectively and to their full potential by the human rights community.[10] Moreover, the LOSC is a global convention of which the scope *ratione*

[7] ECtHR, *Hirsi Jamaa and Others v. Italy*, supra, note 6, para. 65.

[8] D. Nelson, "Reflections on the 1982 Convention on the Law of the Sea", in D. Freestone, R. Barnes and David M. Ong (eds.), *The Law of the Sea: Progress and Prospects*, (Oxford: Oxford University Press, 2006) 28–39.

[9] S. Scott, "The LOS Convention as a Constitutional Regime for the Oceans", in Alex G. Oude Elferink (ed.), *Stability and Change in the Law of the Sea: the Role of the LOS Convention*, (Leiden: Martinus Nijhoff Publishers, 2005) 9–38.

[10] Oxman, supra, note 4 (1997), 377–404; G. Bastid-Burdeau, "Migrations clandestines et droit de la mer", in V. Coussirat Coustère(ed.), *La mer et son droit: Mélanges offerts à Laurent Lucchini et Jean-Pierre Quéneudec*, (Paris: Editions A. Pedone, 2003) 57–66; P. Tavernier, "La Cour européenne des droits de l'Homme et la mer", in V. Coussirat Coustère (ed.), *La mer et son droit: Mélanges*

loci and *ratione materiae* rivals that of all but the most comprehensive of global human rights conventions.[11] Also, from the perspective of ratification, it equals most of the successful global human rights conventions as 162 States are party to the Convention.[12]

As early as the Preamble, the LOSC seeks to advance the interests of humanity by establishing "a legal order for the seas and oceans which will facilitate international communication, and will promote the peaceful uses of the seas and oceans, the equitable and efficient utilization of their resources, the conservation of their living resources, and the study, protection and preservation of the marine environment" and by contributing "to the realization of a just and equitable international economic order which takes into account the interests and needs of mankind as a whole".[13] Thus, several community rights are being promoted in the LOSC. The best known example is the declaration that the international seabed area and its resources are the 'common heritage of mankind'.[14] Therefore, the development of the resources must be carried out for the benefit of mankind as a whole.[15] But also the protection of archaeological and historical objects found at sea,[16] the protection and preservation of the marine environment[17] and the obligation of transparency[18] are reflected in the Convention.

Concerning the protection of individuals, the LOSC requires States to prevent and to punish the transport of slaves in ships flying their flag and also declares with respect to the high seas and the exclusive economic zone (EEZ) that a slave taking refuge on board a ship – whatever its flag – shall *ipso facto* be free.[19] Another example is the prohibition of imprisonment or forms of corporal punishment for fisheries violations and the requirement that parties who take action and impose penalties after arresting and detaining foreign vessels promptly notify the flag State of these ships.[20] For this contribution however, the most important provision in

---

offerts à Laurent Lucchini et Jean-Pierre Quéneudec, (Paris: Editions A. Pedone, 2003) 575–589; B. Vukas, The Law of the Sea: Selected Writings, (Leiden: Martinus Nijhoff Publishers, 2004), 71–79; Cacciaguidi-Fahy, supra, note 5, 1–21; T. Treves, "Human Rights and the Law of the Sea", 28 *Berkeley Journal of International Law* (2010) 1–14.

[11] Oxman, supra, note 4 (1997), 379.

[12] UN, "Status of the United Nations Convention on the Law of the Sea, of the Agreement relating to the implementation of Part XI of the Convention and of the Agreement for the implementation of the provisions of the Convention relating to the conservation and management of straddling fish stocks and highly migratory fish stocks", Table recapitulating the status of the Convention and of the related Agreements (20 September 2011), available at: http://www.un.org/depts/los/reference_files/status2010.pdf

[13] LOSC, Preamble paras. 4–5.

[14] LOSC, Art. 136.

[15] LOSC, Art. 140 (1).

[16] LOSC, Art. 303.

[17] LOSC, Art. 192.

[18] See for example: LOSC, Artt. 16, 94(7), 205, etc.

[19] LOSC, Art. 99.

[20] LOSC, Art. 73(3) and 73(4).

the Convention is the duty to render assistance, also a legal obligation for States under customary international law.[21] It will be discussed in detail in Sect. 7.2.3 of this article.

7.2.2 The International Tribunal for the Law of the Sea

The International Tribunal for the Law of the Sea (ITLOS) is the specialized international judicial tribunal that was created to deal with disputes concerning the interpretation and the application of the LOSC. The LOSC provides in Article 287 that a State may choose – by a written declaration – any one or more of the following means for the settlement of disputes: ITLOS, the International Court of Justice (ICJ), an arbitral tribunal or a special arbitral tribunal for disputes relating to fisheries, protection and preservation of the marine environment, marine scientific research or navigation, including pollution from vessels and from dumping. In case the parties to a dispute have accepted the same procedure for the settlement of the dispute, it may be submitted only to that procedure, unless the parties otherwise agree. If the parties to a dispute have not accepted the same procedure for the settlement of the dispute, it may be submitted only to arbitration. ITLOS has a residual compulsory jurisdiction with respect to the prompt release of vessels (Article 292 LOSC) and the prescription of provisional measures under Article 290(5). The majority of disputes that have been submitted to ITLOS fall under these two categories.

In its prompt release judgments, ITLOS has underlined the importance of the LOSC for the protection of individuals. In the *Camouco Case*[22] as well as the *Monte Confurco Case*[23] – both judgments from 2000 – ITLOS gave a broad interpretation of the notion 'detention', as applied to the shipmaster and his crew. It ruled that the practice of court supervision during a pending case in Réunion – whereby the master had to surrender his passport and the authorities were obliged to verify his presence on a daily basis – amounted to 'detention' for the purpose of the prompt release proceedings under Article 292 LOSC as the master was not in a position to leave Réunion. Two other judgments – the *Juno Trader Case* (2004)[24] and the *Hoshinmaru Case* (2007)[25] – also paid special attention to the freedom of the master and crew.

---

[21] MSC, "Review of safety measures and procedures for the treatment of persons rescued at sea", *IMO Doc.* MSC 76/22/8 (31 July 2002), Annex "Report-Record of Decisions on the United Nations Inter-Agency Meeting on the Treatment of Persons Rescued at Sea", para. 6.

[22] ITLOS, 7 February 2000, The Camouco Case, *Panama v. France*, *ITLOS Reports* (2000).

[23] ITLOS, 18 December 2000, The Monte Confurco Case, *Seychelles v. France*, *ITLOS Reports* (2000).

[24] ITLOS, 18 December 2004, The Juno Trader Case, *Saint Vincent and the Grenadines v. Guinea Bissau*, *ITLOS Reports* (2004).

[25] ITLOS, 6 August 2007, The Hoshinmaru Case, *Japan v. Russian Federation*, *ITLOS Reports* (2007).

Although in both cases the restrictions to the freedom of movement had been lifted, the master and crew were still present on the territory of the prosecuting State. Therefore, ITLOS stressed that the master and crew were free to leave without any condition. Even though the persons were not in a state of detention under Article 292 LOSC, ITLOS wanted to eliminate all possible obstacles, bureaucratic or otherwise, to the departure of the ship. This shows how keen ITLOS is to protect the rights of the individuals involved in the cases submitted to it.[26] In the Juno Trader judgment, it was stated: "[t]he obligation of prompt release of vessels and crews includes elementary considerations of humanity and due process of law. The requirement that the bond or other financial guarantee must be reasonable indicates that a concern for fairness is one of the purposes of this provision."[27] 'International standards of due process of law' were also invoked in the 2007 *Tomimaru Case*[28] in order to assess whether the confiscation of a vessel had been made in such a way as to permit ITLOS to consider that the prompt release proceedings concerning the confiscated vessel were without object.

The aforementioned human rights principles or considerations are directly stated in the LOSC or can be inferred from its provisions. However, such principles may become applicable in a case concerning the application and interpretation of the LOSC even when they do not appear in the latter's provisions. ITLOS first considered the protection of human rights in the *M/V Saiga Case* (1999). It ruled that considerations of humanity must apply in the law of the sea as they do in other areas of international law.[29] ITLOS justified integrating international law beyond the scope of the LOSC by making reference to Article 293 LOSC, which permits the application of other rules of international law not incompatible with the Convention.

7.2.3 The Duty to Render Assistance in the Law of the Sea

7.2.3.1 Establishing a Legal Duty to Assist

The moral obligation to render assistance to persons in peril or lost at sea is one of the oldest and most deep-rooted maritime traditions. Early maritime law was

---

[26] Treves, supra, note 10, 4.

[27] ITLOS, 18 December 2004, The Juno Trader Case, *Saint Vincent and the Grenadines v. Guinea Bissau*, *ITLOS Reports* (2004), para. 77.

[28] ITLOS, 6 August 2007, The Tomimaru Case, *Japan v. Russian Federation*, *ITLOS Reports* (2007).

[29] ITLOS, 1 July 1999, The M/V Saiga Case (No. 2), *St. Vincent and the Grenadines v. Guinea*, *ITLOS Reports* (1999), para. 155. In the *Corfu Channel Case* (1949), the ICJ had already reflected the relevance of elementary conditions and considerations of humanity as a general principle of international law. See ICJ, 9 April 1949, Corfu Channel Case, *United Kingdom of Great Britain and Northern Ireland v. People's Republic of Albania*, *ICJ Reports* 4 (1949).

concerned with the preservation of maritime property, rather than with the protection of seafarers.[30] However, by the mid-ninetieth century, one in five British mariners died at sea. Among sailors, mortality was higher than in any other occupation. Between 1861 and 1870, as much as 5,826 ships were wrecked off the British coast with the loss of 8,105 lives.[31] In 1880, the legal obligation of rendering assistance at sea was recognized in the *Scaramanga v. Stamp Case*, where it was decided: "To all who have trust themselves to the sea it is of the utmost importance that the promptings of humanity in this respect should not be checked or interfered with by prudential considerations which may result to a ship or cargo from the rendering of needed aid."

The Brussels Salvage Convention of 1885 was the first formal international convention that addressed rendering assistance at sea. In 1897, the Comité Maritime International (CMI) held its first international conference in Brussels to advance issues regarding collisions and salvage, as well as the duty to render assistance at sea. As a result, the new text of the Brussels Convention on Salvage was signed on 23 September 1910.[32] In 1989, the IMO concluded the International Convention on Salvage, which replaced the 1910 Brussels Convention.[33] The provisions in these conventions expressly articulate an unqualified duty to render assistance to 'persons' or to 'any person' 'in distress' or 'in danger of being lost at sea'.[34] However, the exact scope of the assistance itself is not defined. Also, the LOSC contains a similar provision. Article 98 LOSC reads:

1. Every State shall require the master of a ship flying its flag, in so far as he can do so without serious danger to the ship, the crew or the passengers:
   (a) To render assistance to any person found at sea in danger of being lost;
   (b) To proceed with all possible speed to the rescue of persons in distress, if informed of their need of assistance, in so far as such action may reasonably be expected of him;
   (c) After a collision, to render assistance to the other ship, its crew and its passengers and, where possible, to inform the other ship of the name of his own ship, its port of registry and the nearest port at which it will call.

---

[30] E. Gold, A. Charcot, and H. Kindred, Maritime Law, (Toronto: Irwin Law, 2003), 193–195.

[31] N. Jones, The Plimsoll Sensation: The Great Campaign to save Lives at Sea, (London: Little Brown, 2006).

[32] International Convention for the Unification of Certain Rules of Law related to Assistance and Salvage at Sea and Protocol of Signature (adopted 23 September 1910, entered into force 1 March 1913), 4 *ACTS* 6677.

[33] International Convention on Salvage (adopted 28 April 1989, entered into force 14 July 1996), 1953 *NUTS* 194 [1989 Salvage Convention]. Article 10 stipulates: "(1) *Every master is bound, so far as he can do so without serious danger to his vessel and persons thereon, to render assistance to any person in danger of being lost at sea.* (2) *The States Parties shall adopt the measures necessary to enforce the duty set out in paragraph 1.* (3) *The owner of the vessel shall incur no liability for a breach of the duty of the master under paragraph 1.*"

[34] Cacciaguidi-Fahy, supra, note 5, 6.

2. Every coastal State shall promote the establishment, operation and maintenance of an adequate and effective search and rescue service regarding safety on and over the sea and, where circumstances so require, by way of mutual regional arrangements cooperate with neighbouring States for this purpose.

Although this article deals with situations on the high seas, rendering assistance is also a duty in the EEZ[35] and in the territorial sea.[36] There are a variety of acts that may constitute 'assistance', such as towing the vessel to safety, extricating a grounded vessel, fighting a fire aboard a ship, providing food and supplies, embarking crewmen aboard to replace the tired or the missing, securing aid or assistance from other nearby ships, or simply standing-by to provide navigational advice.[37] The obligation for flag States and shipmasters to render assistance is an obligation of conduct, not an obligation of result.[38] An important element is that assistance must be given to 'any person'. Therefore, the duty remains unaffected by, for example, the nationality – or lack of nationality – of the persons, the status of the persons, the mode of transport or the number of people involved. As a result, this duty extends to migrants.

The words of Article 98(2) indicate that coastal States shall promote – not provide – a certain level of search and rescue services. Indeed, search and rescue services have to be 'adequate and effective'. However, it is not always clear what 'adequate and effective' means. Moen gives the example of the recent Arctic luxury eco-tourism. Cruise ships – icebreaking vessels that need no escort to navigate – now take advantage of ice-free conditions during the summer months to sail from Iceland to Alaska through the Northwest Passage. Nevertheless, travelling along the Northwest Passage still imposes serious risks, making the potential for a humanitarian disaster real. Canada should therefore adapt its search and rescue services in order to adequately and effectively deal with these new risks.[39]

Article 98 LOSC remains quite vague as it does not give any definitions of what exactly 'distress' or 'rescue' mean, nor does it say what to do with the persons after they are on board the rescuing ship. Therefore, it is difficult to apply in practice. Nevertheless, adapting the LOSC in order to meet new challenges such as migration by sea is not an option. As the LOSC embodies a carefully negotiated balance of interests, it contains several provisions specifically designed to preserve its

---

[35] LOSC, Art. 58(2).

[36] LOSC, Art. 18(2) (implicitly).

[37] M. Norris, The Law of Salvage, (Mount Kisco NY: Baker/Voorhis, 1958), 15–31; I. Wildeboer, The Brussels Salvage Convention: Its Unifying Effect in England, Germany, Belgium, and The Netherlands, (Leiden: A.W. Sijthoff, 1965), 95; F. Kenney and V. Tasikas, "The Tampa Incident: IMO Perspectives and Responses on the Treatment of Persons Rescued at Sea", 12 *Pacific Rim Law & Policy Journal* (2003), 143–177, 151–152.

[38] E. Papastavridis, "Rescuing Migrants at Sea: The Responsibility of States under International Law", Working Paper Series Social Science Research Network, 2011, available at: http://papers.ssrn.com/sol3/papers.cfm?abstract_id=1934352.

[39] A. Moen, "For Those in Peril on the Sea: Search and Rescue under the Law of the Sea Convention", 24 *Ocean Yearbook* 2010, 377–410.

integrity.[40] Not only are reservations or exceptions only allowed when expressly permitted by the Convention,[41] inter se agreements between State Parties must be compatible and notice must be given to other State Parties.[42] Moreover, amendment procedures are very strict and it is unlikely that they will ever be used.[43] Nevertheless, there are still some other instruments in the law of the sea that can provide help in applying the duty in practice.

7.2.3.2 Beyond the Law of the Sea Convention: The SAR and SOLAS Conventions

The primary objective of the 1974 Convention on the Safety of Life at Sea (SOLAS) is the prevention of the loss of life at sea.[44] Consequently, it also deals with situations of distress at sea. The 1979 Convention on Search and Rescue (SAR) on the other hand,[45] imputes multi-State coordination of search and rescue systems. Both treaties are monitored by the IMO.

Until the adoption of the SAR Convention, there was no international system covering search and rescue operations. Consequently, in some areas there was a well-established organization able to provide assistance promptly and efficiently, but in others there was nothing at all. The SAR Convention thus aims at developing an international search and rescue plan. As a result, no matter where an accident occurs, the rescue of persons in distress at sea will be co-ordinated by a search and rescue organization and – when necessary – by co-operation between neighbouring search and rescue organizations.[46] Basically, the world's oceans are divided into 13 search and rescue areas, in each of which the coastal States concerned have delimited search and rescue regions for which they are responsible.[47] States must ensure that sufficient Search and Rescue Regions (SRR) are established within each sea area. These regions should be contiguous and – as far as practicable – not overlap.[48]

---

[40] A. Boyle "Further Development of the 1982 Convention on the Law of the Sea", in D. Freestone, R. Barnes and D. Ong (eds.), *The Law of the Sea: Progress and Prospects*, (Oxford: Oxford University Press, 2006), 43.

[41] LOSC, Art. 309.

[42] LOSC, Art. 311.

[43] LOSC, Arts. 313–314.

[44] International Convention for the Safety of Life at Sea (adopted 1 November 1974, entered into force 25 May 1980) 1184 *UNTS* 278. [SOLAS Convention].

[45] International Convention on Maritime Search and Rescue (adopted 27 April 1979, entered into force 22 June 1985) 405 *UNTS* 97. [SAR Convention].

[46] IMO, "Search and rescue", available at: http://www.imo.org/OurWork/Safety/RadioCommunicationsAndSearchAndRescue/SearchAndRescue/Pages/Default.aspx

[47] IMO, "SAR Convention", available at: http://www.imo.org/OurWork/Safety/RadioCommunicationsAndSearchAndRescue/SearchAndRescue/Pages/SARConvention.aspx

[48] SAR Convention, Annex Chapter 2 para. 2.1.3.

The actual distress phase is defined by the SAR Convention as: "A situation wherein there is reasonable certainty that a person, a vessel or other craft is threatened by grave and imminent danger and requires immediate assistance."[49] When exactly a situation is identified as requiring immediate assistance can be different according to which State is handling the situation. For some States the vessel must really be on the point of sinking.[50] However, the International Law Commission stated that although a situation of distress may at most include a situation of serious danger, it is not necessarily one that jeopardizes the lives of the persons concerned.[51] As every situation is different, an assessment of whether a person is in distress can only be made on a case-by-case basis. Although the definition of distress is quite vague, this allows shipmasters and States to take all relevant elements into account. Their discretionary power to decide whether persons are in distress or not is regarded as essential. However, one element that is indisputable is that the existence of an emergency should not be exclusively dependent on or determined by an actual request for assistance.[52] 'Rescue' is also defined in the SAR Convention as "an operation to retrieve persons in distress, provide for their initial medical or other needs, and deliver them to a place of safety."[53] Thus, this definition tells us what to do with the persons after they have been saved, namely bring them to a place of safety. However, what exactly this 'place of safety' requires, is not clear.

Following a number of incidents that highlighted concerns about the treatment of persons rescued at sea[54] – in particular undocumented migrants, asylum seekers and

---

[49] SAR Convention, Annex Chapter 1 para. 1.3.13.

[50] European Commission Proposal for a Council Decision of 27 November 2007 supplementing the Schengen Borders Code as regards the surveillance of the sea external borders in the context of the operational cooperation coordinated by the European Agency for the Management of Operational Cooperation at the External Borders, COM (2009) 658 final, Explanatory Memorandum, para. 2.

[51] ILC (1979), Yearbook of the International Law Commission, New York: ILC 1979, 135, para. 10, available online: http://untreaty.un.org/ilc/publications/yearbooks/Ybkvolumes%28e%29/ILC_1979_v2_p2_e.pdf. Although this definition was given during the discussions on the concept of 'distress' as one of the grounds for excluding wrongfulness with regard to the Draft Articles on State Responsibility, the definition is often being used to describe the situation of distress of persons at sea. See for example: R. Barnes, "Refugee Law at Sea", 53 *International & Comparative Law Quarterly* (2004), 47–77, 60.

[52] Council Decision (EU) No. 2010/252 of 26 April 2010 supplementing the Schengen Borders Code as regards the surveillance of the sea external borders in the context of the operational cooperation coordinated by the European Agency for the Management of Operational Cooperation at the External Borders, *OJ* L 111/20 of 4 May 2010, Annex Part II para. 1.4.

[53] SAR Convention, Annex Chapter 1 para. 1.3.2.

[54] For example the case of the Norwegian container ship M/V Tampa (2001). The captain rescued as many as 438 asylum seekers from drowning in international waters between Christmas Island (Australia) and Indonesia. It lasted for weeks until all the countries involved came to a solution for the disembarkation problem, painfully demonstrating the insufficiency of the international legal framework. See: S. Derrington and M. White, "Australian Maritime Law Update 2001", 33 *Journal of Maritime Law & Commerce* (2002), 275–291; P. Mathew, "Australian Refugee Protection in the Wake of Tampa", 96 *American Journal of International Law*(2002), 661–676; C. Bailliet, "The Tampa Case and its Impact on Burden Sharing at Sea", 3 *Human Rights Quarterly*(2003) 741–774.

refugees – Amendments to the SOLAS and SAR Conventions were adopted in May 2004. They entered into force in 2006. The purpose of these amendments is to help ensure that persons in distress are assisted, while minimizing the inconvenience to assisting ships and ensuring the continued integrity of SAR services.[55] Concerning the rescued persons, the amendments stipulate that the obligation of assistance applies regardless of their nationality or status or the circumstances in which they are found.[56] Furthermore, within the capabilities and limitations of the ship, all embarked persons shall be treated with humanity.[57] The owner, the charterer, the company operating the ship or any other person shall not influence (because of financial motives for example) the shipmaster's decision concerning what – in his professional judgment – is necessary for the safety of life at sea.[58] Governments have an obligation to co-ordinate and co-operate to ensure that masters of ships providing assistance by embarking persons in distress at sea, are released from their obligations with minimum further deviation from the ship's intended voyage.[59] Lastly, although there is no actual duty for States to allow disembarkation onto its own territory –a State can refuse disembarkation or make this dependant on certain conditions[60] – disembarkation of the persons has to be arranged as soon as reasonably practicable.[61] The new amendments – drafted with the help of *inter alia* the United Nations High Commissioner for Refugees (UNHCR)[62] – were definitely an improvement.

But what exactly is the relationship between Article 98 LOSC and the relevant articles in the SAR and SOLAS Conventions? Several provisions of the LOSC reflect principles compatible with those already included in IMO treaties and recommendations adopted prior to the LOSC; such indeed is the case with certain provisions in the 1979 SAR and 1974 SOLAS Conventions. The active participation of the IMO Secretariat at the Third United Nations Conference on the Law of the Sea has ensured that no overlapping, inconsistency or incompatibility exist between the LOSC and IMO treaties.

---

[55] MSC, "Guidelines on the Treatment of Persons Rescued at Sea", MSC Resolution 167(78) (20 May 2004), para. 2.3.

[56] SOLAS Convention, Chapter V Regulation 33 para 1.

[57] Ibid, 33 para 6.

[58] Ibid, 34–1.

[59] Ibid, 33 para 1–1; SAR Convention, Chapter 3 para 3.1.9.

[60] G. Goodwin-Gill, The Refugee in International Law, (Oxford: Clarendon Press, 1996), 157.

[61] SOLAS Convention, Chapter V Regulation 33 para 1–1; SAR Convention, Chapter 3 para 3.1.9.

[62] In 2002, a High-Level Inter-agency Group was set up to deal with the problem of migrants at sea. The IMO, the UNHCR, the United Nations Division for Ocean Affairs and the Law of the Sea (UNDOALOS), the United Nations Office on Drugs and Crime (UNODC), the United Nations Office of the High Commissioner for Human Rights (OHCHR) and the International Organization for Migration (IOM) were all participating in this Inter-Agency Group. The conclusions of the Interagency Group meetings were the basis for the 2004 SOLAS and SAR Amendments. See for example: MSC, "Review of Safety Measures and Procedures for the Treatment of Persons Rescued at Sea", *IMO Doc*. MSC 76/22/8 (31 July 2002).

What about the 2004 SAR and SOLAS Amendments? The IMO is explicitly mentioned in only one of the articles of the LOSC, namely Article 2 of Annex VIII. Several other provisions refer to the 'competent international organization' in connection with the adoption of international shipping rules and standards in matters concerning maritime safety, efficiency of navigation and the prevention and control of marine pollution from vessels and by dumping. The expression 'competent international organization' – when used in the singular of the LOSC – applies exclusively to IMO, bearing in mind the global mandate of the organization as a specialized agency within the United Nations system.

The wide acceptance and uncontested legitimacy of IMO's mandate is indicated by the universality of the organization, as the 170 sovereign States that are member of IMO represent all regions of the world. They may participate in the meetings of the IMO bodies responsible for drafting and adopting safety and anti-pollution rules and standards. New IMO conventions are normally adopted by consensus. Numerous provisions in the LOSC refer to the mandate of several organizations in connection with the same subject matter. Sometimes, activities set forth in these provisions may involve IMO working in co-operation with other organizations.[63]

As the LOSC is regarded as an 'umbrella convention', most of its provisions – being of a general kind – can be implemented only through specific operative regulations in other international agreements.[64] This is reflected in several provisions of the LOSC which require States to 'take account of', 'conform to', 'give effect to' or 'implement' the relevant international rules and standards developed by or through the 'competent international organization' (i.e. IMO). The latter are variously referred to as 'applicable international rules and standards', 'internationally agreed rules, standards, and recommended practices and procedures', 'generally accepted international rules and standards', 'generally accepted international regulations', 'applicable international instruments' or 'generally accepted international regulations, procedures and practices'.[65] Despite the fact that in many cases the LOSC contains general obligations to apply rules and standards contained in IMO Conventions, IMO rules and standards, which are very precise technical provisions, cannot be considered as binding among States unless they are parties to the treaties where they are contained. The LOSC provisions concerning maritime safety aim at the effective implementation of substantive safety rules, but in the end they remain basically provisions which regulate the features

[63] IMO Legal Committee (LEG), "Implications of the United Nations Convention on the Law of the Sea for the International Maritime Organization", *IMO Doc.* LEG/MISC.6 (10 September 2008), 7–8. The Division for Ocean Affairs and the Law of the Sea (UNDOALOS), Office of Legal Affairs prepared a table on 'Competent or relevant international organizations' in relation to the LOSC. The table lists subjects and articles in the sequence in which they appear in the Convention, together with the corresponding competent organizations. See: Law of the Sea Bulletin No.31, 81–95.

[64] LEG, supra, note 63, 8.

[65] Ibid.

and extent of State jurisdiction and not the enforcement of measures regulated in IMO conventions.[66]

However, in Article 98 LOSC there is no reference to rules established by the 'competent international organisation'. As a result, the obligations under the LOSC concerning search and rescue at sea are exhausted by the provisions in Article 98 LOSC. Relevant IMO conventions – such as the SAR and SOLAS Conventions – can therefore only be used as an interpretative tool pursuant to Article 31(3) of the 1969 Vienna Convention on the Law of Treaties (VCLT). Concerning the interpretation of treaties, the VCLT provides in Article 31(3) that (a) subsequent agreements, (b) practice and (c) relevant rules of international law between the Parties to a treaty are relevant to its interpretation.[67]

Nevertheless, the use of such interpretative methods has to remain faithful to the ordinary meaning and context of the treaty in light of its object and purpose.[68] Although the ICJ has acknowledged that treaties have to be interpreted and applied within the framework of the entire legal system prevailing at the time of the interpretation, it also accepted that there is a primary necessity of interpreting an instrument in accordance with the intentions of the parties at the time of its conclusion.[69] In combining both the evolutionary and the inter-temporal element, the ICJ reflects the opinion of the International Law Commission when commenting on the draft text of Article 31(3)(c) VCLT.[70]

However, this approach is based on the view that the concepts, terms and provisions in question were by definition evolutionary. Therefore, it cannot be applied with regard to a general revision or re-interpretation of a treaty. As a result, evolutionary interpretation does not entitle a court or a tribunal to engage in a process of constant revision or updating of a treaty – such as the LOSC – every time a newer treaty is concluded that relates to similar matters.[71] Many of the terms in the LOSC are likely to be inherently evolutionary, such as the definition of pollution of the

---

[66] A. Mihneva-Natova, "The Relationship between United Nations Convention on the Law of the Sea and the IMO Conventions", Paper within the Framework of The United Nations and The Nippon Foundation of Japan Fellowship, 2005, 14, available at: http://www.un.org/depts/los/nippon/unnff_programme_home/fellows_pages/fellows_papers/natova_0506_bulgaria.pdf

[67] Vienna Convention on the Law of Treaties (adopted 23 May 1969, entered into force 27 January 1980), 1155 *UNTS* 331. [VCLT].

[68] VCLT, Art. 31(2).

[69] ICJ, (Namibia Advisory Opinion), 21 June 1971, Legal Consequences for States of the Continued Presence of South Africa in Namibia (South West Africa) notwithstanding Security Council Resolution 276 (1970) *ICJ Reports* 16 (1971), para. 53; ICJ, 19 December 1978, Aegean Sea Continental Shelf Case, *Greece v. Turkey*, *ICJ Reports* 3 (1978); ICJ, 6 November 2003, Oil Platforms Case, *Islamic Republic of Iran v. United States of America*, *ICJ Reports* 161 (2003), paras. 40–41.

[70] ILC, "The Law of Treaties", Commentary to draft Article 27, para. 16, in Watts, A. (1999, Vol. II, 690).

[71] ICJ, 25 September 1997, Gabcikovo-Nagymaros Case, *Hungary v. Slovakia*, Separate Opinion of Judge Mohammed Bedjaoui, *ICJ Reports* 120 (1997), para. 12.

marine environment.[72] The effectiveness of any such development is dependent upon a general acceptance by the States Parties to the LOSC, either through widespread participation in treaty-making processes or acquiescence.[73]

Although the 1979 SAR and 1974 SOLAS Conventions have respectively 101 and 161 State parties,[74] the implementation of the 2004 Amendments – containing several humanitarian considerations – proved to be more difficult than expected. States like Finland and Malta have not even signed the amendments yet. As there is no general acceptance of the provisions contained in the 2004 Amendments, the latter cannot be used to re-interpret Article 98 LOSC. States that did not sign the amendments will thus not be bound by them. Italy, however, is a party to the LOSC, the 1979 SAR and 1974 SOLAS Conventions and the 2004 SAR and SOLAS Amendments.

7.2.3.3 The Role of Soft Law Provisions

To meet the practical obstacles of implementation and in order to assist States in meeting their existing commitments, a wide range of soft law instruments concerning migrants at sea have been developed. They contain certain elements which are unlikely to find their way into a treaty because of the opposition of some States to binding agreements, but also because of their aim. For example, the 2004 IMO Guidelines on the Treatment of Persons Rescued at Sea were especially developed to provide guidance to Governments and shipmasters with regard to humanitarian obligations and obligations under the relevant international law relating to treatment of persons rescued at sea. These guidelines are considered to be associated with the 2004 SAR and SOLAS Amendments, as they were adopted at the same time. The term 'Government' that is used in these Guidelines, should be read to mean Contracting Government to the International Convention for the Safety of Life at Sea (SOLAS), 1974, as amended in 2004, or Party to the International Convention on Maritime Search and Rescue, 1979, as amended in 2004.[75]

The 2004 IMO Guidelines state that a place of safety can be defined as a location where rescue operations are considered to terminate, where the survivors' safety or life is no longer threatened, basic human needs (such as food, shelter and medical needs) can be met and transportation arrangements can be made for the survivors' next or final destination.[76] Disembarkation of asylum-seekers recovered at sea, in territories where their lives and freedom would be threatened, must be avoided.[77]

[72] Boyle, supra, note 40, 46.

[73] Barnes, supra, note 3, 111.

[74] IMO, "Status of Conventions summary" (31 August 2012), available online: http://www.imo.org/About/Conventions/StatusOfConventions/Pages/Default.aspx

[75] MSC, "Guidelines on the Treatment of Persons Rescued at Sea", MSC Resolution 167(78) (20 May 2004), para. 1.1.

[76] Ibid., para. 6.12.

[77] Ibid., para. 6.17.

This requirement is applicable regardless where the persons were found, thus also on the high seas.

Although these provisions are not binding, a soft law instrument can also contain an agreed interpretation of a treaty provision (Article 31(3)(a) VCLT). Subtle evolutionary changes in existing treaties may thus come about through the process of interpretation under the influence of soft law. Therefore, there is not always the need to attempt turning a soft law provision into a 'rule' of international customary law or to enshrine it in a binding treaty.[78]

It is submitted that States that have adopted the 2004 SAR and SOLAS Amendments have also agreed upon the associated 2004 IMO Guidelines as a tool of interpretation. Malta, for example, did not sign the 2004 Amendments, because they do not agree with the provisions in the 2004 Guidelines. On 22 December 2005, the IMO received a communication from the Ministry of Foreign Affairs of Malta declaring that Malta "is not yet in a position to accept these amendments".[79] According to Malta there is a safe place in terms of search and rescue and there is a safe place in terms of humanitarian law.[80] The 2004 Guidelines, however, do state that a place of safety has to fulfil certain humanitarian requirements too.

7.2.3.4 The Impact of Regional Agreements

The regional development of the law of the sea is not merely envisaged but also encouraged in the LOSC.[81] Article 98(2) LOSC states: "Every coastal State shall promote the establishment, operation and maintenance of an adequate and effective search and rescue service regarding safety on and over the sea and, where circumstances so require, by way of mutual regional arrangements cooperate with neighbouring States for this purpose." Regional arrangements help accommodate the special needs and varying circumstances in certain areas.

In 2010, the IMO Secretary-General proposed to develop a pilot project for a regional solution in the Mediterranean. On the one hand, the system of rescuing migrants in the Mediterranean Basin has to be improved. On the other hand, these persons also have to be disembarked at a place of safety in accordance with the SAR and SOLAS Conventions.[82] If this project works, it could be applied in other parts

[78] Boyle, supra, note 40, 51–52.

[79] IMO, "Status of multilateral conventions and instruments in respect of which the International Maritime Organization or its Secretary-General performs depositary or other functions" (31 October 2011), available at: http://www.imo.org/About/Conventions/StatusOfConventions/Documents/Status%20-%202011.pdf

[80] S. Klepp, "A Double Bind: Malta and the Rescue of Unwanted Migrants at Sea, A Legal Anthropological Perspective on the Humanitarian Law of the Sea", 23 *International Journal of Refugee Law* (2011), 538-557 at 549.

[81] Boyle, supra, note 40, 44.

[82] LEG, "Report of the Legal Committee on the work of its ninety-eight session", *IMO Doc.* LEG 98/14 (18 April 2011), para. 13.25.

of the world.[83] Meanwhile, the IMO is even waiting to take steps at the international level – for example amending the FAL Convention[84] – until the results of this Regional Agreement are ready.[85]

In the Terms of Reference it was concluded that the development of the regional agreement was to[86]:

1. Establish and strengthen co-operation among Parties to enable them to cope with incidents involving persons rescued at sea;
2. Establish a system of communication between the countries in the region to exchange information on the movement of persons by sea;
3. Ensure the safety of persons rescued at sea, pending a decision as to the place where such persons will be safely delivered, taking into account the prevailing weather and other conditions, including the safety of the delivering ships and the capacity of the places where they are delivered to provide care as may be necessary under the circumstances;
4. Arrange that delivery of persons takes place without undue delays to the rescuing ships which should be allowed to promptly proceed to their destination once the delivery operation is over; and
5. Promote co-operation for the delivery of persons rescued at sea to a port of a place of safety.[87]

At the moment there is only a draft text available. The ultimate goal here will be the development of a Regional Agreement in the form of a Memorandum of Understanding (MoU) on concerted procedures relating to the disembarkation of persons rescued at sea.[88] A MoU is a well-accepted type of legal instrument in international law and practice, identified as "an informal but nevertheless legal agreement" between two or more parties.[89] Whether this MoU is meant to be binding is not clear at the moment.

During the meetings, it was stressed that the development of a regional agreement should be restricted to purely maritime matters, in view of IMO's primary concern for the integrity of the search and rescue.[90] Nevertheless, there are some important elements within the draft text. For example, the place of safety has to be

---

[83] COMSAR, "Report to the Maritime Safety Committee", *IMO Doc*. COMSAR 14/17 (22 March 2010), paras. 10.1–10.26.

[84] Convention on Facilitation of International Maritime Traffic (adopted 9 April 1965, entered into force 5 March 1967) 591 *UNTS* 265. [FAL Convention].

[85] COMSAR, "Report to the Maritime Safety Committee", *IMO Doc*. COMSAR 15/16 (25 March 2011), para. 10.3.

[86] MSC, "Measures to protect the safety of persons rescued at sea", *IMO Doc*. MSC 89/INF.23 (12 April 2011), para. 6.

[87] Ibid., Annex.

[88] FAL, "Address of the Secretary-General at the Opening of the Thirty-Seventh Session of the Facilitation Committee", *IMO Doc*. FAL 37/INF. 5 (5 September 2011), 3–4.

[89] Arnold McNair, *The Law of Treaties* (Oxford: Clarendon Press, 1961), 15.

[90] MSC, "Measures to protect the safety of persons rescued at sea", *IMO Doc*. MSC 89/INF.23 (12 April 2011), para. 9.

determined based on the 2004 IMO Guidelines. This means that if Malta will be a part of this regional agreement, it will have to accept these guidelines. To avoid non-acceptance of the regional agreements by Malta, the draft text also mentions the respective capacities of a State when providing a place of safety and the particular circumstances of the case.[91]

Moreover, at the end of 2011, the UNHCR developed a Draft Model framework for cooperation following rescue at sea operations. This framework contains principles of burden and responsibility-sharing among States during and after rescue.[92] It could be complementary or supplementary to the regional MoU.

7.3 The European Convention on Human Rights and the Law of the Sea

7.3.1 Judgments of the European Court of Human Rights

Although the European Convention for the Protection of Human Rights and Fundamental Freedoms (ECHR)[93] makes no direct reference to the law of the sea or maritime law, the European Court of Human Rights (ECtHR) has already considered several cases concerning both. On the one hand, it involves cases related to state jurisdiction in maritime zones: how can the ECHR be applied in a maritime context? Thus, these cases deal with the application of Article 1 ECHR that says: "The High Contracting Parties shall secure to everyone within their jurisdiction the rights and freedoms defined in Section I of this Convention."

Jurisdiction in international law is generally framed territorially.[94] Nevertheless, extraterritoriality does not prevent human rights obligations from being engaged in particular circumstances.[95] The ECtHR considers the exercise of 'effective control'

[91] H. Hesse, "Persons rescued at Sea", Presentation by the Senior Deputy Director, IMO Maritime Safety Division at the Expert Meeting on Refugee and Asylum Seekers in Distress at Sea (8–10 November 2011), available online: http://www.unhcr.org/4ef3061c9.html.

[92] UNHCR, "Refugees and Asylum-Seekers in Distress at Sea – How Best to Respond?", Background paper (8–10 November 2011), available online: http://www.unhcr.org/4ec1436c9.html. The Model Framework is based on and further develops the UNHCR's 10 Point Plan of Action on Refugee Protection and International Migration. See: UNHCR, "Refugees and Asylum-Seekers in Distress at Sea – How Best to Respond?", Summary Conclusions (8–10 November 2011), available at: http://www.unhcr.org/4ede2ae99.html, para. 13.

[93] European Convention for the Protection of Human Rights and Fundamental Freedoms (adopted 4 November 1950, entered into force 3 September 1953) 213 *UNTS* 222. [ECHR].

[94] ECtHR, 12 December 2001, No. 52207/99, *Bankovic and Others v. Belgium and Others*, para. 73.

[95] For a detailed discussion see: V. Moreno-Lax, "Seeking Asylum in the Mediterranean: Against a Fragmentary Reading of EU Member States' Obligations Accruing at Sea", *23 International Journal of Refugee Law*(2011) 174–220.

over the territory (for example the *Loizidou Case*[96]) or over the persons concerned (for example the *Issa Case*[97]) to be the crucial element giving rise to state responsibility. For example, in the *Medvedyev Case,*[98] the ECtHR noted that from the date on which the vessel Winner was seized and its crew arrested and until it arrived in Brest, the Winner and its crew were under the control of French military forces. Although they were outside French territory, they were within the jurisdiction of France for the purposes of Article 1 ECtHR. What remained unclear – until the *Hirsi Case* that will be discussed in Sect. 7.3.2 – is whether situations other than those amounting to detention or arrest, constitute an exercise of control over persons on board vessels sufficient to trigger human rights responsibility.

On the other hand, the ECtHR judgments concern cases on the protection of the applicant's human rights within the context of the law of the sea. In the *Medvedyev Case*[99] (2008) and the *Rigopoulos Case*[100] (1999), ships flying the Cambodian and the Panamanian flags, respectively, were apprehended on the high seas by Navy ships of France and Spain. Each seizure was conducted in the framework of the fight against drug trafficking and with the authorization of the flag State. As a result, the crew members were taken into custody on the Navy ship, brought to a port of the arresting State, and were later submitted to criminal proceedings. However, the crew members claimed that the State detaining them had violated Article 5(3) ECHR according to which arrested or detained persons "shall be brought promptly before a judge or other officer authorized by law to exercise judicial power." The time elapsed between the moment the crew members were taken into custody and the point at which they were presented to a judge (16 days in the Rigopoulos Case and 13 in the *Medvedyev Case*) was claimed to be incompatible with the requirement of "promptitude". However, the Court held that there was no violation of Article 5(3) ECHR as the 'exceptional circumstances' prevailed in both cases. Indeed, the arrest was carried out on the high seas at a distance of thousands of kilometres from the French and Spanish territory. Both cases demonstrate the relevance of maritime situations in interpreting a human rights law provision.

Nevertheless, in order to reach a decision, the ECtHR has sometimes taken certain steps in its reasoning that raise doubts in the minds of international lawyers specializing in the law of the sea. In the *Medvedyev Case*, the crew members claimed a violation of Article 5(1) ECHR, according to which: "No one shall be deprived of his liberty save in the following cases and in accordance with a procedure prescribed by law." The applicants argued that the actors making the arrest did not satisfy the requirement of a procedure described by law. The ECtHR decided that the legality of the seizure of the vessel depended on the flag State's consent.

However, the ECtHR did not seem to adopt as a starting point the idea that the flag State is free to authorize other States to exercise some or all its powers on its

[96] ECtHR, 23 March 1995, No. 15318/89, *Loizidou v. Turkey*.

[97] ECtHR, 16 November 2004, No. 31821/96, *Issa and Others v. Turkey*.

[98] ECtHR, 10 July 2008, No. 3394/03, *Medvedyev and Others v. France*, para. 50.

[99] ECtHR, 10 July 2008, No. 3394/03, *Medvedyev and Others v. France* .

[100] ECtHR, 12 January 1999, No. 37388/97, *Rigoupoulos v. Spain*.

ships, and that all States are free to request such authorization to the flag State. On the contrary, the approach seemed to be that a request for and the granting of an authorization needs a legal basis, *in casu* Article 108 LOSC that says: "Any State which has reasonable grounds for believing that a ship flying its flag is engaged in illicit traffic in narcotic drugs or psychotropic substances may request the cooperation of other States to suppress such traffic".

In the *Women on Waves Case,*[101] the ECHR considered another aspect of the law of the sea. In this case, the Borndiep – a ship flying the Dutch flag – carried out a trip aimed at conducting activities in favour of legalizing abortion. However, as abortion was prohibited in Portugal at that time, the Portuguese government sent a warship to deny the Borndiep access to its waters. The NGOs that had chartered the Borndiep, claimed that Portugal had violated their right of expression and freedom of peaceful assembly and of association under Articles 10 and 11 of the ECHR.

The Portuguese government argued that its interference with the right of innocent passage of the Borndiep was legal under Articles 19 and 25 of the LOSC as the passage entailed violations of Portuguese law. Furthermore, the measures corresponded to restrictions on passage "prescribed by law as are necessary in a democratic society … for the protection of health or morals" in conformity with Articles 10(2) and 11(2) of the ECHR. Although the ECHR accepted the view that the interference of the Portuguese Government was prescribed by law in Articles 19(2)(g) and 25 LOSC, it held that the acts of interference with the navigation of the Borndiep were not necessary in a democratic society. The ECHR noted: "the State certainly had at its disposal other means to attain the legitimate objectives of defending order and protecting health than to resort to a total interdiction of entry of the Borndiep in its territorial waters, especially by sending a warship against a merchant vessel."Treves doubts whether this argument would be valid in a case regarding interference with innocent passage that was submitted to a court or tribunal that had jurisdiction over cases concerning the interpretation and application of the LOSC.[102]

A last case that will be discussed is the *Mangouras Case,*[103] in which the ECtHR had to determine whether a guarantee of three million Euros – fixed by the Spanish judicial authorities for release from detention of Captain Mangouras of the vessel Prestige – constituted a violation of Article 5(3) ECHR. Article 5(3) guarantees release of detainees prior to trial with allowance for reasonable bail. The ECtHR affirmed that, although the amount fixed for release of the captain was admittedly high, it did not contravene the ECHR. One of the reasons was the growing and legitimate concern for marine pollution, inter alia as expressed in the law of the sea. Thus, values emerging in the law of the sea are assessed by the ECtHR to determine whether they should be balanced against values set out in the ECHR.

---

[101] ECtHR, 3 February 2009, No. 31276/05, *Women on Waves and Others v. Portugal.*

[102] Treves, supra, note 10, 11.

[103] ECtHR, 8 January 2009, No.12050/04, *Mangouras v. Spain.*

7.3.2 *The Hirsi Case*

7.3.2.1 The Content of the ECtHR Judgment

The extraterritorial applicability of the principle of non-refoulement – which is implicitly present in Article 3 of the Convention for the Protection of Human Rights and Fundamental Freedoms (ECHR) – was decided by the European Court of Human Rights (ECtHR) on 23 February 2012 in *Hirsi Jamaa and Others v. Italy*.[104] The applicants – 11 Somali and 13 Eritrean nationals – were part of a group of about 200 individuals who left Libya aboard three vessels with the aim of reaching the Italian coast. However, after they were noticed by ships of the Italian Revenue Police (*Guardia di finanza*) and the Coastguard, the persons on board were transferred onto Italian military ships and returned to Tripoli. This return was carried out based on a bilateral agreement between Italy and Libya.[105]

The applicants relied on Article 3 ECHR to argue that the decision of the Italian authorities to intercept the vessels on the high seas – and send the applicants straight back to Libya – exposed them to the risk of ill-treatment there, as well as to the serious threat of being sent back to their countries of origin (Somalia and Eritrea), where they might also face ill-treatment. Although the ECtHR affirmed that only in exceptional cases could acts of the Member States performed or producing effects outside their territories constitute an exercise of jurisdiction by them. It held that in this case there had been a violation of Article 3 ECHR because the applicants had been exposed to (1) the risk of ill-treatment in Libya and (2) of repatriation to Somalia or Eritrea. Indeed, the ECtHR found that the applicants had fallen within the jurisdiction of Italy since in the period between boarding the Italian warships on the high seas and being handed over to the Libyan authorities, the applicants had been under the continuous and exclusive *de jure* and *de facto* control of the Italian authorities. The fact that none of the applicants were actually returned to these countries was irrelevant since it was the existence of the risk that mattered.[106]

Additionally, the ECtHR stated that the transfer of the applicants to Libya had been carried out without any examination of each individual situation, and thus constituted a form of collective expulsion in breach of Article 4 of Protocol No. 4 ECHR. Italy argued that none of the migrants had actually requested international protection on board the military ships. Nevertheless, the ECtHR considered the national

---

[104] ECtHR, *Hirsi Jamaa and Others v. Italy*, supra, note 6. See also: UNHCR, "UNHCR's oral intervention at the European Court of Human Rights Hearing of the case *Hirsi and Others v. Italy* (Application No. 27765/09), Strasbourg, June 22, 2011", available at: http://www.unhcr.org/refworld/pdfid/4e0356d42.pdf.

[105] ECtHR, *Hirsi Jamaa and Others v. Italy*, supra, note 6, paras. 9–13.

[106] Ibid., para. 70 *et seq*. Already before this ECtHR judgment, Guilfoyle concluded that – based on Australian and Spanish state practice – the *non-refoulement* principle will be applicable on the high seas when persons are removed onto a government vessel. See: Douglas Guilfoyle, Shipping Interdiction and the Law of the Sea, (Cambridge: Cambridge University Press, 2009), 231.

authorities – faced with a situation in which human rights were being systematically violated – to have an obligation to find out about the treatment to which the applicants would be exposed after their return.[107] Thus, it seems that there will now be a violation of the Convention in case of forced return in violation with Article 3, as long as the risk of such a treatment is 'sufficiently real and probable',[108] whether or not the applicant has notified the deporting authorities of this risk, as long as these authorities should have been aware of the risk.[109]

7.3.2.2 A Law of the Sea Perspective

As a preliminary matter, it has to be kept in mind that the 'rights' in the law of the sea are generally not enforceable by or against individuals under the LOSC. In many circumstances, they are articulated as duties owed by a State to other State parties. Thus, they may be enforced by those States pursuant to the compulsory dispute settlement provisions in the LOSC. As a treaty has to interpreted in good faith in accordance with the ordinary meaning to be given to the terms of the treaty in their context and in the light of its object and purpose,[110] there is no room to interpret that the individuals aboard a vessel in distress have a positive 'right' to be rescued under Article 98 LOSC. Nor do seafarers have a 'right' to expect that adequate and effective search and rescue services will be made available to them by coastal States in case of a distress situation.[111] Furthermore, many of the LOSC provisions are not self-executing. As such, these provisions must be implemented through domestic legislation before they give rise to legally enforceable rights and duties, at least as far as private persons are concerned.[112] Other States, from their side, may have little interest in ensuring third State compliance with international law concerning search and rescue at sea.[113]

The ECtHR decided: "Speculation as to the nature and purpose of the intervention of the Italian ships on the high seas would not lead the Court to any other conclusion." However, from a law of the sea perspective, this would be a very important question to start with. In the parties' submissions, the Italian Government stressed that they intercepted the vessels in the context of a rescue on the high seas under Article 98 LOSC. According to them, in no circumstances could it be described as a maritime police operation. As Italy itself submits that it was a rescue, it should also fulfil its obligations under international law concerning search and rescue.

---

[107] ECtHR, *Hirsi Jamaa and Others v. Italy*, supra, note 6, para. 133.

[108] Ibid., para. 136.

[109] M. Dembour, "Interception-at-Sea: Illegal as currently practiced – Hirsi and Others v. Italy", Strasbourg Observers Blog, 2012, available at: http://strasbourgobservers.com/2012/03/01/interception-at-sea-illegal-as-currently-practiced-hirsi-and-others-v-italy/

[110] VCLT, Art. 31(1).

[111] For an extensive discussion see: Moen, supra, note 39, 377–410.

[112] Barnes (2004), supra, note 51, 50.

[113] Barnes (2010), supra, note 3, 107.

Italy signed and ratified the LOSC, as well as the 2004 SAR and SOLAS Amendments. Therefore, when carrying out a rescue operation, a place of safety has to be provided to the persons. According to the guidelines – which are associated with the 2004 SAR and SOLAS Amendments and thus can be used to interpret the amendments – there is a need to avoid disembarkation in territories where the lives and freedoms of those alleging a well-founded fear of persecution would be threatened, also when the persons are found on the high seas.[114] We can conclude that also under the law of the sea it is forbidden to disembark the applicants in Libya, as Libya could not be regarded as a place of safety.

7.3.2.3 Remaining Questions

The *Hirsi Case* was unanimously adopted by the ECtHR Grand Chamber. The latter accepts cases that raise a serious question affecting the interpretation or application of the Convention or the protocols thereto, or a serious issue of general importance.[115] As the principle of non-refoulement, as well as the prohibition of collective expulsion, have attained the status of customary international law, the decision can be expected to have a jurisprudential impact beyond the reach of the European Convention.[116] Nevertheless, there are still some problems that remain unsolved.

A first issue is whether there will be effective control in a case involving the diversion of a ship on the high seas. When diverting a migrant vessel, a State exercises the right of visit (Article 110 LOSC). The right of visit is an exception to the general principle of the exclusive jurisdiction of the flag State over ships flying its flag, set out in Article 92 LOSC. It entails the right of every warship or other duly authorised vessel to board the vessel and, more importantly, the right to search the vessel in circumstances of extreme suspicion.[117] As a diversion of boats to a certain destination is indisputably a form of actual physical interference with the vessel, it must fulfil the conditions of the right of visit to be regarded as lawful.[118] Article 110 LOSC stipulates that the right of visit is only justified – next to the situation where the flag State has given its consent – when there is reasonable ground for suspecting that the ship is engaged in piracy, in the slave trade, in unauthorised broadcasting and when the ship is without nationality or though flying a foreign flag or refusing to show its flag, the ship is, in reality, of the same nationality as the warship. The absence of nationality in Article 110(1)(d) LOSC seems to be the most relevant ground for the interdiction of

[114] MSC, "Guidelines on the Treatment of Persons Rescued at Sea", MSC Resolution 167(78) (20 May 2004), para. 6.17.

[115] ECHR, Art. 43.

[116] J. Hessbruegg, "European Court of Human Rights Protects Migrants Against "Push Back" Operations on the High Seas", 2012, ASIL Insights, available at: http://www.asil.org/pdfs/insights/insight120417.pdf

[117] LOSC, Art. 110.

[118] Papastavridis, supra, note 38, 155.

vessels with migrants on board.[119] The right of visit is based upon the fact that the migrant boats are considered to be stateless vessels. As the result of a diversion by an Italian warship for example, it could happen that the migrant vessel is actually forced to return to Libya. However, the persons were never brought onto an Italian vessel. Is there effective control in this case? Also the law of the sea remains silent on whether the principle of non-refoulement is applicable when exercising the right of visit.

Secondly, what if interception operations on the high seas are being coordinated by Frontex? Frontex is the European External Border Agency that organizes joint surveillance operations at sea to interdict such migrant boats, helping States to cope with the problem.[120] Although Frontex is a specialized and independent body, the responsibility for the control and surveillance of external borders lies with the Member States.[121] When human rights violations result from joint maritime operations, the independent responsibility of each participating EU Member State may be invoked.[122] This is how the ECtHR proceeded in the *Xhavara Case,*[123] attributing exclusive responsibility to Italy for the acts it perpetrated in international waters, as a result of the convention concluded with Albania authorizing it to patrol both international and Albanian waters for the purpose of migration control. However, as there is a lack of transparency concerning the Frontex operations, it will not always be easy to know which Member State had effective control.

7.4 Conclusion

Human rights concerns are intertwined with concerns of the law of the sea. These two fields are not separate planets rotating in different orbits, but rather meet on many situations. ITLOS takes into account human rights considerations, just as the ECtHR considers the law of the sea when appropriate. It was interesting to see – be it theoretically – how the law of the sea would have dealt with the *Hirsi Case*. While

---

[119] Papastavridis also discusses the 'slave trade' argument as a possible legal basis for interception of human beings on the high seas. Ibid. 159. See also Barnes, supra, note 3, 130; G. Goodwin-Gill and J. McAdam, The Refugee in International Law, (Oxford: Oxford University Press,2007), 272; M. Pallis, "Obligations of States towards Asylum Seekers at Sea: Interactions and Conflicts Between Legal Regimes" 14 *International Journal of Refugee Law* 2002, 329–364 at 350–353.

[120] Council Regulation (EC) No. 2007/2004 of 26 October 2004 establishing a European Agency for the Management of Operational Cooperation at the External Border of the Member States of the European Union, *OJ* L 349/1 of 25 November 2004; Regulation (EU) No. 1168/2011 of the European Parliament and of the Council of 25 October 2011 amending Council Regulation (EC) No. 2007/2004 establishing a European Agency for the Management of Operational Cooperation at the External Borders of the Member States of the European Union, *OJ* L 304/1 of 22 November 2011.

[121] Council Regulation (EC) No. 2007/2004 of 26 October 2004 establishing a European Agency for the Management of Operational Cooperation at the External Border of the Member States of the European Union, *OJ* L 349/1 of 25 November 2004, Preamble, para. 4.

[122] See for example: Moreno-Lax, supra, note 95, 174–220.

[123] ECtHR 11 January 2001, No. 39473/98, *Xhavara and Others v. Italy and Albania.*

individuals cannot directly benefit from the law of the sea provisions, it is surprising that these rules already provide protection, be it outside the ECHR and the 'effective control' theory. When a State – such as Italy – is party to the 2004 SAR and SOLAS amendments, it cannot disembark rescued persons in territories where the lives and freedoms would be threatened, even though they were found on the high seas.

Next to this, it is remarkable that there is a lacuna in both fields, namely in case of the diversion of vessels on the high seas. As this situation does not constitute a rescue, the law of the sea rules on search and rescue are not applicable. Diversion towards a place where the persons' life could be threatened is therefore not explicitly prohibited. As there is probably no effective control either – since the persons are not transferred onto a vessel of the diverting State – there will still be some discussion on whether the ECHR will be applicable in these cases.

Chapter 8
New Frontiers in American Capital Punishment Litigation

Eric M. Freedman

Abstract This chapter summarizes two significant developments influencing capital punishment in the United States. First, in *Atkins v. Virginia* (2002) and *Roper v. Simmons* (2005), the Supreme Court of the United States held that the death penalty could not be inflicted upon, respectively, mentally retarded persons and persons under the age of eighteen because the characteristics of those groups rendered them insufficiently culpable to justify the punishment. Influential professional groups have proposed extending the principle to mentally ill persons, a proposal that is likely to be adopted case-by-case by the Supreme Court. Second, *Cullen v. Pinholster* (2011) limited the power of a federal court reviewing a death sentences to examine the state court record independently. But *Martinez v. Ryan* (2012) for the first time allowed a petitioner seeking federal court review to attack the quality of legal assistance he received in the later stages of state court review. As a result the positive and negative incentives for states to have robust systems of post-conviction review have increased. These two developments should accelerate the existing downward trend in executions.

8.1 Background

The Eighth Amendment to the United States Constitution prohibits the infliction of "cruel and unusual punishments." The Supreme Court of the United States has ruled that the infliction of capital punishment is not a per se violation of this prohibition,[1] but may be one in particular circumstances.

[1] *Gregg v. Georgia*, 428 U.S. 153 (1976)

E.M. Freedman (✉)
Professor of Constitutional Law, Maurice A. Deane School of Law of Hofstra University, Hempstead, USA
e-mail: Eric.M.Freedman@Hofstra.edu

Y. Haeck and E. Brems (eds.), *Human Rights and Civil Liberties in the 21st Century*, Ius Gentium: Comparative Perspectives on Law and Justice 30,
DOI 10.1007/978-94-007-7599-2_8,

For example, it is well-established that a death sentence which is the product of an arbitrary selection system – one that fails to assign the most severe punishment to the most culpable crimes – is unconstitutional.[2] Moreover, it is inherently cruel, and therefore forbidden, to punish by death crimes less serious than murder.[3]

8.2 Emerging Substantive Issues

In a series of cases during the last decade, the Supreme Court has determined that the legitimate aims of the death penalty, retribution and deterrence, are poorly served by the execution of certain categories of offenders. Hence, the infliction of capital punishment in their cases violates the Eighth Amendment because it is simply the pointless imposition of suffering – particularly in light of the fact that the characteristics of those offenders render them especially likely to be wrongfully convicted. Specifically, the Court held in 2002 that the Constitution forbids the execution of mentally retarded offenders[4] and reached the same conclusion in 2005 with respect to those who were less than 18 years old at the time of their crimes.[5]

These developments quickly led concerned professional groups to consider what additional categories of offenders might be added to the list.[6]

8.2.1 Defining Mental Retardation Functionally

One obvious candidate for inclusion on an expanded list of exemptions emerges from the observation that the concerns expressed by the Supreme Court in *Atkins* are not limited to defendants whose condition meets the strict clinical definition of mental retardation,[7] but rather extend to anyone whose functioning is the equivalent

[2] *Furman v. Georgia*, 408 U.S. 238 (1972)

[3] *Kennedy v. Louisiana*, 554 U.S. 407 (2008) (rape of a juvenile); *Coker v. Georgia*, 433 U.S. 584 (1977) (rape of an adult).

[4] *Atkins v. Virginia*, 536 U.S. 304 (2002), overruling *Penry v. Lynaugh*, 492 U.S. 302 (1989).

[5] *Roper v. Simmons*, 543 U.S. 551 (2005), overruling *Stanford v. Kentucky*, 492 U.S. 361 (1989). See also *Graham v. Florida*, 130 S.Ct. 2011 (2010) (juveniles may not be sentenced to life without parole for non-homicide offenses).

[6] See American Bar Association Resolution 122A and accompanying report on exempting those with severe mental illness from the death penalty, 8 August 2006, available at: http://www.deathpenaltyinfo.org/documents/122AReport.pdf. An almost identical resolution has been endorsed by the American Psychiatric Association, the American Psychological Association and the National Alliance for the Mentally Ill.

[7] In *Atkins v. Virginia,* supra, note 4, the Court quoted with approval the American Psychiatric Association's definition of mental retardation contained in its *Diagnostic and Statistical Manual of Mental Disorders*, at 41 (4th ed. 2000) ("DSM-IV"): "The essential feature of Mental Retardation is significantly subaverage general intellectual functioning (Criterion A) that is accompanied by

of one who qualifies for the diagnosis. As the American Bar Association and its partner organizations have noted, "dementia and traumatic brain injury [are] disabilities very similar to mental retardation in their impact on intellectual and adaptive functioning except that they always (in the case of dementia) or often (in the case of head injury) are manifested after age 18. Dementia resulting from the aging process is generally progressive and irreversible, and is associated with a number of deficits in intellectual and adaptive functioning, such as agnosia (failure to recognize or identify objects) and disturbances in executive functioning connected with planning, organizing, sequencing, and abstracting."

Simply put, if a person suffers a severe head injury at the age of 19 that causes brain damage resulting in significantly subaverage general intellectual functioning and significant adaptive limitations, there is no defensible basis for holding that he is eligible to be executed for a crime that he commits at the age of 20 even though he would not be so eligible if the head injury had happened when he was 17.

The definitions contained in the Diagnostic and Statistical Manual of Mental Disorders (DSM), published by the American Psychiatric Association, have nothing to do with the Eighth Amendment. They are created by an often-contentious public interchange among various stakeholders[8] (including pharmaceutical companies, health insurers, associations of health providers, patient advocacy groups and many others), and change regularly. For present purposes the definition of mental retardation needs to be functional – a description of symptomology rather than a diagnostic label.

It is a reasonable prediction that, if a suitable case presents itself in the next few years, the Supreme Court will agree.

8.2.2 *Exempting Mentally Ill Offenders from Execution*

Following the same line of thinking, there are many offenders within the concerns expressed in *Atkins* who fall into the class by reason of mental illness rather than mental retardation. The need for a functional definition in this context is particularly acute, not only for the reasons already described but also because

---

significant limitations in adaptive functioning in at least two of the following skill areas: communication, self-care, home living, social/interpersonal skills, use of community resources, self-direction, functional academic skills, work, leisure, health, and safety (Criterion B). The onset must occur before age 18 years (Criterion C). Mental Retardation has many different etiologies and may be seen as a final common pathway of various pathological processes that affect the functioning of the central nervous system."

[8] See, e.g., B. Carey, "Psychiatry Manual Drafters Back Down on Diagnoses", *New York Times*, 8 May 2012, available at: http://www.nytimes.com/2012/05/09/health/dsm-panel-backs-down-on-diagnoses.html?_r=1&hp, K. Franklin, "Hebephilia Update: DSM-5 Workgroup Stubbornly Clinging to Pet Diagnosis", *Forensic Psychologist*, 5 May 2012 blogpost available at: http://forensicpsychologist.blogspot.be/2012/05/hebephilia-update-dsm-5-workgroup.html); P.J. Caplan, "Psychiatry's Bible, the DSM, is Doing More Harm Than Good", *Washington Post*, 27 April 2011, available at: http://www.washingtonpost.com/opinions/psychiatrys-bible-the-dsm-is-doing-more-harm-than-good/2012/04/27/gIQAqy0W1T_story.html?

many millions of Americans suffer from some diagnosable mental disorder and if (in defiance of all political possibility) they were to be included in the class, the exception would swallow up the rule. Whatever definition is to be adopted, it must not only be functionally based, but should isolate a class whose disabilities are severe, permanent and rare.

The resolution adopted by the American Bar Association and allied groups[9] proposes that "Defendants should not be executed or sentenced to death if, at the time of the offense, they had a severe mental disorder or disability that significantly impaired their capacity (a) to appreciate the nature, consequences or wrongfulness of their conduct, (b) to exercise rational judgment in relation to conduct, or (c) to conform their conduct to the requirements of the law." This formulation seeks to combine the traditional elements of an insanity defense with the learning of *Atkins* so as to describe a group of offenders who are not too impaired to be convicted at all (otherwise they would have an insanity defense to guilt) but too impaired for consideration of their condition to be left to the judgment of individual juries.[10]

How the Supreme Court will react to this proposal is not yet known as it has not so far exercised its discretionary authority to hear such a case. A number of litigants have attempted to press the claim[11] in the lower courts but have been uniformly rebuffed on the basis that no case authority supports it.[12]

The logic of the argument is strong, however, and the Court will certainly understand that. Yet it has presumably learned a lesson from having been forced to abandon its previously-held views in both *Atkins* and *Roper*. Hence, in dealing with a mental illness exclusion from capital punishment, the Court might chose to pretermit broad pronouncements. Confronted with a severely impaired but not mentally retarded offender, it could simply announce that the exection of this particular

[9] See American Bar Association Resolution 122A, supra, note 6.

[10] Before it changed its view in *Atkins*, the Supreme Court had held in *Penry v. Lynaugh*, supra, note 4, that mentally retarded defendants were entitled only to jury consideration of their condition, not to a categorical exemption from execution.

[11] In addition to the Eighth Amendment argument many of them have also asserted that to exempt mentally retarded offenders but not mentally ill ones violates the command of the Fourteenth Amendmendment that "No State shall … deny to any person within its jurisdiction the equal protection of the laws."

[12] This logjam is the consequence of a much-criticized Supreme Court case, *Teague v. Lane*, 489 U.S. 288 (1989), whose practical effect is that only the Supreme Court, whose case-handling capacity is miniscule compared to that of the lower federal courts, can create new constitutional rules of criminal procedure. See E.M. Freedman, "Federal Habeas Corpus in Capital Cases", in J. Acker, R.M. Bohm and C.S. Lanier (eds.), *America's Experiment With Capital Punishment: Reflections on the Past, Present and Future of the Ultimate Penal Sanction*, 2nd ed., (Durham, NC: Carolina Academia Press, 2003) at 553, 566–567 (Explaining and criticizing *Teague*). Thus it has happened several times over the last 25 years that literally dozens of people have been executed despite presenting a claim that the Supreme Court eventually found meritorious. Examples are to be found in E.M. Freedman, "Mend It or End It?: The Revised ABA Capital Defense Representation Guidelines as an Opportunity to Reconsider the Death Penalty", 2 *Ohio State Journal on Criminal Law* (2005), 663, 673 n.53, available at: http://law.hofstra.edu/_site_support/files/pdf/directory/faculty/fulltime/EFreedman/Ghent/ohrecon.pdf

individual would constitute cruel and unusual punishment. Then it could do the same in the next case. Only after a series of such individual rulings might it attempt to formulate a general rule.

8.3 Emerging Procedural Issues

8.3.1 Background

The procedural path taken by a typical defendant convicted and sentenced to death in a state court may be represented this way:

UNITED STATES SUPREME COURT
(*certiorari* - review at discretion)

↗	↑	↖
HIGHEST STATE COURT ↘	HIGHEST STATE COURT ↘	U.S. COURT OF APPEALS
↑	↑	↑
(appeal as of right)	(appeals procedure varies)	(appeal as of right after initial showing of merit)
↑	↑	↑
STATE TRIAL COURT	STATE TRIAL COURT	U.S. DISTRICT COURT
TRIAL, SENTENCING AND DIRECT APPEAL	**STATE POST-CONVICTION**	**FEDERAL HABEAS CORPUS**
(Column 1)	(Column 2)	(Column 3)

The procedures in Column 1 are mandated by the United States Constitution and are fully subject to the Bill of Rights. This means among other things that the state is obligated to provide competent counsel to the accused if, as is invariably the case, he is indigent.[13] The state is also obligated to produce to the defense without demand all material information that may be favorable to the accused with respect to either guilt or sentence.[14]

The procedures in Column 2 are purely a matter of state law. They need not exist at all, although, for historical reasons, they do in fact exist in every state. Following

[13] U.S. Constitution, Sixth Amendment (1791) ("In all criminal prosecutions the accused shall enjoy the right … to have the assistance of counsel for his defence"), XIV, Sec. 1 (1868) (No state shall "deprive any person of life liberty or property without due process of law"); *Powell v. Alabama,* 287 U.S. 45(1932) (Due process requires State to provide counsel to indigent capital defendant); *Gideon v. Wainwright*, 372 U.S. 335 (1963) (Rule extended to all felony defendants). The right extends to the final appeal as of right in state court but not to the application for review by the United States Supreme Court, *Ross v. Moffitt*, 417 U.S. 600 (1974).

[14] *Brady v. Maryland*, 373 U.S. 83 (1963).

those procedures is a threshold requirement for access to the federal review provided in Column 3,[15] and issues not properly raised during state post-conviction procedures will ordinarily not be considered by the federal courts.[16] However, the Supreme Court has refused to extend the Constitutional right to counsel to Column 2.[17] Indeed not until recently had it even stated explicitly that fundamental norms of due process apply to state post-conviction systems (and are to be vindicated by system wide litigation rather than in individual cases).[18] With respect to Column 3, state capital defendants are assured competent counsel by federal statute.[19]

8.3.2 Right to Fair State Post-conviction Review

By the terms of restrictive legislation passed in 1996, a federal habeas corpus court may only grant relief if the state court proceedings "resulted in a decision that was contrary to, or involved an unreasonable application of clearly established Federal law," or that "was based on an unreasonable determination of the facts."[20] In *Cullen v. Pinholster*,[21] the Court, in an apparent defeat for defendants, ruled that the prisoner needed to meet these standards solely based on the record compiled in state court; only after he had done so could the federal court hold an evidentiary hearing.

The Court, however, was at pains to note that the prisoner had not contested the fact that he had been given a full and fair opportunity to develop his claims in state post-conviction proceedings. Had the fact been otherwise, the ruling would certainly have been otherwise as well. There would be various legal routes by which

[15] 28 U.S.C. Sec. 2254 (b).

[16] See, e.g., *Coleman v. Thompson*, 501 U.S. 722 (1991) (Because defendant filed appeals papers in state post-conviction proceedings three days late, federal courts would not review claims that the Constitution was violated during his trial). In technical language the federal courts often say that if the state courts determine that the defendant committed a "procedural default" during the state proceedings, the federal courts will in the exercise of their sound discretion honor that determination by refusing to reach the merits of the federal constitutional claims.

[17] *Murray v. Giarratano*, 492 U.S. 1 (1989). The practical result, as *Coleman* shows, is that counsel may forfeit all of a defendant's rights but the defendant may not attack counsel as ineffective for having done so. Not suprisingly, this line of cases has been subject to sustained criticism by the profession, see, e.g., E.M. Freedman, "Giarratano is a Scarecrow: The Right to Counsel in State Capital Post-conviction Proceedings", 91 *Cornell Law Review* (2006) 1079, and has been flatly rejected by the American Bar Association. See American Bar Association, "Guidelines for the Appointment and Performance of Counsel in Death Penalty Case", Guideline 1.1, reprinted in 31 *Hofstra Law Review* (2003) 919 (Standards to provide high quality legal representation to capital defendants apply to all stages of proceedings) available at: http://www.americanbar.org/advocacy/other_aba_initiatives/death_penalty_representation/resources/aba_guidelines.html.

[18] See *Skinner v. Switzer,* 131 S. Ct. 1289, 1296 (2011)*; Dist. Atty's Office v. Osborne,* 129 S. Ct. 2308, 2320 (2009).

[19] 18 U.S.C. Sec. 3599 (2).

[20] 28 U.S.C. Sec. 2254 (d).

[21] 131 S.Ct. 1388 (2011).

to reach this conclusion but the underlying principle is that ever since the passage of the Fourteenth Amendment – binding the states by the Bill of Rights, which previously had only applied to the federal government – an individual must be given at least one fair forum, whether state or federal, in which to make a federal constitutional attack on his conviction.[22] Furthermore, as noted above, it is now clear that a state post-conviction system must provide due process or be subject to a structural attack.[23]

The result of these two converging lines of precedent is that the incentives for states to have robust systems of post-conviction review have increased. If the states create such systems, the federal courts will treat their individual outcomes with greater respect than before, but if the states do not create such systems the failure is more vulnerable to system wide attack than before. The federal government, for its part, has every reason to desire the state courts to examine federal constitutional claims fully because the federal courts will have to do the work if the state courts do not.

8.3.3 Right to Assistance of Counsel in State Post-conviction Review

In its most recent relevant case, the Court has re-visited the problem of fair state post-conviction procedures in a context that reflects the concerns just discussed, while addressing one of the most severe problems presented by the cases described in Sect. 3.1.

Recall that a state has a constitutional obligation to provide a defendant with effective counsel for trial and direct appeal.[24] In many states, however, claims of ineffective assistance of counsel must be asserted during post-conviction review rather than on direct appeal,[25] a context in which, as discussed in Sect. 3.1, the state does not have an obligation to appoint counsel. Yet, if the state fails to appoint effective counsel during post-conviction review to assert the claim that trial counsel was ineffective, then the state has managed to render its duty to appoint effective trial counsel nugatory.

---

[22] For a more detailed discussion, see E.M. Freedman, "State Post-Conviction Remedies in the Next Fifteen Years: How Synergy Between the State and Federal Governments Can Improve the Criminal Justice System Nationally" 24 *Federal Sentencing Reporter* (2012) 298 available at: http://law.hofstra.edu/_site_support/files/pdf/directory/faculty/fulltime/EFreedman/Ghent/fed-sent.pdf.

[23] See supra, note 18.

[24] See supra, note 13.

[25] This rule is based on the perfectly sensible rationales that (a) the same counsel is likely to handle all the proceedings in Column 1, and (b) the direct appeal is supposed to focus on errors in the record while claims of ineffective assistance will necessarily involve investigating the record that counsel failed to make. See *Massaro v. United States*, 538 U.S. 500 (2003).

Recall also that the most common effect of ineffective performance of counsel in Column 2 is that the federal courts will hold that federal constitutional claims, in this instance a claim of ineffective assistance of trial counsel, has been procedurally defaulted.[26] But the doctrine of procedural default is a product of the courts' discretion and can be modified for good cause.

That is precisely what happened on March 20, 2012 in *Martinez v. Ryan.*[27] Without making any change in its views respecting a constitutional right to counsel in state post-conviction proceedings, but aware of the need to enforce the states' duties to provide effective assistance of counsel at trial, the Court ruled by 7-2 that if a state does not provide effective counsel to raise that claim during state post-conviction proceedings, the federal courts will excuse the resulting procedural default.

This ruling is likely to have significant effect. Both because of the acknowledged reality that trial counsel is ineffective in far too many capital cases[28] and doctrinal entanglements created by the Supreme Court,[29] virtually every federal habeas corpus petition in a capital case contains a claim of ineffective assistance of trial counsel.[30] The more such cases will be examined by the federal courts instead of being refused, the more they will be found to be meritorious.

Moreover, the logic of *Martinez* is not limited to claims of ineffective assistance of trial counsel, but extends to any claim of constitutional violation at the trial stage that can only be vindicated through state post-conviction proceedings. Examples might include a breach by the prosecution of its duty under *Brady v. Maryland* to turn over exculpatory information to the defense[31] or to inform the defense of incentives given to prosecution witnesses[32] – not to mention even more serious misconduct such as knowingly using perjured testimony[33] or threatening defense witnesses to prevent them from appearing.[34]

---

[26] See supra, note 16.

[27] 132 S.Ct. 1309 (2012).

[28] For a discussion of subsequent developments see E.M. Freedman, "Enforcing the ABA Guidelines in Capital State Post-Conviction Proceedings After *Martinez* and *Pinholster*," 41 *Hofstra Law Review* (2013) available at http://ssrn.com/abstract=2251529. See Freedman, supra, note 12, at 668–670.

[29] Under the ruling in *Murray v. Carrier*, 447 U.S. 478 (1986), a defendant confronted with a claim in federal court that an issue has been procedurally defaulted at trial, and who wishes to assert that any such default was the fault of trial counsel, needs to plead and prove that the overall performance of that counsel was constitutionally ineffective under the stringent standards of *Strickland v. Washington*, 466 U.S. 668 (1984), which remain in place despite intense criticism, see American Bar Association, Guidelines, supra, note 17, at 930.

[30] See id., Commentary to Guideline 10.13, reprinted in 31 *Hofstra Law Review* 1074, 1075 n.324, available at: http://www.americanbar.org/advocacy/other_aba_initiatives/death_penalty_representation/resources/aba_guidelines.html.

[31] See supra, note 14.

[32] See *Giglio v. United States*, 405 U.S. 150 (1972).

[33] See *Mooney v. Holohan*, 294 U.S. 103 (1935).

[34] See *Pyle v. Kansas*, 317 U.S. 213 (1942).

8.4 Implications

The number of both death sentences and actual executions in the United States has dropped sharply since peaking in 1999,[35] and five states in the past 5 years have abolished capital punishment outright. The reasonable outlook is that the developments described above will accelerate this downward trend. The expansion of the class of offenders exempt from execution should result in fewer executions, while the need to provide more rigorous post-conviction review will increase the states' costs of capital prosecutions, which should reduce their number.

[35] See http://www.deathpenaltyinfo.org/documents/FactSheet.pdf

Chapter 9
The Impact of European Human Rights on Childbirth

Marlies Eggermont

Abstract In accordance with Article 8 of the European Convention of Human Rights (ECHR), each Member State has to offer a legal framework to future parents to make a free choice concerning the place of birth of their baby (in a hospital or at home). If complications occur during the delivery and damage is done due to a medical fault, the responsible healthcare worker has to be made accountable. In order to be in conformity with Article 2 ECHR, every Member State has to set up a judicial system which offers the procedural guarantees to the parents to examine and finally determine the liability of the healthcare worker. The Belgian legislation offers the parents a real free choice and has a legal system which can result in criminal, civil and disciplinary sanctions in case of medical negligence.

9.1 Introduction

Child care is one of the ground rules of our society. Caring starts in the prenatal phase, which has an important influence on the motoric and intellectual development at a later age. An important milestone between life "in utero" and life outside the womb is birth. The place of birth, in a hospital with a doctor and a midwife or at home with an independent midwife, is one of the choices that a future mother/father has to make. In *Ternovszky v. Hungary* the European Court of Human Rights considered that a Member State should provide an adequate regulatory scheme concerning the right to choose in matters of child delivery (at home or in a hospital), in accordance to Article 8 ECHR, the right to respect for private life.[1]

[1] ECtHR 14 December 2010, No. 67545/09, *Ternovszky v. Hungary.*

M. Eggermont (✉)
Lecturer at the Artevelde University College of Ghent, Ghent, Belgium

Practice Assistant at the Department of Social Law, Ghent University, Ghent, Belgium
e-mail: Marlies.Eggermont@UGent.be

Y. Haeck and E. Brems (eds.), *Human Rights and Civil Liberties in the 21st Century*, Ius Gentium: Comparative Perspectives on Law and Justice 30,
DOI 10.1007/978-94-007-7599-2_9,

A birth without complications after a normal prenatal development offers the best opportunity of a good "outcome" and further evolution of the child. In Europe, the majority of the births present little complications and a good outcome for mother and child. Presuming that the baby dies after the delivery or is damaged (for example brain damage) due to a medical fault, one may ask what the options are for the parents to hold the responsible healthcare worker accountable. Article 2 ECHR, which protects everyone's life by law, entails that a Member State has to set up an effective independent judicial system so that the cause of death of patients in the care of the medical profession can be determined and those responsible made accountable? This contribution stresses how the regulatory scheme in Belgium conforms with Articles 8 and 2 ECHR. Does Belgium provide the legal certainty to a future mother/father to choose the place of birth? Does the Belgian law provide a judicial system which leads to the liability of the healthcare worker for medical mistakes and a financial compensation for the parents?

9.2 The Choice Concerning the Place of Birth

Article 8 ECHR provides that everyone has the right to respect for his private life and that the authorities will not interfere with the exercise of this right:

1. Everyone has the right to respect for his private and family life, his home and his correspondence.
2. There shall be no interference by a public authority with the exercise of this right except such as is in accordance with the law and is necessary in a democratic society in the interests of national security, public safety or the economic well-being of the country, for the prevention of disorder or crime, for the protection of health or morals, or for the protection of the rights and freedoms of others.

"*Private life*" is a broad term, encompassing aspects of an individual's physical and social identity, including the right of personal autonomy, personal development and the establishment of relationships with other human beings and the outside world.[2] Also the right to respect for both the decisions to become and not to become a parent is incorporated in the term "private life".[3] The right concerning the decision to become a parent includes the right of choosing the circumstances of becoming a parent. If the public authority has interfered with this right, it can be to benefit the health of the mother or the child.

In *Ternovszky v. Hungary,*[4] the European Court has considered that a Member State should provide an adequate regulatory scheme concerning the right to choose in matters of child delivery. In the context of homebirth, regarded as a matter of

[2] ECtHR 24 July 2002, No. 2346/02, *Pretty v. United Kingdom.*

[3] ECtHR (GC) 10 April 2007, No. 6339/05, *Evans v. United Kingdom.*

[4] ECtHR, *Ternovszky v. Hungary*, supra, note 1.

personal choice of the mother, this implies that the mother is entitled to a legal and institutional environment that enables her choice. The State has to ensure that the legal protection is foreseeable and accessible, not prone to arbitrariness. The right to choose includes the legal certainty that the choice is lawful and not subject to direct or indirect sanctions of the healthcare worker.

Mrs. Ternovszky, a pregnant woman who intended to give birth at home, alleged the violation of Article 8 ECHR, because she is of the opinion that the Hungarian national law prohibited a healthcare worker (a midwife) to assist a home delivery, as the Government Decree no. 218/1999 (XII.28) stipulated that a healthcare worker assisting a homebirth runs the risk of conviction for a regulatory offence. In her view, while there is no comprehensive legislation on homebirth in Hungary, this provision effectively dissuades healthcare workers from assisting those opting for homebirth. The Court decided that the Hungarian legislation violated Article 8 ECHR, considering that there is a contradiction between the Health Care Act 1997, which recognizes the patients' right to self-determination, in particular the free choice to accept or reject certain treatments, and the Government Decree no. 218/1999 (XII.28), which penalizes the healthcare worker who carries out activities within his/her qualifications in an incompatible manner with national legislation or his license.

Ternovszky v. Hungary opens the debate on the matter of childbirth in Europe and specifically the involvement of the assisting healthcare worker, the midwife.[5] To determine if the regulatory scheme in Belgium concerning the choice of child delivery is in accordance with Article 8 ECHR, it is necessary to look at the legal base to practice midwifery, the sanctioning mechanism (liability) in case of medical negligence (see Sect. 9.2) and the possibility for the expectant mother to use certain patients' rights. Does Belgium provide the legal certainty to a mother that the midwife can legally assist a homebirth?

Royal Decree No.[6] 78 of 10 November 1967 concerning the exercise of the healthcare professions (*KB nummer 78 betreffende de uitoefening van de gezondheidszorgberoepen*) provides that a doctor and midwife (*"vroedvrouw/accoucheuse"*) practice obstetrics.[7] The midwife is competent to practice autonomously normal obstetrics, which includes prenatal guidance, delivery and providing postnatal care to mother and child at home or in a hospital. The midwife can cooperate with the doctor-gynecologist and act under his/her responsibility in the field of pathological obstetrics, which includes fertility problems, pathological pregnancies/deliveries and babies needing intensive care. In order not to lose her license, the midwife should follow a permanent training of 75 h over 5

[5] For information on the maternity models (midwifery and obstetrics in practice) in Europe: ICM. 2005. *Multidisciplinary Collaborative Primary Maternity Care Project. Current practice in Europe and Australia. A descriptive study.* ICM. July 2005, available at: www.mcp2.ca/english/documents/IntlReptFinal9Jul05.pdf

[6] A Royal Decree number is equivalent to a law in Belgium.

[7] The midwives are represented by the Belgian Midwives Association, available at: www.belgianmidwives.be

year to keep up with the obstetrical evolutions. Royal Decree No. 78 also determines the educational programme of a midwife.[8] The violation of the Royal Decree can be penalized.

The Royal Decree of 1 February 1991 concerning the exercise of the profession of a midwife (*KB betreffende de uitoefening van het beroep van vroedvrouw*) provides that the Belgian midwife is competent to practice normal obstetrics, which includes prenatal guidance, doing the delivery and postnatal care. To give adequate care she has to possess the necessary material and implement an obstetrical file. The Royal Decree sums up the permitted and forbidden acts during the follow-up of the pregnancy/delivery. For ultrasounds, the midwife has to refer to a gynecologist. At the notice of any pathology, the midwife is obliged to refer the person concerned to a hospital/doctor. A civil liability insurance is not legally obliged, but every independent midwife takes an insurance.

The attachment to the Royal Decree of 14 September 1984 concerning the listing of medical acts on the obligatory insurance for medical care and benefits is also called "nomenclature of medical acts" (*nomenclatuur der geneeskundig everstrekkingen*). The nomenclature contains a list of numbers, which represent acts of doctors, independent midwives, independent nurses (and any healthcare worker), which gives the patient the right to compensation from public insurance. Article 9 lists the medical acts of an independent midwife: injections, prenatal care, supervising/assisting labour, assisting/doing the delivery at home/hospital and postnatal care (including assistance with breastfeeding).

The National Law of 22 August 2002 concerning the rights of the patient (*Wet betreffende de rechten van de patiënt*) provides, apart from o the right to information and informed consent (or refusal), the right to quality care and free choice of healthcare worker.[9] In the matter of child birth, this enables the mother to choose between a midwife or a doctor (gynecologist) to assist her delivery.

As for obstetric care, this means that any pregnant woman in Belgium can choose between a midwife and a doctor for the follow-up of her pregnancy and child delivery. Therefore, we can conclude that there is a legal environment for the mother concerning child birth and that the choice of home delivery is lawful. Although the regulatory scheme in Belgium concerning the choice of child delivery is very clear and certain, and definitely in accordance with article 8 ECHR, few mothers choose to deliver their baby at home with an independent midwife (less than 1 % in 2010).[10] One of the reasons for this could be the

[8] The Belgian midwifery education implies a 3-year study in the Flemish region and a 4-year study (1 year of nursing) in the Walloon region. The provision on the obligated 4-year study (240 ECTS) is not in force yet.

[9] Valueplus, Patients' rights in the European Union. 2009, available at http://www.eu-patient.eu/Documents/Projects/Valueplus/Patients_Rights.pdf. Accessed 10 October 2012.

[10] The Centre for Operational Research in Public Health (CORPH) is a research unit of the Scientific Institute of Public Health (IPH)'s Unit of Epidemiology. This centre received a mandate from the Flemish and French Community to develop a software application called SPMA (Standardized Procedures for Mortality Analysis), available at: www.iph.fgov.be/epidemio/spma.

medicalization of child birth and the mothers' fears of the consequences for the baby if complications occur during the delivery.

In this connection, the Court of Appeal of Antwerp decided on 30 June 2009 that an independent midwife and a general practitioner were not liable contractually for the delivery at home of a baby with brain paralysis caused by perinatal asphyxiation. The Court considered that the choice of delivery at home entails certain risks concerning the follow-up of the labour and delivery and less medical interventions are possible. For example, reducing the damage by performing a caesarean section is not possible in a home environment.[11]

In other Member States such as Germany, The Netherlands, France and the United Kingdom national legislation also respects the right to private life.[12] This is the conclusion of a topical comparison of the legal base to practice midwifery, the sanctioning mechanism (liability) in case of medical negligence and the possibility for the expectant mother to use certain patients' rights in these States. None of the States have imposed any restrictions. Private matters, such as the lack of insurance (Germany, the United Kingdom and France) and the acceptance of risks for the parents (the United Kingdom and France) could endanger the "real free choice" of child delivery (except in The Netherlands).

9.3 The Legal Procedure in Case of Medical Negligence

Article 2 ECHR which provides the protection of life by law is one of the most fundamental provisions in the Convention:

1. Everyone's right to life shall be protected by law. No one shall be deprived of his life intentionally save in the execution of a sentence of a court following his conviction of a crime for which this penalty is provided by law.
2. Deprivation of life shall not be regarded as inflicted in contravention of this article when it results from the use of force which is no more than absolutely necessary:
   (a) In defence of any person from unlawful violence;
   (b) In order to effect a lawful arrest or to prevent escape of a person lawfully detained;
   (c) In action lawfully taken for the purpose of quelling a riot or insurrection.

This entails that each Member State has to take appropriate steps to safeguard the lives of those within its jurisdiction.[13] The positive obligations require each Member State to draft national regulations for hospitals to adopt appropriate measures for the

[11] Court Antwerp, 30 June 2009, *Tijdschrift voor Gezondheidsrecht* 2010/11, 2, 140–148.

[12] M. Eggermont, "The choice of child delivery is a European human right", 19 *European Journal of Health Law* 2012, 257–269, 269.

[13] ECtHR 9 June 1998, No. 23413/94, *LCB v. United Kingdom*.

protection of patients' lives. Therefore, an effective independent judicial system has to be set up so that the cause of death of patients in the care of the medical profession, can be determined and those responsible made accountable.[14] The procedural obligation is not an obligation of result but an obligation of means.[15]

9.3.1 European Case-Law Concerning Procedural Guarantees

In the case of *Calvelli and Ciglio v. Italy*[16] the applicants alleged the violation of Italian law with Article 2 (and 6) ECHR, maintaining that a legal procedure in which the prosecution of a homicide offence was time-barred as a result of the malfunctioning of and delays in the judicial system, could not be compatible with the European Convention on Human Rights.

The parents of a newborn baby who suffered from brain damage (post-asphyxia syndrome) and died 2 days after birth, lodged a complaint to the Cosenza Public Prosecutor's office on 10 February 1987 (1 day after the death of the baby). A criminal procedure was started and experts submitted their report. The investigating judge charged the responsible doctor EC for involuntary manslaughter. The hearing for the Criminal Court was set down several times. Eventually doctor EC was found guilty *in absentia* on 17 December 1993. His sentence was suspended. Nevertheless, EC appealed. On 3 August 1994 the Catanzaro Court of Appeal declared the appeal inadmissible. The Court held that EC had failed to give his lawyer the authority to act as required under the rules applicable in such cases, noting that EC had been tried *in absentia* at first instance. The Court of Cassation overturned this decision on 22 December 1994 because EC had been present at the beginning of his trial, so he could not be convicted *in absentia*. The criminal procedure was terminated with a judgment of the Court of appeal on 3 July 1995 that prosecution of the offence was time-barred. Three months before this judgment, on 27 April 1995, the applicants entered into an agreement with the insurance company of the doctor and the hospital, after the applicants had served a summons requiring the doctor to appear before the civil court.

Considering this agreement, the Court decided that Italy had not violated the European Convention: "where a relative of a deceased person accepts compensation in settlement of a civil claim based on medical negligence, he or she is in principle no longer able to claim to be a victim".[17] The Court also noted that the Italian law system provides injured parties with criminal, civil and even disciplinary proceedings to make healthcare workers accountable. If the infringement of the right to life is not caused intentionally (usually not in medical negligence) Article 2 does not

[14] ECtHR 26 October 1999, No. 37900/97, *Eriksson v. Italy*; ECtHR 4 May 2000, No. 45305/99, *Powell v. the United Kingdom*; ECtHR 7 November 2002, No. 53749/00, *Lazzarini and Ghiacci v. Italy;* ECtHR 27 June 2006, No. 11562/05, *Byrzykowski v. Polen*.

[15] ECtHR 14 March 2002, No. 46477/99, *Paul and Audrey Edwards v. the United Kingdom*.

[16] ECtHR 17 January 2002, No. 32967/96, *Calvelli and Ciglio v. Italy*.

[17] ECtHR, *Powell v. the UK*, supra, note 13.

necessarily require a criminal law remedy in every case.[18] And in this case the procedural shortcomings did not prohibit the national courts to operate effectively in practice and complete their examination. The national legislation was effectively administered on the applicants.

In a very recent case, *Spyra and Kranczkowski v. Polen*,[19] the applicants (mother and son) alleged that the sons' disability had been caused by a lack of appropriate medical treatment during his hospitalization at the time of his birth, and especially by the medical staff's failure to comply with the medical norms for newborns. The applicants also alleged a lack of effectiveness in the procedures conducted by the Polish courts to ascertain the origin of the second applicant's disability. Sir Kranczkowski was born premature (29 weeks) on 25 September 1999. He was intubated and given oxygen in an incubator. His transport to the neonatal intensive care unit happened without an incubator. He was in hospital for a long time. In August 2000 he was diagnosed with brain paralysis and in 2002 he was declared 100 % disabled from birth.

The civil procedure was terminated by the Court of Appeal of Gdansk on 2 December 2005 who confirmed the judgment of 29 March 2005 of the Civil Court. The handicap was caused by the premature birth (immaturity of the longs) and not during the transport. There was no connection between the acts of the healthcare workers and the actual damage. Disciplinary proceedings showed no violations of the responsible doctor. Although the criminal complaint dates from 20 September 2006, the criminal proceedings is still pending before the Court of First Instance. The Minister of Justice has meanwhile intervened.

Similar to the *Calvelli and Ciglio case,* the Court cannot assess national legislation *in abstracto,* and neither can it make a general evaluation of the compatibility of the judicial system and the practice of healthcare. The Court needs to evaluate if the relevant national legislation or proceedings were effectively applied to the applicants (analogue to *Ruza v. Latvia*,[20]). The Court decided that the rights of the applicants were not violated, considering that there is no national or international rule which determines that the transport of a premature baby has to be done with an incubator. The fact that a criminal procedure was still pending after civil and disciplinary proceedings, convinced the Court that the Polish judicial system was in accordance with the European Convention.

9.3.2 The Belgian Liability Procedure

Belgium has set up an effective independent judicial system to determine who is responsible for damage to patients or their death. A civil procedure starts with a

---

[18] If a persons' life is damaged intentionally criminal proceedings are included in an effective judicial system. See ECtHR 28 March 2000, No. 22492/93, *Kiliç v. Turkey*; ECtHR 28 March 2000, No. 22535/93, *Mahmut Kaya v. Turkey*,

[19] ECtHR 25 September 2012, No. 19764/07, *Spyra and Kranczkowski v. Polen.*

[20] ECtHR 11 May 2010, No. 33978/05, *Ruza v. Latvia.*

summons to court of the responsible healthcare worker and/or hospital. Unique in Belgium is the provision in the law on the patients' rights (2002) of a central hospital liability. This means that the applicant does not have to identify the responsible healthcare workers. If the damage was caused in a hospital were the healthcare workers were practicing, the hospital can be summoned. Similar to other European States the Belgium judicial system provides the possibility of a criminal procedure against all healthcare workers.

Only doctors can receive disciplinary sanctions, not midwives or nurses. According to Royal Decree No. 79 of 10 November 1967, possible disciplinary sanctions are caution, censure, reprimand, suspension or occupational ban.

If the healthcare worker does not offer quality care or violates one of the patients' rights, he/she is also risking liability and penalization in France, Germany, the Netherlands and the United Kingdom. In all aforementioned Member States a midwife is exposed to civil and criminal liability. In the Netherlands, France and the United Kingdom, she also risks disciplinary sanctions.[21]

9.3.3 Belgian Case Law Concerning Medical Faults During Child Birth

In July 1991, a newborn baby had suffered severe brain damage due to a rupture of the uterus. It was a second baby, the first baby being born by caesarian section because it was in a breech position. Next to the scar in the uterus there was also the problem of a narrow pelvis, which is why the delivery was labeled to be "at risk for complications".

The parents of the baby lodged a criminal complaint 2 months after the delivery. The public prosecutor accused the midwife and the gynecologist of involuntary assault and battery. The Court of Appeal in Ghent acquitted them,[22] after a conviction of the gynecologist for the Criminal Court of Ghent.[23] The Court of Cassation overturned this decision on the civil matter.[24] On 4 November 2004, the Civil Court of Appeal in Brussels held the midwife and the gynecologist accountable for the brain damage of the baby.[25] For the damage to the mother only the gynecologist was liable. The Court based its judgment on the fact that, considering the risks, the gynecologist himself should have done the follow-up of his patient so that he could perform a caesarian immediately before the uterus rupture occurred. The negligence of

[21] Eggermont, supra, note 12.

[22] Court of Appeal Ghent 27 June 1996, No. 80594, unpublished.

[23] Criminal Court of Ghent 11 October 1995, No. GE.46.90.3502/91, unpublished.

[24] Court of Cassation 15 December 1998, No. P.96.1206.N.

[25] Civil Court of Appeal Brussels 4 November 2004, No. 1061, unpublished.

the midwife consisted of the "unnecessary delay" to inform the gynecologist. The midwife first consulted a colleague and checked the fetal heart beat with a new monitor. Only then she informed the gynecologist of the decreasing fetal heart beat, the non-progressive labor, the heavy contractions and the heavy pains of the mother. Precious time was lost and brain damage occurred. The gynecologist had also asked the midwife to assist the patient continuously, which pointed to the need for a "quick response" to any signs of abnormality.

The Court of Cassation rejected the appeal of the midwife and the gynecologist and their liability became final.[26]

In a second case, the civil procedure concerning facts that occurred in September 1983 is still pending before the Court of Appeal of Mons.[27] The Court of Appeal needs to determine if the responsible healthcare workers caused the damage unintentionally (professional negligence) at the birth of the premature baby.

Legally there is no doubt that the two nurse-midwives involved, the pediatrician and the hospital have committed no intentional errors (guilty absenteeism). The criminal Court of Huy acquitted the healthcare workers of all charges on 7 February 1986.[28] The experts who had to give their advise held that it was a case of negligence of the pediatrician and the nurse-midwives. Considering the blue nails and lips of the baby and the insufficient feeding, the nurse-midwives had to notify the pediatrician, especially after the mother had sharply insisted on doing that. Only in the late evening, the pediatrician was called to intervene by a concerned governess. The pediatrician misdiagnosed the serious sugar shortage (hypoglycemia), which led to mental retardation and developmental disorders.

The parents appealed the decision but decided to end the proceedings.[29] On 10 October 2003, the Court of Cassation overturned this judgment, considering that a civil party does not have to end the criminal proceedings before starting civil procedure (distance of procedure).[30] The Court of Appeal of Brussels[31] determined that the claim of the parents was unfounded, considering that the acquittal of the healthcare workers was based on the same facts as the civil claim. Again the Court of Cassation[32] overturned this decision, because the authority of the criminal judgment does not entail the civil claims based on unintentional errors.

These two cases illustrate that Belgium has set up a judicial system which guarantees victims of medical mistakes, specifically in the obstetric care, the right to bring a case against the responsible healthcare worker, in accordance with Article 2 ECHR.

[26] Court of Appeal 26 April 2005, No. P.04.1614.N/1, unpublished.

[27] Court of Appeal of Mons, No. 2011/AR/1044.

[28] Criminal Court of Huy 17 February 1986.

[29] Court of Appeal Liege 8 October 2001.

[30] Court of Cassation 3 October 2003, No. C.02.0186.F/1.

[31] Court of Appeal Brussels 25 September 2008, No. 2005/AR/1103

[32] Court of Cassation 30 June 2011, No. C.09.0160.F/1

9.4 Conclusion

Belgium provides future parents with an adequate regulatory scheme to make a real free choice concerning the place of birth of their baby. A homebirth is possible and does not lead to the sanctioning of the assisting midwife. The judicial system of Belgium has procedural rules which can lead to criminal, civil and disciplinary sanctions for medical negligence of healthcare workers in accordance with the European Convention.

Chapter 10
Res Interpretata: Legal Effect of the European Court of Human Rights' Judgments for other States Than Those Which Were Party to the Proceedings

Adam Bodnar

Abstract States that were not a party to proceedings in a case before the European Court of Human Rights should take into account judgments and decisions issued with respect to third states. Indeed, judgments and decisions establishing a new legal principle or standard should have a persuasive authority for other states. They should be an incentive for state parties to change their law or practices in order to avoid similar issues being brought against them. Such judgments should have a *res interpretata* effect, a notion to be distinguished from the typical *res judicata* effect of judgments. As such, *res interpretata* may become one of the most important tools reinforcing the principle of subsidiarity underlying the entire European Convention and thereby also limit the number of applications brought to the European Court. The *res interpretata* effect may therefore be a good instrument of constant fine-tuning of third states' legal system.

10.1 Introduction

In view of the crisis of the European system of human rights' protection, based on the machinery created under the European Convention on Human Rights (hereinafter ECHR or Convention), there is a much stronger search for new solutions that would make the system more efficient. One of them is to "bring the Convention back home", i.e., create instruments that would encourage the High Contracting Parties to comply to a greater extent with the Convention. State parties should take more responsibility for compliance with obligations stemming from the Convention and the case-law of the European Court of Human Rights (hereinafter European Court,

A. Bodnar (✉)
Associate Professor of Human Rights at Warsaw University,
Helsinki Foundation for Human Rights, Warsaw, Poland
e-mail: a.bodnar@wpia.uw.edu.pl

Y. Haeck and E. Brems (eds.), *Human Rights and Civil Liberties in the 21st Century*,
Ius Gentium: Comparative Perspectives on Law and Justice 30,
DOI 10.1007/978-94-007-7599-2_10,

Court or ECtHR). Under Article 46 of the Convention, state parties are obliged to comply with judgments issued with respect to them. However, state parties should attribute importance and take into account not only "own" judgments but also judgments and decisions issued with respect to third states.[1] States that were not a party to proceedings before the Court should take guidance from such judgments, thanks to which they may avoid similar violations in future. If a given state party would know standards stemming from the Strasbourg jurisprudence in cases concerning other states, it would and even should make the appropriate changes to its legal system or practice, and thereby also limit the number of applications brought to the European Court. Standards in their domestic law or practices would then be changed earlier (rather than after the judgment concerning this particular state as regards relevant issues), to the benefit of individuals under the jurisdiction of that state.

During a speech at the Skopje Conference, Christos Pourgourides gave two interesting examples indicating how state parties fail to consider judgments concerning other states. He underlined that after *Marckx* it took France 20 years to wait for a judgment concerning equal inheritance rights for children born out of wedlock, before taking action itself. Indeed, the famous judgment in *Marckx v. Belgium*[2] was issued in 1979, while *Mazurek v. France*[3] was only rendered in 2000. Similarly, the decriminalization of homosexual conduct was declared a Convention standard in 1981.[4] However, Cyprus did not make appropriate changes in law and was found violating the Convention as late as 1983.[5]

Judgments and decisions that establish a new legal principle or standard should have a persuasive authority for other states. They should be an incentive for state parties to change their law or practices in order not to violate human rights in a next judgment against them, concerning the same or similar issue. Such judgments should have a *res interpretata* effect. This notion should be distinguished from a typical *res judicata* effect of judgments, stemming from Article 46 of the Convention.

The *res interpretata* effect is not regulated precisely in the Convention. One may only interpret it from general clauses included into the ECHR (such as Article 1 and 19 of the Convention), from *soft law* documents or from the ECtHR jurisprudence,

---

[1] The ECtHR issues judgments and decisions. New legal principles are formulated both in judgments and decisions. Decisions thus do not have a purely procedural character. Some of them, especially in precedent cases, include comprehensive reasoning that constitutes an interpretation of the Convention. A good example is the inadmissibility decision in *Köpke v. Germany* (5 October 2010, No. 420/07), in which the Court interpreted the scope of applicability of Article 8 ECHR to include video surveillance of employees suspected of theft. Material reasoning having impact on interpretation of the Convention may be included, both in admissibility and non-admissibility decisions. Even if the ECtHR does not declare a certain application admissible, the reasoning about the scope of the protected rights under the Convention is important for building the case-law. Also, the ECtHR in its jurisprudence refers both to judgments and decisions, and approaches them as a unified case-law informing on the Convention interpretation.

[2] ECtHR 13 June 1979, No. 6833/74, *Marckx v. Belgium.*

[3] ECtHR 1 February 2000, No. 34406/97, *Mazurek v. France.*

[4] ECtHR 22 October 1981, No. 7525/76, *Dudgeon v. United Kingdom.*

[5] ECtHR 22 April 1993, No. 15070/89, *Modinos v. Cyprus.*

which suggest compliance with "general human rights standards" as they are developed by the Court, and not only with judgments concerning a given state.

The debate on *res interpretata* is currently pending in Europe. Most importantly, the Interlaken Conference (18–19 February 2010) called upon the Member States to commit themselves to take into account:

> the Court's developing case-law, also with a view to considering the conclusions to be drawn from a judgment finding a violation of the Convention by another State, where the same problem of principle exists within their own legal system. (point B.4.c).

In the Brighton Declaration (19–20 April 2012), emphasis was placed on the duty to apply the Convention's case-law by courts. According to the Declaration, national implementation of the Convention should be effected through *inter alia*:

> Enabling and encouraging national courts and tribunals to take into account the relevant principles of the Convention, having regard to the case law of the Court, in conducting proceedings and formulating judgments; and in particular enabling litigants, within the appropriate parameters of national judicial procedure but without unnecessary impediments, to draw to the attention of national courts and tribunals any relevant provisions of the Convention and jurisprudence of the Court (point 9.c.iv).

The *res interpretata* effect may become one of the most important tools reinforcing the principle of subsidiarity. If state parties start to care more about standards stemming from judgments issued with respect to other states, it will limit the workload of the Court. Also, the Council of Europe may develop tools encouraging state parties to take the whole ECtHR case-law into account.

One should, however, not overestimate the significance of the *res interpretata* effect of judgments. It is only a supplementary tool to enhance the compliance with the Convention by state parties. Currently, a number of them do not comply with judgments issued with respect to them, are systemic violators of certain human rights, or do not introduce efficient domestic remedies. The Council of Europe cannot fully concentrate on such sophisticated instruments like *res interpretata*, as it has a problem with the timely review of enforcement of cases under Article 46 of the Convention. Nevertheless, for many other countries, which do not have such systemic problems, the *res interpretata* effect may be a good instrument of constant fine-tuning of their legal system.

This contribution is divided into the following sections. First, the legal background of the *res interpretata* effect will be analysed. The second part will concentrate on factors that should be taken into account when defining the scope of the *res interpretata* effect. Not every ECHR judgment has the same authoritative value. Not every ECHR judgment is repeatable – as to the substance – in some other legal system. Third, the *res interpretata* effect will be analysed from the point of view of obligations of the state. A source of such obligations may be found in those soft law instruments or other pronouncements that suggest the necessity for member states to take into account judgments issued with respect to third states. Finally, practice of different state parties will be analysed. Some of them already rely on judgments issued with respect to third states, and take them into account when changing the legal system or practice.

10.2 Legal Basis for the *Res Interpretata* Effect of ECtHR Judgments

10.2.1 Introductory Remarks

10.2.1.1 European Convention on Human Rights

According to Article 46 ECHR, final judgments of the Court are only binding to states that were a party to the proceedings. Such judgments are commonly known as having *res judicata* status and are binding *inter partes*. In most of the international courts and tribunals, judgments have a similar legal effect – they are binding only for the state that was a party to the proceedings.[6]

The ECHR does not provide a direct interpretation of what is the legal value of judgments issued with respect to third states, which did not participate in the proceedings. There is no legal norm providing an answer to this question.

Due to the fact that neither Article 46 ECHR nor any other provision govern the issue of legal effects of judgments issued with respect to states not participating in proceedings, one has to look into the general provisions of the Convention in order to determine the legal effects of such judgments.

Article 1 ECHR includes the general obligation of the High Contracting Parties to secure compliance with rights and freedoms guaranteed in the Convention.[7] This provision should be read together with Article 19 ECHR, which provides the setting up of the European Court of Human Rights, functioning on a permanent basis in order "to ensure the observance of the engagements undertaken by the High Contracting Parties in the Convention and the Protocols thereto".

The ECtHR has been created in order to secure compliance with the Convention. It is also the duty of the Court to interpret the Convention and its particular provisions. If states are bound by the Convention (or Protocols) they are bound by material provisions, as the Court – the sole interpreter of the Convention – interprets them.

The ECtHR interprets the Convention in its day-to-day jurisprudence. The whole body of case-law constitutes the system of the Convention. However, certain provisions of the Convention provide additional powers to the Court in this respect. First, the Grand Chamber of the ECtHR will only take on a case "if the case raises a serious question affecting the interpretation or application of the Convention or the Protocols thereto, or a serious issue of general importance" (Article 43(2) ECHR). This provision

---

[6] Compare: "Article 59 of the Statute of the International Court of Justice states: The decision of the Court has no binding force except between the parties and in respect of that particular case"; Article 68(1) American Convention on Human Rights states: "The States Parties to the Convention undertake to comply with the judgment of the Court in any case to which they are parties"; Article 30 Protocol on the establishment of the African Court of Human Rights states: "The States parties to the present Protocol undertake to comply with the judgment in any case to which they are parties within the time stipulated by the Court and to guarantee its execution".

[7] Article 1 ECHR states: "The High Contracting Parties shall secure to everyone within their jurisdiction the rights and freedoms defined in Section I of this Convention".

provides the competence to accept or reject a request for referral to the Grand Chamber to the panel of five judges of the Grand Chamber, and in fact defines, at the same time, the legal value of judgments issued by the Grand Chamber (as compared to the Chamber judgments). Second, following the entry into force of Protocol No. 14, the Committee of Ministers would be able to request an additional interpretation of the judgment given by the Court.[8] The Committee of Ministers has not exercised this competence yet.

Article 1 in conjunction with Article 19 ECHR is in fact the sole source of legal authority of judgments issued with respect to third states. The general clause included into Article 1 ECHR should be interpreted in accordance with the principles of public international law. If state parties declare that they are bound by the ECHR (including Article 1), they should comply with this international agreement in good faith. Such an obligation stems from Article 26 of the Vienna Convention on the Law of Treaties.[9] Under public international law, state parties are prohibited to adopt measures contrary to international obligations. They are obliged to implement judgments and other decisions resulting from the application of the international treaty. State parties are also obliged to interpret domestic law in accordance with the international treaty (Article 27 of the Vienna Convention).[10] State parties have also an obligation to implement judgments and other decisions that are the result of the application of the international treaty.[11] Furthermore, under Article 12 of the Draft Articles on Responsibility of States for Internationally Wrongful Acts 2001, states have an obligation of result as regards implementation of provisions of international treaties and not an obligation of due diligence.[12]

10.2.1.2 The *Res Interpretata* Effect as Observed by the European Court of Human Rights

The ECtHR did not make an unequivocal statement that its judgments should have *res interpretata* value. However, in a number of cases it underlined their value as precedents and that state parties should monitor and observe the development of the

[8] Article 46(3) ECHR states: "If the Committee of Ministers considers that the supervision of the execution of a final judgment is hindered by a problem of interpretation of the judgment, it may refer the matter to the Court for a ruling on the question of interpretation".

[9] Article 26 Vienna Convention on the Law of Treaties states: "Every treaty in force is binding upon the parties to it and must be performed by them in good faith".

[10] Article 27 Vienna Convention on the Law of Treaties states: "A party may not invoke the provisions of its internal law as justification for its failure to perform a treaty. [...]".

[11] Advisory opinion of the International Court of Justice of 13 July 1954 in case "Effect of Awards of Compensation Made by the United Nations Administrative Tribunal", available at: http://www.icj-cij.org/docket/index.php?p1=3&p2=4&code=unac&case=21&k=d2

[12] International Law Commission, *Draft Articles on Responsibility of States for Internationally Wrongful Acts*, November 2001, Supplement No. 10 (A/56/10), chapter IV.E.1. See also commentary to Draft Articles on Responsibility of States for Wrongful Acts (points 11 and 12 – Article 12), available at: http://untreaty.un.org/ilc/texts/instruments/english/commentaries/9_6_2001.pdf

case-law. The first case in which the ECtHR specified the precedential value of its judgments was *Ireland v. United Kingdom*.[13] It underlined that judgments of the Court "serve not only to decide those cases brought before the Court but, more generally, to elucidate, safeguard and develop the rules instituted by the Convention, thereby contributing to the observance by the States of the engagements undertaken by them as Contracting Parties (Article 19)".[14] This statement was repeated in later jurisprudence.[15]

In *Pretty v. United Kingdom*,[16] the ECtHR stated that "judgments issued in individual cases establish precedents albeit to a greater or lesser extent".[17] Consequently, it rebutted the argument of the applicant that finding a violation of the Convention would be only of an individual character and would not create any risk to others. The ECtHR underlined that the decision cannot be framed in a way that would prevent application in later cases.

In the domestic violence case *Opuz v. Turkey*,[18] the ECtHR indicated that in its scrutiny of compliance with the Convention it will examine "whether the national authorities have sufficiently taken into account the principles flowing from its judgments on similar issues, even when they concern other States."[19] Here, the ECtHR quite directly indicated that it is the obligation of state parties to analyze principles shaped by the jurisprudence regarding cases originating from different states. Accordingly, compliance with this obligation becomes the obligation not only in the light of the Council of Europe's soft law, but also a standard required by the ECtHR.

In *Karner v. Austria*,[20] the ECtHR reiterated its statement on the role of the ECtHR to:

> elucidate, safeguard and develop the rules instituted by the Convention.

In the opinion of the Court:

> Although the primary purpose of the Convention system is to provide individual relief, its mission is also to determine issues on public-policy grounds in the common interest, thereby raising the general standards of protection of human rights and extending human rights jurisprudence throughout the community of Convention States.[21]

Please note that the ECtHR is referring to "general standards of protection of human rights", which are formed by virtue of its jurisprudence. A similar general

---

[13] ECtHR 18 January 1978, No. 5310/71, *Ireland v. United Kingdom*.

[14] Ibid., para 154.

[15] ECtHR 6 November 1980, No. 7367/76, *Guzzardi v. Italy*, para. 86.

[16] ECtHR 29 April 2002, No. 2346/02, *Pretty v. United Kingdom*.

[17] Ibid., para. 75.

[18] ECtHR 9 June 2009, No. 33401/02, *Opuz v. Turkey*.

[19] Ibid., para. 163.

[20] ECtHR 24 July 2003, No. 40016/98, *Karner v. Austria*.

[21] Ibid., para. 26.

statement was included in *Capital Bank AD v. Bulgaria*[22] and in *Rantsev v. Cyprus and Russia*.[23]

10.2.2 The Res Interpretata *Effect in Soft Law Documents*

The *res interpretata* effect of the ECtHR judgments has not been specifically referred to in different soft law instruments of the Council of Europe. Most of them, quite naturally, concentrate on the enforcement of the ECtHR judgments issued with respect to a given state, as it is the primary obligation under Article 46 of the Convention.[24] However, in some recommendations of the Committee of Ministers one may notice a clear distinction between judgments having *res judicata* and the more general term "case-law of the European Court of Human Rights". Obviously, "case-law of the ECHR" includes not only judgments concerning the given state, but encompasses all the ECtHR judgments as a whole system of the Convention, and does not refer specifically to obligations arising with respect to judgments concerning other states.

In particular, reference to the "case-law of the European Court of Human Rights" is made in recommendations of the Committee of Ministers in connection with the need for state parties to verify their laws and administrative practices.[25] Furthermore, certain duties are recommended as regards dissemination of the ECtHR case-law.[26]

Another soft law document that should be mentioned here is the resolution of the Parliamentary Assembly (hereinafter PACE) of the Council of Europe No. 1516 (2006) on the implementation of judgments of the European Court of Human Rights.[27] The resolution, when defining the scope of obligations, refers in general to the "Court's judgments". Most importantly, it recommends to national parliaments

[22] ECtHR 24 November 2005, No. 49429/99, *Capital Bank AD v. Bulgaria*, paras. 78–79.

[23] ECtHR 7 January 2010, No. 25965/04, *Rantsev v. Cyprus and Russia*, para. 175.

[24] E.g. Recommendation Rec(2000)2 on the re-examination or reopening of certain cases at domestic level following judgments of the European Court of Human Rights; Recommendation Rec(2004)6 on the improvement of domestic remedies; Recommendation Rec(2004)4 on the European Convention on Human Rights in university education and professional training; Recommendation Rec(2004)6 on the improvement of domestic remedies.

[25] Recommendation Rec(2004)5 of the Committee of Ministers to member states on the verification of the compatibility of draft laws, existing laws and administrative practice with the standards laid down in the European Convention on Human Rights, available at: https://wcd.coe.int/wcd/ViewDoc.jsp?id=743297

[26] Recommendation Rec(2002)13 of the Committee of Ministers to member states on the publication and dissemination in the member states of the text of the European Convention on Human Rights and of the case-law of the European Court of Human Rights., available at: https://wcd.coe.int/wcd/ViewDoc.jsp?Ref=Rec(2002)13&Language=lanEnglish&Site=COE&BackColorInternet=DBDCF2&BackColorIntranet=FDC864&BackColorLogged=FDC864

[27] Parliamentary Assembly of the Council of Europe Resolution 1516 (2006), available at: http://assembly.coe.int/Main.asp?link=/Documents/AdoptedText/ta06/ERES1516.htm

the introduction of specific mechanisms and procedures to effectively oversee the implementation of the Court's judgments on the basis of regular reports by the responsible ministries.[28] In the progress report prepared under this resolution,[29] the PACE identified that a good practice in this respect exists in The Netherlands. It underlined that the Dutch practice not only monitors compliance with judgments issued with respect to The Netherlands, but also monitors compliance with judgments concerning other states. The PACE was aware that it is outside the scope of strict implementation, but nevertheless acclaimed such practice:

> While the latter aspect does not strictly fall within execution of Strasbourg judgments, but rather a broader obligation to observe the Convention and the Court's interpretation thereof, it is nevertheless a valuable preventative procedure, demonstrating a strong commitment to adhere to Convention standards.[30]

Specifically, the *res interpretata* value of the ECtHR judgments was underlined at the meeting of the PACE Committee on Legal Affairs and Human Rights organized in December 2009 in preparation to the upcoming Interlaken Conference.[31] It was underlined that there is:

> a need to enhance the authority and direct application of the Strasbourg Court's findings in domestic law. Rather than refer to the *erga omnes* effect of Grand Chamber judgments of principle, it is probably more accurate to refer to its interpretative authority (*res interpretata*) within the legal orders of states other than the respondent state in a given case.[32]

The PACE Committee on Legal Affairs and Human Rights was not the only entity which noticed the importance of the *res interpretata* effect of the ECtHR judgment as a method to enhance the meaning of the principle of subsidiarity. Such voices have been also heard from other stakeholders, such as the Steering Committee on Human Rights of the Council of Europe,[33] the Council of Europe Secretary

[28] Ibid., para. 22.1.

[29] Progress report by Rapporteur Christos Pourgourides of 31 August 2009 on Implementation of judgments of the European Court of Human Rights, PACE Committee on Legal Affairs and Human Rights, AS/Jur (2009) 36, available at: http://assembly.coe.int/CommitteeDocs/2009/ejdoc36_2009.pdf

[30] Ibid., para. 29.

[31] Conclusions of the Chairperson, Mrs Herta Däubler-Gmelin, of the hearing of the PACE Committee on Legal Affairs and Human Rights, held in Paris on 16 December 2009 on the future of the Strasbourg Court and enforcement of ECHR standards: reflections on the Interlaken process, AS/Jur (2010) 06, available at: http://assembly.coe.int/CommitteeDocs/2010/20100121_ajdoc06%202010.pdf

[32] Ibid., at 15.

[33] Opinion of the Steering Committee for Human Rights: Issues to be covered at the high-level conference on the future of the European Court of Human Rights, in *Preparatory Contributions to the High-level conference on the future of the European Court of Human Rights organised in Interlaken, Switzerland on 18 and 19 February 2010*, Directorate General of Human Rights and Legal Issues, Council of Europe, 2010, 15–24. One of the issues to cover during the Interlaken conference should be the interpretative value of the ECtHR judgments. In general, the knowledge of the ECHR case-law should be increased at a domestic level, as well as interaction between the European and the national level.

General,[34] the Commissioner for Human Rights[35] and NGOs.[36] It seems that the most progressive voice in this regard was from the then President of the ECtHR, Jean-Paul Costa, who even suggested that the ECtHR judgments should have *erga omnes* effect.[37] In his opinion, giving binding effect to the Court's judgments in respect of their interpretation of the Convention:

> would strengthen the states' obligation to prevent Convention violations. It is no longer acceptable that states fail to draw the consequences as early as possible of a judgment finding a violation by another state when the same problem exists in their own legal system. The binding effect of interpretation by the Court goes beyond *res judicata* in the strict sense. Such a development would go hand in hand with the possibility for citizens to invoke the Convention directly in domestic law ("direct effect") and the notion of ownership of the Convention by the states.[38]

Please note that this idea was identified as a mid-term goal. Certainly, changing the legal character of the ECtHR judgments (in the direction of typical constitutional court powers) would require the amendment of the Convention. Therefore, Jean-Paul Costa discerns that such a change would be "a new step in the evolution of Convention law".[39]

---

[34] Contribution of the Secretary General of the Council of Europe to the preparation of the Interlaken conference, in *Preparatory Contributions to the High-level conference on the future of the European Court of Human Rights organised in Interlaken, Switzerland on 18 and 19 February 2010*, Directorate General of Human Rights and Legal Issues, Council of Europe, 2010, 36–48. According to the CoE Secretary General, states should take into account principles stemming from the ECtHR judgments concerning other states. They should also build an institutional system or mechanism allowing for analysis of potential effects of such judgments on the domestic legal system or practices.

[35] Memorandum of the Commissioner for Human Rights for the Interlaken Conference, in *Preparatory Contributions to the High-level conference on the future of the European Court of Human Rights organised in Interlaken, Switzerland on 18 and 19 February 2010*, Directorate General of Human Rights and Legal Issues, Council of Europe, 2010, 26–27. See also the Commissioner's Recommendation on systematic work for implementing human rights at a national level, CommDH (2009) 3, 18/02/2009. The Commissioner for Human Rights proposed to identify leading judgments of the ECtHR, irrespectively of the state that they concern, to form a basis for a general study on compliance with international human rights commitments. Such a study should be made in every member state of the Council of Europe.

[36] NGOs in the joint appeal suggested that the lower number of cases may be a result of the implementation by state parties of also those judgments that were issued with respect to other states. Joint NGO appeal: Human rights in Europe: decision time on the European Court of Human Rights, 7 December 2009, in *Preparatory Contributions to the High-level conference on the future of the European Court of Human Rights organised in Interlaken, Switzerland on 18 and 19 February 2010*, Directorate General of Human Rights and Legal Issues, Council of Europe, 2010, 32–35, at 33.

[37] J.P. Costa, Memorandum of the President of the European Court of Human Rights to the states with a view to preparing the Interlaken conference, in *Preparatory Contributions to the High-level conference on the future of the European Court of Human Rights organised in Interlaken, Switzerland on 18 and 19 February 2010*, Directorate General of Human Rights and Legal Issues, Council of Europe, 2010, 5–14.

[38] Ibid., at 13.

[39] Ibid.

The Interlaken Declaration of 19 February 2010[40] is a document of extreme importance for the development of the idea of the *res interpretata* effect of the ECtHR judgments. For the first time, with a high level of clarity in the political documents of the Council of Europe, this effect of judgments was defined, as well as the corresponding obligation of state parties. The *res interpretata* effect was declared as one of the aspects of the principle of subsidiarity and shared responsibility between state parties and the Council of Europe for the effectiveness of the Convention system.

In its Action Plan, the Interlaken Declaration, among others, called upon the state parties to commit themselves to:

> taking into account the Court's developing case-law, also with a view to considering the conclusions to be drawn from a judgment finding a violation of the Convention by another State, where the same problem of principle exists within their own legal system.[41]

The Interlaken Conference provided the mandate for the Council of Europe organs to undertake activities in order to implement the Action Plan. The first effect was the Resolution of the Parliamentary Assembly of the Council of Europe of 29 April 2010 on the effective implementation of the European Convention on Human Rights: the Interlaken process.[42] The PACE underlined that the so-called Interlaken process should especially take into account such actions that do not require a change of the Convention. They include:

- The need to strengthen implementation of Convention rights at the national level (including the *res interpretata* authority of the Court's case law);
- Improvement of the effectiveness of domestic remedies in states with major structural problems; and
- The need to rapidly and fully execute the judgments of the Court.

On 11 May 2010, the Committee of Ministers also adopted a decision relating to the Interlaken process.[43] It reminded that state parties, the ECtHR and the Committee of Ministers share the responsibility for full and effective implementation of the Interlaken Declaration and the Action Plan. The Committee of Ministers encouraged state parties to undertake actions aiming to implement the Action Plan, especially by introducing domestic remedies, increasing the knowledge of the Convention and the ECtHR case-law.

The Brighton Declaration reminded state parties that their primary duty is to secure compliance with the Convention. It repeated major indications to state

---

[40] The Interlaken Declaration is available at: http://www.eda.admin.ch/etc/medialib/downloads/edazen/topics/europa/euroc.Par.0133.File.tmp/final_en.pdf

[41] Point B (c) – Interlaken Declaration. Action Plan.

[42] Parliamentary Assembly of the Council of Europe Resolution 1726 (2010): Effective implementation of the European Convention on Human Rights: the Interlaken process, resolution available at: http://assembly.coe.int/Mainf.asp?link=/Documents/AdoptedText/ta10/ERES1726.htm

[43] Decision of the Committee of Ministers of the Council of Europe of 11 May 2010: Follow-up to the High-level Conference on the Future of the European Court of Human Rights, CM(2010)PV Addendum 1.

parties regarding the enforcement of judgments. In the context of the *res interpretata* effect, the Brighton Declaration referred specifically to the case-law of the Convention in the context of the operation of courts and tribunals. In particular, it encouraged the state parties to take specific measures in order to enable and encourage courts and tribunals to:

> take into account the relevant principles of the Convention, having regard to the case law of the Court, in conducting proceedings and formulating judgments; and in particular enabling litigants, within the appropriate parameters of national judicial procedure but without unnecessary impediments, to draw to the attention of national courts and tribunals any relevant provisions of the Convention and jurisprudence of the Court.[44]

Since the Brighton Declaration, the reform of the ECHR system got a new impetus. As a result, a Draft Protocol No. 15 has been prepared, as well as a Draft Agreement on Accession of the EU to the European Convention on Human Rights. With respect to the *res interpretata* effect, there is no significant change. This issue is still not a subject of broader consideration, although it should.

10.2.3 The **Res Interpretata** *Effect as Interpreted by Domestic Constitutional Courts*

The legal effect of the ECtHR judgments for states that were not party to proceedings, was the subject of interest in some states. In Germany, the Federal Constitutional Court referred to this problem in the case of *Görgülü*.[45] It underlined that ECtHR judgments issued with respect to third states, give only other states that are not party to proceedings the opportunity to verify their own legal system and their compliance with the Convention. If changes are needed, such ECtHR judgments have a value of orientation.[46] According to the German Federal Constitutional Court, the system of the Convention does not include a provision, which may be similar to § 31 (1) of the German Law on the Constitutional Court, according to which all federal and state constitutional organs, as well as all courts and public authorities, are bound by the judgments of the Federal Constitutional Court.[47] Article 46 of the

[44] Brighton Declaration, point 9 (c) (iv).

[45] German Federal Constitutional Court 14 October 2004, No. 2 BvR 1481/04, *Görgülü*.

[46] The German Federal Constitutional Court referred to a publication by G. Ress, "Wirkung und Beachtung der Urteile und Entscheidungen der Straßburger Konventionsorgane", *Europäische Grundrechte-Zeitschrift* 1996, 350, German Federal Constitutional Court 14 October 2004, No. 2 BvR 1481/04, para. 39. See also G. Ress "The Effects of Judgments and Decisions in Domestic Law", in R. St. J. Macdonald, F. Matscher, H. Petzold (eds.) *The European System for the Protection of Human Rights*, (Dordrecht: Martinus Nijhoff Publishers, 1993), 801–851, at 810–812.

[47] Article 31 Sect. 1 of the German Constitutional Court states: "The decisions of the Federal Constitutional Court shall be binding upon Federal and Land constitutional organs as well as on all courts and authorities."

Convention provides that only state parties that were party to proceedings are bound by its final judgments[48] before the ECtHR.

A similar view on the problem of orientation value of the ECtHR judgments issued with respect to third states, is held by German legal doctrine.[49] According to H.-J. Papier, ECtHR judgments have a precedent effect by virtue of Article 32(1) of the Convention, giving the ECtHR the power to interpret and develop the system of the Convention.[50] Therefore, in his opinion leading ECtHR judgments have a function of normative direction and orientation.[51]

This issue is also subject of discussion in Greece. However, Greek legal doctrine is divided. It is claimed that the ECtHR case-law does not constitute a source of law in the meaning of the Greek Constitution. At the same time, judges are obliged to follow the Constitution and statutes. However, taking into account the importance of the Convention for a given state and the interpretational value of the ECtHR judgments (stemming from Article 1 and 32 of the Convention), Greek authors claim that domestic courts should take the ECtHR case-law into account and if possible refer to it when deciding legal disputes. Such conclusion may be drawn additionally from Article 93 Sect. 3 of the Greek Constitution, which obliges a court to justify substantively its decisions.[52] According to E. Psychogiopoulou, argumentations included in the ECtHR judgments may lead the state to correct its dysfunction in the protection of the rights and freedoms guaranteed by the Convention when shaping its own legal system.[53]

Also the Italian Constitutional Court referred to the importance of the ECtHR judgments and their interpretational value. In decision No. 348/2007, the Italian Constitutional Court made the following statement:

> Since legal norms live in the interpretation that legal professionals give to them, in particular judges, the obvious consequence of Article 32, Paragraph 1, of the European Convention is that among the international obligations Italy entered into by executing and ratifying the ECtHR there is the obligation to adapt its domestic legislation to the provisions of this treaty, as interpreted by the [European] Court, which has been introduced specifically to perform their interpretation and application.[54]

---

[48] *Görgülü*, supra, note 45, para. 39.

[49] J. Meyer-Ladewig, *EMRK Europäische Menschenrechtenkonvention. Handkommentar* 2nd ed., (Baden-Baden: Nomos verlag, 2006), Note No. 14 to Article 46 of the Convention. See also H.-J. Papier, "Execution and Effects of the Judgments of the European Court of Human Rights from the Perspective of German National Courts", 27 *Human Rights Law Journal* (2006), 1–5.

[50] Article 32(1) ECHR states: "The jurisdiction of the Court shall extend to all matters concerning the interpretation and application of the Convention and the Protocols thereto [...]."

[51] Papier, supra, note 49, at 1.

[52] K. Xrysogonos, "H (mi) efarmogi tis ESDA apo ta ellinika dikastiria", 5 *To Syntagma* (2002), available at: http://tosyntagma.ant-sakkoulas.gr/afieromata/item.php?id=726. Article referred to in the report by Evangelia Psychogiopoulou, *Strasbourg Court Jurisprudence and Human Rights in Greece: An Overview of Litigation, Implementation and Domestic Reform*, prepared within JURISTRAS project, available at: http://www.juristras.eliamep.gr/wp-content/uploads/2008/09/greece.pdf, footnote 138, at 26–27.

[53] Ibid., at 27.

[54] Translation as included in F. Biondi Dal Monte and F. Fontanelli "The Decisions No. 348 and 349/2007 of the Italian Constitutional Court: The Efficacy of the European Convention in the Italian Legal System", *9 German Law Journal* (2008), 889–932, at 921.

According to commentators, this statement clearly indicates that the Italian Constitutional Court is aware of the importance of the interpretation of the Convention made by the ECtHR in the context of sources of international law. They underlined that the scope of obligations under the Convention is changing all the time as a result of jurisprudence. It should, however, be accepted in Italy's constitutional system, because the existence of an organ – equipped by international agreement – to make an official interpretation of the Convention, is a natural thing for public international law.[55]

10.3 Factors Influencing the *Res Interpretata* Effect of the ECtHR Judgments

10.3.1 Introduction: General Problem of Legitimacy of the ECtHR Judgments

The *res interpretata* effect of the ECtHR judgments depends on the legitimacy of the European Convention on Human Rights and the ECtHR judgments themselves. There is a lot of literature concerning the legitimacy of supranational adjudication, explaining why states tend to follow judgments of international courts, despite the fact that they influence democratic choices. In general, the system of the Convention is in this respect unique on a global scale. There is no similar regional system of human rights protection that would have a similar level of compliance. Every international tribunal may be attributed with a different theory why states comply with its judgments.[56] It seems, however, that the Convention is complied with mainly because its norms were internalized by states and currently form a permanent part of the European legal landscape.[57] There are states which do not comply with the ECtHR judgments and states which violate human rights systematically. There are different reasons for this. Some states were not really democratic at the moment of accession to the ECtHR and some states' practices remained unchanged since that time (it applies especially to some former USSR countries). Other states in general implement judgments, but have certain systemic problems due to the lack of effective internal reforms (e.g., Italy or Poland). In some other states, the non-enforcement of judgments is rather incidental and is a result of a different domestic perception of certain issues or of ideological constraints. Non-implementation of ECtHR judgments is a point of serious concern within the Council of Europe and most of the reforms (including the Interlaken process) address this problem.

[55] Ibid., at 922.

[56] R.P. Alford, "Proliferation of International Courts and Tribunals" *American Society of International Law Proceedings*, (2000) 160–165, at 163–164.

[57] Ibid.

State parties *have to* implement all the ECtHR judgments issued with respect to them (by virtue of Article 46 of the Convention). As regards judgments concerning other states, state parties are not obliged, but *may* implement them, thus increasing standards of human rights protection (and avoiding future violations in similar cases). This distinction between "obligation" and "possibility" is important here. Authority of judgments may not be read by using the zero one approach – binding or non-binding (as is the case of most *res judicata* judgments[58]). Such an approach may be intellectually attractive, because of its logical simplicity. However, reality is much more complicated and such an approach specifically cannot be applied to *res interpretata* judgments, which may have different levels of compliance pull. Therefore, the better approach is to search for different factors influencing the level of authority and persuasion of such judgments.

There is no doubt that ECtHR judgments in general are treated as precedents and should be followed in subsequent cases. Although the ECtHR takes a certain distance from the theory of precedents, it is aware that principles of legal certainty and legal equality require a consistent approach to adjudication and following earlier judgments:

> Even though the Court is not bound by precedent, legal certainty and legal equality require that the Court's case law be both consistent and transparent as well as reasonably predictable in so far as the facts of the case are comparable to those of earlier cases.[59]

Precedent value of the ECtHR judgment is important, not only to the Court itself, but also to state parties who are bound by the Convention and its interpretation made by the Court. Nevertheless, even in case of precedents, the level of implementation of such judgments may differ. The ECtHR precedent judgments establish the general standards of human rights protection. Accordingly, courts (in adjudication), executive bodies (in practice) or legislature (when assessing laws) should follow them. It seems that such *passive* use of precedent judgments is already widely accepted (see further). However, the major problem lies with the *active* use of precedents, i.e., a voluntary attempt to change laws or practices following the establishment of a new legal principle in an ECtHR judgment issued with respect to other states.

---

[58] In this article, we deal with the legal effects of ECHR judgments for states that were not a party to proceedings. Please note, however, that also the level of authority of *res judicata* judgments may be questionable. There have been many a number of instances in the practice of the ECtHR where the state did not want to comply with the judgment, claiming that the ECtHR insufficiently assessed the situation in question. See the discussion on compliance with the judgment in ECtHR 26 February 2002, No. 38784/97, *Morris v. United Kingdom*. The case concerned rules that govern the role of junior officers as members of martial courts. Following the criticism of the judgment, the Grand Chamber issued a judgment in ECtHR 16 December 2003, No. 48843/99, *Cooper v. United Kingdom*. In this judgment, the position of the ECtHR has changed. See L. Garlicki, "Cooperation of courts: The role of supranational jurisdictions in Europe", 6 *International Journal of Constitutional Law* (2008) 509–530, at 517.

[59] ECtHR 23 April 1997, Nos. 21363/93; 21364/93; 21427/93; 22056/93, *Van Mechelen and Others v. Netherlands*.

10.3.2 Grand Chamber Judgments v. Chamber Judgments

One of the most important factors influencing the authoritative value of judgments having *res interpretata* status is whether the Chamber or the Grand Chamber issued them.

There is no doubt that Grand Chamber judgments have the status of precedents. Article 43(2) ECHR indirectly indicates the character of such judgments. They are issued "if the case raises a serious question affecting the interpretation or application of the Convention or the Protocols thereto, or a serious issue of general importance". This provision providing for the competence of the Panel of five judges of the Grand Chamber in fact defines at the same time the legal value of judgments issued by the Grand Chamber.

The Chambers may not depart from the Grand Chamber judgment and the interpretations it has adopted. The Grand Chamber judgment becomes binding as the most authoritative statement on the application or interpretation of the Convention.

The Court may also give judgments, acting as a Committee of three judges or as a Chamber of seven judges. It seems that as to judgments issued by the Committee of three judges, there is no significant theoretical difficulty from the point of view of their potential *res interpretata* value. Article 28(1)(b) ECHR states clearly that such judgments are issued only when "the underlying question in the case, concerning the interpretation or the application of the Convention or the Protocols thereto, is already the subject of well-established case-law of the Court." This procedure is used for repetitive cases, in which standards already exist and the task of the Court is just to assess individual applications in light of established case-law. One cannot thus expect much new thinking or new legal principles in this type of judgments.

However, what is the value of the Chamber judgment from the point of view of their potential interpretative value? The picture here is quite blurred. There are some arguments in favour of their *res interpretata* value. First, many cases are resolved only by way of Chamber judgments. Many important principles of law are shaped only in Chamber judgments and they have a profound impact on the development of the system of the Convention.[60] At the same time, there is not a big chance that subsequently a Grand Chamber judgment will be issued, because cases are rarely referred to the Grand Chamber. If parties submit a motion to refer the case to the Grand Chamber, in most of the cases the Panel of five judges does not admit it. Similarly, only in very selected cases Chambers decide to relinquish jurisdiction to the Grand Chamber. Second, if the case has not been transmitted by the Panel of five judges of the Grand Chamber for resolution by the Grand Chamber, it may mean that most probably the adopted solution was not controversial in the Court and is shared by a majority of judges. Third, the Chamber judgment should be seriously taken into

[60] For example, leading Polish cases of last years, having significant impact on the system of the Convention, were inter alia the following Chamber judgments: ECtHR 20 March 2007, No. 5410/03, *Tysiąc v. Poland*, (access to therapeutic abortion); ECtHR 3 May 2007, No. 1543/06, *Bączkowski and Others v. Poland*, (ban on gay prides); ECtHR 15 June 2010, No. 7710/02, *Grzelak v. Poland*, (lack of education on ethics in Polish schools).

account, because one cannot expect any Grand Chamber judgment concerning the giving issue. They would be the only pronouncement establishing a legal principle.

However, there are also arguments against attaching too much interpretative value to the Chamber judgments. Most importantly, one may claim that by virtue of the Convention only the Grand Chamber has a power to make final interpretations of the Convention. Therefore, one should not take the Chamber judgment into account too seriously as regards its interpretative value, especially if there is a chance for the Grand Chamber to adjudicate on the same or a similar issue. Second, the Court is currently composed of five sections. The volume of work and caseload creates a situation in which it is highly difficult even for members of the Court to follow judgments issued by their colleagues. The natural consequence of such a situation may be a discrepancy in judgments, different assessment of similar situations and even the creation of slightly different standards as regards similar issues. Also the language barrier may be a problem. Although judges and Registry staff are required to speak English and French, it may happen that some of them will follow only those judgments and decisions issued in their working language.

Yet another perspective affecting the *res interpretata* value is the section in which the Chamber judgment was given. If a state which is not participating in the proceedings considers the effect of the judgment issued with respect to another state, the inclusion of this state into the same section does matter. When a similar issue will be heard, it is quite probable that the same section applies similar standards. Therefore, states should be more willing to observe the Chamber judgments from their own section.[61]

10.3.3 Comparability of Legal Systems or Legal Institutions in Different States and Its Impact on Possible Enforcement

Similarity of legal norms as well as social and political conditions in which they operate should encourage states to implement ECtHR judgments even if they did not participate in specific proceedings before the ECtHR. The orientation value of such judgments is thus greater than judgments having crucial importance for human rights standards in a state being subject to examination by the ECtHR, but with respect to issues that are not similar to situations in other states.

Such an approach imposes on the state certain obligations. If the state contemplates implementation of the ECHR judgments issued with respect to other states, it should first make the assessment if the given legal institution (assessed by the ECtHR) is similar to the domestic legal institution. In the same way, if a certain violation happened as a result of wrongful application of the law, and the source of the violation is rather administrative practice than legal provisions as such, the assessment should be made whether such wrongful administrative practices occur in the domestic context.

[61] It may be also a strategy of lawyers litigating cases before the ECtHR to observe what is the approach of judges belonging to a given section to certain issues, as it may have an impact on future judgments.

Such assessment requires the fulfilment of two conditions:

- Possession of knowledge by the relevant public authorities on new standards of human rights established in the jurisprudence of the ECtHR[62];
- Regular analysis of the extent to which ECtHR judgments concerning third states require domestic legal changes or changes in the administrative practice. Such analysis requires the use of a comparative approach and the comprehensive knowledge of domestic law, in order to properly assess the ECtHR judgment issued with respect to other legal systems and its potential consequences for domestic law and practice.[63]

Only in case of knowledge of the ECtHR standards and a certain level of comparability between the legal and social situations in a state that was a party to the proceedings and the state wishing to implement the ECtHR judgment, it is possible to undertake actions aiming to enforce such judgment. The selection of methods of implementation should be the second step and depend upon the specific character of a given judgment.

10.3.4 Clarity of Reasoning of ECtHR

According to Hermann Mosler, ECtHR judgments only have orientation value to states that were not a party to the proceedings, and they are an indication of how such states should act. Such judgments impose a special duty on the ECtHR. It has to convince by way of the correctness of its reasoning in order to attract compliance.[64]

During the Interlaken Conference, the Greek Delegation indicated that an important factor influencing the use of the ECtHR case-law is that the Court has to make sure that its judgments are consistent and clear. The examples of *Kudła v. Poland*[65] and *Eskelinen v. Finland*[66] were given. In the Greek Delegation's opinion, the reasoning in

[62] Compare the response by the ECtHR to the Report of the Wise Men: "Although its judgments do not, strictly speaking, have *erga omnes* effect (see Article 46 of the Convention), all States should take due notice of judgments against other States, especially judgments of principle, thereby preempting potential findings of violations against themselves." Document available at: http://www.echr.coe.int/NR/rdonlyres/26457EAB-2840-4D71-9ED7-85F0F8AE0026/0/OpinionoftheCourtontheWisePersonsReport.pdf

[63] A good example is the activity of the Office of Research and Analysis of the Supreme Court in Poland, which regularly publishes the Review of European Jurisprudence in Criminal Cases (prepared by Dr. Małgorzata Wąsek-Wiaderek). It is the only regular review prepared by public authorities in Poland that provides a comprehensive analysis of the ECtHR cases concerning other states than Poland and their potential importance for the Polish criminal justice system. The Review is available at the website of the Supreme Court: www.sn.pl.

[64] H. Mosler, "Report on the Result of the Colloquy", in I. Meier (ed.) *Protection of Human Rights in Europe. Limits and Effects. Proceedings of the Fifth International Colloquy about the European Convention on Human Rights*, (Heidelberg: C.F. Müller Juristischer Verlag, 1982), 333–347, at 344–345.

[65] ECtHR 26 October 2000, No. 30210/96, *Kudła v. Poland.*

[66] ECtHR 8 August 2006, No. 43803/98, *Eskelinen and Others v. Finland.*

these cases permits for the conclusion of general and succinct principles which are easily applicable, not only by the respondent state (the state party to the proceedings) but by all state parties.[67] Also the UK Delegation regarded the clear reasoning as one of the pre-conditions for securing respect of the ECHR by national courts.[68]

Recent literature suggests that, in practice, the Court is not very consistent in the application of different canons and methods of interpretation, such as the principle of proportionality, the margin of appreciation or the principle of subsidiarity. J. Christoffersen suggests that there is a great need for a certain consistency in the use of different concepts by the Court.[69]

In the recent Brighton Declaration, a long paragraph was devoted to the need for consistency in the ECtHR jurisprudence (para. 23):

> Judgments of the Court need to be clear and consistent. This promotes legal certainty. It helps national courts apply the Convention more precisely, and helps potential applicants assess whether they have a well-founded application. Clarity and consistency are particularly important when the Court addresses issues of general principle. Consistency in the application of the Convention does not require that States Parties implement the Convention uniformly.

The Brighton Declaration indicated that one of the measures to change the situation in this respect is the procedure for selecting judges, but also changes regarding the state party's possibility to object to the wish of a Chamber to relinquish jurisdiction in favour of the Grand Chamber. The latter changes are proposed by the recently adopted PACE Draft Protocol No. 15 to the ECHR.

10.3.5 Unanimous Judgments v. Judgments with Dissenting Opinions

One of the factors influencing the authority of the ECtHR judgments is whether the given judgment has been adopted unanimously or with dissenting or concurring opinions. By virtue of Article 45(1) ECHR, judges are entitled to deliver a separate opinion.[70]

---

[67] Statement by Mr. Fokion Georgakopoulos, Head of the Greek Delegation, Interlaken Conference Proceedings, p. 57.

[68] Statement by Lady Patricia Scotland, Head of the UK Delegation, Interlaken Conference Proceedings, at 106.

[69] J. Christoffersen, *Fair Balance: Proportionality, Subsidiarity and Primarity in the European Convention on Human Rights*, (Series: International Studies in Human Rights, Vol. 99) (Leiden-Boston: Martinus Nijhoff Publishers, 2009).

[70] There is already a comprehensive literature on the dissenting and concurring opinions in the ECtHR: F. Bruinsma and M. de Blots, "Rules of Law from Westport to Wladiwostok. Separate Opinions in the European Court of Human Rights", 15 *Netherlands Quarterly of Human Rights* (1997), 175; F. Rivière, *Les opinions séparées des juges à' la Cour europenne des droits de l'homme*, (Brussels: Bruylant, 2004); F. Bruinsma, "Judicial Identities in the European Court of Human Rights", in A. van Hoek (ed), *Multilevel Governance in Enforcement and Adjudication*, (Antwerp: Intersentia, 2006); R.C.A. White and I. Boussiakou, "Separate opinions in the European Court of Human Rights", 9 *Human Rights Law Review* (2009), 37–60.

Please note that with respect to judgments having *res judicata* status this problem is not so important. Irrespective of the number of dissenting opinions, in case of the finding of a violation by the majority of the Court, the state party to the proceedings has to implement this judgment. Such judgments may raise a lot of controversy, but as long as they are final, they have to be implemented.[71]

However, the *res interpretata* significance of judgments issued with dissenting opinions is certainly lower than unanimous judgments. The existence of dissents may suggest that the assessment of the Convention standards was not the same by all the judges, that there are discrepancies in thinking and approach. Such considerations, especially if they apply to controversy on legal issues, may deter some state parties from modifying their laws in accordance with such newly established standard. The *res interpretata* value relies greatly on the level of authority of the judgment itself. If some judges, already at the issuance of the judgment, undermine some of its aspects, there undoubtedly might be hesitance on the part of the states that potentially were willing to follow quite voluntarily such new standards.

The situation of judgments with concurring opinions is much different. Here, individual judges agree with the majority as regards the outcome of the case. They have, however, a different view on the approach to the case. In most of the cases, concurring opinions should not have such a significant impact on the level of authority of the given judgment. Nevertheless, one may imagine a situation where the concurring opinion gives a blow to the reasoning of the majority, which lowers the authority of the Court.[72]

10.3.6 Judicial Composition and Authority of Certain Judges

The quality of judges was raised as one of the crucial issues during both the Interlaken and Brighton Conferences. According to the UK Delegation, one of the pre-conditions for the ECtHR to command the respect of national courts is to have the very best judges nominated by the member states.[73]

Following the Interlaken Declaration, the Parliamentary Assembly of the Council of Europe in its resolution No. 1726 (2010) of 29 April 2010 reiterated that the "authority of the Court is contingent on the stature of judges and the quality and coherence of the Court's case law." The PACE underlined that it is the Assembly's

---

[71] Compare ECtHR 15 September 2009, No. 10373/05, *Moskal v. Poland*, adopted with a 4 to 3 majority. See the case note to *Moskal* case by Ewa Łętowska in the forthcoming book in honour of Maria Matey-Tyrowicz.

[72] For example, the ECHR may find a violation of Article 8 ECHR by analysis of certain wrongful practices. At the same time, the concurring opinion may suggest that Article 8 ECHR was in fact violated, but because of the wrongful regulation of a certain invasion of privacy, and thus violation of a requirement "provided by law". The effect is the same – violation of Article 8, but the majority judgment has a much more limited scope of application.

[73] Statement by Lady Patricia Scotland, Head of the UK Delegation to Interlaken Conference, *Interlaken Conference Proceedings*, 6.

authority to elect judges of the highest calibre. However, in compliance with the PACE resolution on this issue,[74] it is also an obligation of the states to make a proper selection of the best three candidates, Similarly, in the Brighton Declaration it was underlined that:

> The authority and credibility of the Court depend in large part on the quality of its judges and the judgments they deliver.
>
> The high calibre of judges elected to the Court depends on the quality of the candidates that are proposed to the Parliamentary Assembly for election.[75]

In this respect, the Brighton Declaration suggested certain reforms aimed to increase the quality of the candidates proposed by state parties for future ECtHR judges.

There is no doubt that judicial composition and authority of individual judges may have impact on the authoritative value of judgments, especially those issued by the Chamber. If the judgment establishing a legal principle is issued by a panel composed of judges with prominent careers as scholars, domestic judges, law professors, or judges with long experience at the Court, it has a certain impact on the quality and clarity of reasoning, method and depth of legal argumentation. In consequence, it is much more probable that such judgment would have a higher persuasive effect.[76]

10.3.7 Lapse of Time from the Date of Judgment

Another factor influencing the *res interpretata* effect of judgments is the time factor. If the standard is well established in the jurisprudence of the Court (even if it is a Chamber judgment) it should cause the state to modify its practices as soon as possible. Obviously, it may be difficult for the state to make a comprehensive review of existing legislation from the point of view of all judgments of principle. One can imagine only regular checks of legislation.[77]

---

[74] Parliamentary Assembly of the Council of Europe Resolution 1646 (2009) on the nomination of candidates and election of judges to the European Court of Human Rights, available at: http://assembly.coe.int/main.asp?Link=/documents/adoptedtext/ta09/eres1646.htm

[75] Brighton Declaration, points 21–22.

[76] Judgments of the European Court of Human Rights do not indicate who was a judge rapporteur. On the one hand, this strengthens the authority of the Court (especially if judgments are issued unanimously). On the other hand, if the judgment has been written by a prominent expert, one cannot rely on this fact and search for some additional persuasive value. One should take into account that in many constitutional courts, the fact that a certain judgment was written by a specific judge increases its legitimacy (and *vice versa* if the judge is not highly regarded in the legal society).

[77] E.g. in Spain, the Ombudsman in his annual reports reviews the compatibility of certain Spanish laws with the Strasbourg decisions. The Ombudsman's activities proved to be a very useful tool to encourage legislative amendments or changes in the behaviour of the administrative authorities. See M. Candela Soriano, "The reception process in Spain and Italy" in H. Keller and A. Stone-Sweet (eds.), *A Europe of Rights: The Impact of the ECHR on National Legal Systems*, (Oxford:

The lapse of time from the date of issuance of judgment is certainly a factor pushing for changing domestic practices or legislation. In order to avoid a situation of being behind in current standards of human rights protection, states should rather monitor on a day to day basis the changing jurisprudence of the ECHR, the establishment of new standards, and should modify their law or practices adequately. It seems that it is the only way to cope with the massive number of judgments, including those dealing with new principles.

10.3.8 Subsidiarity and Use of Margin of Appreciation

Another factor influencing the *res interpretata* effect of the judgment is the use by the Court of the principle of subsidiarity and margin of appreciation in its adjudication.

One of the aspects of subsidiarity is the limitation of the freedom in adjudication by the Court. The Court has to rely on the case on the basis of submitted documents, assessments of facts, collected evidence by domestic courts, and it has to adjudicate within limits of complaints. Sometimes, due to this, the case may be so specific that it is difficult to draw general conclusions that may form part of the legal principle to be followed in the general system of the Convention.

A good example is the *Moskal v. Poland* case.[78] The ECtHR in the Chamber judgment created a new principle of good governance in cases involving social security issues (as part of property rights). However, the judgment was adopted by a majority of 4–3. Second, its reasoning was clearly affected by domestic procedures, collected evidence and assessment of certain facts. Following such case, the question is whether the principle of good governance should be "exported" to other state parties to the Convention having problems with effectiveness of administrative bodies, or it is only a reflection on the condition of the Polish social security institutions.

The margin of appreciation doctrine allows the Court to assess the situation by reference to local, social, political, historical or legal conditions. If the state has a margin of appreciation in a given field, it means that the ECHR is not going to enter with its control machinery into this field. However, if the state oversteps this margin of appreciation, then the ECHR may find a violation.

The question is to what extent such judgments – based on the assumption of inherent margin of appreciation (and its overstepping) may be a basis for construing a legal principle of universal applicability (in order to have the *res interpretata* effect). Is the check made by the ECHR somehow blurred by this initial assumption

---

Oxford University Press, 2008) at 431–432. A regular check of legislation is also made in The Netherlands and in the United Kingdom (the Parliament's Joint Human Rights Committee). See D. Feldman, "The Impact of Human Rights on the UK Legislative Process", 25 *Statute Law Review* (2004), 91–115.

[78] *Moskal v. Poland*, supra, note 71. See comment to the judgment by A. Bodnar and B. Grabowska, "Glosa do wyroku ETPCZ w sprawie Moskal przeciwko Polsce" *Praca i Zabezpieczenie Społeczne [*'*Work and Social Security' journal]*, (2010) 6.

of margin of appreciation? How would certain measures be assessed if the ECHR would not have to use the margin of appreciation doctrine at all? What kind of legal principle would then be construed?

Those questions cannot be answered with a sufficient clarity. Everything would rather depend on a particular judgment and the situation in question. For example, when resolving disputes on criminal responsibility for defamation the ECtHR admits that states have a margin of appreciation in providing such responsibility. However, by virtue of judgments it eliminates certain penalties (such as imprisonment) or limits their severity (by finding that certain judgments were too onerous and thus states crossed the margin of appreciation). On the basis of such cases, one may draw a general principle of universal applicability (there should be no prison for defamation[79]), but the margin of appreciation doctrine does not allow to formulate any more specific principle to be applicable in legislative context. The principle of proportionality that is usually used to assess sanctions imposed on journalists may be a general guideline on how the legislation should be reformed,[80] but it does not provide a sufficiently clear and precise direction of such changes. Using this particular example, as long as the ECtHR declares that criminal sanctions for journalists are per se contrary to Article 10 of the Convention, such responsibility would stay in criminal codes and the assessment whether a sanction in a given case was proportional would be delegated to courts.

Following the Brighton Declaration, the role of the margin of appreciation doctrine increased, as it will be inserted into the Preamble to Protocol No. 15 to the ECHR. There is a risk that the ECtHR will use this doctrine more often. As a result, in some fields (such as religious freedom), the ECtHR may avoid the creation of new standards to be followed by other state parties.

10.3.9 Participation of Third State in Proceedings Leading to the Judgment Concerning Other State (as Intervener)

Under Article 36 ECHR, state parties have a possibility to submit written comments and to take part in hearings, if they are invited to do so by the President of the Court in the interest of proper administration of justice. The right to third party intervention allows state parties to comment on the issues involved in the resolution of the case.

States who are being interveners are not regarded as *"parties to the case"* under Article 46 ECHR. Accordingly, acting as interveners does not extend the *res judicata* effect on them. The question is, however, whether participation in proceedings as interveners has any influence on the activities of the state, following the issuance of the judgment. Does the fact of intervention increase or decrease the authoritative

---

[79] ECtHR 23 April 1992, No. 11798/85, *Castells v. Spain.*

[80] ECtHR 24 February 2009, No. 23806/03, *Długołęcki v. Poland.*

value of such judgment? Does it exert more compliance pull on the part of such intervening state?

In most of the cases, the intervention by the state is made in order to present a certain position on a problem, being a reflection of internal practices or political approach. Interventions may have both a positive character (the ECHR should establish a new standard, find violation of the Convention, etc.) and a negative one (the ECHR should not deal with the issue, human rights are not violated, states should be allowed to act within the margin of appreciation).

In case of a positive approach, one cannot expect problems with compliance, because such intervening states usually have domestic practices which are more advanced than those proposed by the ECHR. The real problem is when the state is suggesting a solution that is contrary to later ECHR judgment.

On a pure formal level, of course, an intervening state does not have a clear obligation to implement such judgment, because it does not have a *res judicata* status. However, it cannot ignore this judgment either. The mere fact of intervention indicates that the state is aware of the problem, has knowledge of the ECHR standard (participated in proceedings, was notified about the judgment), and certain awareness of domestic legislation and practices. However, the practical outcome may be much more different that ideal the situation of a *bona fides* implementation of such judgment.

10.4 Obligations of States with Respect to ECHR Judgments Concerning Third States

10.4.1 Introductury Remarks

The ECHR case-law creates a body of standards that are commonly shared by common courts, administrative courts and constitutional courts in the Member States. They very often rely on the jurisprudence of the ECHR, without even considering which state was party to proceedings in a case. It is especially visible in freedom of speech cases or in criminal defence rights.

However, the *res interpretata* effect of the ECHR judgments requires something more. First, Member States should carefully follow the jurisprudence concerning other states. Such practice requires special mechanisms, such as offices responsible for the constant ECHR compliance check of the existing and proposed legislation. Such compliance check should not be made superficially. It requires the knowledge of domestic legislation and practice and the ability to make an effective comparison with the situation in a state that was subject to proceedings. Only very few states have such practice (most notably The Netherlands). It should be noted that not all judgments concerning other states might be easily implemented in other states. Sometimes the assessment made by the ECHR concerns very specific and local circumstances.

Second, if non-compliance with a certain ECHR judgment is found, there should be a mechanism of coordination within the government. The Government Agent, other special governmental or parliamentary units or even national human rights institutions, may fulfil such a role.

Third, there must be an understanding in the Government that the *bona fides* implementation of the Convention may sometime require adequate changes in law and practice following the ECHR judgment concerning other states.

10.4.2 Obligation to Have Full Knowledge of ECHR Jurisprudence

The most important obligation of the state parties in order to consider the *res interpretata* effect at all is knowledge of ECtHR jurisprudence. This obligation was clearly stated in the ECtHR answer to the Report of Wise Persons:

> Although its judgments do not, strictly speaking, have *erga omnes* effect (see Article 46 of the Convention), all States should take due notice of judgments against other States, especially judgments of principle, thereby preempting potential findings of violations against themselves.[81]
>
> The above principle was underlined also in *Scordino v. Italy*[82]:
>
> … domestic courts must … be able, under domestic law, to apply the European case-law directly and their knowledge of this case-law has to be facilitated by the State in question.

Please note that in order to have a full knowledge of jurisprudence and to identify legal principles in judgments concerning third states, certain methodological knowledge is required. Legal principles are usually formulated in the reasoning part of the judgment. Grounds to judgments are a primary source of information on how the ECtHR is interpreting a certain provision of the Convention. It creates a certain problem from the point of view of enforcement. The ECtHR usually in addition to the *ratio decidendi* contained in the grounds, tends to include some general *obiter dicta* remarks. The correct implementation of such judgment requires a good methodological approach and the proper distinction between *ratio decidendi* and *obiter dicta*.

10.4.3 Obligation to Translate Most Important ECHR Judgments and to Disseminate Them

The most important obligations of the states as regards translation and dissemination of judgments are formulated in Recommendation Rec(2002)13 of the Committee of Ministers on the publication and dissemination in the member states of the text of the European Convention on Human Rights and of the case-law of the

---

[81] Available at: http://www.echr.coe.int/NR/rdonlyres/26457EAB-2840-4D71-9ED7-85F0F8AE0026/0/OpinionoftheCourtontheWisePersonsReport.pdf

[82] ECtHR 29 July 2004, No. 36813/97, *Scordino v. Italy*.

European Court of Human Rights.[83] Among the many recommendations, the Committee of Ministers recommended that Member States should ensure that:

> judgments and decisions which constitute relevant case-law developments, or which require special implementation measures on their part as respondent states, are rapidly and widely published, through state or private initiatives, in their entirety or at least in the form of substantial summaries or excerpts (together with appropriate references to the original texts) in the language(s) of the country, in particular in official gazettes, information bulletins from competent ministries, law journals and other media generally used by the legal community, including, where appropriate, the Internet sites.

This specific recommendation is very general in nature. It should be underlined, however, that it does not only refer to judgments binding for a particular state (judgments requiring "special implementation measures"), but also to "judgments and decisions that constitute relevant case-law development". According to this recommendation it is up to the Member State to decide whether such judgments are translated in their entirety or only summaries of them are prepared, and where they are published.

The recommendation to translate the most important judgments concerning other states appeared in the statement of the Polish National Council of Judiciary of 16 December 2011. In particular, the Council recommended:

> making an analysis and translation of important judgments in non-Polish cases, which significance extends over the state concerned and has a meaning for Polish law and practice.[84]

10.4.4 Obligation of the State to Consider Whether Third State ECHR Judgments Have an Impact on Domestic Practices

Recommendation Rec(2004)5 of the Committee of Ministers clearly indicates that the primary obligation of the Member States under Article 46 ECHR is to comply with judgments issued in cases against them. However, it underlines in the preamble that "further efforts should be made by Member States to give full effect to the Convention, in particular through a continuous adaptation of national standards in accordance with those of the Convention, in the light of the case-law of the Court." Just in this context, the Committee of Ministers outlines a set of measures that may serve verification of laws or practices with respect to compliance with the Convention.

Such an approach – the necessity of compliance of the legislation with the ECHR standards – was underlined by the ECtHR itself in *Maestri v. Italy*:

> in ratifying the Convention the Contracting States undertake to ensure that their domestic legislation is compatible with it. Consequently, it is for the respondent State to remove any

[83] Recommendation Rec(2002)13 is available at: https://wcd.coe.int/wcd/ViewDoc.jsp?Ref=Rec(2002)13&Language=lanEnglish&Site=COE&BackColorInternet=DBDCF2&BackColorIntranet=FDC864&BackColorLogged=FDC864

[84] Statement of the Polish National Council of Judiciary on the enforcement of judgments of the European Court of Human Rights of 16 December 2011, point 4.

obstacles in its domestic legal system that might prevent the applicant's situation from being adequately redressed.[85]

Under Recommendation Rec(2004)5, states should establish mechanisms allowing for systematic and regular verification of draft laws, binding laws and administrative practices. Recommendation Rec(2004)5 suggests a number of solutions that may be adopted for this purpose. With respect to verification of existing laws, the Recommendation directly refers to judgments issued with respect to third states:

> While member States cannot be asked to verify systematically all their existing laws, regulations and administrative practice, it may be necessary to engage in such an exercise, for example, as a result of national experience in applying a law or regulation or following a new judgment by the Court against another member State.[86]

This statement is a clear indication of the scope of potential obligations. The Committee of Ministers indicates that it would be too burdensome to regularly verify all existing laws and practices. However, if new ECHR judgments are rendered against another Member State this should be a good opportunity to check one's own legislation or practices in this respect. The Committee of Ministers, as good practice indicates that such an effort is made in some states by ministers who are responsible for the initiation of legislation. Their role is also to verify existing regulations and practices. This, in turn, requires knowledge of the "latest developments in the case-law of the Court."[87]

Recommendation Rec(2004)5 also suggests that developments of case-law should also be notified by governmental agencies to independent bodies, especially courts.[88] Recommendation Rec(2004)5 provides, as good practice, that competent organs of the State have to ensure that those responsible in local and central authorities take into account the Convention and the case-law of the Court, in order to avoid violations.[89]

10.4.5 Prohibition to Pass a Law That Would be Contrary to the ECHR Judgment Issued with Respect to Third States

The mere existence of an ECHR judgment establishing certain human rights standard may also be interpreted as a prohibition to pass any law that would be contrary to such standards. Such approach may be expected from Member States as a *bona fides* application of the international treaty. This obligation was formulated explicitly

---

[85] ECtHR 17 February 2004, No. 39748/98, *Maestri v. Italy*.

[86] Appendix to the Recommendation Rec(2004)5, point 25.

[87] Appendix to the Recommendation Rec(2004)5, point 26.

[88] Appendix to the Recommendation Rec(2004)5, point 26.

[89] Appendix to the Recommendation Rec(2004)5, point 26.

in a judgment of the German Federal Constitutional Court, which underlined that the legislature, without clearly stating so, cannot deviate from public international legal obligations of the Federal Republic of Germany or make violations of such obligations possible.[90] According to the German Federal Constitutional Court "the case-law of the European Court of Human Rights serves as an aid to the interpretation of content and scope of fundamental rights as well as principles of the rule of law under the Federal Constitution." Consequently, statutes have to be interpreted in harmony with international legal obligations of Germany. The Convention standards must be applicable even if the statute was enacted later than the Convention, because it is just a consequence of public international law requirements.

Once again there is the question whether the state may deviate from international obligations by passing certain laws, not being aware that it contravenes human rights standards.[91] It seems that such a situation may happen even quite often, due to the growing number of significant judicial pronouncements and a corresponding insufficient number of domestic institutions equipped to verify the compliance of laws with the ECHR. It seems that such unknowing adoption of legislation that is contrary to standards, would not be interpreted as a violation of international law obligations, because one should assume that the state acted *bona fides* when passing the law. However, if the state intentionally adopted legislation that is contrary to standards (despite legal opinions or comments indicating a necessity to amend the legislation), then such approach should be regarded as a violation of international law obligations.

10.4.6 Obligation to Take into Account the Whole Case-Law of the ECHR When Adjudicating

In those states that adopted laws incorporating the European Convention on Human Rights into their domestic legal system or provided for mechanisms of enforcement, one may find provisions relating to the *res interpretata* effect of judgments concerning other states.

Very extensive obligations in this respect are provided in the 2006 Ukrainian Act.[92] Article 17 Sect. 1 states that, while adjudicating cases, courts shall apply the

---

[90] BVerfGE, vol. 74, 358 (at 370).

[91] According to Frowein, one cannot imagine a situation where the German federal legislator adopts willfully a law that is in contravention of the ECHR standards. The only problem may appear when the legislator is not aware of specific obligations stemming from the ECHR case-law. See J.A. Frowein, "Incorporation of the Convention into Domestic Law", in J. P. Gardner (ed.), *Aspects of Incorporation of the European Convention of Human Rights into Domestic Law*, (London: British Institute of International and Comparative Law & British Institute of Human Rights, 1993) 3–11, at 6–7.

[92] Law on the Enforcement of Judgments and the Application of the Case-Law of the European Court of Human Rights, Law No.3477-IV of 23 February 2006.

Convention and the case-law of the Court as a source of law.[93] Furthermore, by virtue of Article 19 Sects. 3, 4, and 5, it is the duty of the Government Agent to make a regular examination of the legislation as regards compliance with the Convention and the Court's case-law. If he finds inconsistencies, the Agent has to submit proposals to the Cabinet of Ministers of Ukraine to amend the legislation. Also ministries and departments should systematically control compliance of administrative practice with the Convention and the Court's case-law.

In the United Kingdom and in Ireland, where the ECHR has been incorporated into domestic law, emphasis is put on the use of the Convention and the case-law by domestic courts.

In the United Kingdom, by virtue of the Human Rights Act 1998, a court or tribunal determining a question which has risen in connection with a Convention right, must take into account any judgment, decision, declaration or advisory opinion of the European Court of Human Rights, if it is relevant to the proceedings in which that question has arisen (Sect. 10.2.1.1). The Human Rights Act, by referring to the ECtHR pronouncements, uses the phrase "whenever made or given", which suggests that there are no special limits as regards applicability of standards stemming from the ECtHR jurisprudence concerning other states.[94]

Lord Bingham has interpreted this provision in the so-called *Ullah* judgment.[95] According to this interpretation:

> national court subject to a duty such as that imposed by section 2 should not without strong reason dilute or weaken the effect of the Strasbourg case law. It is indeed unlawful under section 6 of the 1998 Act for a public authority, including a court, to act in a way which is incompatible with a Convention right. It is of course open to member states to provide for rights more generous than those guaranteed by the Convention, but such provision should not be the product of interpretation of the Convention by national courts, since the meaning of the Convention should be uniform throughout the states party to it. The duty of national courts is to keep pace with the Strasbourg jurisprudence as it evolves over time: no more, but certainly no less.[96]

Nevertheless, in some judgments the highest court in the United Kingdom provided for additional criteria to determine to what extent courts should follow the ECHR jurisprudence. Most notably in *R v. Horncastle and others*,[97] the UK Supreme Court indicated the limits of influence of the Strasbourg standards on domestic decisions. It stated

---

[93] 2006 Ukrainian Law was annexed to the Parliamentary Assembly Report on the implementation of judgments of the European Court of Human Rights, prepared by Mr. Erik Jurgens, 18 September 2006, Assembly Doc. 11020. It is available in English at: http://assembly.coe.int/main.asp?Link=/documents/workingdocs/doc06/edoc11020.htm#P1169_169391

[94] The Human Rights Act 1998 is available at: http://www.legislation.gov.uk/ukpga/1998/42/data.pdf

[95] *R (Ullah) v Special Adjudicator* (2004) 2 AC 323, per Lord Bingham, available at: http://www.publications.parliament.uk/pa/ld200304/ldjudgmt/jd040617/ullah-2.htm

[96] Ibid., para. 20.

[97] *R v Horncastle and others* [2009] UKSC 14, available at: http://www.supremecourt.gov.uk/decided-cases/docs/UKSC_2009_0073_Judgment.pdf

that, in general, courts should follow the principles clearly established by the ECtHR. However, there are:

> rare occasions where this court has concerns as to whether a decision of the Strasbourg Court sufficiently appreciates or accommodates particular aspects of our domestic process. In such circumstances it is open to this court to decline to follow the Strasbourg decision, giving reasons for adopting this course. This is likely to give the Strasbourg Court the opportunity to reconsider the particular aspect of the decision that is in issue, so that there takes place what may prove to be a valuable dialogue between this court and the Strasbourg Court.[98]

It means that while the Ullah principle opened the way for using ECHR standards in the jurisprudence of UK courts, the Horncastle principle limits their applicability (in rare situations), and opens the way to a discussion between courts. It should, however, be underlined that both under the Human Rights Act 1998 and under said judgments, the ECtHR case-law is treated in its entirety, without distinction to any special categories of cases with limited scope of applicability.

Similar provisions as in the United Kingdom are provided in the Irish legislation. In Ireland, Sect. 10.4a of the European Convention on Human Rights Act 2003[99] provides that:

> judicial notice shall be taken of the Convention provisions and of any declaration, decision, advisory opinion or judgment of the European Court of Human Right [...] and a court shall, when interpreting and applying the Convention provisions, take due account of the principles laid down by those declarations, decisions, advisory opinions, opinions and judgments.

10.4.7 Reference by Party in Domestic Court Proceedings to the ECtHR Judgments Issued with Respect to Third States: Obligations of the Court

One of the states' obligations relating to giving respect to judgments concerning third states, would be to require an appropriate reaction by courts. If the party is referring to the legal principle stemming from the ECtHR judgment, courts should have an obligation to properly consider the application of such principle to the case. If they decide not to apply it, they should provide an adequate reasoning for their decision. It is unacceptable when courts ignore ECHR standards in their decision-making. They may not agree with the argumentation presented by one of the parties, but they should treat the ECHR standards seriously as one of the most important sources of law (in some countries being equal to the constitutional norms).

One may imagine that ignoring the reliance by parties on ECtHR judgments may be regarded as a sufficient argument to undermine the validity of the decision made by domestic courts (e.g., in a cassation appeal). It should be a duty of the

---

[98] Ibid., para. 11.

[99] The European Convention on Human Rights Act 2003 is available at: http://www.oireachtas.ie/documents/bills28/acts/2003/a2003.pdf

supreme courts in different states to establish such an approach to ECHR jurisprudence. It may be one of the most efficient methods to secure the domestic enforcement of the ECHR.

10.4.8 Necessity to Take into Account ECtHR Judgments (Including Third Country Judgments) in the Activity of the Constitutional Courts

In most countries, ECtHR jurisprudence is treated as a whole body of case-law, without distinguishing between judgments having *res judicata* or *res interpretata* status. It is especially visible in the practice of constitutional courts, where judgments are a source for interpretation of the Convention. Constitutional courts, when exercising judicial review, act in a passive role (as compared to the legislator). Accordingly, it is much easier for them to take into account the whole body of case-law and standards that emerge from them.

A good example of such approach is the practice of the Polish Constitutional Court (hereinafter PCC). Under the Polish Constitution, the Convention has the status of the ratified international agreement and in case of conflict takes precedence over statutory norms. The Polish Constitutional Court commonly uses the whole case-law of the ECtHR when adjudicating, mostly in cases where it has to interpret domestic constitutional provisions. The case-law of the ECtHR is used as a subsidiary source or guideline for such interpretation. Such practice is especially visible in cases concerning the right to court, criminal defence rights, the prohibition of torture, inhuman or degrading treatment, the freedom of speech and the freedom of assembly. Please note, however, that with respect to some issues, Polish standards are more advanced than ECHR standards. In the judgment of 18 October 2004, No. P 8/04, the Constitutional Court underlined that the necessity to take into account the existence of a ECtHR judgment by internal organs, creates also an obligation for the Constitutional Court to apply principles and methods of interpretation which lead to smoothe potential collisions between Polish standards and those formulated by the ECtHR.

The PCC has a practice of controlling the challenged provisions with the ECHR standards, even if the petitioner did not request it. It applies especially to cases where the constitutional standard is the same as required by the Convention, e.g., defence rights in criminal trials.[100] The same applies if the scope of protected rights under the Convention and the Constitution is similar.[101]

---

[100] Polish Constitutional Court (hereinafter) 3 June 2008, No. K 42/07, OTK ZU of 2008, No. 5A, item 77. An English summary of the judgment is available at: http://www.trybunal.gov.pl/eng/summaries/documents/K_42_07_GB.pdf

[101] PCC 19 December 2002, No. K 33/02, OTK ZU of 2002, No. 7A, item 97; the PCC referred directly to Art. 1 Prot. 1 ECHR and Art. 64 of the Constitution. English summary available at: http://www.trybunal.gov.pl/eng/summaries/documents/K_33_02_GB.pdf

In case the PCC does not have a relevant ECtHR precedent on which it may rely, it refers to the general principles that were taken into account by the ECtHR in a similar case. E.g., the PCC relied on the need to balance public interest and the protection of individual rights (as used in *Mellacher v. Austria*[102]) in order to determine the constitutionality of the regulation restricting the amount of lease fees in private houses.[103]

The PCC relies also on jurisprudence of the ECtHR in order to seek justification for declaring certain domestic provisions as being in compliance with the Constitution. In 2009, the PCC declared that the right to submit preliminary reference questions to the European Court of Justice does not violate the right to fair trial standards, in particular it does not create unduly lengthen proceedings.[104] In this regard, the PCC relied on earlier jurisprudence of the ECtHR, which confirmed that the state might not be responsible for the waiting period for answering to the preliminary reference question.[105]

The *res interpretata* effect is achieved to the greatest extent with respect to the Polish constitutional court when the latter treats the whole body of the ECtHR case-law as the source of interpretation of the Convention provisions. If the Convention (or similar constitutional norms) is used by the court as a verification tool of constitutional compliance, there is no special reason to make exceptions between selected judgments.

However, in some situations the ECHR standards could be made on the basis of a specific situation in a given country. Constitutional courts should be aware of the specific context (legal, social, political or historical) in which a certain judgment has been issued and should take it into account accordingly. Such methodological approach is especially needed when there is only a single judgment establishing a legal principle, when there is a lack of an established line of precedents regarding certain issues. In such a situation, the constitutional court should take proper care of determining the context of issuing the judgment by the ECtHR, and whether the state that was party to proceedings has a similar institution as compared to the institution under the constitutional court's review. To put it simply, constitutional courts may not just cite a standard from some judgment and rely on it. They have to make a proper contextual analysis of such new standard. Only in case of finding similarities, the constitutional court may apply such new standard to the examination of the domestic legal norm.

---

[102] ECtHR 19 December 1989, Nos. 10522/83, 11011/84 and 11070/84, *Mellacher and Others v. Austria*.

[103] PCC 12 January 2000, P 11/98, OTK ZU of 2000, No. 1, item 3. English summary available at: http://www.trybunal.gov.pl/eng/summaries/documents/P_11_98_GB.pdf

[104] Judgment of the Polish Constitutional Court of 18.02.2009, No. Kp 3/08, OTK ZU of 2009, No. 2A, item 9. Full text of the judgment (in English) is available at: http://www.trybunal.gov.pl/eng/summaries/documents/Kp_03_08_GB.pdf

[105] ECtHR 26 February 1998, No. 20323/92, *Pafitis and Others v. Greece*; ECtHR 30 September 2003, No. 40892/98, *Koua Poirrez v. France*.

In judicial review there is a risk of abusing the ECHR standards. By giving power to constitutional courts to examine the compliance of domestic norms with the Convention and the ECHR standards, constitutional courts may cherry-pick and select only those judgments (or even phrases) that are the most suitable for the overall solution of the case. They may misinterpret certain principles included into judgments. Such an approach may be a result of either lack of sufficient knowledge of the ECHR standards and legal argumentation (which may be quite natural in many countries), or acting in bad faith. In the latter case, the ECHR standards (as misinterpreted or wrongly construed by the domestic court) would be used as an additional source of legitimacy for the judgment, and would support the intended outcome of the case.[106] Obviously such an approach should be condemned and may be regarded as a breach of international obligations. For that reason, the methodology of using the ECtHR case-law in judicial review is of utmost importance, as it limits the possibility of abuse of standards.

10.4.9 Possibility to Re-open Domestic Proceedings After the ECtHR Judgment Concerning Third States Which Establish a New Legal Principle or Standard

A common way to redress a violation of the Convention is the possibility to re-open proceedings in a case. Such possibility, if allowed by domestic law, usually refers to persons who were victims of human rights violations and then successfully litigated their case before the ECtHR. A judgment finding a violation of the ECHR gives them a possibility to re-open proceedings. Re-opening in criminal cases is a common feature among state parties to the Convention, and may be regarded as a human rights standard.[107] Common standards, however, still do not exist as regards civil or other type of proceedings, despite a recommendation of the Committee of Ministers.[108]

[106] Compare the *amicus curiae* brief submitted by the Helsinki Foundation for Human Rights in the case concerning deprivation of special benefits of the former secret police members, case No. K 36/09; *amicus curiae* brief, available at: http://www.hfhr.org.pl/przeszlosc-rozliczenia/opinie-przyjaciela-sadu-amicus-curiae/opinia-amicus-curiae-dla-trybunalu-konstytucyjnego-w-sprawie-o-sygn-k-36-09-dezubekizacja.html

[107] In the case ECtHR 20 April 2010, Nos. 12315/04 and 17605/04, *Laska and Lika v. Albania*, the ECtHR suggested that there should be a possibility to re-examine a case or re-open criminal proceedings, and it would be the best way to redress the applicants and to repair the situation of violation. The ECtHR indicated that such possibility does not exist in the domestic legal system, and indirectly pointed out the need to establish a new remedy for victims of the right to fair trial.

[108] Recommendation of the Committee of Ministers No. R (2000) 2 on the re-examination or reopening of certain cases at domestic level following judgments of the European Court of Human Rights, available at: https://wcd.coe.int/wcd/ViewDoc.jsp?id=334147&Site=CM

An interesting question, but raised only in some jurisdictions, is whether a possibility to re-open criminal proceedings should be allowed not only to persons who successfully brought a case to the ECtHR, but also to other persons, who are in a similar legal and factual situation. For example, we can imagine a case in which applicant X claims that the use of a certain type of evidence violates the right to a fair trial. The ECtHR finds a violation of Article 6 of the Convention and as a result applicant X may re-open proceedings. The problem is whether persons Y and Z, who may have final criminal verdicts due to the use of similar type of evidence may claim the re-opening of proceedings or whether they should initiate their individual application.

As a general rule, a judgment of the ECtHR is binding only between parties to the proceedings and it does not have an *erga omnes* effect. But in the situation described above, it could be reasonable to allow persons to claim re-opening of proceedings.[109] Second, sometimes a case reaching the ECtHR is one of massive and systematic violations, indicating a structural problem. The question is then whether the state should wait for the ECtHR review of all cases or should create remedies (which may include re-opening) to a bigger group of individuals.[110]

Nevertheless, this matter is rather a question of scholarly interest at the moment, and there is not yet a universal standard in this regard. One may, however, expect that the future development of the *res interpretata* effect may give ground to consider the re-opening of proceedings in individual cases, as the ECtHR judgments would have *erga omnes* effect. If such possibility is allowed, it may apply both to individuals originating from a given jurisdiction, and from other jurisdictions (especially if similar standards exist in certain countries and were in the same way neglected).

The decision to re-open proceedings is always a matter of discretion for the given court. We are, thus, not discussing the obligation to re-open proceedings following the ECtHR judgment in every similar case when the convicted person requests it. Rather, we are discussing the creation of a mere possibility to examine whether leave to re-open a case should be granted.

---

[109] See F. Czerner, "Inter partes – versus erga omnes – Wirkung der EMGR-Judikate in den Konventionsstaaten gemäß Art. 46 EMRK. Eine Problemanalyse auch aus strafverfahrensrechtlicher Perspektive", 46 *Archiv des Völkerrechts*, (2008), 345–367, at 363–364; see also for a similar view: B. Nita, "Orzeczenie ETPCz jako podstawa wznowienia postępowania karnego [The ECtHR judgment as the basis for re-opening of criminal proceedings]", *Europejski Przegląd Sądowy [European Court Review]* (2010)9, 4–10, at 7. In the opinion of Barbara Nita, re-opening criminal proceedings concerning another person than the one which had his case before the ECtHR, is possible when the violation of the Convention standard is identical. It is the limitation which should be equally applicable also to re-opening if a judgment was rendered with respect to other states than the state in which re-opening is claimed.

[110] Explanatory Memorandum to Recommendation R(2002)2 clearly specifies that it does not address the special problem of "mass cases", i.e. cases in which a certain structural deficiency leads to a great number of violations of the Convention. In such cases, it is in principle best left to the state concerned to decide whether or not reopening or re-examination are realistic solutions or, whether other measures are appropriate.

10.4.10 Dissemination of "Specific Relevance" Judgments

Recommendation Rec(2002)13[111] also includes the general recommendation to ensure the rapid dissemination among appropriate public bodies and non-state entities, such as bar associations, professional associations etc., of those judgments and decisions which may be of specific relevance to their activities. Such dissemination should happen together with an explanatory note or a circular. It should be underlined that Recommendation Rec(2002)13 does not differentiate between judgments having *res judicata* or *res interpretata* status. The emphasis is put on the "specific relevance" of judgments for activities of different bodies. It means that if there is a judgment concerning third states that should be regarded in the interpretation of certain rights guaranteed under the Convention, such judgment should also be disseminated along with a special circular outlining its importance.

10.5 *Res Interpretata* Effect: Practical Active Implementation

10.5.1 Introductory Remarks

As it was mentioned, we can distinguish two types of *res interpretata* effect – a passive effect and an active one. The passive effect occurs when the state party is using the whole body of the ECtHR case-law in its legislative, executive or judicial practice. It means that the ECtHR judgments, irrespectively of the concerned state, are used as general standards of human rights protection and serve to verify legislation, administrative practice or are used in the process of adjudication by ordinary courts or constitutional courts. Such passive use of the ECtHR standards is pretty common in Europe, especially among courts. It is much more rare among the legislative or executive bodies.

The active effect requires something more on the part of the state. States should actively obtain knowledge on new ECtHR standards (e.g., as a result of analysis of judgments of principle) and thereafter adequately change their laws, practice or existing lines of precedent. It means that states should treat judgments having *res interpretata* status in a similar manner as judgments issued with respect to them. If they identify that their legislation or practice has the same problem as the one identified by the ECtHR in a case concerning another state, they should implement such judgment. Implementation should depend on the nature of the available means and the specific domestic situation. However, in most of the situations it will require a change of laws, including sometimes also a change of the Constitution.

[111] Recommendation Rec(2002)13 of the Committee of Ministers to member states on the publication and dissemination in the member states of the text of the European Convention on Human Rights and of the case-law of the European Court of Human Rights.

Such active voluntary implementation of judgments concerning other states is very rare in the Member States of the Council of Europe. Only a few may indicate their positive experience in this regard. Below we will give an overview of international practice. A special section is devoted to Poland, where extremely interesting discussions concerning the implementation of a few ECtHR judgments are now pending.

10.5.2 International Practice

In recent years there have been some examples of state parties to the Convention that amended their domestic legislation or practice following an ECtHR judgment concerning other states, by taking due notice of standards established therein.[112]

The most notable example is a change in many countries following the *Hirst v. United Kingdom (No. 2)*[113] judgment concerning prisoners' right to vote. At the time of issuance, not only the United Kingdom was in default but also other states. The review of states and their different approach to voting rights of prisoners was made even by the Court itself (paras. 33–34). Electoral laws were changed in Cyprus[114] and Ireland.[115] Quite interestingly, this judgment has not been implemented by the United Kingdom itself. Therefore, the ECtHR recently issued a pilot judgment finding a systemic violation of the Convention and calling for amending the legislation imposing a blanket ban on voting rights to prisoners.[116] A similar problem with voting rights exists also in other states, where the implementation of the judgment would necessitate an amendment of the Constitution.

In this context, one should mention the activity of the Venice Commission. In its advisory function as regards laws under consideration in the Council of Europe Member States, the Venice Commission is referring to standards of the ECtHR. The judgment in *Hirst v. United Kingdom (No. 2)* was referred to in the opinion on

[112] One of the recent documents in which one can find a review of relevant cases was the Background document to the intervention made by Mr. Christos Pourgourides, Chairperson of the Committee on Legal Affairs and Human Rights (AS/Jur) of the Parliamentary Assembly of the Council of Europe at the conference: "Strengthening Subsidiarity – Integrating the Court's Case-Law into National Law and Judicial Practice" (Skopje, 1–2 October 2010), available at: http://assembly.coe.int/CommitteeDocs/2010/20101125_skopje.pdf

[113] ECtHR 6 October 2005, No. 74025/01, *Hirst v. United Kingdom (no. 2)*.

[114] In Cyprus, amendments were passed before parliamentary elections in May 2006, see Council of Europe document DH-PR (2006)004 rev Bil., available at: http://www.coe.int/t/e/human_rights/cddh/3._committees/02.%20improving%20of%20human%20rights%20protection%20%28dh%2Dpr%29/03.%20working%20documents/2006/2006_004rev_en.asp#TopOfPage

[115] Electoral (Amendment) Act 2006, No. 33 of 2006, 11 December 2006, available at: http://www.oireachtas.ie/documents/bills28/acts/2006/a3306.pdf

[116] ECtHR 23 November 2010, Nos. 60041/08 and 60054/08, *Greens and M.T. v. United Kingdom*. Please note that this judgment has not been implemented by the United Kingdom until now and was one of the reasons for the introduction of the discussion on the margin of appreciation doctrine in the agenda of the Brighton Conference.

the new electoral code in Georgia. The Venice Commission protested against the total exclusion of prisoners from voting rights.[117]

In The Netherlands, following *Salduz v. Turkey*,[118] legal practice was amended. The Supreme Court, in a judgment of 30 June 2009, made a detailed examination of the implications of the *Salduz* judgment for judicial practice in The Netherlands.[119]

Also after *Goodwin v. United Kingdom*,[120] the Dutch Supreme Court changed its approach as regards the protection of journalistic sources. This was clearly noted in *Sanoma v. The Netherlands,* dealing with similar issues.[121]

In the early history of the ECtHR, there were some incidental changes of law following the ECtHR judgments concerning other states. Below you will find some examples. In France,[122] laws regulating costs of translation in a criminal trial were amended. This was implemented following the case of *Luedicke v. Germany.*[123]

The case of *Piersack v. Belgium*[124] and *De Cubber v. Belgium*[125] led to a lively debate in Dutch law journals on whether the Dutch system of juvenile judges taking pre-trial decisions, could be considered compatible with Article 6 ECHR. After those cases, the Dutch juvenile judges decided to stand down as a trial judge in case their pre-trial involvement had been substantial.[126] The cases of *Piersack v. Belgium*[127] and

---

[117] Opinion of the European Commission for Democracy through Law (Venice Commission) and OSCE Office for Democratic Institutions and Human Rights – joint opinion on the Election Code of Georgia as amended in March 2010, Opinion No. 571 / 2010, CDL-AD(2010)013, available at: http://www.venice.coe.int/docs/2010/CDL-AD(2010)013-e.pdf

[118] ECtHR 27 November 2008, No. 36391/02, *Salduz v. Turkey* .

[119] Speech of Mr. Geert Cortens, President of the Supreme Court of The Netherlands, "Dialogue between Judges", seminar organised by the Strasbourg Court, 29 January 2010. Original French version: http://www.echr.coe.int/NR/rdonlyres/B7BAA2F0-EAB2-4B27-9298-781BB0FB310E/0/20100129_Discours_President_Corstens_Seminaire.pdf

[120] ECtHR 27 March 1996, No. 17488/90, *Goodwin v. United Kingdom.*

[121] See ECtHR 14 September 2010, No. 38224/03, *Sanoma Uitgevers B.V. v. Netherlands*, para. 36: "[…] The principle [that a journalist had to disclose his sources when asked as a witness]" was overturned by the Supreme Court in a landmark judgment of 10 May 1996 on the basis of the principles set out in the Court's judgment of 27 March 1996 in the case of *Goodwin v. United Kingdom.* In this ruling, the Supreme Court accepted that, pursuant to Article 10 of the Convention, a journalist was in principle entitled to non-disclosure of an information source unless, on the basis of arguments to be presented by the party seeking disclosure of a source, the judge was satisfied that such disclosure was necessary in a democratic society for one or more of the legitimate aims set out in Article 10 para. 2 of the Convention, *Nederlandse Jurisprudentie* [Netherlands Law Reports] 1996, no. 578.

[122] Decree No. 87-634 of 4 August 1987

[123] ECtHR 28 November 1978, Nos. 6210/73; 6877/75; 7132/75, *Luedicke, Belkacem and Koç v. Germany.*

[124] ECtHR 1 October 1982, No. 8692/79, *Piersack v. Belgium.*

[125] ECtHR 26 October 1984, No. 9186/80, *De Cubber v. Belgium.*

[126] Source: Information provided by Roeland Böcker, Government Agent for The Netherlands on the questionnaire concerning effective implementation of the ECtHR judgments. 18 February 2009.

[127] *Piersack v. Belgium*, supra, note 124.

De Cubber v. Belgium[128] led also to changes in the jurisprudence of the Swiss Federal Court[129] as well as in Spain (deletion of unconstitutional provision by the Constitutional Court[130]).

In France, after *Burghartz v. Switzerland*,[131] a law of 4 March 2002 established egalitarian rules regarding the attribution of the family name.[132]

As a result of *Brogan v. United Kingdom,*[133] the Netherlands has changed its legislation concerning the time in which an arrested person should be brought before a judge.[134] When this judgment was issued, the authoritative commission (the Moons Commission) was instructed to give an emergency opinion to the legislature, which then took the necessary steps. The new rule provided for an Article 59a of the Code of Criminal Procedure, which entered into force on 1 October 1994. Interestingly, the enforcement authorities did not wait for the amendment to take effect. The Public Prosecution Service had already laid down a policy to be followed in practice on the basis of the *Brogan* judgment.[135]

In The Netherlands changes were made in the laws on succession for children born out of wedlock after the judgment of *Marckx v. Belgium.*[136] The Dutch law had a retroactive effect from 13 June 1979 (i.e., the date of the judgment). This case is regarded as an example of a very quick implementation of the ECtHR judgment. The Netherlands was even quicker than Belgium, which implemented the judgment as late as 1987.[137] Similar changes were made in the case-law of the Luxembourg courts.[138]

---

[128] *De Cubber v. Belgium*, supra, note 125.

[129] Swiss Federal Supreme Court 4 June 1986, No. 112 IA 290.

[130] Spanish Constitutional Court 12 July 1988, No. 145/1988, available at: http://www.boe.es/aeboe/consultas/bases_datos/doc.php?coleccion=tc&id=SENTENCIA-1988-0145

[131] ECtHR 22 February 1994, No. 16213/90, *Burghartz v. Switzerland.*

[132] E. Lambert Abdelgawad and A. Weber, "The reception process in France and Italy" in H. Keller and A. Stone-Sweet (eds.), *A Europe of Rights: The Impact of the ECHR on National Legal Systems*, (Oxford: Oxford University Press, 2008), 126.

[133] ECtHR 29 November 1988, Nos. 11209/84; 11234/84; 11266/84; 11386/85, *Brogan and Others v. United Kingdom.*

[134] R. Ryssdal, "The enforcement system set up under the European Convention on Human Rights" in M.K. Bulterman and M. Kuijer (eds.), *Compliance with judgments of international courts. Proceedings of the symposium organized in honour of HG Schermers*, (Hague/Boston/London: Martinus Nijhoff Publishers, 1996) 50, at 62.

[135] G. Corstens, President of the Supreme Court of The Netherlands, in *Rights. Dialogue Between Judges. Seminar "The Convention is yours" Proceedings* (2010), 11–16, at 14.

[136] E. de Wet, "The reception process in The Netherlands and Belgium" in H. Keller and A. Stone-Sweet (eds.), *A Europe of Rights: The Impact of the ECHR on National Legal Systems*, (Oxford University Press, 2008), 275.

[137] T. Barkhuysen and M. van Emmerik, "A Comparative View on the Execution of judgments of the European Court of Human Rights", in T. Christou and J.P. Raymond (eds.) *European Court of Human Rights. Remedies and Execution of Judgments*, (London: British Institute of International and Comparative Law, 2005), at 11.

[138] Court of Cassation of Luxembourg 17 January 1985, No. 2/85, as noted in Rolv Ryssdal, *The enforcement system set up under the European Convention on Human Rights*, at 62, footnote 10.

An interesting aspect of the *res interpretata* effect of judgments was a consequence of *Kudła v. Poland.*[139] In this case, the ECtHR determined for the first time that the lack of domestic remedy allowing submission of a complaint on the length of proceedings, constitutes a violation of Article 13 of the Convention. Following this case, Poland had to pass a law establishing a domestic remedy. However, the *Kudła* case was also an incentive for other states to pass relevant legislation.[140] However, one should not underestimate the pressure put by the Council of Europe to pass relevant legislation or amend existing legislation (especially in Italy). Some legislative actions were speeded up due to own cases (like Slovenia[141]). Some violations for lack of an effective domestic remedy were only recently established by way of a pilot judgment (like Germany[142]). One may argue that, while the typical *res interpretata* effect is to a great degree voluntary (states amend the legislation or practice acting *bona fides*), in case of improvement of domestic remedies, they are pressurized as a lack of them has a significant effect on the ECtHR workload increase.

10.5.3 Practices in Poland

Following *Copland v. United Kingdom*[143] the Polish Ombudsman initiated a discussion on the need to regulate in detail different aspects of privacy of employees at the workplace.[144] Scholars, NGOs as well as the General Inspector of Data Protection, have followed up this issue. The *Copland* standard was also referred to in one of the leading cases concerning the collection of biometric data by employers.[145] As a result, a need to change the Labour Code and to precisely regulate issues of employees' privacy was seriously discussed at the government level. Unfortunately, no changes were proposed.

Nearly two weeks after the Chamber judgment in *Kiss v. Hungary* was issued,[146] the Ombudsman requested the statement by the Minister of Justice as regards compliance of the Polish Constitution (Article 62 Sect. 2) with the Convention.[147]

---

[139] *Kudła v. Poland,* supra, note 65.

[140] See e.g. *The improvement of domestic remedies with particular emphasis on cases of unreasonable length of proceedings. Workshop held at the initiative of the Polish Chairmanship of the Council of Europe's Committee of Ministers*, Directorate General of Human Rights, Council of Europe 2006, available at: http://www.echr.coe.int/NR/rdonlyres/82597AB6-124F-48D5-8BBB-792899EB0C6A/0/AmeliorationsRecours_EN.pdf

[141] ECtHR 6 October 2005, No. 23032/02, *Lukenda v. Slovenia.*

[142] ECtHR 2 September 2010, No. 46344/06, *Rumpf v. Germany.*

[143] ECtHR 3 April 2007, No. 62617/00, *Copland v. United Kingdom.*

[144] Letter by the Ombudsman to the Minister of Labour of 20 December 2007, letter No. 561580-III-07/MRP.

[145] Polish Supreme Administrative Court of 1 December 2009, I OSK 249/09.

[146] ECtHR 20 May 2010, No. 38832/06, *Alajos Kiss v. Hungary.*

[147] Statement by the Deputy Ombudsman Stanisław Trociuk to the Minister of Justice of 1 June 2010, No. RPO- 647849- I/10/AB.

The Constitution deprives all persons with mental incapacity (*ubezwłasnowolnienie*) of the right to vote. A similar regulation is issued in Hungary (Article 70 Sect. 5 of the Hungarian Constitution). The ECtHR declared that such automatic deprivation of the right to vote violates Article 3 of the Convention. A discussion on the need to change the Polish Constitution is now pending.[148] Also the Ministry of Labour, in the name of the Government, declared that work is under way concerning the potential implementation of *Kiss v. Hungary*.[149]

Following the Chamber judgment in the case of *Uzun v. Germany*,[150] a discussion has started on whether Poland should regulate in detail the ways of using the GPS system in surveillance of suspects.[151] It seems that Polish law is well behind German standards in this regard. It is an interesting example, because the ECtHR did not find a violation of Article 8 of the Convention. However, the assessment of the quality of the German legislation made by the ECtHR should also be taken into account by other states in order to avoid future violations of the Convention. The Helsinki Foundation for Human Rights (Warsaw), relying on the above judgment, requested appropriate changes in Polish law and a strict regulation of how and when different technical means of surveillance may be used by police and special services.[152] The *Uzun v. Germany* case was specifically referred to in the motion to the Constitutional Court submitted by a group of left-wing party deputies and by the Ombudsman, challenging the compliance with the Constitution of the relevant imprecise provisions.

Recently, one of the most discussed cases in Poland is *M. v. Germany*[153] concerning preventive detention. However, in this context the ECtHR judgment is referred to more as a problem to overcome than as an inspiration to some positive, pro-human rights changes.

---

[148] A. Bodnar, "Zmiana Konstytucji jako konsekwencja wykonania wyroku Europejskiego Trybunału Praw Człowieka. Glosa do wyroku Europejskiego Trybunału Praw Człowieka w sprawie Alajos Kiss przeciwko Węgrom [Necessity to change the Constitution as a consequence of implementation of the judgment in the case of Kiss v. Hungary]", *Europejski Przegląd Sądowy [European Court Review]*, (2010)10; see also a commentary in the Polish press: E. Siedlecka, "Ubezwłasnowolniony też wyborca [Incapacitated person is also a voter]", *Gazeta Wyborcza*, 20 May 2010, available at: http://wyborcza.pl/1,75478,7912624,Ubezwlasnowolniony_tez_wyborca.html

[149] Statement by Jarosław Duda, Undersecretary of State in the Ministry of Labour of 18 August 2010, directed to the Helsinki Foundation for Human Rights, available at: http://www.hfhrpol.waw.pl/precedens/images/stories/Odpowiedz_MPiPS_18_08_2010.pdf

[150] ECtHR 2 September 2010, No. 35623/05, *Uzun v. Germany*.

[151] See e.g. comment at leading blog of Mr. Piotr Waglowski devoted to issues at intersection of law and IT technologies, available: http://prawo.vagla.pl/node/9193. See also E. Siedlecka, "Całe nasze życie na podglądzie [Whole Our Life Under Surveillance]", *Gazeta Wyborcza* of 7 October 2010, available at: http://wyborcza.pl/1,75478,8475018,Cale_nasze_zycie_na_podgladzie.html

[152] See the letter by the Helsinki Foundation for Human Rights to the Prime Minister of 14 October 2010, available at: http://www.hfhrpol.waw.pl/precedens/images/stories/file/pismo_2538_2010_DP.pdf

[153] ECtHR 17 December 2009, No. 19359/04, *M v. Germany*.

10.6 Conclusions: Shared Responsibility for *Res Interpretata* Effect

State parties have a special duty with respect to judgments having *res interpretata* status. However, one may ask what the duty of the Council of Europe organs should be in this respect. If respect for the correct functioning of the enforcement machinery is shared responsibility between state parties and the Council of Europe, then one should expect that certain actions should also be taken by organs of the Council of Europe.

Without any doubt, the Committee of Ministers is currently overloaded with work. It would be unrealistic to expect from the Committee to take on itself the additional responsibility of monitoring compliance with *res interpretata* judgments (even with the use of some soft law instruments, because "hard" competence would require a change of the Convention). Zooming in on Article 46 of the Convention, such judgments do not have a binding force. Therefore, their enforcement does not constitute a direct international obligation. State parties may be rather pressurized to implement such judgments, but they cannot be compelled.

However, the Committee of Ministers, as well as the Parliamentary Assembly of the Council of Europe, may inspire state parties to take into account more often judgments with *res interpretata* status. The best way to do so is to adopt a recommendation which would suggest, on the basis of existing good practices, what kind of practical measures states may adopt in order to take such judgments into account. The Committee could also propose a set of methodological tools which make it easier to identify judgments of principle.

Also the ECtHR may put more emphasis on identification of judgments with such precedential value. In practice it is currently done by way of annual reports outlining the most significant judgments. However, one can predict that the Court is additionally signalling judgments of universal value, which may potentially have impact on many state parties. Nobody should expect from the Court any special analysis of consequences of judgments for specific states (not being part of proceedings). But the general indication that a certain judgment may be important for many state parties, may be crucial in taking a pro-active approach by the state as regards its implementation.

Printed by Printforce, the Netherlands